To Carolyn
a gift fro

May you always fin[d]
great joy from God's
deep wells of salvation
Christmas 2013

Downstream from Eden

The Amazing Gift of Water for a Thirsty World

David L Knight

David L Knight

WestBow Press
A Division of Thomas Nelson

ISBN: 978-1-4497-4565-3 (sc)
ISBN: 978-1-4497-4564-6 (hc)
ISBN: 978-1-4497-4566-0 (e)

Library of Congress Control Number: 2012906588

WestBow Press books may be ordered through booksellers or by contacting:

WestBow Press
A Division of Thomas Nelson
1663 Liberty Drive
Bloomington, IN 47403
www.westbowpress.com
1-(866) 928-1240

Printed in the United States of America

WestBow Press rev. date: 05/24/12

Permissions

Grateful acknowledgement is given for permission to use the following:

The Baptismal Prayer from the *Book of Alternative Services*, 1985 is used by permission of ABC Publishing.

The poem "Reluctant Prophet" is used by permission of the author, from the book *Polishing the Petoskey Stone*, (Copyright Luci Shaw, Regent College Publishing, 2003).

Dr. Tom Baskett's "Lifta: a poem" is used by the author's permission.

The photograph of the sculpture "All that the Rain Brings" is used with the permission of the sculptor Mary Fox and photographer Janet Dwyer.

Mary Fox is represented by the Jonathon Bancroft-Snell Gallery-Galerie in London Ontario.

The drawing "Moses Crosses the Red Sea" is used with the kind permission of North Carolina artist, Benjamin Lewis and his parents.

Cover Photograph – David Knight, Hvita River, Iceland, enhanced by In-Sun Kim, Waterloo Ontario. Cover Design by the Graphic Department at WestBow Press.

Dedication:

To Jennifer,

Joanna and Timothy

Jeff and Jolene:

You have made my life like a well-watered garden,

like a spring whose waters never fail.

Isaiah 58:11

Contents

Acknowledgements

Long before I was aware, this book was embryonic inside me.

To my late father, Leslie Knight, I owe my love affair with words and with the Bible. My mentor and one-time boss Don Posterski and our late friend Jim Berney encouraged me to write and opened doors for me. Ruth Lewis predicted 15 years ago that I would one day write a book about springs – you had no idea, my friend.

To the wonderful congregations of Westview in Montreal and Lincoln Road Chapel in Waterloo Ontario who helped me honestly to explore the interface between an ancient text and the challenges of contemporary life – you shaped many of the ideas in this book. To my brothers and sisters: Kathy for critiquing the text, Ian, Phil and Dan for your suggestions and fan-support, to Pauline for photos that spurred the blog and book along. And to Glenn for a thousand prayers and warm enduring friendship.

I owe more than I know to my colleagues Gord, Bruce and Debbie who pulled extra weight when my brain was immersed in water. Thanks to my daughter Jennifer and my friends Bruce and Chris for your science lens and to Nicole Fisher and Katharina Walton for cleaning up the text in ways beyond number.

And to my wonderful wife Tiffany for sharing your life and home with me. Your work as a hydrogeologist opened up new horizons to me to see creation in ways I had never known and became the inspiration for this book. You have endured and sacrificed much as I labored to bring this baby of ours to birth. For that and for your boundless enthusiasm for life and your untiring love, I am forever grateful.

So fair art thou, my bonnie lass
So deep in love am I;
And I will love thee still, my dear,
Till a' the seas gang dry.

Introduction

I splashed my way from the shore to the lifeguard raft – and made it! Halfway back, though, my stamina gave out. Maybe it was the cold that undid me, or maybe my fear, but suddenly I was sinking like stone and gulping saltwater. This swim test was not going well.

I was thirteen, so everyone assumed I could swim. I knew better; my lessons the year before hadn't really helped. Now I was in trouble. I was going down a second time when something buoyant scooped under me from behind and thrust me towards shore – a vigilant lifeguard. My feet found bottom and I stood up, coughing and scared, but thankfully alive. It was the start of a great summer camp.

This was my first West Coast camping experience on the Straits of Georgia between Vancouver Island and the British Colombia coast. I learned the J-stroke for canoeing; we caught crabs and cooked them fresh for lunch, and my swimming slowly improved. And that summer at Pioneer Pacific Camp something happened somewhere in my soul, and I've been on an adventure with God ever since.

This book explores the convergence of water and spirituality. It's a book I never expected to write, but it flows naturally out of the surprising twists and turns of my life adventure which like many journeys has had its share of good weather, a few dark forests and more than I realized about water.

Beginnings

I was born just south of the Thames River in London England, not that I remember anything of the experience. But forty years later, standing on Westminster Bridge watching the Thames flow east towards the sea, it dawned on me that this river had been flowing continuously since I was born. It was a mystical moment that connected me with my roots.

Another water wonder in my life happened each time I saw my children being born. When my wife Mary Lynn was in labor with our first daughter, her friend and midwife announced to her after several fruitless hours of labor, 'I'm going to break your water; that will get things moving.' Within minutes the contractions accelerated, and a couple of hours later we held little Jennifer in our arms. Water is the vital matrix for the first nine months of our life, but the time comes to leave the matrix. My second daughter, Joanna, is now a mother of four and a maternity nurse with her own collection of water breaking stories.

A month before my son Jeff was due to be born, his protective amniotic sac ruptured while we were camping high in the Rocky Mountains. By the time we reached Foothills Hospital in Calgary, there wasn't a drop of fluid left. Without fluid, the doctors feared infection, but they also wanted to keep the baby gestating as long as possible. The importance of water and the urgency that comes when it's lacking is a global water issue, but for us it was very personal, and we felt its life-and-death implications. A week later Jeff was born premature but healthy, and he has grown to become a father himself. And through it all his parents drank deep of God's goodness and grace through the sunshine and mist of each part of their adventure.

Fast-forward to a cold January morning in 2005 when Mary Lynn succumbed to cancer. My children lost their mother and I lost my closest friend; it was a brutal stretch of white water for us all. A few weeks before she died, Mary Lynn wrote about feeling that she was being carried down a river in a floating chair. The current was turbulent and there were dark tunnels ahead, but she had a strong sense of being carried safely along.

A year after Mary Lynn died, I met Tiffany and eventually we married. Tiffany is a hydrogeologist and introduced me to her world of groundwater. I assumed that groundwater meant rivers and ponds, but it turns out that groundwater is actually *under*ground water – wells and aquifers. I didn't even know what an aquifer was, but I began to learn. For a wedding gift, Tiffany gave me a beautiful notebook to encourage my writing. And to fill the notebook, I began writing about water. The more I wrote, the more I learned. And so began this book.

Kaleidoscope

Water is every-which-way marvelous and amazing. From icebergs and toilet bowls to thunderstorms and fresh-brewed coffee, water is a quick-change artist. It's a chameleon that takes on the colors around it, but under a breeze it becomes a kaleidoscope of colors, shapes and textures[1]. Firemen, surgeons, priests and baristas all use water in such different ways. Visually, the wide expanse of Lake Michigan or the ocean stretching to the horizon expands our imagination; the splendor of dewdrops on a spiderweb dazzles our aesthetic sense. The roar of Niagara energizes us, and the serene snow-laden forest calms our spirit. Endlessly, water fascinates and serves us.

Biologically, our bodies are about 60% water; newborns are closer to 75% but by their first birthday, they're down to about 65%. Our brains stay around the mid-70's and blood is 83% water.[2] Every cell in our body contains water and every cell membrane has a meticulous arrangement for allowing water in and keeping it out so cells don't just disintegrate. Water is the crucial mechanism for transporting nutrients to our cells and shipping away the waste. In a number of extraordinary ways water is 'biophilic' as my friend Chris teaches his high school biology students. The chemical structure and behavior of water is uniquely suited to the biological needs of all living things from blue-green algae to blue whales and other large warm-blooded organisms like human beings.[3]

The complexity and power of water humbles us. Our utter dependence on it helps us appreciate the gift of water that keeps us alive to enjoy life. Gratitude and humility, amazement and awe – water excites all these responses. As St. Francis of Assisi wrote eight hundred years ago, "Praised be my Lord for our sister water; who is very serviceable to us and humble and precious and clean."[4]

Besides our fascination with it, water stirs our curiosity. What makes ice float? Why are clouds white and oceans blue? Where did all this water come from? How can we get more of it when the rains don't come? How can we hold it back when floodwaters rise? Engineers in India research how to harvest monsoons to prevent flooding and to enhance Indian agriculture; marine biologists wrestle to manage cod stocks; politicians and engineers agonize over inadequate sanitation and water supply in Gaza and urban slums all over the world. Water brings us a thousand challenges, and the need to know leads to serious focused enquiry, research, initiative and discovery.

All these are expressions of the human spirit at work. *Downstream from Eden* probes some of these tributaries of wonder and perplexity. It ponders the marvels of water and explores some of the complex issues of living in a water dependent world.

Water for Life

Water links us in a profound way with other people. Seven billion of us from Europe to Australia, from Alaska to the Himalayas, from the Amazon to Antarctica, all need water. We all wash in it, drink it – and pass it. It flows in our blood, sweat and tears. Our common humanity is traced in water. We all have to share the well.

Over the past one hundred years, the global human family tripled in size. Africa's population grew by 570%. As agriculture intensified and industrialization spread across the globe, the strain on the earth's water resources steadily increased. Demand continues to swell. Rural people are migrating into the world's cities, which places even greater strain on water delivery systems. Water has become an urgent global concern in both rural and urban contexts.

Almost ten thousand people die every day from waterborne diseases; more than half of these are children. Over 800 million people live in parched conditions or without access to safe water and adequate sanitation. One of the Millennium Development Goals for the world was to cut this number by half.[5] For this reason, the United Nations named the years 2005 – 2015 the 'Water for Life Decade'.

Part of our human spirituality is expressed in our response to other people, our empathy or lack of it, our commitment to justice and compassion. Throughout this book, we'll explore relevant social justice issues as well as environmental themes; we'll look at some of the politics and economics of water; and we'll look at the issue of gender, especially since finding and bringing water in many places is the work of girls and women.

Send My Roots Rain

But there's another dimension to the human spirit that's much harder to calibrate or define. It has to do with deeper questions of the heart, questions of God and our purpose in life, questions about what satisfies our thirst for inner peace, belonging and meaning. What attitudes and actions make us most truly human? "Interestingly, water is one of the common metaphors people have found to express and explore these questions of the soul. Irish poet Gerard Manley Hopkins concludes his soul-searching sonnet "Thou

Art Indeed Just, Lord" with the plea that God would 'send his roots rain'.[6] This is another theme woven through the following pages.

Rabbi Abraham Heschel laments that our culture has lost its awe of God, our wonder before creation and our radical amazement at life. The natural world, he says, gives us a hint, a faint hint, of God's own grandeur, and Heschel invites us to stand in wonder before God's creation. We need to cultivate a sense of embarrassment, he says. Our lack of embarrassment before God and God's creation is at the heart of our indifference and cruelty. Recovering a healthy 'embarrassment' will lead us back to "gratitude, true appreciation and awe"[7] and a stronger sense of community.

That's what this study of water has done for me, opened my eyes, enlarged my world and deepened my appreciation and awe of God for this profuse and marvelous gift of water.

Downstream from Eden

In its early pages the Bible describes a garden of paradise in Eden as the first home of the human family. Every kind of beautiful and fruitful vegetation flourished. A river flowed through the garden watering it and enhancing the beauty of the landscape. The name Eden evokes a sense of pristine perfection, an uncorrupted paradise, the world as God intended it.

Our world today is no longer pristine and uncorrupted, but it is still a place of incredible beauty and vitality. The gifts of Eden flow down to us in a thousand ways. As Elizabeth Barrett Browning wrote, "Earth's crammed with heaven and every common bush afire with God." Open your eyes, she says, take off your shoes. That's a spiritual response of gratitude and awe.

But spirituality isn't naïve; clearly we do not live in Eden. We've lost our innocence; the purity of the world is tainted; pollutants foul our waters and the food-chain, as well as our politics and our souls. We're banished from the garden and we've drifted way downstream. Many of the human family live in environments that make mockery of the Eden ideal. But God has not abandoned us. Living downstream means living in our imperfect world between a curse and a promise.[8] If the beauty of our post-Eden world evokes gratitude and awe; the brokenness of the world should humble us and arouse in us empathy and compassion for those who are most deprived of Eden's gifts.

The Design of the Book

Downstream from Eden is about water and life and faith in the real world. Part One is called 'Feast and Festival'. It reflects on water as a marvelous gift of creation and one of the gifts of Eden. It explores how water in its various forms pervades the world and serves the world. Our environment, indeed, our very bodies, are utterly dependent on water and flourish marvelously because of water. We discover a lot about the power and creativity of our Creator from the wonders of water. This section celebrates this festival of water; it also naturally introduces some of the downstream environmental issues and challenges that are particularly relevant in our day.

Part Two is the heart of the book. It's an extended story that I've nick-named "A River Runs Through It"[9]. The twelve chapters in this section explore a hundred or more water related stories in the Bible. They move more or less chronologically along the narrative plot-line that flows through the Bible from the Garden of Eden to the persecutions at the end of the first century of the Christian era.

Unlike the Vikings, Greeks or Polynesians, the ancient Hebrews were not seagoing people. Most of their water stories are not about the high seas, but about rivers and rainfall – or the lack of them. Every home needs water and the Bible tells numerous stories of women coming to wells and finding more than water. Isaac's wife Rebecca, Jacob's wife Rachel and Moses' wife Zipporah were all 'discovered' at the well. And Jesus has a most interesting conversation with a despised woman at the well in Samaria.

There's something very contemporary and universal in many of these stories of ancient wells and rivers, drought and harvest; they dovetail with the stories of our own hopes and dreams. I hope they help you to connect your own story with God's story.

Part Three invites us to plunge into God's river and experience its radical life-giving power. The eight chapters in this section distill wisdom for the journey from another sixty references or allusions to water in the Bible about how to live the great adventure of life as the Creator intended life to be lived.

Living "downstream" means living our "one wild and precious life"[10] in a less-than-ideal setting – which is where we all live, where people cheat, crops fail and life sometimes gets hijacked by cancer or divorce. It's a world where rivers flood, investments tank, water-mains burst, bosses and neighbors are not always neighborly and industries degrade rivers. Our private souls go dry and we wonder what can quench a thirst that burns deeper than the throat.

The Christian story is about Jesus paddling downstream with us, living his "one wild and precious life" among us on the river of the real world, and inviting us to join him in his mission to bring healing to both river and land, redeeming the curse and replacing it with promise and ultimately, with fulfillment, transforming "the waterless waste into splashing creeks" (Isaiah 41:18 MSG).

Rounding out the book is a 'Manifesto for Action', ten principles or disciplines for living 'downstream from Eden', a sort of 'how-to-do-it' for living ethically in light of the challenges and opportunities water brings us both personally and globally. I wrote this section to summarize the suggestions for response threaded through the pages of the book; I also wrote it to challenge myself so that the words of this book might become flesh, not just passive ideas, warm thoughts, interesting connections. I hope these ten practical disciplines will help you as well as me to translate our inclinations and convictions into action. As an Irish proverb says, "Nodding the head does not row the boat."

A Vigorous Dialogue

I write as a Christian pastor with a background in literature. I've always enjoyed the stories of the Bible, the travels and travails, the tragedies and triumphs of its heroes and heroines. But I was surprised to discover that the Bible is so awash in water, that the Biblical narratives, songs, poetry and other texts include many hundreds of references to rivers, clouds, springs and wells, thirst, dew, rain, ice and snow, floods, drought, oceans, storms, water for washing, baptism, agriculture and drinking, Jesus walking on water, turning water into wine and calling himself 'living water' – the list goes on and on.

Downstream from Eden is a dialogue between three worlds – the natural world of water, the ancient world of the Bible and the contemporary world where we live out our values, hopes and dreams. I hope you enjoy the overlap and the dialogue between these worlds.

With my focus on the Judeo-Christian writings, I am not suggesting that other faith traditions or a secular world-view have nothing important to say about water or human spirituality. No doubt they do, but that is a book someone else would have to write. I have written about the world I know best, and I have tried to write in a way that respects readers from other traditions.

As we explore connections between water and God, the interface between an ancient story and the demands of planet Earth in the 21st century, I hope you'll discover wonders you have never known or seen before about water. I hope you'll come to appreciate the ecology of the created world and of your own life and soul in fresh ways.

In writing these reflections, I was often moved to respond in prayer. I have included some of these prayers in the text. Other times I felt the text asking questions or dazzling my mind with wonder. I've kept some of these too, and you'll see traces of them in the questions or exclamations of *wonder* scattered through these pages. I hope these reflections, prayers and questions give you a good place to dive in and swim around, or provide a restful riverbank where you can listen to the birdsongs or to the questions of your own heart. Perhaps you will hear your heart calling out to God in new ways. If you do, I am certain God will listen and respond. Drink deep and enjoy!

He makes springs pour water into the ravines;
it flows between the mountains.
They give water to all the beasts of the field;
the wild donkeys quench their thirst.
The birds of the air nest by the waters;
they sing among the branches.
He waters the mountains from his upper chambers;
the earth is satisfied by the fruit of his work.
Psalm 104:10-13

Praised be my Lord for our sister water,
Who is very serviceable to us and humble and precious and clean.
St. Francis of Assisi, "Canticle of the Sun"

The poor and homeless are desperate for water,
their tongues parched and no water to be found.
But I'm there to be found, I'm there for them,
and I, God of Israel, will not leave them thirsty.
I'll open up rivers for them on the barren hills,
spout fountains in the valleys.
I'll turn the baked-clay badlands into a cool pond,
the waterless waste into splashing creeks. . . .
Isaiah 41:17-18 MSG

On the last day, the climax of the festival, Jesus stood and shouted to the crowds, "Anyone who is thirsty may come to me! Anyone who believes in me may come and drink! For the Scriptures declare, 'Rivers of living water will flow from his heart.'"
John 7:37-38 NLT

Part One:
FEAST AND FESTIVAL:

The GIFT of Water in Creation

"All that the Rain Brings"

Sculpture by Mary Fox

I will send rain on your land in its season,
both autumn and spring rains,
so that you may gather in your grain, new wine and oil.
I will provide grass in the fields for your cattle,
and you will eat and be satisfied.
Deuteronomy 11:14-15

ALL NATURE IS GIFT. Sun, wind, mountains and rain – the four elements of Fire, Air, Earth and Water – they were all here before we arrived. We didn't have to create them, and they just keep coming. Rain falls and rivers flow; around and around they go, the great feast and festival of creation[11].

The Bible consistently describes God as a lavish and generous giver. Every good and perfect gift comes to us from God – "rivers of light cascading down from the Father of Light" (James 1:17 MSG). One of the psalms says, "you open your hand and satisfy the desires of every living thing" (Psalm 145:15). Another says, "you fill our tankards with Eden spring water. You're a fountain of cascading light" (Psalm 36:8-9 MSG).

Water not only refreshes us, but we could hardly ask for a more perfect gift. The chemistry of water is especially well-suited to the stringent requirements of biological life.

Warm-blooded mammals like us need water in liquid form to stay alive; so do fish and fowl, coral and oak trees. Thankfully, flowing water is what we get across the temperature gradient of much of the earth. The liquid band between vapor and ice is far wider than for most elements in the universe, which allows us to survive. Water retains heat remarkably well, so oceans help keep the world warm in winter and cool in summer. The electrical polarity of water molecules which makes it the best solvent in the world also lets them ship nutrients along our bloodstream and through cell membranes.

Water has an unusually high surface tension which enables trees to lift water from underground roots to their highest branches; it swells grain and bursts open seedpods. It forms our tears and aids perspiration. It lets water seep into fissures in rock – and then in a rare but critical maneuver, just before freezing, it expands and cracks open crevices in the rock and releases minerals for downstream life.

And because ice expands, lakes and rivers freeze from the top down rather than from the bottom up, allowing fish to survive and life to resume when the sun returns in the spring.

Biochemist and theologian Alister McGrath notes that these and many other distinctive properties of water are "indispensible for the functioning of proteins and biological cells."[12] No other known liquid combines all of these properties in this systemic manner.[13] Water is a crucial, unique and life-sustaining gift.

A sculpture called *All That the Rain Brings* by British Columbia ceramic artist Mary Fox helps me to reflect on what an extraordinary gift water is.

The uppermost of the three bowls is tilted downwards. Rain comes to us as sheer gift. It falls freely from above and what it brings is life-giving. It sustains us biologically and emotionally as surely as the wavy ceramic column supports the bowl physically and artistically. Other times I see the top bowl and its supporting stem as a hand lifting up an empty bowl in supplication for rain.

The downward flow of the three bowls follows the flow of rain from cloud to earth and streams and back to the sea. The three bowls suggest various ways we use rain – for drinking, washing and planting and a hundred other activities of life. The bowls are positioned erratically suggesting that the rain is not a neat and tidy process. We can't control when the rains come; they may be late or early; sometimes they are too much or too little. None of the bowls is level as if to remind us that we can't hold on to water.

This sculpture looks to me like a haggard old woman, and perhaps that's all we are as we wait for this unpredictable gift. We do our best to catch it and keep it, and we manage it as we can, but at best we're at the mercy of the elements. We are receptors of nature's bounty.

Maybe that's part of what the rains bring us, both the extravagant gift of water and a humble reminder of our true identity. That's not a trivial gift. As dramatically as rains bring the dry land back to life, so this generous gift renews hope and energizes life.

As all art does, this sculpture reveals that there is far more in this gift of water than meets the eye. No wonder the Bible is so focused on giving thanks in return for this lavish and elegant gift.

Chapter 1

Seven Day Symphony and Other Creation Songs

1.1 The Waters

AT FIRST THERE WAS just ... water! The opening chapter of the Bible is a fascinating seven day symphony celebrating the emergence of life on our glorious planet earth. Fifteen times it speaks of water, first as a deep, dark empty abyss, but by the end, the home of "every living and moving thing with which the water teems" (Genesis 1:21).

In its opening stanza it uses two words 'formless' and 'empty', *tohu* and *bohu,* to describe the "soup of nothingness" (Genesis 1:2 MSG) out of which the material world emerged. God's Spirit moved like wind over this deep abyss which is called 'the waters' – *mayim* in Hebrew.

This formless expanse of *mayim* is the womb of the cosmos, and hovering over this unformed sea of possibilities was the Spirit of God, the breeze that flutters, the brooding Dove. The voice of God rang out through the emptiness: *"Light!"* and light shattered the darkness, radiating glory and energy everywhere.

All stories are edited, and the Bible certainly leaves out a lot of details: how energy was released in waves or particles to make light and give shape to atoms and galaxies, how the elements formed and blended to create the stuff of the universe. These are some of the deep questions and complex processes that engage cosmologists and physicists.

And there are plenty of puzzles in the universe to keep them awake at night. In the summer of 2011, astronomers announced the discovery of the largest and oldest mass of water ever detected in the universe, a gigantic, 12-billion-year-old cloud harboring 140 trillion times more water than all of Earth's oceans combined. This cloud of water vapor surrounds a massive black hole located 12 billion light-years from Earth. This discovery, they say, shows that water has been prevalent in the universe for nearly its entire existence.[14]

Wonderfully, through the creative energy of God, somewhere in the process, hydrogen and oxygen bonded and formed H_2O, an exquisite elixir that would become vital to every form of life on the planet. There is simply no life without water! The complex properties of water and every other structure of creation celebrated in this symphonic story, demonstrate the wisdom and power and purposefulness of God. What was formless and empty is now beautifully formed and full of potential. *Hallelujah!*

So the opening chapter of Genesis tells us that on this first day of creation, it was God who gave nature its dynamic capabilities. It was the pulsating power of God that energized creation and brought it to birth. The universe bears the imprint of its creator.

Just as the cosmos was birthed out of the original 'waters', so every human being begins their life in the waters of the womb. And like the cosmos, we need the spark of Life, the energizing touch of God – and then untold creative possibilities emerge from that igniting touch in our lives.

There is a lot more that follows in this 'seven day symphony', but first we should look at something that predates even the water.

1.2 Wisdom Song

Solomon was Israel's first naturalist and nature philosopher. He pondered the mystery of Earth's origins and motions. He observed extraordinary patterns of craftsmanship and design in the world of nature and wrote a poem in praise of it. He personified this genius as Lady Wisdom, who calls aloud in the noisy streets of the city (Proverbs 1:20 and 8:1). Here she sings about her participation with God in the creation:

> The LORD formed me from the beginning,
> before he created anything else.
> I was appointed in ages past,
> at the very first, before the earth began.
> I was born before the oceans were created,
> before the springs bubbled forth their waters.
> Before the mountains were formed,
> before the hills, I was born—
> before he had made the earth and fields

and the first handfuls of soil.
I was there when he established the heavens,
when he drew the horizon on the oceans.
I was there when he set the clouds above,
when he established springs deep in the earth.
I was there when he set the limits of the seas,
so they would not spread beyond their boundaries.

And when he marked off the earth's foundations,
I was the architect at his side.
I was his constant delight,
rejoicing always in his presence.
And how happy I was with the world he created;
how I rejoiced with the human family!

And so, my children, listen to me,
for all who follow my ways are joyful.
Proverbs 8:22-30, 32 NLT

If the opening chapter of Genesis is a symphony with God's Spirit hovering over the waters, this 'Wisdom Song' is like its Overture.[15] It goes back 'before the beginning', before the first drop of water, "when there were no oceans ... and no springs abounding with water" (verse 24), and it tells us about something even more vital than water.

Solomon identifies Wisdom as the elemental power undergirding all of nature, a wisdom that is found deep within the Earth, its true meaning hidden from a casual and superficial glance".[16] Wisdom is the creativity and purpose that brought creation from design to fruition. Even before the water, Wisdom flowed in the mind and heart of God. She was "brought forth as the beginning of God's works... before the world began" (verse 22).

Water, though, serves as the temporal benchmark before which Wisdom was birthed, perhaps because water is such a critical component for everything in life. It is absolutely vital for the continued existence of all life forms, plant, animal or human. No water, no life. And in every form of water there is evidence of such wisdom that scientists often speak of the 'mystery' of water.

Solomon's Wisdom song goes on to celebrate the oceans, rivers and rains that sustain the world, but its central focus is the wisdom and joy that brought about their creation. Here we see the earthy spirituality of Israel. Inherent within the material world, and undergirding it, is a relational power of love. The formation of the world as we know it is not seen as an impersonal process, but as an intentional act of divine love and creativity.

It may surprise us that Wisdom does not rhapsodize about the skill of the creator or the complexity of creation, but about the privilege of being a participant with God throughout the entire creative process, someone who exuberantly watched every move God made and delighted with God in each expression of artistry. Old Testament scholar David Hubbard notes that this is a startlingly different view of creation from the Babylonian myths (which we'll look at in Chapter 5) as well as more contemporary mechanistic views. This is "high comedy applauded and enhanced by wisdom herself."[17]

In the Hebrew mind, Wisdom is not a philosophical abstraction or merely technical skill. Wisdom is being attentive to God and living in harmony with God's purpose. Solomon personified Wisdom as God's companion and a fellow merry-maker, who celebrated with God "day after day", the joy, delight and wonder of the created world. Someone has said that God and Wisdom 'rejoiced' the cosmos into existence.[18]

Prayer:
God of Wisdom, I rejoice at the ingenious creativity of all your works in earth and sky, oceans and rivers and in the apparent fluidity of my own life.

Give me wisdom to ponder your handiwork, childlike curiosity that delights to explore its intricacy, fresh eyes to see its simplicity, complexity and beauty. Give me humility to know the limits of my understanding and to trust you with the mysterious fountains of the deep places in my life.

Teach me to watch for – and participate in – your ongoing creativity in the world, and may I, like Lady Wisdom, rejoice with you in all the works of your hands. Amen.

1.3 If It Weren't for the Sky

Meanwhile, back in the Genesis creation song, the story of days two and three unfold two stunning wonder-of-water events, the emergence of the atmosphere and the separation of dry land from surrounding oceans, two crucial environmental events that define the Earth as we know it!

As fish need water, the rest of us need air. So God spoke a word, and a space – an expanse – opened up to buffer Sky above from Ocean below. The ancients thought of it as a dome; we might identify it as the *troposphere,* or as we commonly call it, *sky,* but it includes the air around us. It is a fragile and invisible membrane between us and the cold dark, a roof over our heads. Professor Marva Dawn says, "it is like a womb in which the earth safely dwells."[19]

A mere 9 miles (15 km) of space between sea-level and the highest clouds holds most of our air. That's where clouds and wind form and carry out a creative dance that produces most of our weather. If the earth were a basketball, this membrane would be thinner than a cellophane wrapping. Even the 30 mile (50 km) band out to the ozone layer is proportionately thinner than an apple skin is to the apple, but it is a complex and highly functional domain.

Clouds soar over our heads in an intricate balance of physics: pressure, temperature and other forces that sustain a crucial water cycle of evaporation and precipitation. This is the factory where water vapor is collected, stored, transported and recycled to earth as rain, snow or hail. Air is sturdy enough to let birds and airliners fly, yet light enough for us to inhale. It carries fog to the canopy of redwood forests, ruggedly dismantles meteorites and deflects radiation, yet translucent to display starlight, moonlight and rainbows and the spark of fireflies.

The Genesis creation song says succinctly, "God said, let there be a space between the waters, to separate the waters of the heavens from the waters of the earth. And that is what happened" (Genesis 1:6-7 NLT). That's a very compacted narrative, simplistic to the scientific mind that searches out how things happen. But the ancients were not particularly concerned with the process by which our atmosphere came into being. To their mind everything in nature was infused with spiritual power and was controlled by a complex web of gods, spirits and astral powers. So it is profoundly significant that Israel's story ascribed everything to the Creator's word.

Whose is this voice who claims to have called into being such enormous forces of nature? Whatever deities human beings might imagine ruled their world, they meet their match in the One whose singular word evokes such a spectacular response.[20] All creation answers the bidding of this voice. For ancient Israel, this is the key to the story being told in this seven day symphony. There is one God, not many, and this God has single-handedly fashioned for us a stunningly beautiful and functional world. The emergence of the 'expanse' or atmosphere is one movement of the symphony and it plays a vital role in the ordered process of the natural world.[21]

Astrophysicist Hugh Ross says that the chances of getting the physics and chemistry of this atmosphere right were less than one in a billion![22] Whew! Lucky us! Take a deep breath – and thank Earth-Maker for Air and for such creative, generous hospitality! Air is not only a wonderful gift, it is a gift full of *wonder*! Normally we're as oblivious to air as fish are to water. We take it for granted. But let the weather change, or let human mismanagement degrade air quality or disrupt the delicate carbon balance of the atmosphere and we can be in serious trouble, as friends with asthma can tell you.

This wonder of the world, our delicate finely tuned, vital atmosphere is both gift and responsibility. As with every molecule of the universe, it calls forth awe and appreciation. This is the reason the opening chapter of Genesis is written the way it is, as a kind of prose poem or song[23], with a carefully crafted symmetry, repeated phrases and above all a cry of wonder:[24] God's assessment that everything is Good! It's as much a song of exultation as an explanation.

Theologian Marva Dawn calls it 'a liturgy that draws us into worship' because in the darkness of void and emptiness, the Creator God is present and active, causing brilliant things to appear.[25] Another great wonder is that we have been invited to participate in the drama. Does that not stir in your heart a deep sense of privilege, a response of gratitude and praise?

1.4 Land and Sea

The next dazzling water event in the Genesis creation song is the emergence of the earth out of the sea at the voice of God – the transformation of a featureless ocean into a sculptured landscape! "God said, Let the waters beneath the sky flow together into one place, so dry ground may appear" (Genesis 1:9).

Imagine the forces that came into play to bring about this transformation – tremors ripping through the earth's crust, trenches gashing across the sea-floor, hollowing out deep marine basins, and giant crags of rock thrusting up through the surface of the sea, catching the glint of the sun. The Genesis song doesn't explore how this process occurred, but a twenty-first century imagination can't help but wonder how it might have unfolded, and we can't help but stand in awe of the One who caused it all to happen and to consider what a gift the outcome is to us today.

The dry land gives us a place to stand, to build and grow. The earth buffers us from the ocean waves, yet it drinks in the rain and holds enough water to sustain grasslands and cedar forests. Trees and people need to be rooted, as do cities and civilizations. We need the land just as we need water.

The first day gave us Light; the second, Air and Sky; the third day divided Land from Sea. I capitalize these words to convey their significance as unique domains, environments wonderfully designed as venues for life. God explicitly names them (verses 5, 8 and 10) and identifies their purpose in the functioning of the world: Sky designed for clouds and eagles, gnats, hummingbirds and rainbows; Sea for coral, dolphins and octopus; Land for elk and elephants, willow and sequoia, scorpions and humans. Each domain has its own variety of habitats beautifully suited to the needs and capabilities of a vast biodiversity. And God expresses his pleasure at the harmony of the emerging world: "and God saw that it was good" Genesis 1:12).

All will need the water, and the water is tamed and stored in place to serve its life-enabling role. Safeguarded out in the open seas, in glaciers and on ice rimmed mountain peaks, in lakes and rivers, in clouds and aquifers, ready to serve the needs of all the world's future inhabitants.

It will become a wonderful and intricate ecosystem – and breathtakingly beautiful, for this creator is both artist and engineer. God looked on this magnificent panorama of Sky-Ocean-and-Land in the same way that artists, adventurers, lovers and poets have looked at it ever since the dawn of creation, and God declared it 'good'.

In fact, twice in the stanza of day three (verse 10 and 12), the song tells us that God saw that it was good. In this context, the Hebrew word *'tov'* means both functionally good like a good car, and aesthetically pleasing like good wine. It implies excellence in quality and potential as well as moral goodness. In every way, the creation earned gold medal status for elegance of both form and functionality.

The visual contrast of water, sky and land is a photographer's stock-in-trade. Every Caribbean sunset, every Yosemite waterfall, Antarctic glacier and Norwegian fjord confirms not only the awesome power of the Creator, but also that this Creator is an artist with an exquisite eye for splendor and magnificence.

We'll come back to the Genesis creation song, but let's take another detour into the Wisdom library of the Bible, including the Psalms, Proverbs and Book of Job and some interesting insights from their reflection on the wonder of water. They help us to see behind the power of nature, the mystery and majesty of nature's God.

1.5 Birthing the Sea

On November 12, 1970, a cyclone with gusts of 130 mph (over 200 km/h) roared inland from the Bay of Bengal generating a storm surge 33 feet (10m) high and a hundred miles (160 km) wide. It smashed into the coast of Bangladesh and the Ganges Delta as the deadliest tropical cyclone ever recorded. More than 300,000 people drowned, largely because of the intensity of the ocean surge. The people of Bangladesh know the fearful unpredictable, untamable power of the sea.

It's no wonder the seagoing Greeks considered Poseidon, god of the sea, as moody and irritable, easily offended and relentless in exacting revenge on his foes. No wonder other cultures saw the sea as the domain of Chaos.[26] Despite the enormous power of ocean winds and waves, Israel's theology boasted that Yahweh was supreme master of the sea as we see in a fascinating passage in the Book of Job.

Job and four friends are engaged in a lengthy debate about great questions of life – suffering, morality and the justice of God when God suddenly joins the conversation. God dwarfs their imagination and challenges their credentials to pontificate on such weighty matters by asking them what they really know about the mysteries of the world. Who was in charge of the creation? God asks. "Who shut up the sea behind doors when it burst forth from the womb? (Job 38:8-9). It's a bizarre picture – imagining the sea as an enormous infant confined *in utero* until it burst forth out of the womb!

As I mentioned in the Introduction, I was present at the birth of all three of my children, and none of them 'burst forth from the womb'. They had to be pushed and pulled and prodded. Even then they took their sweet time. When a human mother gives birth naturally, the amniotic sac ruptures and about 3 cups of fluid (600 mls) drain out. But in the poetry of Job, the entire oceans of the world burst forth! What a baby! What a mother!

Who was this mother? What midwife broke her water to release this enormous child into the world? Rhetorical questions, like the ones God asked Job and his friends, draw our attention to the obvious: for all its prodigious power, the sea is not the ultimate force in the universe. It came into being 'maternally'. The word 'nature' comes from the Latin word for birth, *natura*, and the Bible unabashedly uses this metaphor of God birthing the creation: "from whose womb comes the ice? who gives birth to the frost ...?" (Job 38:29) and "before the mountains were born or you brought forth the earth and the world, from everlasting to everlasting, you are God" (Psalm 90:2).

Then, expanding on the birth metaphor, God describes wrapping this newborn sea-child the way a mother swaddles an infant. "I made the clouds its garment and wrapped it in thick darkness" (verse 9). Thick darkness – imagine dense ocean fog. Who can see through it? Who can see beyond the horizon or penetrate the silence of all that lies in the deep darkness of the sea? What a rich metaphor for the mystery of the oceans, their vast distances, beyond our sight and knowledge!

The darkness of this 'blanket' is not an ominous gloom, but the generous swaddling bands of an immensely powerful and caring mother! The extravagance of the metaphor exposes how preposterous it is for us to think we could master the seven seas. Or death. Or even our own thoughts and fears half the time.

1.6 Baby Grows Up

In the next stanza, the personified sea is no longer a passive infant but a defiant force in need of restraint. God asks Job if he was there "when I fixed limits for [the sea] and set its doors and bars in place, when I said, 'This far you may come and no farther; here is where your proud waves halt' (Job 38:10-11).

Like an adolescent who needs boundaries to restrict her intemperate excesses, the sea needs to have limits imposed on her. Sure enough, the continental shelf fills the bill, along with vast rims of sandy shoreline, mangrove swamps, reefs and rocky coastlines, and the cliffs of Dover, Gibraltar, Moher, Oregon and Tierra del Fuego. They all provide fixed limits for the boundless energy of the sea.

This high-energy, impulsive and reckless youth called Ocean has her rash powers contained. Oh, she still serves up some mighty tantrums every season. She shows off her vibrant boisterous energy at world-class surfing basins. Her tidal dynamics and powerful currents shape our weather and shorelines and she makes breathtaking photography. Perhaps someday engineers will develop the technology to harvest the ocean's currents, waves and tides as a viable clean and affordable energy source for coastal cities. But still she will remain a formidable, fearsome force.

Robert Frost vividly describes the collision of sea against the land in his poem "Once By the Pacific." The poem opens with

> The shattered water made a misty din.
> Great waves looked over others coming in,
> And thought of doing something to the shore
> That water never did to land before.[27]

Frost sees the ocean as a reckless, even malevolent, force. He goes on to observe how the shore is lucky to have the cliff and the continent behind it to stand up against the destructiveness and 'dark intent' of the waves. Even then, 'someone had better be prepared for rage' he says. Perhaps the 'someone' Frost has in mind is actually God who should understand our human rage against the disappointments of life. Frost seems to suggest that such violence will dominate the world until ultimate darkness descends.

The hostile sea embodies Frost's theme, and yet he uses the sonnet form with its carefully structured lines and meter to paint this picture of wild energy and shattered illusions. The deeply troubling world is not eliminated by the poet's craft, but the poet uses words as a window through which we can safely view and ponder the dangerous storm. And in a similar way the Creator has provided geographic restraints that prevent this adolescent from overwhelming the world!

There are limits to human understanding of the mysteries of life. This text prompts me to ask myself, if God is the great maternal life-giver, why am I always trying to be God's midwife, telling God what is best, trying to manage the outflow of God's creative work in my life?

Like Job and his companions, I try to get my head around profound questions of suffering and injustice, trying to figure out what is fair and noble, what is right, what is most human and humane. Yahweh challenges me to recognize the limits of my understanding and power and submit to a parental purpose more profound than I could ever imagine. This is not to rebuke my curiosity about the world or to blunt my questions, but to teach me to live in trusting relationship with God even when God says to me "'this far you may come and no farther" (verse 11).

Ultimately, God intends that our lives should be governed internally by the power of the Spirit of God. The character qualities of the Spirit include graces like love, joy and peace, but they culminate with self-control (Galatians 2:22). There is no way human beings can ever exercise responsible relationship to the world around us unless we learn to master ourselves, to restrain our reckless impulse to master others. This is why Jesus tells us to seek first the reign of God in our lives and in the world around us (Matthew 6:33). God's reign in our lives disciplines our impulses and releases in us a robust life-giving creativity.

I was vacationing one summer on the New Jersey shore when a significant storm blew in, short of the destructive fury of a hurricane, but the kind of storm that showcases the raw power of nature, the wind wild in your face and the waves roaring and relentless. Standing on the shore, surrounded by all that energy, I yearned to be a part of it, to feel its strength within me. The sea sang to me about "the deep, deep love of Jesus, vast, unmeasured, boundless, free, rolling as a mighty ocean in its fullness over me!" I thought of all the ways God's goodness flows into my life, 'grace upon grace' and 'wave after wave after wave of inexhaustible joy', as I described it later in my journal.

Experiences like that usually come upon us without warning, triggered by a thunderstorm or a birdsong, a child's smile or some other unexpected glimpse of the beauty or power of the world. Such moments are gifts. They are given and we resonate to them because we both come from the hand of God.

1.7 Boundaries

The prophet Jeremiah sees another kind of significance in this well designed, God-designed, geography. Just as the shoreline provides physical boundaries so the sea cannot destroy the land, so God has put moral boundaries in place to protect human life and society. Jeremiah speaks for God saying,

> I made the sand a boundary for the sea,
> an everlasting barrier it cannot cross.
> The waves may roll, but they cannot prevail;
> They may roar, but they cannot cross it.
> But these people have stubborn and rebellious hearts;

they have turned aside and gone away.
They do not say to themselves, 'Let us fear the LORD our God'
Jeremiah 5:22-24

The moral laws of the world are as real and nonnegotiable as physical laws. Ethical boundaries are designed to restrain our natural instincts and promote the flourishing of society. But Jeremiah's contemporaries stubbornly resisted God's laws and refused to limit their personal freedoms. Jeremiah sees that ultimately as self-destructive; he foresees complete disaster ahead for them.

I'm not sure I always know where these boundaries are, but as a father I learned that my kids were are always pushing them. It's human instinct to resist limitation. The creative energies of the adventurous spirit impel us 'to strive, to seek, to find and not to yield.'[28] But the drive for self-control and self-advancement inevitably collides with the ethical laws of life that protect truth and justice, fidelity and honor, mercy and compassion.

In his book *The Seven Habits of Highly Effective People,* Stephen Covey writes about principles of human character and effectiveness as laws in the human dimension that are as established and unchangeable as gravity in the physical world. He relates an incident during naval exercises when the commander of an aircraft carrier challenged the operator of another ship and ordered it to move aside to avoid collision – until the other 'ship' identified itself as a lighthouse. The aircraft carrier wisely changed course. Covey says that principles of character are like lighthouses, bedrock laws that cannot be broken. He quotes Cecil B. de Mille's observation about the Ten Commandments: "it is impossible for us to break these laws; we can only break ourselves against them."[29]

Early in the poetic drama of the Book of Job, Job asks, "Am I the sea, or the monster of the deep, that you put me under guard?" (Job 7:12). Job feels he is being disciplined like a reckless irresponsible youth and he resents it.

"Well, yes, Job, in a way you are the sea. No, you are not being punished for unruly misbehavior; you've been a model of a self-governed righteous life, of spiritual maturity. But in another way, Job, you are very much like the sea. Every human being is a deep oceanic arena of self-will. You have powers and capacities and motivations within you that God has yet to harness for their full potential. Like Abraham, well past 100 years of age, you still have room to grow. God intends to form and transform you into a rich wholeness of being beyond what you can imagine. Having begun that good work in you, God will continue it to the end. And growing into deeper, richer maturity in knowing God always involves a journey into mystery.

1.8 Terra Firma

The famous Leaning Tower of Pisa began tilting by the time the second floor was being built in 1178. The cause: a weak foundation and unstable subsoil. By contrast, the Golden Gate Bridge withstands enormous tides and currents and survived the 1989 Loma Prieta earthquake unscathed, in part because it sits on solid foundations: at the north end, on a bedrock ledge twenty feet under the water and at the south end on a deep pier the size of a football field.

Gibraltar, the Alps and Himalayas are symbols of our rock solid world. Unlike clouds that are wispy and ephemeral, the earth is firm, solid and stable. We call it *terra firma,* although earthquakes, large and small, remind us that even 'terra firma' is a relative term. Nevertheless, Everest and the Matterhorn and Mount Fuji symbolize to us the steadfast immovable realities of the world.

Israel looked at mountains as eloquent expressions of God's power. When so much of our social and political world is in flux, it is reassuring to be on solid ground and the poet credits this stability to God. In that light it is particularly interesting to consider the words of Psalm 24:

> The earth is the Lord's and everything in it
> for he founded it upon the seas
> and established it upon the waters.
> Psalm 24:1

What in the world does the writer mean by the earth is 'founded on the seas'? How can anything be established on water? The poetic image, of course, comes from the Genesis creation song where the solid earth rose out of the sea at God's command and became firmly established. The poet celebrates God's power as the authority that prevents the sea from overwhelming the land, making the inhabitable world secure. People living in Manhattan, London and Amsterdam today rely on that geophysical reality.

We hear the same confidence celebrated in Psalm 93:

> The LORD reigns, he is robed in majesty; [...]

> The world is firmly established; it cannot be moved. [...]
>
> The seas have lifted up, O LORD, the seas have lifted up their voice;
> the seas have lifted up their pounding waves.
> Mightier than the thunder of the great waters,
> mightier than the breakers of the sea-- the LORD on high is mighty.
> Psalm 93:1-4

Psalms 24 and 93 share the conviction that Yahweh has mastered the physical world and established it firmly. Then Psalm 24 turns to consider the implications of Yahweh as creator and king; it turns our attention from physical foundations to ethical ones. It asks 'what are the fundamentals of a moral life?

> Who may climb the mountain of the Lord?
> Who may stand in his holy place?
> Only those whose hands and hearts are pure,
> who do not worship idols
> and never tell lies.
> Psalm 24:3-4 NLT

Clean hands, pure heart and truthful speech give stability to our lives and give us secure standing in God's holy place. A rock solid world points to stable moral foundation. A thousand years ago Celtic Christians echoed this link between God's self-revelation in the created world and our personal response to God. In the prayer commonly called *St. Patrick's Breastplate,* they prayed each morning:

> I bind unto myself today
> The virtues of the starlit heaven,
> The glorious sun's life giving ray,
> The whiteness of the moon at even,
> The flashing of the lightning free,
> The whirling wind's tempestuous shocks,
> The stable earth, the deep salt sea
> Around the old eternal rocks.

That's the basis of a durable faith with unwavering ethics, as constant as '*the stable earth, the deep salt sea around the old eternal rocks!*' In contrast, Isaiah sees the restlessness of people without God, the instability of undisciplined lives of people who reject moral restraint:

> The wicked are like the tossing sea, which cannot rest,
> whose waves cast up mire and mud.
> "There is no peace," says my God, "for the wicked."
> Isaiah 57:20-21

Of course, the relative stability of the earth is discernable only within the short span of human awareness. If we changed the scale to geologic time we would see that the lithosphere of planet earth is constantly in motion, drifting, colliding, separating and reconfiguring. Only 130 million years ago, the mountains of western Morocco and what is now eastern Nova Scotia were lying cheek by jowl in the supercontinent of Pangaea until the fledgling Atlantic began to flow between them and the seafloor began spreading apart. Mount Everest continues to rise from below and erode at the same time. Tectonic plate studies tell us that everywhere things are on the move, though so creepingly as to be largely inconsequential to our daily concerns, except when the earth shudders with Richter-scale adjustments.

Psalm 90 recognizes that even within the shifting realities of geologic time, God is the ultimate stability.

> Lord, through all the generations
> You have been our home.
> Before the mountains were born
> Before you gave birth to the earth and the world
> From beginning to end, you are God.
> Psalm 90:1-2 NLT

1.9 Water Warehouse

The Genesis creation song describes the power and artistry of God creating the world. Derek Kidner calls it 'effortless mastery'[30]. Psalm 33 describes the formation of galaxies the same way. Imagine, "by the word of the LORD were the heavens made, their starry host by the breath of his mouth" (Psalm 33:6). The formation of the earth is similarly succinct and graceful, "for he spoke and [the earth] came to be. He commanded and it stood firm" (Psalm 33:9). God speaks and things happen: light, sky, ocean, land, grass – just like that! – effortless, effective and orderly.

But then the psalm goes on to depict God working hard to organize nature. It describes God as a warehouse manager . . . "He gathers the waters of the sea into jars; he puts the deep into storehouses" (Psalm 33:7). It's a picturesque metaphor – the vast inventory of the oceans collected and compressed into barrels or skins, stacked up and stored in place so that human life can prevail on the earth – vivid language to express the majesty of Yahweh's governance over the world with purpose.

God is indeed a warehouser of water. The high seas are kept in the great deep. Glaciers and ice-caps and permafrost are huge reservoirs, locking away two-thirds of the world's fresh water in cold storage. It's an arrangement that energetically moderates the earth's atmospheric temperature. The rest of the fresh water is dispersed through a lacework of lakes, rivers and marshlands, hidden under the earth in aquifers, and couriered about in clouds to fields and forests the world over to sustain life everywhere.

Psalm 33 is not only about God's prodigious power in creation but also God's love for humanity. The earth is "full of God's unfailing love" (verse 5). The Hebrew word here is *hesed,* a wonderful word that occurs 250 times in the Bible. It refers to steadfast unfailing love, covenant loyalty and faithfulness.

When we got married, Tiffany and I had our wedding rings inscribed with this word '*hesed*'. Even better, we work to ensure that our relationship reflects that unfailing love. Without *hesed,* marriage partners just go through the motions. But a home or marriage that is full of *hesed* is a vibrant, secure, joyful place to live. The psalmist looks at the way Yahweh has made the world and says 'the earth is full of his unfailing love.' Water is just one of the evidences that the earth is literally a storehouse of faithful, never-failing love.

Do you notice the present tense of this description? For this poet and for the whole Biblical witness, creation is not just an ancient prehistoric event, but a continuing work-in-progress. God 'gathers' the waters (present tense) and stores them away (verse 7). This portrays Yahweh as actively providentially engaged in the world. The prophet Amos expresses the same thought when he says

> It is the Lord who created the stars, the Pleiades and Orion.
> He turns darkness into morning and day into night.

> He draws up water from the oceans and pours it down as rain on the land.
> Amos 5:8 (and repeated in Amos 9:5)

Just as God created the oceans long ago, so God sustains their mechanisms, gathering up the tides and releasing them, collecting evaporated mists into clouds day after day, century after century. Unfailing love, stored up and released, gathered again, warehoused and released again and again and again.

1.10 Form and Fullness

The symphony of Genesis 1 that celebrates the wonder of creation exudes a sense of profusion and abundance. This fullness is highlighted by the structure of the hymn in two parallel triads. During the first three days God set the stage for life and established the structures or domains essential to our life on earth: light, sea and sky, dry land and vegetation. But the stage, so to speak was empty.

On days four, five and six, those empty spaces were filled up with good things. Light (day one) was filled out on day four by sun, moon and stars. Sea and sky (day two) were filled on day five with fish and birds. The dry land and vegetation of day three was filled on day six with animals and humans. The world came forth from formless emptiness to full and overflowing! That's the story the symphony celebrates.

What an awesome creation – there is no lack or scarcity in sight. We don't get just stars, but galaxies by the billion. At the midpoint of the symphony when life emerges – grass on day 3 and fish and birds on day 5 – it's a massive effusion. Not just a few fish, but hundreds of thousands of species; birds and butterflies without number. Words associated with abundance gush forth in the account of day five: 'let the water *teem* ', '*great* creatures of the sea', '*every* living and moving thing with which the water *teems*'. There's fullness in quantity, size and variety. And if that were not enough, God tells them to 'be fruitful and *increase* in number and *fill* the water in the seas'. The Creator is on a roll. God delights in abundance and empowers his creatures to continue the process: "*fill* the water in the seas and let birds *increase* on the earth" (Genesis 1:22).

Okay, maybe God overdid it a bit with mosquitoes, but even they are lunch for the birds. No wonder Psalm 33 urges people everywhere to respond in worship for his power and goodness!

> Let all the earth fear the LORD,
> Let all the people of the world revere him!
> Psalm 33:8

Another psalm invites heaven and earth and sea to join in praise:

> Praise him, you highest heavens
> and you waters above the skies.
> Praise the LORD from the earth,
> you great sea creatures and all ocean depths,
> lightning and hail, snow and clouds,
> stormy winds that do his bidding.
> Psalm 148:7-8

This song anticipates the ones we will hear in Revelation 4 and 5 as the entire cosmos reverberates with praise to its Creator.

1.11 Ocean Vents

In every conceivable area of creation we can see expressions of God's continuing creativity in the world: in the beauty of sunsets and infants, the bounty of agriculture, the mystery of coincidence and miracles, the capacity of human bodies to heal – the list of breath-taking wonders goes on. Listen again to Solomon who was such an astute observer of nature. In his Song of Wisdom he celebrates the amazing design he sees in the very fabric of our complex world. He particularly singles out the wonders of water and how consistently water functions.

I was there . . . when he marked out the horizon on the face of the deep, when he established the clouds above and fixed securely the fountains of the deep, when he gave the sea its boundary so the waters would not overstep his command (Proverbs 8:27-29).

As we have seen, oceans are enormous but measurable and well regulated. Despite tidal variations and gale force winds, gravity holds the sea in place. Above us, clouds, which are the epitome of freedom in motion, are nevertheless 'established', operating by consistent principles.

Below us, the 'fountains of the deep' are 'securely fixed'. This doesn't mean that geological fissures never shift, but that laws of hydrology are constant and reliable. Aquifers store water and release their stores to the world above in ways that well-drillers can rely on. These 'fountains of the deep' show the complexity and consistency of nature – and of Wisdom. They reveal her bounty and, surprisingly, the continuing creativity of the world.

Only recently scientists have discovered geothermal vents under the ocean, upwelling jets of superheated water bursting out of vents in the sea floor. Subterranean molten magma heats water below the seafloor to extremely high temperatures, causing it to spew out in nutrient rich springs. Aquatic life forms of incredible variety and complexity never before seen live in these warm water zones. Creation itself continues as an infinitely creative work-in-progress, amazing wonders of nature. Perhaps Solomon's poetry spoke more than he knew, or perhaps he knew more than we give him credit for knowing.

Human beings, too, are 'fearfully and wonderfully made' (Psalm 139:14) with creativity flowing out of our pores. That is why Wisdom sings us her song, pleading with us to use our creative capacity as artists, parents, educators, researchers, engineers, caregivers, laborers, etc., but to use it wisely and joyfully in serving God and our fellow creatures.

And then, perhaps the greatest wonder of all, God entrusted the entire enterprise to his fledgling human apprentices. "Take charge!" God told them; "be responsible for fish in the sea and birds in the air, for every living thing that moves on the face of Earth" (Genesis 1:28). What a mandate! God blessed them as he had blessed the other animals and urged them to multiply life across the earth. But to us he added this royal mandate of stewardship.

1.12 Crescendo

The seven-day symphony reaches its crescendo with God resting from his work. This is not the rest of fatigue or exhaustion, but the celebration of the creation of the cosmos "in all its vast array" (Genesis 2:1). God blessed the seventh day and made it holy, which implies that the crowning act of creation was not the creation of human beings or even humans fulfilling their tasks, but our being invited to rejoice in the vibrancy of God's creation, to relax and trust God, to define ourselves not by our achievements in the world, but by God's gifts to us and by God's sovereignty over our time.[31]

The symphony began with the primal waters dark and formless. The sea becomes a restless force (Isaiah 57:20) and Isaiah speaks about the troubled restlessness of those who resist God's rule in their lives, but the symphony of creation culminates in a deep tranquility that invites us into rest. God's reign is an environment of peace from Genesis all the way to Revelation. There in the last book of the Bible, we get a vision of heaven as God's throne, and in front of God's throne is "a shiny sea of glass, sparkling like crystal" Revelation 4:6 NLT), a serene untroubled sea that we'll explore more in Chapter 20 and 24.

So this grand symphony that opens our Bible celebrates the vast panorama of God's creative work and sets the tone for us to enjoy it and to cherish it just as God does. And before we leave this chapter, let's consider one more song with lyrics about water that celebrates God's marvelous creation.

1.13 Fountain of Life

Yellowstone National Park in Wyoming is home to more geysers than any other place in the world. Half of the world's 1000 known geysers are there.

Geysers occur only in particular hydrogeological conditions, usually near active volcanic zones, where surface water works its way down to where it meets up with hot rocks. The resultant boiling of the pressurized water produces the dramatic geyser effect. Every ninety minutes or so, Yellowstone's most famous geyser, Old Faithful, serves up a fountain of 4,000 – 8,000 gallons (15,000 to 30,000 liters) of boiling water and spews it 150 feet (45m) into the air – thunderous power and surprise, dramatic beauty and unfailing reliability.

The word 'geyser' is Icelandic for 'gush'. The town of Geysir in Iceland sits on a geothermal zone with lots of steam vents and a geyser called *Stokkur* that erupts 12-15 times every hour. That's ten times more frequently than Old Faithful and almost as large by volume!

So, on a Friday morning in August, sightseeing in Iceland, my wife and I found ourselves in Geysir standing with perhaps forty or sixty other tourists, eagerly awaiting the next dramatic 'gush'. We stood in near silence, the suspense fueling our anticipation. Then a brief swelling of the water in the ten-foot (3m) wide basin, a sudden explosive *fffwoooooosh!* – and a plume of white-hot water and steam shot 120 feet (36m) into the air! Cameras snapped and the crowd of silent watchers instantly celebrated with a simultaneous cheer. A momentary community of joy was born as strangers exchanged chatter with strangers.

We watched several reprises of the spectacle until we had to leave, but the earth never tires of the process. It recycles the water and does it all over again within two, four or six minutes – and again and again. Spectacular geothermal hydrologic power on display day and night, year after year. As we drove away from Geysir, I thought of the words of King David.

The poet-king David never visited Iceland or Yellowstone Park, but in *Psalm 36* he wrote about his experience of God with equally dramatic nature imagery.

> Your love, O LORD, reaches to the heavens,
> Your faithfulness to the skies.
> Your righteousness is like the mighty mountains,
> Your justice like the great deep.
> How priceless is your unfailing love!
> We drink from your river of delights.
> You are the fountain of life.
> In your light we see light.
> Psalm 36:5-9

I love that kaleidoscope of God qualities: love that towers above the clouds, righteousness rock solid as the Himalayas, justice more profound than the oceans, faithfulness that beggars human wealth. These flow out of God like a life-giving fountain that invigorates David and gives him a fresh vision for his own life. He contrasts this experience of a God-energized life with the alternative, a God-avoiding life that becomes myopic, scheming and false. David chooses a life inspired and illuminated by God.

I love how Eugene Peterson renders David's Psalm 36 in *The Message*:

> God's love is meteoric,
> his loyalty astronomic,
> His purpose titanic,
> his verdicts oceanic.
>
> How exquisite your love, O God!
> as you fill our tankards with Eden spring water.

> You're a fountain of cascading light,
> and you open our eyes to light.
> Psalm 36:5-9 MSG

And I pray . . .

Magnificent eye-opening God, I don't want to drift through your world with eyes glazed over. I don't want to miss a thing. Surprise me each day with the glory of your work all around me. Lift my eyes to the towering dimensions of your truth. Faithful fountain of life, energize me so I will erupt and overflow every day with God-warmth and geyser-glory. Amen.

Chapter 2

What a Wonderful World!

Centuries before Louis Armstrong painted "skies of blue and clouds of white" with his gravelly voice, artists and poets, children, lovers and scientists have stood speechless at the beauty of our elegant world.

Psalm 104 is a majestic creation praise song, a melodic retelling of the opening of Genesis, tracing its way through the six days of the creation story. Over and over again it shows us the glory of God in "sister water" as St. Francis called it. In the same material creation of which we are a part, we see our Creator's heart as well as his handiwork.

In its first glimpse of the creator in Psalm 104 we see God as Earth-maker, robed in sunlight, setting up tent in the blue sky with cloud chariots and wind couriers at the ready.

> O LORD my God, you are very great;
> you are clothed with splendor and majesty.
> He wraps himself in light as with a garment;
> he stretches out the heavens like a tent
> and lays the beams of his upper chambers on their waters.
> He makes the clouds his chariot and rides on the wings of the wind.
>
> He set the earth on its foundations; it can never be moved.
> You covered it with the deep as with a garment;
> the waters stood above the mountains.
> Psalm 104:1-6

Ocean depths below reflect the grandeur of sky above. The physical world mirrors the glory of its Creator. We see God first as a homebuilder, radiating sunlight; then as a tender mother, swaddling her new creation with a blanket of Ocean, reminiscent of the maternal portrait of God in Job as mother of the oceans.

2.1 Roaring God

Then, dramatically, God is a Commander snapping fingers, ordering Ocean to retreat, allowing Land to rise:

> At your rebuke the waters fled,
> at the sound of your thunder they took to flight;
> they flowed over the mountains, they went down into the valleys,
> to the place you assigned for them.
> You set a boundary they cannot cross;
> never again will they cover the earth.
> Psalm 104:7-9

Picture the scene as continents lift like blue whales breaching, rising out of the ocean depths. Seawater falls away; streams flow down mountains, as water always does, seeking out the lowest places on the planet.

As this psalm celebrates God's creative exploits, there's nothing tame about its vision. God roars a rebuke and nature obeys in a powerful tectonic drama. These are not impersonal geological mechanisms, but nature responding to its creator's command, like an orchestra following the conductor's baton.

Geology is a fascinating record of this process of earth formation – the interaction of rock, heat, water and time. The Hebrew vision captures the energy and drama of these processes, but it also identifies the maker as an artist with life-creating, life-protecting purpose and determination.

I wonder what we can learn from watching how God works, because I'm convinced that our part in creation is not just to be admiring spectators. I wonder how God's rebuke might sound in response to a major oil spill or some other ecological travesty. I wonder what I can do today to help Earth-maker's purpose to prosper?

2.2 Respect and Restraint

Two things stand out to me in this portrait of God's activity. First, notice how God uses creative power for constructive life-supporting purposes. God's rebuke is not timid, nor haughty or defensive as human rebukes often are. Rather, it is empowering and developmental. Oceans and rivers exult in God's initiative and ingenuity; they sustain life on our planet and enable living things to flourish. Second, God imposes limits and boundaries to protect what he has created.

Both of these God actions are instructive for us, inviting us to echo God's example. The first response is one of *respect*. We show respect for God as Earth-maker by treating our environment with care. We should be as deliberate and focused in caring for the earth as God was in creating it, wrapping it, so to speak, with dignity. Nature is fragile, and too often we have ignored its need and its call for supportive care. We should be as immediate in response to nature's call or rebuke as the waters were in this story to the Creator's authoritative word. If the waters accepted their assigned place in the created order and continue to carry out their purpose in the world, surely we who have received a role of such immense privilege and honor should use our capacity to serve the purposes of the One who made us.

The second response is *restraint*. God imposed limits on the sea in order to sustain life on earth. Without consistent boundaries Chaos inevitably breaks through. Neglect and the law of entropy are the default positions in all of nature. Our capability to destroy is vastly greater than our creative capacities. Vigilance and restraint are crucial. Boundaries are essential to good order. And what a crucial lesson was learned from the ravages of Hurricane Katrina in New Orleans in 2005 about the importance of investing in sound boundaries and the steep price of ignoring those levees and limits of life!

In this great project of earth-making and earth-keeping, restraint is balanced with initiative. At the culmination of Psalm 104's eloquent recital of all God's amazing creative activity, as the sun rises and lions steal back to their dens, "then people go out to their work, to their labor until evening" (verse 23). The great high privilege of human beings is to partner with God in God's creation initiative. There is no stewardship without engagement.

The psalm concludes with a prayer that creation will continue to reflect God's beauty and that God will forever be able to rejoice in how the creation is being sustained.

> May the glory of the LORD endure forever;
> may the LORD rejoice in his works!
> Psalm 104:31.

I believe these words invite us to join our efforts in support of God's amazing handiwork in creation.

Around the world there are thousands of scientists, engineers and conservationists constantly and creatively at work designing appropriate strategies to protect and preserve the natural world. Dr. Steven Hall is an agricultural engineer in Louisiana who, along with others, has launched initiatives to protect the fragile Louisiana shoreline both before and since Hurricane Katrina. They have developed bioengineered reefs that are better suited to the Gulf Coast environment than heavy rock breakwaters. These placements not only reduce wave erosion and protect the marshes and shore, but also enhance ecological restoration, the regeneration of oyster populations and the growth of small fish and other desired organisms and assist in coastal wetland restoration.

This evening as I write this piece, my wife and I attended a charity dinner sponsored by Canadian high school students who are raising funds to build a school in eastern Sri Lanka that was devastated by the tsunami in 2004. When the sea convulses and wreaks havoc against humanity, it is the glory of our race to respond like our Creator God, to bring hope out of despair and make new life possible.

These are only a couple of examples among thousands of initiatives around the world that illustrate how we can partner with God, supporting God's purposes so that water and earth can enhance each other for the flourishing of life everywhere. Unfortunately, too often we leave it to other people to do the earth-keeping for us.

2.3 Cool Mountain Streams

Ten of Asia's largest rivers begin in the Himalayan glacial fields. It is the largest supply of frozen water on the planet after the two polar regions, sometimes called "the third pole". The ice-melt from these vast reservoirs helps feed over 2 billion people – a third of the earth. Psalm 104 celebrates God's power and love as vibrant mountain springs spill out of the ground and course down through streams and rivers, lakes and wetlands.

> He makes springs pour water into the ravines;
> it flows between the mountains.
> They give water to all the beasts of the field;
> the wild donkeys quench their thirst.

> The birds of the air nest by the waters;
> they sing among the branches
> Psalm 104:10-12.

Proportionately rivers and streams are a miniscule drop in the global water bucket. Over 97% of the world's water is ocean and most of what remains lies frozen in snowpack or glaciers or stored underground in aquifers, leaving one-third of one percent of the earth's freshwater in streams and rivers, marshes, lakes and swamps, vapor and living things like people and trees.[32] Only five percent of this, a mere 508 cubic miles (2,120 cubic kms),[33] flows down the Amazon, Nile, Congo and Mississippi, the Danube and Rhine, the Yangtze and Yellow, the St Lawrence, Volga, Ganges and Brahmaputra, Mackenzie, Murray and Mekong, the Rio Grande and the thousands of tributaries that feed them and hundreds of other rivers like them, draining the highlands to irrigate the thirsty plains below.

Vast ecosystems depend on these rivers. Grasses, flowers, shrubs and trees grow in the water or along the shore; insects swarm above them; fish ply the currents, graze the stony riverbed, and procreate in quiet places while other fish come in from the ocean to spawn in ponds upstream; birds feed on the grasses or fish or insects; snakes and frogs, turtles and alligators and mammals large and small quench their thirst or satisfy their hunger from the river's bounty. All these interact in a dynamic balance of nature. All of them call the river 'home'. And sometimes they need our help to protect their homes from the impact of human interference.[34]

I love the terse two lines of verse 12 with which this psalm describes the river habitat:

> The birds of the air nest by the waters;
> they sing among the branches.

What a delightful picture of nature contented and harmonious – a bird-watcher's delight. Perhaps such a scene is what Jesus had in mind when he said, "Consider the birds of the air that neither sow or reap or gather into barns, yet your heavenly Father feeds them. Are you not much more valuable than they?" (Matthew 6:26).

Psalm 104 praises God for the beauty and fruitfulness of the earth, and prays that this will endure for all time and that God himself will find as much pleasure and joy in the work of his hands as we do:

> May the glory of the LORD endure forever;
> may the LORD rejoice in his works!
> Psalm 104:31

Humans depend on rivers for food, drinking water and sanitation, the reason so many cities grow up along rivers. Rivers serve industry, commerce, travel and recreation. The power of gravity that causes a river to flow is harnessed both for industry and for recreation. Picture waterwheels running mills; picture children floating downstream on inner tubes or collegiate rowers at sunrise on the Thames or whitewater rafters navigating raging gorges in New Zealand! Add the aesthetic beauty of rivers, whether the roaring majesty of Victoria Falls or the peaceful quiet of a woodland stream; rivers are one of God's wonder filled gifts for nourishing the human soul!

Exploring a river in Iceland one day I received a glimpse into infinity. My wife and I were hiking along the Skógá River above Skogafoss, one of Iceland's most striking waterfalls. The falls are postcard perfect: an impressive 200 foot (60m) sheer drop, higher than Niagara, into a thundering pool, often with a double rainbow effect. The rugged rocks on either side and the jet-black sand on the flat plain along the river below the falls give a dramatic framing. No wonder legends of buried Viking gold grew up around this place; no wonder tourists shoot a zillion photos.

Climbing 380 steps to see the falls from above drew us into an adventure of discovery. A stile over a fence at the top beckoned us further up and further in. Little did we know the wonders that awaited. The Skógá is a glacial melt river with head-waters several miles upstream on the slopes of Eyjafjallajökull, the mountain that erupted in 2010 disrupting air traffic all over Europe. The volcano was quiet when we visited, but the river was very much alive, tumbling down twenty-three cataracts and rapids before its final drop and leisurely flow another 3 miles (5 kms) to the Atlantic.

Rounding a curve in the path, the first of these caught us by surprise, the sounds and sights of a triple ledge cascade. More photos, ooh's and ahh's and we walked on. Suddenly the rock strewn canyon below became another torrent of white water with a wide flume twisting in a 180^0 corkscrew – and more exclamations of wonder! Above that, around another bend, a fourth and then a fifth wide chute. The sixth was a tumbling swath of rapids.

Tumbling water is always exhilarating, but in that rugged green and black landscape it was breath-stoppingly awesome. Every swirl of water was a study in beauty, an infinite kaleidoscope of white, blue and gray. And clinging to the edge of the rocks, the tiniest of flowers were drinking in the mist from the river below. Add the symphonic sounds echoing through the canyon and you get a hint of why I say we had a brush with the infinite.

At this point we had surfeited our capacity for beauty and wonder. We had to turn back at the sixth cataract, knowing there were amazing worlds beyond us. We thought of C.S. Lewis's words in *The Last Battle* about "the Great Story . . . which goes on for ever: in which every chapter is better than the one before."[35]

Ecclesiastes 3:11 says "He has made everything beautiful in its time and set eternity in our hearts, but still we cannot fathom what God has done." But that limitation, that human finitude and frailty, can't stop us from reveling in the marvels of creation and the One who created it all! Twenty-three cataracts carved over centuries of continuing geological and divine creativity! No wonder the Psalmist says "Great is the LORD and most worthy of praise; his greatness no one can fathom" (Psalm 145:3).

Perhaps that is why an infinite God has promised eternity to share the pleasure of his creation with us at leisure. But we live our lives in the constraints of time. And time is what the great Tibetan glaciers are running out of. They are shrinking rapidly and it makes me wonder. I wonder what it's all going to look like a hundred years downstream from here. And I wonder how to pray for those who depend on these waters.

2.4 Rain, Rain, Rain

The annual migration of Serengeti wildlife is a desperate drama – two million desperately thirsty elephants and lions, monkeys and wildebeest travel hundreds of miles in search of the life-giving rains. Without the rains, they die. So do we all.

Ancient Israel's Earth-maker hymn, Psalm 104, celebrates rain as a sign of God's generous providence. And as Jesus noted, rain does not discriminate; it falls on "the evil and the good" alike! (Matthew 5:45),

> He waters the mountains from his upper chambers;
> the earth is satisfied by the fruit of his work.
> Psalm 104:13

On any given day, about 330 cubic miles (1370 kms^3) of rain or snow falls on our planet[36]. Just for reference, that's about 360 trillion gallons. 87% of this volume evaporated out of the ocean, but only 79% of the rain falls there. The 8% difference – averaging 30 cubic miles (126 km^3 or 33 trillion gallons) of moisture every day – replenishes the land, recharging rivers and aquifers, watering mountain forests, open grasslands, rice paddies and golf courses.

We measure rain locally by inches or millimeters, but the benefit it brings to the landscape and human society both locally and globally is beyond measure. This daily hydrological 'windfall' provides us the critical water that sustains our lives both physically and emotionally.

A hydrogeologist friend returned from a year in Central and South America, seeing both rain forests and bone-dry drought regions. She wrote of the sheer joy of experiencing rain in the tropics:

> I loved the rain, the peace of the environment being awakened by an almost deafening sound all around you. It is like a curtain has been drawn and suddenly the rest of the world has been cut off from you. The heavens open and so much water falls that it seems like the land will not dry up, but then suddenly the rain stops, the world becomes quiet again but you get a feeling of nourishment, that everything has been replenished. You can almost feel the land and the plants soak up the life sustaining water. … God has created such a magnificent and beautiful world; in such a miraculous way it sustains us and it sustains itself!

As recipients of this lavish gift that comes so freely and profusely to replenish body and soul, we have endless reasons to be both humble and grateful to God as rain-maker. It ought also to prompt within us an instinctive neighborly response when people elsewhere experience the calamity of extreme rain – drought or monsoon flooding.

The psalm goes on to cite the benefit first of open-plain grasslands for grazing animals, and then the cultivated crops for human consumption.

> He makes grass grow for the cattle,
> and plants for man to cultivate –

bringing forth food from the earth:
wine that gladdens the heart of man,
oil to make his face shine,
and bread that sustains his heart.
Psalm 104:14-15

Agriculture was one of the key developments that led to the rise of human civilization and continues to be the foundation of almost every nation's economy, especially those that are able to manage the gift of rain.

The psalm mentions olive oil, barley and wine as specific examples of rain's bounty. Israel has been famous for its grapes since the time of Moses and Joshua, and today is enjoying resurgence in the production of its wineries. Grainfields and vineyards are nourished and nourishing all because of Earth-maker's gift of rain that falls from the sky.

Psalm 104 celebrates God's creative production of a lavish smorgasbord out of water and soil – rain from above combining with nutrients from the earth below to produce "wine to gladden our hearts, oil to make our faces shine and bread to keep us well-fed and hearty" (verse 15 MSG). Food is not a given but a gift.[37]

This is where Israel finds its traditional mealtime blessing:

Blessed are You, Lord, our God,
King of the Universe
who brings forth bread from the earth.

This is creation spirituality, embodied and earthy, not a hint of theoretical religion in this vision of the world. Like rain, faith has to be either down-to-earth or it's meaningless.

- *I wonder . . .* what I can learn about generosity from Earth-maker's lavish gift of rain?
- *I wonder. . .* how to think about extreme weather – drought and monsoons and the dire effects they have on my global neighbors?
- *I wonder. . .* if there's a Serengeti drought zone in my life, thirsting for rain?

2.5 Rain Forest

Forests are the lungs of planet earth. They consume our carbon dioxide and they exhale oxygen. They filter our pollution and purify the air; they recycle back to the atmosphere vast amounts of water through transpiration and thus help to regulate the climate patterns for the world.

Deforestation is like planetary lung cancer; it takes our breath away. We simply can't survive without the forests. We didn't plant them but they serve us day and night; they breathe for us. Reckless logging and large-scale burning for agriculture destroys a crucial balance of soil, water and air. In the two decades between 1990 and 2010, a quarter of Ghana's forest cover was felled for timber export, firewood or to create land for cocoa cultivation.[38] We all pay the price of that wanton short-sightedness. As Scott Sabin explains, though, in his book *Tending to Eden,* many of the world's poor and landless farmers often have no choice but to destroy forests to eke out a living, He shows how re-forestation and agroforestry can help to break the cycle of poverty and create more virtuous and more productive communities.[39]

Israel's Earth-maker hymn Psalm 104 celebrates the forest as God's garden–

> The trees of the LORD are well-watered,
> the cedars of Lebanon that he planted.
> There the birds make their nests;
> the stork has its home in the pine trees.
> Psalm 104:16-17

A rain-forest ecosystem is a complex marvel of mutually-supporting organisms. In fact, tropical rainforests support the greatest biodiversity on the planet.[40] Forests provide huge economic resources and medicinal treasures far beyond what we know today. Harvesting these riches without deforestation, without killing the goose that lays the golden eggs, is an almost impossible project. Recreation and tourism leaders remind us to leave only our footprints behind, but that seems to be a tough challenge for most people.

Sustainable development is the gold standard of responsible stewardship, but as a human race, our greed and impatience gets the better of us every time. Beneath the forest floor lie huge deposits of minerals, oil and gas, the extraction of which almost always fouls the environment. And that brings us again to the delicate balance that wisdom demands of good stewardship: *respect* and *restraint*.

As Israel's song says,

> How many are your works, O LORD!
> In wisdom you made them all;
> The earth is full of your creatures.
> Psalm 104:24

In his 2009 Massey Lectures, *The Wayfinders*, anthropologist and ethnobotanist Wade Davis tells a fascinating story of the people of the Anaconda who live in the northwest Amazon rainforest in the eastern foothills of the Andes in Colombia. For them the forest is not a material resource to seize and exploit, but a living homeland to treasure and enjoy, to cultivate and preserve. Whether they sing Israel's song or not, they have a similar conviction that their canopied world is not of their own making, and that it is full of wonderful mystery and has been entrusted to them to cherish and honor.[41]

Ponder for a moment what a marvelous and intricate gift a forest is. Thank God for its glory, color and vibrancy. Consider what a generous classroom a forest can be for wisdom and humility. Pray that we will value and conserve the forests of the earth for generations to come.[42] As for Ghana's forests, thank God for organizations like A Rocha who are working with local residents on re-forestation projects, restoring hundreds of acres with native trees and other species.[43]

2.6 Blue Marble

From space our planet looks like a "blue marble" – 75% of it covered by water, "the ocean wrapping the world in its sapphire scarf" as poet Luci Shaw puts it[44]. The vast blues of the oceans are laced by swirling white clouds showcasing the beauty and symmetry of God's creation. Psalm 104 revels in Earth-maker's workmanship – sky, clouds and rain, rivers and wetlands, wildlife and forests – and now, finally, the wide blue oceans.

> There is the sea, vast and spacious,
> teeming with creatures beyond number—
> living things both large and small.
> There the ships go to and fro,
> and the leviathan, which you formed to frolic there.
> Psalm 104:24-26

The Hebrews were not a seagoing people, so biblical oceans usually roar wild and restless. In this song, though, while the ocean is vast and spacious, it is not intimidating. It is hospitable and "teems with creatures beyond number, living things, both large and small" (verse 24), from tiny microbes and plankton to dolphins and manta rays, from corals and conchs to octopus and sperm whales. Yet despite the fullness of the sea, it is not crowded; there is plenty of room for ship traffic and for whales to cavort, calve, graze and migrate.

Perhaps the most uncharacteristic detail of the elaborate seascape in this Hebrew poem is the portrait of leviathan as a frolicking animal, a bath-toy for the Creator.[45] When the Book of Job describes leviathan (Job 41), we see a thrashing menacing creature of the deep – shark, whale, crocodile or mythic sea monster. But this psalm pictures leviathan as a playful specimen, a show-piece of God's exuberant pleasure and enjoyment. Ours is a lively well-ordered world where God has made every creature for joyous creative purpose. The world is not an alien place for us. God made it for us and we share it with a marvelous array of fellow creatures.

From the seas, as from the land, we reap a harvest far beyond what we have sown. Every summer we visit the North Carolina coast where my wife loves to go fishing. Her best catch so far was a 36 inch (91 cm) bonnethead shark, '*the finest eating in the sea*' according to the locals.

Under the sea, a bountiful harvest is continually being cultivated for hungry mouths. Kelp beds dance in tidal rhythms providing a nursery for plankton, algae and worms and countless invertebrate creatures, and a smorgasbord that invites diners with voracious appetites to their feast – snails, sea urchins and fish galore – even human ice cream lovers who benefit from '*algin*', a gooey compound extracted from kelp just for us!

Examine every habitat on the planet and you find a similarly dazzling intricacy of harboring and harvesting, helping and exploiting, eating and being eaten. Even the most inhospitable spots have become home to the strangest of creatures. Taken all together the world is wonderfully balanced and interdependent – a most ingenious ecology. What an eminently practical Creator!

In the light of this celebration of the bounty of the seas and its Creator, it is vital that we turn our wonder into responsible action. We are fellow creatures with the sea, but according to the Bible, uniquely charged with the task of "ruling over the fish of the sea and all that swim the paths of the sea" (Psalm 8:5). 'Ruling' with integrity means safeguarding fish stocks and seal herds; it means stewarding underwater minerals, not over harvesting or extracting them recklessly. Who else will preserve the habitats of penguins and cormorants, polar bears and blue whales if we are indifferent to how we are treating them?

We ought to demonstrate our appreciation for this beautiful bountiful blue gift by protecting its shorelines and by acting not only as stewards of earth and sea, but as worshippers of a generous Creator, worshippers who value what we've been given and who want to give something back.

> God of Oceans,
> Everything comes from you;
> Everything happens through you;
> Everything ends in you;
> Always glory! Always praise!
> Yes. Yes. Yes.
> Adapted from Romans 11:36 MSG

Psalm 104 celebrates the beauty and fruitfulness of the earth, and attributes it all to God. It prays that this glory will endure for all time and that God will find as much pleasure and joy in it as we do –

> The glory of GOD—let it last forever!
> Let GOD enjoy his creation!
> Psalm 104:31 MSG

Wonder... Reflect for a moment on the stunning visual beauty of our world and the dynamic power of nature, either around you right now or depicted in this song. Pause and be restful; sense the joy throbbing in creation – and an ache behind the joy, and thank God for the immense privilege of being part of it.

2.7 Nile in the Sky

Many of Israel's psalms are attributed to David or some other musical poet. Not so Psalm 104. We don't know who first wrote it, but it is almost certainly an example of an ancient cultural rip-off – or perhaps a high culture replica. Fourteen centuries before Christ, hundreds of years before Israel's worship leaders assembled the Book of Psalms, the Egyptian pharaoh Akhenaten penned a hymn to his god, Aten. This pharaoh abandoned traditional Egyptian polytheism and introduced a more monotheistic form of worship featuring Aten as a solar deity above the mere gods.

We don't know how original Akhenaten's song was or how popular it became, but the similarities between that hymn and Psalm 104 are remarkable. Equally remarkable are the differences between the two songs[46]. Both songs are monotheistic and both attribute the beauty, joy and vibrancy of the world to the One who created it. We live in an awesome wonderful world and we have Someone to thank for that. To the Egyptian, that was Aten, to the Hebrews it was Yahweh, the one who "'wraps himself in light as with a garment" (verse 2)[47]

Nor do we know how Israel became aware of this poem, but I have my own take on the process, admittedly, a purely fanciful one. I like to imagine a Hebrew child a hundred years before Moses, singing the words of the sun god song she has learned from her Egyptian friends. Her parents are outraged at the theology their child has absorbed from the foreign culture, but they can't stop her from humming the melody. So instead, they co-opt the sun god song and refit it with strands of the well-loved Hebrew story until it sparkles with the glory of God and all his works. Of course, that scenario is pure speculation.

But clearly, Psalm 104 is a great example of transforming culture, using a familiar cultural art form, perhaps even a pagan one, to express and transmit God's redemptive truth in a recognizable idiom. Martin Luther is said to have done the same thing a couple of millennia later.[48]

The original Egyptian poem praises the sun as the light that makes possible the water based delights of "boats sailing upstream and downstream, where every highway is open and visible in the daylight, where fish leap for the light and the sun's rays color the great green sea." It speaks of "a Nile in the sky for the strangers and for the cattle of every country", a picturesque and culturally relevant way to describe rain as the atmospheric counter-part to the life-giving Nile, recognizing the divine gift that sustains people and wildlife both locally and to the ends of the earth.

The Hebrew psalm also revels in all these gifts; it begins and ends with a joyous exclamation of the heart – "Praise Yahweh, O my soul" – and invites us to make that praise a life-long practice and a vibrant source of inner joy.

I will sing to the Lord all my life;
I will sing praise to my God as long as I live.
May my meditation be pleasing to him
As I rejoice in the Lord.
Psalm 104:35

Chapter 3

Rain – The Immeasurable Gift

3.1 Evaporation

It happens in coffee shops day and night around the world. It wafts from the breath of every person on the planet. Mist rises from golf courses and wetlands. Steam soars from industry stacks and treetops. Water evaporates from the Bay of Bengal and transpires from plants. Round and around it goes, steaming up as vapor and then falling as rain or snow. It's the hydrologic cycle and it goes on endlessly day after day, night after night all over the world.

The Water Cycle is a fascinating process, a powerful perpetual-motion self-sustaining procedure for circulating water, purifying the air and nourishing life.

As oceans and land absorb energy from the sun, water transforms into gas and evaporates into the air. Warm air rises ... and expands. Expansion causes it to cool and eventually clouds form. The engineering design is brilliant and self-sustaining. It's the original reuse and recycle process built into the universe. And the scope of the operation boggles the mind.

In his book *When the Rivers Run Dry,* Fred Pearce, water journalist for *New Scientist,* notes that about half a million cubic kilometers of water flow through the evaporation-precipitation cycle in a year[49]. That's 1370 kms^3 a day, or 330 cubic miles a day – or as we noted in the last chapter, 360 trillion gallons a day. That's the entire volume of Lake Ontario every 28 hours! The enormous energy of the sun heats this vast volume of water, turns it into vapor and lifts it into the skies – more than a billion tons (a trillion kgs) of water every minute, day and night![50] The sky stores it and ships it around until it cools sufficiently to begin the process of precipitation. Huge effects on the earth from something as silent as vapor wafting from a teacup! In most religious traditions, smoke is used as an expression of devotion or prayer. Perhaps steaming coffee is our culture's substitute.

Evaporation makes water invisible; but what we cannot see eventually distills and returns to us, often in places where it does more good. There's a metaphor of more than rain in this process – it's an ingenious system indeed!

Long before we had mathematical formulae to explain the complexity of the process, a philosopher named Elihu in the Book of Job marveled how God

> . . . draws up the drops of water,
> which distill as rain to the streams;
> the clouds pour down their moisture
> and abundant showers fall on mankind.
> Who can understand how he spreads out the clouds?
> Job 36:27-29

Indeed who can understand the complex science of nephrology, the study of clouds?

And what an astonishing feat of physics! Moisture, heat, pressure, gravity, electricity and crystal formation combine to float tons of water for miles through thin air, condense them to fall as mist or monsoon, as snow or hail onto the earth below. There's chemistry in there too, making nephrology a very complex science.

3.2 The Clouds Veil

Long before children learn how clouds are formed, they lie in the grass watching them morph from shape to shape. I still love doing that. I recall an evening train ride along the shore of Lake Ontario under a clear sky and the setting sun, watching magnificent clouds for half an hour as they curled and curved under the flow of wind and shifted through red, violet and purple shades. Clouds are nature's poetry in motion.

And what visual spectacle they give us. Flying to the Caribbean you can see enormous cumulus clouds towering hundreds of feet above you. I remember flying through a lightning storm over the Appalachians, as electricity forked from one cloud to another, lighting up the sky in an exhilarating display of power and surprise.

Clouds are also highly functional. At any time, about half the planet is covered by cloud, shading us from scorching sun and helping to insulate the earth. They affect environments and climate everywhere. Job shakes his head at this wonder of water – "God wraps up the waters in his clouds, yet the clouds do not burst under their weight" (Job 26:8). And this goes on day after day, night after night, around the world.

As Job's friends sat around him under the blistering sun in the Mesopotamian desert trying to decipher the mysterious cause of Job's suffering, Job pointed at the clouds above them in the brilliant blue sky and marveled at the paradox of the unexplainable, water bearing clouds that don't burst under their own weight, and the paradox of a glorious but distant God. For Job, clouds were exhibit A of the inscrutable mystery of God's power and purposes.

A few verses later he says, "these are but the outer fringe of his works; how faint the whisper we hear of him! Who then can understand the thunder of his power?" (Job 26:14).

One of Job's friends, Eliphaz, claims that arrogant people look at clouds as proof that God can't see what they're doing. God is so far away, what does God know? Does he judge through such darkness? Thick clouds veil him, so he does not see us as he goes about in the vaulted heavens (Job 22:13-14). The writer of Lamentations sees it from the other side and suggests that God uses clouds to insulate himself against the prayers of undeserving sinners, "You have covered yourself with a cloud so that no prayer can get through" (Lamentations 3:44). Imaginative ideas, but both wrong.

Like Job we stand in awe at this phenomenon of nature in the skies. Like Elihu, we are impressed by the sheer inventiveness of this process and the scope of its benefits for every inhabitant on earth. It is a marvel, he observed, that dwarfs human comprehension and capability. Even with state-of-the-art technical instruments and doctorates in meteorology the complexity cloud behavior still outstrips our capacity to *understand* the skies, let alone *master* them.

Satirist Douglas Adams lampoons the kind of intellectual pretentiousness that masks itself in pseudoscience language:

> I can't comment on the name Rain God . . . We are calling him an example of Spontaneous Para-causal Meteorological Phenomenon . . . or "a Supernormal Incremental Precipitation Inducer". And

> we'll probably want to shove a Quasi in there somewhere to protect ourselves."[51]

So these lofty white fluff balls are eloquent and dramatic parables reminding us that our insight into other deeper mysteries of life is often equally cloudy.

The brilliance and ingenuity of this natural process evokes our humility and wonder. But when the poet asks rhetorically 'who can understand such complexity?' he isn't suggesting that mystery and the limits of our knowledge makes observation and study pointless. Rather it inspires our curiosity to know more, to understand all we can. The more we discover, the more our amazement grows.

But as Rabbi Abraham Heschel observed, awareness of the divine begins with wonder[52]. It is a sense of awe, wonder and amazement that make our souls aware of God. Notice the clouds around you or above you today. Thank God for their beauty and benefits, and let them whisper to you about the Creator's love and power and purpose.

And consider this analogy: imagine this global action of evaporation being a gigantic expression of prayer. Just as nature lifts vast volumes of water into the skies every minute of the day, imagine the pouring out of thanks and praise to the Creator from millions of worshippers in gratitude for the good gifts of life.

Imagine the cumulative prayers of the poor crying out for justice and mercy, the collective yearnings of humble and faithful souls rising like mist from the earth, forming clouds of petition before God.

3.3 Tipping Point

Hurricane Igor slammed into Newfoundland in 2010 with ferocious winds and rain. The weather channel saw it coming but was powerless to stop it or steer it out to sea. An 80 year old man was swept away in the flood along with bridges, roads and homes. We *wonder*. . . and we ask *Why?*

Job and his friends wore themselves out pondering the '*Why?*' question. Sometimes our best explanations don't fit. Eventually God steps into their conversation and asks more questions. Chapters 38-39 of Job contain a dazzling barrage of twenty case studies from nature. Take ten minutes and read them over. God asks who has the wits to design sunsets and dawn?

Who can redirect Orion? Who can tame dragons or manage hurricanes, inventory the clouds or command rains to start or stop?

> Can you raise your voice to the clouds
> and cover yourself with a flood of water?
> Do you send the lightning bolts on their way? . . .
> Who has the wisdom to count the clouds?
> Who can tip over the water jars of the heavens?
> Job 38:34-38

I love the picturesque language of this rhetorical question, "who can tip over the water jars of the heavens?" (Job 38:38). People accidentally knock over pails of water and glasses of milk, but even with the greatest effort, who can bring clouds to the tipping point? Even when the need is urgent, when soil becomes cracked and parched, we simply cannot command the rain.

Nor can Job – or we – demand an explanation for our suffering. Job would love to tip over the jars of heavenly secrets and make sense of what has happened in his life. But that power is beyond him.

Like Job we are fragile creatures in a vast universe; we have no bragging rights before God. But God does not humiliate us with our frailty; he gives us dignity. An almighty God chooses to involve us, frail as we are, as trusted partners in amazing, mind-bending high purposes.

Clouds – and all of nature beyond our control, are visible signs to us of God's grace. The power, beauty and mystery of God's creation give us a hint that there is a similar authority, beauty and moral order in the universe. That's the *tipping point* that leads us to a mature relationship with God and a deeper, wiser view of the way the world works.

Even if God never explains the mysteries of our life, we can know – or try to learn – that God is trustworthy and good. *The Cloud of Unknowing* is a book of contemplation by a 14th English Christian mystic who wrote that God is hidden to us behind a cloud. He argues that God may not be known by reason, He may not be gotten by thought, nor concluded by understanding; but He may be loved.

Like Job, we will never fully comprehend God, but we can enjoy relationship with God. There is amazing dignity in that.

3.4 What Goes Up . . .Must Come Down

Every day about 10% of the vapor in the atmosphere falls to the earth – about 60 billion tons of water every hour, and is replaced by a fresh supply. Ancient Elihu also saw God's active hand in the transforming effects of evaporation and precipitation – "He pulls water up out of the sea and distills it" (Job 36:27 MSG). Almost a billion tons of water – that's how much evaporates every minute of every day.

As the water vapor in this air mass cools it begins to condense on particles like dust, ice, and salt. This forms small droplets or ice crystals, as small as a one-hundredth of a millimeter in diameter. When surrounded by billions of other such droplets they become visible as clouds which reflect back the sunlight, giving a cloud its characteristic white color.

But before clouds can drop their freight of water to the earth, a massive 'clobber & clump' operation has to occur so these tiny ice crystals can combine with one another to produce minute droplets which combine to form larger droplets large enough to fall out of the suspended air mass as rain, sleet or snow.

3.5 Multiplier Effect

And everywhere this enormous gift of rain or snowfall accomplishes a variety of essential services for our earth by cleansing the air, moderating the temperature and, most obviously, nourishing the plants and animals on the earth. Day and night, it augments alpine and arctic snowpacks, refreshes rainforests and woodlands, nourishes meadows and grainfields and then returns by evapotranspiration into the skies to do it all again. Some of the rain infiltrates into the ground and trickles down into sand and gravel aquifers that serve as storage beds for later use or flows down through streams and rivers back to the sea.

What it accomplishes along the way is fascinating, cracking open rock fissures and releasing minerals from stone, flushing wetlands. The net benefit of rain and snow is not just the sum total of its various functions. It actually has a multiplier effect. Rainfall leverages a host of related natural environmental outcomes. In excess, it causes avalanches, landslides and floods. Combined with wind it brings blizzards and hurricanes.

But rain also makes possible every form of life on the planet. We drink it and wash in it. It makes corn grow which we can eat today or save and use as seed to multiply the harvest next year. If the rains come in time, apple trees do both – providing both fruit to eat and seeds to sow. Clover turns rain into nectar which bees manufacture into honey, pollinating fields in the process. Oaks turn rain and soil into lumber and acorns and a home for the birds.

This marvelous network of nature is so natural we hardly stop to think about it. But in light of such a beautifully integrated and finely tuned universe, the psalms urge us to respond to the Creator in recognition, praise and gratitude.

> Sing out your thanks to the LORD;
> sing praises to our God with a harp.
> He covers the heavens with clouds,
> provides rain for the earth, and
> makes the grass grow in mountain pastures.
> He gives food to the wild animals
> and feeds the young ravens when they cry.
> Psalm 147:7-9 NLT

Isaiah noticed this variety of effects that come from the rain and the snow. He saw an intriguing parallel to the word and will of God. Both rain and word go out with intentionality; they achieve their purpose, and then return when their assignment is fulfilled. Nothing is wasted; everything is purposeful:

> As the rain and the snow come down from heaven, and do not return to it without watering the earth and making it bud and flourish, so that it yields seed for the sower and bread for the eater, so is my word that goes out from my mouth: It will not return to me empty, but will accomplish what I desire and achieve the purpose for which I sent it Isaiah 55:10-11.

Isaiah's words were directed to the Jewish exiles who lived as strangers in Babylon for two generations. Exile is a frustrating detour in life, where your rights and freedoms are withheld at the whim of others. For Israel it seemed that a foreign emperor had the last word.

But God had a greater word awaiting them, a promise that they would be coming home. As improbable as that sounded, God said, their desert would burst into bloom, just as the parched wilderness blossoms under the rain.

God's word would achieve its transformative purpose, both lifting the hopes of the exiles and convincing the Persian king to reverse imperial policy and send the prisoners home.

Throughout history God has rained down words with varied purpose – words of instruction and promise, rebuke and invitation. Page after page of scripture Paul says, is "inspired by God and is useful to teach us what is true and to make us realize what is wrong in our lives. [...] God uses it to prepare and equip his people to do every good work (2 Timothy 3:16-17 NLT).

Like rain and snow, the Bible is designed by God to have a transforming effect on our lives. One psalm writer 'hid God's word in his heart', like a personal reservoir he could draw on so that his good intentions would not wilt in the summer heat or when moral fatigue set in (Psalm 119:11). Another let the stories of God's way flow over his mind and heart the way a tree rooted near a stream is sustained and nourished (Psalm 1:3).

God's word comes in other ways besides the written scriptures. The Spirit is constantly whispering God's heart into the heart of those willing to listen. Bill Hybels' book *The Power of a Whisper* is a wonderful exploration of God's still small voice. But as Hybels reminds us, we have to be willing to listen and respond.

The book you are reading is a response to such a whisper. As a result of God's prompting, though I didn't recognize it at the time, I began exploring this theme of water in the Bible. Then, after a few more prompts, I began blogging my reflections and learned that people in Poland, Philippines and Pakistan were reading them. Eventually these musings became a book – because of a word from God that did not go back to God empty-handed.

That's the multiplier effect, just like the cumulative effect of rain on the macro environment. God's word comes to us custom designed to achieve effects far into the future beyond what we can see today, beyond what we might consider our immediate needs. Obedience to that word opens up opportunities and possibilities we cannot foresee, like the exiles – something beyond their imagining.

- *I wonder* – how ready am I to welcome God's rain (or reign) into my life?

- Will I let it accomplish God's purpose in my heart and shape my decisions?
- Am I listening to know the tasks God has for me?

If you feel like your life is in a long detour right now, bathe yourself in the rainfall of God's word to you.

3.6 Listen to the Clouds

Job's friend Elihu sounds like a weatherman-turned-theologian. He outdoes himself drawing spiritual lessons from the natural world. He sees God as the power and wisdom behind the clouds. And beyond the power and wisdom he sees God's love. He believes that God directs nature for the benefit of humankind.

> He loads the clouds with moisture;
> he scatters his lightning through them.
> At his direction they swirl around over the face of the whole earth
> to do whatever he commands them.
> He brings the clouds to punish men,
> or to water his earth and show his love.
> "Listen to this, Job; stop and consider God's wonders.
> Do you know how God controls the clouds ?
> Do you know how the clouds hang poised,
> those wonders of him who is perfect in knowledge?
> Job 37:11-16

The Message translates the text this way:

> It's God who fills clouds with rainwater and ... commands them to do what he says all over the world. Whether for discipline or grace or extravagant love, he makes sure they make their mark.

As in Psalm 33:5, the original Hebrew word here is *hesed* – God's extravagant love, covenantal love, love that is loyal and faithful, committed to the well-being of the other. The weather is one of God's gifts of love to the earth. "'God opens his hand and satisfies the desires of every living thing" (Psalm 145:16).

God is not only our benefactor but our moral instructor as well, and he uses clouds to achieve his purpose in both areas. Even when the weather bursts upon us in ferocious intensity, God intends it for our good.

God uses clouds and rain to work out his creative gracious purposes for the world as well as for each nation, city and individual person in the world. Whether it is a hurricane's fury or the cool shadow of a passing cloud on a blistering hot afternoon or the generous summer rains that plump up the Nebraska corn, God is the loving source of it all, "whether for discipline or grace or extravagant love" (Job 37:16 MSG).

Does this mean that God manipulates the clouds like a chess player moves his pawns and bishops and knights? Frankly, I find it a bit hard to believe that every cloud is positioned for personal delivery. Yet I breathe a prayer of gratitude when a cloud brings welcome relief on a sweltering afternoon. I see God's good hand behind the gift, even if God didn't deliberately blow that cloud 6 degrees west just for my benefit, depriving my cross town neighbor of shade.

So Professor Elihu urges us not to take the gifts of nature for granted, but to be attentive to them, "Stop and consider God's wonders" (Job 37:14). Take time to ponder and appreciate the amazing complexity of God's creation and its benefits. Be curious about it; let it temper your pride – do you know how God controls the clouds? Let the clouds and rain lead you to humility not hubris, to reverence not resentment.

3.7 Radical Equality

Another remarkable wonder of water is the way rainfall supports the equal treatment of all regardless of wealth, race, gender or moral virtue. Jesus said, "your Father in heaven causes his sun to rise on the evil and the good, and sends rain on the righteous and the unrighteous" (Matthew 5:45).

Jesus says that God is a large-hearted, even-handed Giver. He points out that God is generous to us regardless of our degree of virtue or vice. Sunshine and rain are gifts from the Creator to his creatures with no moral preconditions. Jesus echoed the Psalmist a thousand years earlier who said "The Lord is good to all; he has compassion on all that he has made" (Psalm 145:9).

St. Paul echoes Jesus when he tells his Greek audience about God signs imbedded in the natural order. "God has shown kindness by giving you rain from heaven and crops in their seasons; he provides you with plenty of food and fills your hearts with joy" (Acts 14:17).

Nature's bounty is the outflow of God's self-giving nature which seeks to multiply joy – even before we respond to God.

What a contrast this is to human nature. We reward our friends and rebuff our adversaries. But God treats us all alike – and he gives gifts of common grace that are not only beneficial, but invaluable – gifts you can't create for yourself or obtain anywhere else. Not only that, but you get your allowance whether you've been bad or good. "He gives his best – the sun to warm, and the rain to nourish – to everyone regardless; the good and the bad; the nice and the nasty" (Matthew 5:45 MSG).

Two farmers receive the same rainfall even though one beats his wife and the other feeds the poor. What's the point of that? Where is the justice? Wouldn't the world work better if God rewarded good people and put the squeeze on those who put the squeeze on others?

Morality *does* matter to God. Performance reviews still count, both in this world and the next. But God is even more passionate about being gracious to us all. This is how God designed human life to be lived. And the radical call of Jesus is to act like God in this extravagant non-discriminating way-raining down kindness even on our enemies. This is a foundational law of nature and the universe. If this is counterintuitive for us, it shows how deeply ingrained our instinct to selective kindness is. This principle has enormous implications in every area of our lives.

Jesus says that if we follow God's lead, we will discover our true selves, our 'God-created selves'. "Live out your God-created identity," he says. "Live generously and graciously towards others, the way God lives towards you" (Matthew 5:48 MSG). One of the distinguishing marks of the image of God in us is our capacity for generous self-giving love.

Prayer:
Generous God, spur me on to more spontaneous love, mentor me to be more openhanded in showing kindness, to reflect your sunshine into the world without filters and to refresh others as generously as you refresh me. Amen.

3.8 Harvesting Fog

Without question the amazing phenomenon of rain certainly teaches us humility and wonder. But as a gift of God's generous providence, the falling rain summons us to action, it calls us into partnership and response. Jesus said, "freely you have received, freely give" (Matthew 10:8)

Since so much creative natural energy is constantly being invested in the supply and delivery side of this vital life-giving process, I think it challenges us as the beneficiaries of this generous windfall to invest similarly creative efforts to harvest and manage the resources of the hydrological cycle.

Living in Belize as a teenager I experienced the benefits of rooftop catchment of rainwater. Our house was better resourced than many and the rains kept our ground level cistern full eight months of the year. If I did my daily hand pumping, the rooftop barrels kept a gravity feed of warm water flowing into our kitchen. When I read about people in Gaza harvesting rainwater from their rooftops, I'm there! Less familiar to me, but even more fascinating are the strategies for harvesting fog in the mountains of Peru and Chile. Rectangular sheets of polypropylene mesh are erected a yard (a meter) above the ground; drops of water collect on the mesh and flow together into receptacles. But this technology is crude and inefficient compared to the ingenious strategies employed by plants and animals living in some of the hottest places on earth.

The Namibian Desert in Southern Africa is dry and hot with scorching sand and very little rain, yet there are several species of beetles that are remarkably well-adapted to this forbidding habitat. The trench beetle, *lepidochora discoidalis,* lives under the sand, but can 'hear' approaching winds; it surfaces just in time to dig long trenches perpendicular to the advancing fog-laden wind and captures water from the air. Another, the fog-basking beetle, *Onymacris unguicularis,* stands on it head and faces the gale force winds and collects droplets of fog that run down grooves on its shell into its mouth. I read somewhere of another species with a fan-shaped tail and a small vial at the base of the tail ridges that collect the tiny drops which it can ingest.

A *Nature* article in November 2001 tells of yet another of these resourceful desert dwellers called *Stenocara* which uses its bumpy shell the same way as the fog-basking beetle without standing on its head. Zoologist Andrew Parker who has studied this beetle thinks its bumpy shell offers a good model for cost-efficient tent coverings and roof tiles that could be used in arid regions.[53] Agricultural and military researchers as well as recreational designers are drawing inspiration and insight from these lowly creatures and applying them to human problems. Human beings have been emulating biological strategies for centuries, but in the search for more efficient methods, 'biomimicry' is enjoying a new era of prestige and promise.[54]

These are just a hint of what can be done – and needs to be done globally. When engineers, hydrologists, politicians, researchers and educators, artists and business people work together with local communities, amazing things can happen. If the ingenuity of nature's unheralded insects and the water cycle earns well-deserved praise for its Creator, we best reflect the Creator's image when we bring our finest creativity to bear on our side of the project.

The water cycle is an enormous priceless legacy freely entrusted to us. And it extends to us unlimited opportunity to develop its capacity for ourselves and others.

Prayer:
Generous and Creative God, you have invested such creative energies in the natural process of providing rain for the earth . . . for us, help us to show our appreciation by partnering with you in the distribution side of the supply chain, so that all your creatures receive the fullest possible benefits of your bounty. Keep us from professing belief in your sovereignty and providence without participating with you in your gracious generosity. Overcome the apathy and indifference in us that prevents us from being worthy coworkers in your enterprise of providence. Amen.

3.9 How Cool is Ice!

Sometimes precipitation turns white and fluffy and comes down in the form of snow, blanketing mountaintops and parking lots, schoolyards and cornfields. Skiers love it and commuters hate it. Snowfall deepens the glaciers and snow-pack reservoirs that are already twenty times the volume of all the earth's rivers combined. Winter bears witness to God's amazing creativity and power every bit as much as spring and summer do.

There is a vivid passage in the Book of Job about a winter blizzard. Eugene Peterson translates the text like a true northerner:

> He orders the snow, 'Blanket the earth!' [...]
> No on can escape the weather. [...]
> Wild animals take shelter, crawling into their dens,
> When blizzards roar out of the north
> and freezing rain crusts the land,
> It's God's breath that forms the ice,
> it's God's breath that turns lakes and rivers solid.
> Job 37:6-10 MSG

Blizzards can be terribly disorienting – even deadly. Animals and people without shelter are in trouble, but amazingly, snow and ice can actually become home. An igloo is a house made of water and the Inuit mastered the art of building snow homes long before the Swedes designed Ice Hotels as a winter novelty.

The same breath of God that gave life to Adam is also credited here with producing ice and snow. Like Adam, ice and snow have characteristics as unique and marvelous as any part of God's creation. Snowflakes are water vapor art. According to physicist Kenneth Libbrecht, the world's foremost snow crystal photographer,[55] every flake is unique.[56] In his 2011 Massey Lectures on Winter, writer Adam Gopnik challenges this commonly asserted belief, citing a study by cloud scientist Nancy Knight in 1988 who took a plane up into the clouds in Wisconsin and found simple snowflakes absolutely identical to each other. Gopnik then describes the tumultuous downward journey of snowflakes through differing humidities, temperatures and wind velocities that play with the crystalline structure of each flake. Gopnik concludes that while snowflakes actually start off all alike, "it is experience that makes each one just different enough to be noticed."[57]

Canadian nature filmmaker Bill Mason wrote "I'll never forget that day in school when the teacher pointed out that as water gets colder it sinks, but just before it reaches the temperature at which it freezes it expands, so ice forms on the surface rather than on the bottom of the lake. I was overwhelmed by that simple fact as the teacher continued to explain that in the northern hemisphere lakes would freeze solid and remain that way if it were not for this characteristic. This fact as well as many others that I learned in science, convinced me that God really knew what He was doing when He created the Earth."[58]

Personally, I'm not a giant fan of winter, but I've seen how God's sub-zero gifts of snow and ice, make winter not just endurable for many, but also an arena for fun. Where would Canadians be without ice hockey, snowboarding, shoe-shoeing, curling, snowmobiling, snow-ploughs, parkas, toques, mitts, skating on the Rideau, snowmen, snow angels, snow forts, snow-banks, hot chocolate, winter carnival, ringette, skiing, ice fishing, tobogganing and shoveling our driveways?

Snow is the proverbial measure of clean, bright purity -- as in Snow White and Ivory Snow laundry soap. I like Mae West's witty quip "I used to be pure as snow, but I drifted." We've all drifted, Mae. Anyone who says otherwise is, shall we say, snowing us. But Isaiah uses the purity of snow to contrast the dark stain of sin: "though your sins are like scarlet, they shall be as white as snow" (Isaiah 1:18). Snow blankets a dirty messy world very nicely; covers it all up all pretty and clean. We like clean. We love the beauty of snow covered gardens, forests, parks. Winter Wonderland. Not many of us would trade the rich spectrum of colors for an all white world, but we do love the beauty of whiteness.

White snow symbolizes purity, but it is also the color of death. Robert Frost's famous poem 'Stopping by Woods on a Snowy Evening' vividly describes the quiet and beauty of snow falling in the forest, but at a deeper level it brings to mind the somber silent eloquence of death. The first references to snow in the Bible are sinister, speaking about leprous limbs "as white as snow" – Miriam in Numbers 12:10 and Gehazi in 2 Kings 5:27.

But white snow equally connotes honor and dignity. In Daniel 7, Daniel has a vision of God as a regal figure, the Ancient of Days. His clothing is as white as snow; the hair of his head is white like wool and his throne ablaze with fire (Daniel 7). In the Book of Revelation, John sees the risen Christ in strikingly similar ways – his head and hair are white like wool, as white as snow, and his eyes like blazing fire (Revelation 1:14). The contrast of snow and fire intensifies the awesome aspect of white brilliance and glory of God.

In his book *McGilloway's Ireland,* nature journalist Olly McGilloway describes the beneficial aspects of the inhospitably cold damp Irish winter.

> Ice and snow will harden and then break up the ground and mercifully kill old and weak wild birds and mammals. For the next few months heavy rains and gales will wash and scour every rock, tree trunk and branch, and remove very dead twig and leaf. And while the ice and snow melt and flow with the rain in spate to refresh the rivers and streams, mighty tides will clean the shorelines.[59]

As I said, winter is not my favorite season, to be sure, but it is part of the Creator's marvelous design for the annual renewal of the earth, and a recurring sign of the faithfulness of God. "As long as the earth endures, seedtime and harvest, cold and heat, summer and winter, day and night will never cease" (Genesis 8:22).

3.10 Storm Glory

There's nothing quite like a raging thunderstorm experienced from the door of your tent while camping in the Adirondak or Muskoka wilderness. (Okay, name your own favorite remote wilderness! But there has to be thunder and lightning!) Lightning has a visual drama all its own. Add the percussion of thunder and the sweep of wind rioting through the trees and the drenching downpour of rain – and there you are in the midst of it all with a mere nylon wall between you and the elements. The shiver of vulnerability is only exceeded by the trembling grandeur and glory of the raw power of nature.

Psalm 29 describes a scene like that. It traces the fury of a thunderstorm blowing in from the sea. It whips through the northern forests of Lebanon, tears across the land and into the Negev in the south. It splits oak trees asunder and shatters the mighty cedars. It strips the forests bare.

> The voice of the LORD echoes above the sea.
> The God of glory thunders.
> The LORD thunders over the mighty sea.
> The voice of the LORD is powerful;
> the voice of the LORD is majestic.
> The voice of the LORD splits the mighty cedars;
> the LORD shatters the cedars of Lebanon.
>
> The voice of the LORD twists mighty oaks
> and strips the forests bare.
> In his Temple everyone shouts, "Glory!"
> Psalm 29:3-5, 9 NLT

The singer revels in the majestic roar of waves and thunder, howling wind, crack of lightning and the reverberation of trees crashing to the ground. Nature is majestic, wild and breath-taking! Water, wind and weather dwarf our pride. People who have to face the weather head-on – sailors, mountain climbers, airline pilots – learn to respect nature's laws.

But this storm-song does more than just dazzle us. It has deep mythic overtones – it echoes the original waters of chaos when God cracked open darkness and called the ordered world into being – God's creative voice. And it echoes God's thundering judgment in Noah's day when nature erupted to purge the world. Scholars believe this psalm was originally a Canaanite hymn; it reflects Canaanite language and mythology, but it has been taken over by Israel and made into a vibrant summons to Yahweh worship.[60]

This psalm challenges our instinct to domesticate God or reduce God to an impersonal force. Eighteen times it names God by name and ascribes nature's awesome power, majesty and beauty to Yahweh. This God speaks with a voice – seven times the voice of Yahweh speaks.

Another instinct in storms is to fear the worst – to give the storm *'god-status'*. In a hurricane or personal upheaval – a medical crisis, family chaos, financial thunderstorm, a mudslide of failure or doubt, the fury of the storm threatens to overwhelm us. We fear it will consume us. This psalm reminds us that above the roar of waves and rain, God thunders, whispers, sings.

The psalm's opening summons everyone in the entire universe with a mind and a will to acclaim Yahweh as worthy of glory and honor. At the end of the psalm, Yahweh sits secure above the floodwaters, restoring strength to his people after the catastrophic storm and blessing them with peace – *shalom* – like the rainbow that arched over Noah and a renewed world.

Israel sings this song because she learned that Yahweh, not Baal is the ultimate Storm-god, ruling over nature powerfully and majestically. The very act of singing this song is a practice of faith and defiance. This psalm reorients faith to sing with confidence and wonder – even during a storm.

> The LORD rules over the floodwaters.
> The LORD reigns as king forever.
> The LORD gives his people strength.
> The LORD blesses them with peace.
> Psalm 29:10-11 NLT

Chapter 4

Spring Harvest – Psalm 65

4.1 Drenched Furrows

THE HARVEST CELEBRATION SONG of Psalm 65 is a perfect text to close this Gift section of a book about Water. Where would the harvest be without rain? But when the rain is plentiful, the harvest is full and everyone sings for joy:

> You take care of the earth and water it,
> making it rich and fertile.
> The river of God has plenty of water;
> it provides a bountiful harvest of grain,
> for you have ordered it so.
> You drench the plowed ground with rain,
> melting the clods and leveling the ridges.
> You soften the earth with showers
> and bless its abundant crops.
> You crown the year with a bountiful harvest;
> even the hard pathways overflow with abundance.
> The grasslands of the wilderness become a lush pasture,
> and the hillsides blossom with joy.
> The meadows are clothed with flocks of sheep,
> and the valleys are carpeted with grain.
> They all shout and sing for joy!
> Psalm 65:9-13 NLT

The gift of water is a sign of God's care for the land and all its inhabitants, people and flocks. Water brings so many gifts – and this psalm celebrates them joyously – rainfall, full rivers, bountiful harvest, beautiful landscape. Let the harvest festival break out with gladness and appreciation for God's bounty! That's the surface story of this song.

But there's another story, a darker one underlying it. We don't know the details, but they were bad. Some kind of spiritual disaster had befallen the nation. The third line speaks of being "overwhelmed by sins", but now the catastrophe is behind them. God has forgiven the past and restored his people. They have turned back to God and have a strong sense of living in God's favor.

> What mighty praise, O God, belongs to you in Zion.
> We will fulfill our vows to you, for you answer our prayers.
> All of us must come to you.
> Though we are overwhelmed by our sins, you forgive them all.
> What joy for those you choose to bring near,
> those who live in your holy courts.
> What festivities await us inside your holy temple.
> Psalm 65:1-4 NLT

Now they are filled with good things, not just the fruit of the field, but good gifts from God's holy temple. Mercy and grace, righteousness and hope are serious expressions of God's care for them just as barley and wine are.

This is a David psalm and it begins with praise, pent-up and bursting for expression by the people of Zion, but its horizon stretches to the ends of the earth. It resonates with the aspirations of people everywhere. This God who hears prayer and answers with active grace and power is something people long for around the globe – 'to you all of us must come' (verse 2). Everyone is eligible.

> O God our savior,
> You are the hope of everyone on earth,
> even those who sail on distant seas (verse 5).

From east to west, "where morning dawns and evening fades" (NIV), God inspires joy. The Creator of the natural world in all its power and productivity is also personally responsive to his creation.

> You formed the mountains by your power
> and armed yourself with mighty strength.
> You quieted the raging oceans
> with their pounding waves
> and silenced the shouting of the nations.

> Those who live at the ends of the earth
> stand in awe of your wonders.
> From where the sun rises to where it sets,
> you inspire shouts of joy.
> Psalm 65:5-8 NLT

Read it over slowly and let the wonder of the God's gift inspire you to 'shout and sing for joy' (verse 13).

4.2 Feast and Festival

Conservationist Wendell Berry speaks of "the great feast and festival of Creation to which we are bidden as living souls."[61] Every summer, Tiffany and I find ourselves 'bidden' afresh to drive or fly south from Canada to spend a week on the Atlantic coast of North Carolina near where her sister lives. Every day on the Oak Island Pier, scores of patient fisher men and women arrive with trolleys of gear and tackle; they come hungry, hopeful and patient; they come to match wits with trout and king mackerel, skate and pompano, bluefish, black drum and flounder; they come to harvest the ocean, to dine at nature's table. For the folks on the pier, creation is a hopeful feast. But for miles on either side of the pier, thousands of others congregate at the same ocean with an entirely different purpose. For them creation is a festival.

Festooned in swimwear in all shapes and sizes of the most vibrant colors, the beach crowd celebrates the playfulness of the ocean; they match wits with the waves, the sun and the seagulls; they run and walk and bathe in the sun, they swim and dig and throw Frisbees, they eat and read and feed sea-gulls. Beachcombers come to the festival searching for treasures. Others come for solitude in the midst of the crowd; others come in the evening to exchange vows under a sunset canopy; leatherback sea turtles come out of the water under cover of night to lay eggs at the edge of the dunes. Creation celebrates its summer festival in a hundred different ways.

Six months later, that same strand of wave-washed sand is virtually desolate – and yet at such a time, on New Year's Day 2010, we enjoyed a most memorable festive moment. It all began with a morning walk, bundled against the brisk breeze under a sullen January sky. The waves pounded their unending percussion and the memories of summer days planted the playful thought of an afternoon polar bear plunge. Thought grew into dare and dare issued a challenge – the way it naturally does in festive settings. By mid-afternoon, the sky still grey, three of us stripped down to our essentials and raced across the sand, clamored crazily over waves and threw ourselves into 'the deep' – a bracing experience of ice-water and nerve endings, a celebration of self-abandonment. Loving wives and in-laws cheered our insanity and bravado. Cameras clicked and video's whirred, and before long we were out of the water buried in towels and fleece sweaters laughing and retelling the tale – a truly festive moment.

Later in the hot tub I thought about Berry's comment about Creation being a festival to which we are invited as living souls. As a Canadian, I personally prefer the summer solstice, but God's four season festival affords a myriad of ways to enjoy creation's bounty, appreciate the Creator's material gifts and celebrate the goodness of life. *Hallelujah!*

As you move into the next section of this book, I hope you will continue to enjoy the feast and the festival that celebrate the good gifts of the Creator, because the Bible continues to revel in this amazing gift of water right to the very last page. In fact, the very last reference to water in the Book of Revelation is about the water of life being a free gift! In this next section we're going to see how this gift of water was experienced by people who found their way into the fascinating narrative of the Bible.

Part Two: A RIVER RUNS THROUGH IT:

The Story of God's People and Water

Moses Crosses the Red Sea

by Benjamin Lewis, age 6

"The waters were divided and the Israelites went through the sea on dry ground, with a wall of water on their right and on their left."

Exodus 14:21-22.

IN THE FIRST SECTION we explored water as a GIFT of nature as celebrated in Biblical songs. The next twelve chapters will unfold the STORY of God's people with water.

I chose a young boy's drawing for this section to illustrate how stories open up our imagination. Myths and folktales, biographies and histories, parables and adventure stories capture the human drama and embody truth for us. They provide a pathway for our understanding. Legendary water stories like *The Odyssey, Adventures of Huckleberry Finn, Moby Dick, The Life of Pi, Treasure Island* and *The Rime of the Ancient Mariner* not only entertain us, they stretch our thinking; they challenge, warn and inspire us – and as we listen to them, find them telling parts of our own stories.

Kenneth Grahame's *The Wind and the Willows,* tells about a mole that encounters a river for the first time in his life and hears stories that hold him hostage.

> [The Mole] thought his happiness was complete when, as he meandered aimlessly along, suddenly he stood by the edge of a full-fed river. Never in his life had he seen a river before – this sleek, sinuous, full-bodied animal, chasing and chuckling, gripping things with a gurgle and leaving them with a laugh, to fling itself on fresh playmates that shook themselves free, and were caught and held again. All was a-shake and a-shiver – glints and gleams and sparkles, rustle and swirl, chatter and bubble.
>
> The Mole was bewitched, entranced, fascinated. By the side of the river he trotted as one trots, when very small, by the side of a man who holds one spellbound by exciting stories; and when tired at last, he sat on the bank, while the river still chattered on to him, a babbling procession of the best stories in the world, sent from the heart of the earth to be told at last to the insatiable sea.
> -Excerpt from *The Wind in the Willows,* Chapter One[62]

The river tells the best stories in the world, sent from the heart of the earth and the sea can't get enough of them. That's the story of water, and the Mole was bewitched. Like the Mole, we love stories, and as we continue our journey downstream, some mighty fine stories about water are waiting to bewitch us.

Stories stir the imagination and powerfully shape our behavior. My earliest memory of water is hearing a missionary from Africa tell how a crocodile pulled an ox into the river and devoured it. I was six years old and that story terrified me. Lake Winnipeg where we were camping hadn't seen crocodiles since the Jurassic Period, but I was certain they were still there and I wasn't about to become lunch.

Two years earlier, as a four-year-old English boy I had spent a week crossing the Atlantic Ocean as we immigrated to Canada. That ocean experience with water was far more significant than the missionary story, but I don't remember even a glimpse of the vast ocean. Perhaps it was too overwhelming, or perhaps my four-year-old consciousness simply accepted and dismissed it as a passing oddity. Or perhaps this illustrates the power of stories to shape our perception – or misperception of the world.

Human beings are irrepressible story makers and storytellers and devoted listeners to stories. Growing up, my children loved to hear stories read to them, but their favorite request was for a spontaneous homemade tale, told in the first person and including them as a central character. One of the splendid things about stories is how we can read ourselves into the stories of others.

A River Runs Through It

The Bible is a great collection of stories. Much of what it tells us about God comes to us in stories, firsthand experiences where people encountered God in some way, or where their encounters with other people disclosed something vital about life. They told and retold these stories and reflected on their significance; they wrote songs about these experiences and sang them to each other and to God.

The Story of God's people in the Bible is book-ended by two beautiful river scenes, the Garden of Eden and the New Jerusalem. They introduce and give crescendo to the grand story of God's 'River of the Water of Life' that flows through the entire drama of the Bible. Throughout the narrative are over a hundred more water related stories that expand on this theme – stories of rivers, lakes, springs, dew, storms, floods and droughts; stories of washing, drowning, walking on water, water turned into wine, meeting strangers at wells and marrying them.

On a warm evening in May 1990, my first wife and I were enjoying a two hour cruise on the Danube River in Budapest. The lights along the river on both sides sparkled like jewels. But what I remember best is the interpretive commentary which was narrated by the River herself. As we travelled along the water that evening we listened as she told us the story of the Danube, the history of the kings and empires that had crossed the river, taxed it, polluted and exploited it. Then she came to the present – May 1990, which was just a few months after the Berlin Wall fell, suddenly releasing the entire communist world including Hungary from Russian domination. The River told us of the enormous sense of freedom that had so recently come over her.

The River that flows through the Bible speaks the same way. It is an epic story of bondage and freedom. If we listen to it carefully we can hear a veritable symphony expounding the grace and goodness of God. It's the narrative Hebrew equivalent of Handel's Water Music. It not only entertains, but it inspires. This story has so much to teach us, and it instructs by plunging us into the experiences of men and women like ourselves who met God, like Jacob met the Wrestler at the Jabbok River, like Jonah met God in the great deep, like the woman in Samaria met a stranger at Jacob's well – they were never the same again. It is a convoluted and colorful storyline. I hope you can read yourself into these stories – or discover yourself already in them.

By the end of this over-arching story we will see how water fulfills its destiny, the purpose and '*telos*' for which it – and the entire cosmos – was made. This was not to return us to a utopian Eden, but to bring us into God's new creation, flowing with water, radiant with light, an urban community with the natural vitality of a garden, but cosmopolitan and alive with culture, justice and joy.

Forget your galoshes – plunge right in and get soaked!

Chapter 5
Epic Sea-Battle

5.1 Marduk

The sea churned furiously as the archetypal hero Marduk waged war against the fierce mythical sea monster who was his mother, and more-menacing-than-death. And in ancient time, everyone within a thousand miles knew the story – or some variation on it.

This myth became one of the central stories of ancient Babylon. In oral form, it predated the reign of Hammurabi (1728-1686 BCE), but at some point it was recorded on clay tablets which then lay buried in the sand for centuries until they were discovered in the mid-1800s in the Iraqi city of Mosul. They were taken and stored in the British Museum and then translated and published in English in 1876. It is the Babylonian creation epic 'Enuma Elish'.

The story goes something like this:

> The primordial sea monster was named Tiamat, which essentially means 'the deep'. She represents the sea, the untamed forces of Chaos, the default condition of the world. Marduk was the ruler of the young gods and one of her offspring. Tiamat was full of fury (as the sea often is) against these gods and organized an all-out assault against them. Marduk stormed out against her with ferocious power, with howling winds, flood and a storm-chariot, thunder and lightning, a bow and a huge net. The sea churned as they engaged in combat. Tiamat opened her dragon mouth to swallow him alive, but with warrior skill Marduk overpowered her, slew her and split her body in two. One half of her carcass he raised up as the Sky and the other became the waters below, the great deep. So the god Marduk created the universe by separating the waters above from the waters below. Then he mixed the blood of the vanquished rebels with clay and made humans to be slaves of the surviving gods.

It's a gruesome story to be sure, but its decisive outcome made it popular in Mesopotamia, because it reflected the political order that came into effect under the emerging civic rulers of Babylon, especially under Hammurabi. It shows the civilizing effects of law and order and the authority of a king who keeps the forces of Chaos from destroying the community. It also reflects the concerns of primitive Mesopotamian 'farmers' who each spring had to endure the annual flooding of the Tigris and Euphrates that wreaked such havoc over their livelihood. That's what myths do; they give people a story that expresses and validates what is important to them.

This story was very familiar to the writers of the Bible. In the pages of the Old Testament we find numerous references to it, but the Bible writers never tell the story directly. In the same way that someone today might refer to Hamlet or Cinderella or Star Wars, so Biblical writers alluded to this cosmic battle story, knowing that their readers and listeners would understand what they were talking about. But they never dreamed that anyone would think they were reporting actual history.[63]

Knowing the Tiamat myth helps us to understand a number of biblical passages. Obviously we hear echoes of it in the familiar Genesis creation story. But the mythological echoes help us to see what a different kind of story the Hebrews told. For the Hebrews, Sky is not the leftover carcass of a defeated monster, but something created by the word of Elohim, the Creator. The waters of the abyss are not deified, and human beings were not made to be slaves so the gods could live in leisure.

As crude and fanciful as the Babylonian story is, it helps us understand what Job means when he says that God powerfully "churned up the sea; by his wisdom he cut Rahab (Tiamat) to pieces and his hand pierced the gliding serpent" (Job 26:12-13). God has subdued Chaos by his sovereign power and wisdom and continues to manifest awesome power far beyond what we know – 'these are but the outer fringe of his works; how faint the whisper we hear of him! Who then can understand the thunder of his power?' (Job 26:14).

The name Rahab for Tiamat is related to the Hebrew word for 'pride' which fits the defiant resistance of chaos against Yahweh's rule. Earlier Job says, "God does not restrain his anger; even the cohorts of Rahab cowered at his feet" (Job 9:13).

5.2 The Mythical Dragon

So Biblical poets and prophets praise Yahweh as the supreme power over the chaotic deep, and they used the pagan myth to illustrate that power. Psalm 74 now makes sense when we read

> It was You who split open the sea by your power; you broke the heads of the monster in the waters. It was you who crushed the heads of Leviathan and gave him as food to the creatures of the desert; It was you who opened up springs and streams; you dried up the ever flowing rivers.
> Psalm 74:13-14

This psalm came out of an intensely dark and bitter time in Israel's history, when the temple had been savagely gutted and the king taken away in chains to Babylon while God had seemingly stood by in silence. It looked to Israel as if the Babylonian monster ruled the world. But instead of losing his faith in the wake of such confusion, the poet recalls earlier times when God overturned Chaos and brought order to the world and when he delivered Israel from Egypt. He urges God to do it again, now that the nation is exiled into a new chaos. God's ancient victories over the waters provide a fulcrum point for faith in the midst of a new crisis.

To Isaiah similarly, the fury of foreign nations that were threatening Israel echoes the futile rage of the mythical dragon, the forces of Chaos.

> Oh, the raging of many nations-- they rage like the raging sea!
> Oh, the uproar of the peoples-- they roar like the roaring of great waters!
> Although the peoples roar like the roar of surging waters,
> when he rebukes them they flee far away
> Isaiah 17:12-13

but their loud proud threats will be silenced before the decisive rebuke of Yahweh, Israel's God.

For Israel the Exodus rivaled the Creation as the greatest of God's mighty deeds. Yahweh's victory over Pharaoh echoed the cosmic victory over Chaos, so Israel used the name Rahab – with all its mythic overtones – in referring to Egypt.

> O LORD God Almighty, who is like you?

> You are mighty, O LORD, and your faithfulness surrounds you.
> You rule over the surging sea;
> when its waves mount up, you still them.
> You crushed Rahab like one of the slain;
> with your strong arm you scattered your enemies.
> The heavens are yours, and yours also the earth;
> you founded the world and all that is in it.
> Psalm 89:8-11

As Derek Kidner says, this victory is as central to the Old Testament as Calvary is to the New.[64]

Isaiah recalled the mighty deeds of both creation and exodus and urges Yahweh to do it again, to bring Israel back again from exile –

> Awake, awake! Clothe yourself with strength, O arm of the LORD; awake, as in days gone by, as in generations of old. Was it not you who cut Rahab to pieces, who pierced that monster through? Was it not you who dried up the sea, the waters of the great deep, who made a road in the depths of the sea so that the redeemed might cross over? The ransomed of the LORD will return.
> Isaiah 51:9-11

In fact, Isaiah sees the telltale tracks of the ancient sea monster all through history wherever monstrous evil erupts against social order, against the poor and the righteous. But he assures us that Yahweh will have the last word: "In that day, the LORD will punish with his sword, his fierce, great and powerful sword, Leviathan the gliding serpent, Leviathan the coiling serpent; he will slay the monster of the sea" (Isaiah 27:1). In the book of Revelation, John expresses the same confidence as the dragon relentlessly rages and wars against the Lamb; but ultimately the Lamb is victorious.

5.3 Churning the Great Waters

Habakkuk is probably the most eloquent in his use of the cosmic battle imagery.

> Were you angry with the rivers, O LORD?
> Was your wrath against the streams?
> Did you rage against the sea
> when you rode with your horses

and your victorious chariots?
You uncovered your bow,
you called for many arrows. Selah
You split the earth with rivers;
The mountains saw you and writhed.
Torrents of water swept by;
the deep roared and lifted its waves on high.

Sun and moon stood still in the heavens
at the glint of your flying arrows,
at the lightning of your flashing spear.
In wrath you strode through the earth
and in anger you threshed the nations.
You came out to deliver your people,
to save your anointed one. . . .
You trampled the sea with your horses,
churning the great waters.
Habakkuk 3:8-15

So whenever you personally feel the forces of chaos surging around you, remember Habakkuk 3:13, "You came out to deliver your people, to save your anointed one." He is the ultimate Dragon-slayer. He has always been so, and always will be.

So we move now from myth to history. The narrative that unfolds in the following chapters gives a progressively expanding picture of the importance of water in people's lives and how they experienced God more fully as a result.

Chapter 6

Catastrophe and Covenant – The Great Flood

6.1 Inundation

EXCEPT FOR THE RIVER reference in Eden, the first story of water in the Bible is the story of the Deluge.

As a teenager I moved from weather perfect California to the coastal city of Belize on the west shores of the Caribbean, where I was suddenly introduced to the terrifying phenomenon called '*hurricane*'. I arrived there a year after Hurricane Hattie had crashed onto the Belize coast with 140 mph (225 km/h) winds, a 14 foot (4.3 m) storm surge and devastating results, banana plantations and crops destroyed, 319 people killed.

I didn't experience it firsthand but the lingering evidence was everywhere, wrecked buildings ripped off their moorings and a refugee camp for homeless survivors. Stories of tragedy and loss and heroism were still foremost on people's minds. Belize sits on reclaimed land exactly at sea level and when the hurricane hit, the entire city was inundated. The calm in the eye of the storm lured stunned people into a false sense of security and despite radio warnings scores perished when the fury of the storm resumed.

Floods are devastating -- overwhelming in every sense, physically, financially and emotionally. Stories of survival and upheaval touch a deep chord in the collective human psyche. People in low-lying countries like Bangladesh and Holland live their lives constantly exposed to the threat of flooding from rivers or the sea.

Traumatic floods occur frequently all over the world, such as the terrible 2010 flood in Pakistan that swamped 20% of the entire nation. Long after the waters subside, the ordeal lingers in the memory of survivors. Big ones become legendary and serve as symbols of all kinds of threats to our survival. This may help to explain the plethora of flood stories around the world.

Many cultures of the world have stories of mythic proportions about a flood that virtually annihilates human civilization. Nineteenth century British Assyriologists, studying clay tablets from Mesopotamia were astonished to discover the similarities between the Epic of Gilgamesh and the more familiar story of Noah in Genesis.

As the science of anthropology grew, researchers discovered that cultures as diverse as Scandinavians and Polynesians, Australian aboriginals and American Navajo, Celts, Mayans and Thai all tell a story of a great inundation, often with similar details -- punishment for an offense, humans and animals saved by a boat, birds being sent out on reconnaissance, and the boat landing on a mountaintop. Here's part of the Genesis narrative:

> Noah and his sons and his wife and his sons' wives entered the ark to escape the waters of the flood. ... In the six hundredth year of Noah's life, on the seventeenth day of the second month--on that day all the springs of the great deep burst forth, and the floodgates of the heavens were opened. And rain fell on the earth forty days and forty nights.
> Genesis 7:7-12

The story of Noah is quite literally a watershed event in the Biblical narrative (Genesis 6-9). It was catastrophic – with human and animal populations all but destroyed. It was like a reversal of creation – the unmaking of earth. How are we to understand this devastating overwhelming of the earth?

In the Babylonian flood story, human beings became so noisy, the gods couldn't sleep, so they deluged the world to wipe out the people. Their motive came from annoyance and inconvenience. In the Bible Yahweh's motive was moral and ethical. "God saw that human evil was out of control" (Genesis 6:5 MSG).

6.2 Flood Story / Love Story

In fact, before we hear about forty days of rain, we hear about three other forms of flood.

First, human imagination became flooded with evil – with attitudes defiant against God and toxically selfish and deviant. Human imagination had run amok and become so destructive it could only be described as corrupt and 'wicked' (6:5). Hubris, vice and perversity were not only deep, but pervasive and constant – "only evil, all the time," the text says in v.5. Like the "great deep" in 7:11, the "great wickedness" of 6:5 had reached avalanche and tsunami proportions.

The New Testament uses similar flood language to describe a profligate lifestyle. "Your old friends," Peter says, "don't understand why you no longer plunge with them into *the flood* of wild and destructive things they do" (1 Peter 4:4 NLT). *Flood* is an apt word for hedonism because the pursuit of pleasure takes so little moral effort; relax all discipline, ignore God and party all night without restraint. The flood is exhilarating, addictive and draws others in, even if it's exhausting and ultimately destructive.

The second form of flood occurred as personal corruption grew into a social norm such that the larger society was engulfed by greed, hostility and violence (Genesis 6:11). Civilization became increasingly uncivil. With a rising tide of social chaos, the world sank steadily deeper into systemic injustice and violence. The culture was in serious jeopardy, past the point of remedial intervention, but no one seemed particularly concerned.

At creation, God blessed the sea and told the fish to "fill the water in the seas with life" (Genesis 1:22). He gave human beings the command to fill the earth and subdue it (verse 28). Instead of filling it with beauty, joy and the glory of God, they filled it with greed, aggression, and fear – and on top of that, denial. Instead of subduing themselves they strove to subdue each other.

These two tragic floods of personal corruption and social demise in Noah's world caused a third and more haunting kind of deluge. The Creator was overwhelmed with grief; anguish flooded the heart of God. This third expression of inundation is the only one described in personal or emotional terms as the narrator says, "The LORD was grieved that he had made mankind on the earth, and God's heart was filled with pain" (6:6), or, as *The Message* says, "it broke God's heart."

Downstream from Eden, something eventually breaks all our hearts. Grief is an all-too-familiar emotion. This tells us that God is no stranger to our pain. When God announced to Noah that floodwaters would destroy "every creature that has the breath of life in it, and that everything on earth will perish," (6:17) we could interpret it as the malicious spite of an enraged deity. But a truer reading of the story reveals a deep sadness. It was the response of a heartbroken Lover, the overflow of what G.K. Chesterton called "the furious love of God"[65].

The inhabited world that God created and cherished had been tragically flooded by evil. God had no choice but to flood it with water to purge the toxic defilement that had taken root in it. Yahweh was not the initiator of the ruin, but the one who initiated the remaking of the earth by using water to expunge the moral and cultural corruption that had degraded it beyond repair[66].

6.3 But Why Wipe It All Out?

We might ask 'why did *everything* have to be destroyed? Had all of creation become that bad? And why a flood and not some other means to wipe out evil and violence?'

The answer, as we have said is that the flood a reversal of creation – the waters that had been corralled and bounded at creation are unleashed. In the same way that human civilization had eroded into Chaos, so the chaotic waters are unleashed to destroy the world. It seems that the story reveals a principle by which God governs divine response to human freedom. God permits us to experience the consequences of the choices we make. In the days of Noah that meant living free from the restraints of God-ordained order. Nature responded in kind.

The flood also highlights the holistic interconnectedness of the world. Our choices and actions affect our neighbors, shape society and impact our environment – animals and rivers, air, grasslands and forests. When we violate the laws of nature and the moral fabric that holds things together, we all suffer.

This lesson of the Noah story for our day is echoed in recent books like Jared Diamond's *Guns, Germs, and Steel,* and Ronald Wright's *A Short History of Progress,* which trace the demise of other civilizations that ignored the impact of unbridled greed, moral complacency and indifference to ecology, squandered their natural resources, turned on one another and continued in denial until they suffered irreversible demise – and how in the twenty-first century we seem to be following the same well-worn path to disaster. Diamond and Wright are warning us that our abuse of the environment today echoes the disastrous presumption of past civilizations as they careened towards extinction. They are no more alarmist than Noah's prophetic voice, warning us to take heed of our stewardship of the earth and of each other. In this sense Noah's flood serves as a metaphor for the catastrophe that flows from human folly. But it also is a metaphor of hope. Noah shows us the way forward.

The Genesis Flood story reveals Yahweh as an ethical and just God, who carries out the purging and remaking of the world even at the cost of personal heartbreak and pain. God's mercy towards Noah introduces a dominant Biblical theme of grace and compassion. And through Noah we see God's preserving care for the whole of creation.

Old Testament scholar Tremper Longman says that what distinguishes the Hebrew story from its Sumarian and Babylonian parallels is the sharp contrast between their respective deities; in the context of divine judgment the Hebrew story revolves around grace which is missing in the other Near Eastern versions.[67]

6.4 One Man . . .

The entire race of humanity was oblivious to the disaster they had caused – with the exception of one man. Noah found grace in the eyes of the Lord (Genesis 6:8). When God directed Noah to gather mating pairs of all the animals, we read that "Noah did everything just as God commanded him" (6:22) – which contrasts the prevailing culture and reinforces the ethical theme of the story.

Then in the next chapter God told Noah "Go into the ark . . . because I have found you righteous in this generation" (7:1) – which is a pretty high commendation. Jewish texts like Ezekiel 14:14 list Noah along with Job and Daniel as three extraordinarily upright worthies. The Christian writer of Hebrews commends Noah for his faith, and Islam counts him as one of the five great prophets. These three religions of ethical monotheism recognize that virtue and righteousness enhance life and that self-serving behavior destroys life. No wonder Noah scores high in religious memory.

But Noah was not a virtuous man in isolation. He lived before God in obedient trust. It's not so much that Noah earned his salvation by his merit; rather it was his responsiveness to a righteous God that brought him under the mercy and faithfulness of God, rather than the floodwaters of judgment. The Hollywood movie *Evan Almighty* humorously portrays the challenge of obeying God in the midst of a disbelieving world.

People in Noah's world, for the most part, were going about business as usual, oblivious to the disintegration going on around them. In Jesus' words, they were "eating and drinking, marrying and giving in marriage, unaware of what would happen until the flood came and took them all away" (Matthew 24:37). Jesus predicted it would be very similar at the coming of the Son of Man.

Frederick Buechner imagines Noah coming to realize how immoral and doomed his society was.

> His thoughts, one imagines, were of water and as the windows of heaven were opened and all the fountains of the great deep burst forth so that the sea crept in over the earth, and where there had been dry land and order all was disorder and violence, perhaps Noah knew that it had always been so. Perhaps Noah knew that all the order and busyness of people had been at best an illusion and that, left to themselves, they had always been doomed. The waters came scudding in over forest and field, sliding in across kitchen floors and down cellar stairs, rising high above television aerials and the steeples of churches, and death was everywhere as death is always everywhere, people trapped alone as they are always trapped, always alone, in office or locker room, bedroom or bar, people grasping out for something solid and sure to keep themselves from drowning, everybody fighting for the few remaining pieces of dry ground. Maybe the chaos was no greater than it had ever been. Only wetter.[68]

Attentiveness to God set Noah apart from the crowd. He is a front runner in the great Biblical motif of the remnant, the pattern of one individual standing against the tide of his or her culture, bearing witness to God's truth, and making a difference in their world. Old Testament scholar Walter Brueggemann calls Noah "the bearer of an alternate possibility, ... a fresh alternative."[69] Because of Noah's faithful obedience to God, the terrible story of destruction became a story of deliverance and hope for humanity and all of God's creation. In this way Noah transcends history and speaks prophetically into our lives today about how we can relate more creatively to God, to one another and to our environment – if we listen with humility, and take heed, and take action.

So Noah built a massive boat – a barge with three floors. It was a microcosm of creation, designed to preserve life through the year of devastation ahead. In this project we see Noah fulfilling the vocation of all humanity –

partnership with God and zealous care for God's creation. He coated the ark inside and out with pitch to keep his fellow passengers dry. The water had to be kept at bay at all costs. Water is a paradox – every animal needs to drink, but that very water, unchecked, threatens its survival. The ark became a place of refuge as water wiped out everything else.

6.5 Breathtaking Disaster

Every day along beaches of the world, children build legendary castles and for an afternoon they own it all. But the tide eventually turns. As the waves creep closer, mothers and fathers are called to help fortify the walls, but the tide is relentless, moats are soon submerged, towers collapse and the ocean reclaims the shore. Within minutes monuments become memories. In miniature that is the story of the great Flood.

Genesis 7 describes the rising floodwaters like escalating waves of bad news, each more unbelievable than the last: "after the seven days the floodwaters came on the earth. [...] On that day all the springs of the great deep burst forth, and the floodgates of the heavens were opened. And rain fell on the earth forty days and forty nights" (Genesis 7:10-12).

First we hear about massive unleashing of water from below and above – "the springs of the great deep burst forth and the floodgates of the heavens were opened" (Genesis 7:11). Falling judgment and rising chaos combined as heaven and hell broke loose, the whole created order coming violently unglued. It calls to mind the chaos that preceded creation and that continually threatens to undermine the created order. In this story of the Great flood, human irresponsibility and divine judgment converge.

Torrents of rain fell from above, geysers and aquifers burst out of the ground; upheaval and deluge. Rain fell for forty days and nights – the symbolic time of purifying. Rain, meant to nourish the earth, became its destroyer, purging the defilement that had poisoned the whole of creation. But the ark was a haven of mercy and peace amid the judgment.

This harrowing judgment prefigures the story of crucifixion where Jesus was engulfed by the betrayal of his own creation and suffered in person the consequences of our treachery.

Twice in Genesis 7 we're told that the flooding was relentless, and twice we're reminded that the ark with its precious cargo of people and animals, remnants of the old creation was being preserved above the waters:

> For forty days the flood kept coming on the earth,
> and as the waters increased they lifted the ark high above the earth.
> The waters rose and increased greatly on the earth,
> and the ark floated on the surface of the water
> Genesis 7:17-18

Hope bobbed like a small cork on a vast and terrifying flood. Where judgment rose to unimaginable depths, grace kept pace with the punishment: "the waters rose greatly on the earth, and all the high mountains under the entire heavens were covered" (verse 19).

Biblical scholars debate about whether this flood was global or local. Evidence in the Biblical record can be interpreted either way. In either case, it is described as a vast unprecedented event that altered the world as the survivors knew it. Listen to the totality of the world's obituary:

> All the living things on earth died—birds, domestic animals, wild animals, small animals that scurry along the ground, and all the people. Everything that breathed and lived on dry land died. God wiped out every living thing on the earth—people, livestock, small animals that scurry along the ground, and the birds of the sky. All were destroyed. The only people who survived were Noah and those with him in the boat.
> Genesis7:21-23 NLT

The devastation was total, literally breathtaking – it is enough to suck the breath right out of our chests as we hear the story or read it, just as surely as those on the outside gasped for air as they drowned. We're meant to be awed and overwhelmed at the extent of it, and sobered into realizing the catastrophic consequences of allowing moral and ethical chaos to overtake our family lives and community and to destroy the earth under our feet.

The Irish poet W. B. Yeats describes the collapse of such a world in his poem 'The Second Coming' when he says,

> Things fall apart; the centre cannot hold;
> Mere anarchy is loosed upon the world,
> The blood-dimmed tide is loosed, and everywhere
> The ceremony of innocence is drowned.[70]

6.6 Interlude

> Now the springs of the deep and the floodgates of the heavens had been closed, and the rain had stopped falling from the sky. The water receded steadily from the earth. At the end of the hundred and fifty days the water had gone down.
> Genesis 8:2-3

For a hundred and fifty days the ark floated on the face of the waters – five months of silence as the lingering waters ensured that the old world was gone forever. The earth which God had called forth out of the original waters had been buried again. It is as if creation's story has been told in reverse as the undoing of God's masterpiece. But Chaos did not win the day. The old earth was purged of all that had defiled it; it was scoured clean. Then we read "but God remembered Noah" (Genesis 8:1).

No doubt Noah and his family wondered many times during that long ordeal if God had forgotten them or abandoned them. It's a common human fear, but eventually the story says "God remembered Noah" (Genesis 8:1). The long silence of God did not mean that God was neglecting Noah. In fact, Noah had been on God's mind every hour of the extended nightmare.

Centuries later, Isaiah spoke of Yahweh 'remembering' Israel's exiles engulfed in a flood of a different kind in Babylon. After years of wondering if God had forgotten them, they heard Yahweh say,

> "Can a mother forget the baby at her breast
> and have no compassion on the child she has borne?
> Though she may forget, I will not forget you!
> See, I have engraved you on the palms of my hands.
> Isaiah 49:15-16

With more maternal awareness and anticipation than a nursing mother, God was preparing Noah and the world for a future Noah could hardly imagine.

6.7 New Beginning

A new beginning got underway as God sent a wind over the earth (Genesis 8:1) to dry up the waters – a clear echo of the first creation story where the Spirit of God – spirit being the same word as wind – hovered and gusted over the waters. In time the floodwaters receded; mountain tops were seen and birds were dispatched to survey the conditions outside the ark, first a raven, then a dove. A week later a dove was sent a second time and we're told "when the dove returned to him in the evening, there in its beak was a freshly plucked olive leaf! Then Noah knew that the water had receded from the earth" (Genesis 8:2-3, 11).

That olive branch has become proverbial – a token of the emerging renewal of the earth – what Frederick Buechner calls "a sprig of hope held up against the end of the world."[71] But as Walter Brueggemann says, "Hope for the future is not premised on possibility thinking or human actualization. Hope will depend on a move from God."[72]

The narrator highlights this new beginning by telling us that "by the first day of the first month of Noah's six hundred and first year, the waters had dried up from the earth" (8:13). The date couldn't be more coincidental! Noah's days are carefully numbered and mercy has preserved him for a new beginning. By sheer mercy and grace the ark and its inhabitants had survived the ordeal.

And by sheer mercy God does this over and over again in our lives. There are experiences in life that overwhelm us and change our world forever. They are not evidence that God has abandoned us, even if we feel that we have been forgotten by God and that the forces of chaos rule the world. God uses such overwhelming experiences to transform us and to re-form us for his new purposes. That's something that truly takes my breath away – and breathes new hope into my soul.

Emily Dickinson describes how hope sings wordlessly into our souls.

> Hope is the thing with feathers
> That perches in the soul,
> And sings the tune without the words,
> And never stops at all.
> Emily Dickinson [73]

A year and ten days after the flood began, God told Noah to leave the ark and to bring all the animals out with him "so they can multiply on the earth and be fruitful and increase in number" (Genesis 8:17). The words 'multiply' and 'be fruitful and increase' mean exactly the same thing, so God seems to be excited about this new beginning!

The 19th century American Quaker Edward Hicks probably painted more renditions of this moment than any other artist. Between 1820 and 1849 he composed 61 variations and revisions of 'The Peaceable Kingdom'. Hicks was strongly influenced by Quaker spirituality and Isaiah's vision of harmony throughout God's creation (Isaiah 11:6-8), and he used his paintings to promote a vision of community peace.

In gratitude for God's protection, Noah built an altar and made an offering to God. We read that God blessed Noah (as he had earlier blessed Adam) and established a covenant with Noah and his family – and, as Genesis 9:10 says, with every living creature on earth – never to destroy the earth again with a flood. As a sign of that pledge, God said, "I have set my rainbow in the clouds. [...] Whenever I bring clouds over the earth and the rainbow appears in the clouds, I will remember my covenant between me and you and all living creatures of every kind" (Genesis 9:13-15).

6.8 Rainbow Radiance

Nothing graces the landscape quite like a rainbow, especially after the gray sky of a storm. Physics tells us that a rainbow is merely the effect of sunlight refracted through the prism of water molecules such as mist or failing raindrops. Water particles cause light waves to bend, and since each color has a different wavelength, each portion of the spectrum is bent through the raindrop at a slightly different angle. So, when the light emerges from the drop, the colors are separated and we see – a rainbow!

That's the hard science, but the mere sight of a rainbow with its lively spectrum of violet, indigo, blue, green, yellow, orange and red, arching across the open space between the viewer and the sky beggars analysis and definition. A rainbow silently offers itself to be noticed, admired, enjoyed, photographed, painted and pursued into the imagination. William Wordsworth wrote "My heart leaps up when I behold a rainbow in the sky". Wordsworth wasn't alone. Color always energizes and brightens a gray day.

It is possible to imagine a monochrome universe devoid of color – like the early years of television and photography. But the artist who crafted our universe used a full palette to paint light. Beauty gave water the properties to refract that invisible light and splash arcs of splendor across the sky. Truly the heavens declare the glory of God and the skies display his handiwork – and rainbows are one of the great displays.

Ezekiel had a vision of the magnificent glory of God. The rainbow gave him a way to express that experience in words: "Like the appearance of a rainbow in the clouds on a rainy day, so was the radiance around him. This was the appearance of the likeness of the glory of the LORD" (Ezekiel 1:28).

The fact that science can explain the rainbow doesn't diminish our wonder when we see one. I remember waking up the morning after a rainstorm aboard a yacht in Desolation Sound, British Columbia. My wife Mary Lynn had died seven months earlier and despite the majestic beauty of the scenery, the name 'Desolation Sound' echoed the recent deluge of loss in my life. As I raised the deck hatch that morning I stared up at a magnificent double rainbow arched across the sky above the shrouds and mast of our boat. My heart leapt as those rainbows silently eloquently proclaimed promise and hope to my soul.

The ancient story of Noah and the Flood is crowned with such a rainbow, not just as a joyous exclamation point, but as a meaningful sign. God said "I have placed my rainbow in the clouds as a sign" (9:13). A sign points to something beyond itself; it indicates something of significance that we might otherwise miss. The rainbow is not just a pretty ribbon in the sky; it signifies a word from God with deep meaning. The word translated rainbow is 'qeshet', literally 'a bow' which usually means a warrior's weapon – and here was God, unilaterally disarming! No matter how vile or violent human society may become in the years ahead, God was refusing the option to wipe out the creation again. Heaven is intimately connected with earth's well-being and the rainbow signals that pledge.

Here was God as Peace-maker, prefiguring the day when swords everywhere will be beaten into ploughshares, and spears into pruning hooks, (Isaiah 2:4 and Micah 4:3), when agriculture will replace aggression, when nations invest their resources in life-giving enterprises and mutual care – when peace, not blood, will flood the earth, when people will no longer "harm nor destroy on all my holy mountain, for the earth will be full of the knowledge of the LORD as the waters cover the sea" (Isaiah 11:9).

Noah's rainbow tells us something crucial about Yahweh's nature as God. This deity is not in love with raw power. Yahweh is a God we can trust; all-powerful, yes, but whose nature and character dictate limits to that infinite capability. The rainbow is a pledge that ties the hands of God. God will not be reckless with the creation; it is sheltered and safe: humanity's habitat protected forever, wrapped with a rainbow promise! If only we human beings would seriously embrace Yahweh's example!

So Noah and his family left the protection of the ark and headed out into the renewed world with the strong promise of this peace-making God. Lesslie Newbigin says, "Humankind sets out under the rainbow arch which is the sacrament of the primal covenant with all humankind and with the created world for humanity's sake."[74]

6.9 Sound Theology

What a reassuring promise this is! Charles Shultz expressed this winsomely in a *Peanuts* cartoon. Lucy and Linus are looking out the window at a driving rain storm. She says, "Boy, look at it rain...What if it floods the whole world?" Linus responds, "It will never do that. In the ninth chapter of Genesis, God promised Noah that would never happen again, and the sign of the promise is the rainbow." She says, "You've taken a great load off my mind." To which Linus replies, "Sound theology has a way of doing that."[75]

The rainbow is *sound theology*. Sound in the sense of being solid and reliable; every occurrence is a faithful echoing of God's sure word of promise. As a visible sign the colors of the rainbow accurately depict God's love of beauty in the material world and the depth of God's unfathomable goodness. Sound theology indeed!

But the theology was deeper than Noah ever imagined. Sally Lloyd-Jones, author of the *Jesus Storybook Bible* for children, notes that

> . . . It wasn't long before everything went wrong again, but God [...] had another plan – a better plan. A plan not to destroy the world but to rescue it – a plan to one day send his own Son, the Rescuer. God's strong anger against hate and sadness and death would come down once more – but not on his people or his world. No, God's war bow was not pointing down at his people. It was pointing up into the heart of Heaven.[76]

Ahh! The *wonder of water,* hidden in the form of a rainbow! Devastation followed by promise, desolation transformed by hope; God-as-Judge now revealed as God-as-Faithful-Protector. The Creator had just undone his creation and was now making it anew and pledging his word that it would never happen again. No wonder the Bible says "the heavens declare the glory of God!"! (Psalm 19:1) And no wonder rainbows cause the heart to leap with joy!

The rainbow and the whole Noah story illustrate the profound interconnection and interdependence of all living creatures for and with one another.

6.10 Full Circle Rainbow

Social groups of every kind have espoused the rainbow to symbolize their aspirations for peace and reconciliation and hope in the world. Daycares and children's playgrounds often display rainbows to denote a place of acceptance, harmony and creativity; political and environmental groups use it to convey inclusion and a respect for nature. The LGBT movement often uses a six-color rainbow flag as its banner in Gay Pride parades. But my favorite use of the rainbow symbol is the picture of heaven in the Book of Revelation: "I saw a throne in heaven and someone sitting on it.[...] And the glow of an emerald circled his throne like a rainbow" (Revelation 4:2-3 NLT).

The throne of God is surrounded by a rainbow – a beautiful picture of God's authority and power circumscribed by covenant faithfulness. Despite the harrowing events and judgments about to engulf the planet and its human population, God has pledged their survival. The Creator will redeem the earth and restore it. Evil will be purged, but the earth will not be destroyed.

The Book of Revelation was written to challenge and to reassure the church. Christians at that time faced fierce and relentless persecution. John himself was in exile for his faith and witness. His churches felt overwhelmed. He wrote to reassure his fellow believers that God had not forgotten or abandoned them – and that they were safe in God's covenant care. The God of Flood and Rainbow was their God, a covenant keeping God, a God who cared for his creation. The rainbow encircled throne is one of the many pictures in John's vision given to bolster and encourage his readers in every generation whatever personal vulnerability or cosmic catastrophe we have to face.

On a few occasions flying above the clouds I've seen the phenomenon called the 'airman's glory', where a full circle rainbow appears on the cloud cover below. The water vapor around the airplane is refracted by the bright sunlight and reflected on the cloud in what looks like a rainbow with the shadow of the airplane in the center of it, encircled by the full spectrum of promise.

Overwhelmed? Not by the threats of enemies or the circumstances of life, but most definitely overwhelmed and undergirded by the strong love of Christ. God's people are always completely secure in that protecting promise:

> in all these things we are more than conquerors through him who loved us. For I am convinced that neither death nor life, neither angels nor demons, neither the present nor the future, nor any powers, neither height nor depth, nor anything else in all creation, will be able to separate us from the love of God that is in Christ Jesus our Lord.
> Romans 8:38-39

I lived for twenty years in Montreal, an island city situated at the confluence of the Ottawa and St. Lawrence rivers. In its first year as a mission colony in 1643, the fledgling outpost was threatened in midwinter by a potentially disastrous flood. Downstream ice dammed the flow of the river swollen by heavy rain, and the freezing waters of the St. Lawrence rose to dangerous levels. Legend has it that the settlement's governor, Paul Chomedy de Maisonneuve, implored the Virgin Mary to stop the flood; he promised to erect a cross on the mountain above the city if the floodwaters abated. The rising waters slowed and then receded. The settlement was spared, and, as the story goes, de Maisonneuve eventually fulfilled his promise and planted a wooden cross somewhere on the hill overlooking the tiny settlement of Ville Marie. Over the centuries that mission station grew into the world-class city of Montreal.

Today, a huge steel cross on the top of Mount Royal commemorates the event. Often regarded as a tourist feature or a tribute to Montreal's past religious character, Christ-followers in that wonderful city see the cross differently. They see it as a sign of God's yearning love for their city. Like the rainbow after the flood in Noah's day, it is a sign of grace. Montrealers today are largely preoccupied with sports, business, entertainment and fashion – culture and commerce without God. But God has not forgotten his people there, nor the mission that they pursue by their daily lives. The Cross is a sign that Christ is Lord, protector and judge of all the earth.

As the 19th century Dutch statesman Abraham Kuyper said, "There is not a square inch in the whole domain of our human existence over which Christ, who is Sovereign over all, does not cry, 'Mine!'"[77]

Chapter 7
The Patriarchs

7.1 Beyond the Fertile Crescent

THE JOURNEY OF ABRAHAM and four generations of his descendents follows the arc of the Fertile Crescent from the famed Tigris-Euphrates valley in the east, or Mesopotamia as it was known, to the Nile Delta in the west.

Mesopotamia, the land between the rivers, was the cradle of one of the earliest civilizations on earth. It already had two thousand years of commerce, culture and tradition when Abraham was born in Ur on the south bank of the Euphrates. Lying just west of the point where the two mighty rivers joined before flowing into the Persian Gulf, Ur was a prosperous and proud city, living off the largess of the two rivers.

Mesopotamia was affluent with water (not just a pun). The Tigris flows down from the Taurus Mountains in Turkey 1,000 miles (1600 km) to the northwest. Less than a hundred miles (150 km) away, the Euphrates begins to flow first to the west, then it curls around to the southeast and flows in a roughly parallel direction to the Tigris, draining a vast region of hills in its early miles and then meandering 600 miles (a thousand kilometers) across the plains, becoming the longest river in Western Asia. Early settlers in Mesopotamia developed extensive irrigation systems and levees to enhance the use of water for agriculture. Traders brought goods and wealth from far afield and the commercial expertise of the Mesopotamians fostered the development of cuneiform script, the earliest known system of writing.

But the Bible is not particularly impressed with Ur or the whole Mesopotamian culture. Instead, it tells the story of a man and his descendents who deliberately left the good life in Ur and travelled west in search of a very different kind of civilization. As Thomas Cahill tells it in *The Gift of the Jews,* it would have seemed to everyone in Ur that this was a migration in the wrong direction. But in fact, this peculiar migration became "a hinge of history changing the way everyone in the world today thinks and feels."[78]

Genesis 12 tells of the summons of a god named Yahweh who said to Abram "Leave your country, your people and your father's household and go [the word could equally be 'come'] to the land I will show you. I will make you into a great nation and I will bless you" (Genesis 12:1-2). Abraham was called to leave this land of abundance and go where water was much less available. In this adventure he would learn that God, the designer of rivers, is also the spring of a different kind of water, living water, and the headwaters of every stream that enriches our lives.

Nevertheless, Abraham had to work hard to support his herds and flocks in a land of minimal rain or surface water. Genesis 12 tells how "he set out for the land of Canaan and arrived safe and sound" (Genesis 12:4 MSG). After traveling through the land he settled in the Negev. Why he chose that challenging terrain we're not told; perhaps because it was more sparsely settled than other areas. Despite the fact that Canaanites occupied the land at the time, God appeared to Abraham and told him "I will give this land to your children" (verse 7). Abraham took hold of that promise and built an altar to God in response. When and how that promise of land and children would be fulfilled, God did not say, and since Abraham had neither at the time, it remained part of the great waiting experience of Abraham's life.

Before long a severe famine in the area forced Abraham to travel east to Egypt in search of food, but he returned when he could to the Negev, settling in the eastern region near Beer-sheva (Genesis 21:22-34). And to support his cattle and sheepherding enterprise in an arid land like this, Abraham needed a significant amount of water, which meant he needed wells. So Abraham's servants did a lot of digging.

7.2 The Well of the Oath

When it became obvious that Abraham intended to settle in the region, the local 'king', Abimelech, proposed a treaty of friendship. This entitled Abraham to register a complaint about a recent conflict he had suffered when Abimelech's servants had seized possession of a well Abraham had dug (Genesis 21:25). Abimelech claimed to know nothing of the offense.

Digging a well was not the same as staking a claim to the land, but it entitled the one who dug the well to use the water that comes from it. The well served as a physical sign of grazing and watering rights. When Abimelech's servants seized Abraham's well and refused him access to the water, they were essentially robbing and expelling him, a significant violation of the code of hospitality.

With a generous gift of sheep and cattle, Abraham sealed a non-aggression covenant with his host Abimelech. He also set aside seven ewe lambs as a special 'addendum' to the agreement, an explicit affidavit concerning the well. "When you accept these seven sheep, you take it as proof that I dug this well, that it is my well" (Genesis 21:30 MSG).

This covenant at Beer-sheva has great significance both in the Genesis story and in the unfolding complex history of Israel and the land. It marks the beginning of a historic cultural relationship with the land even while Abraham resided there as an alien. Abraham named the well Beer-sheva, 'the well of the oath' to commemorate his treaty with the resident king who recognized Abraham's legitimacy.

Some years later, when his wife Sarah died, Abraham negotiated the purchase of a burial site at Hebron, along with official deeds for the property. To this day the Cave of the Patriarchs is considered a sacred site to Jews, Muslims and Christians.

The contested well at Beer-sheva was not the only well Abraham dug to sustain his herds and flocks. A generation later when Abraham's son Isaac settled in the Gerar Valley, (15 miles (24 km) west of Beer-sheva, about 10 miles (15 km) east from modern day Gaza), the locals harassed him by plugging "all the wells that his father's servants had dug in the time of his father Abraham" (Genesis 26:15). Clearly Abraham had kept his well digging crews busily occupied.

Wells and cisterns were crucial in the Negev for economic survival, and Abraham had invested considerable effort to acquire them as means for prosperity. But the wells were not Abraham's primary concern. The tradition tells us that having left the prosperous urban centers of Ur and Haran, Abraham was searching for something no amount of money could buy, a city whose builder and maker was God, a community characterized by godliness.

Abraham was married but childless – seemingly infertile – as he departed the lush lands of the Fertile Crescent. The decades ahead unfold a plot-line that culminates in God promising that Abraham's offspring will be as numerous as the stars in the sky and as the sand on the seashore, *i.e.* innumerable. God promised to ensure Abraham's fruitfulness even in the most barren land. By the end of Genesis, we can begin to see signs of that promise being fulfilled. Abraham's grandson, Jacob blesses his son Joseph as "'a fruitful vine near a spring" (Genesis 49:22) – and we'll explore that blessing at the end of this chapter.

But God's plan went far beyond biological progeny for Abraham, God's mission was the creation of a people who would flourish in every area of life and who would become channels of God's living waters to the rest of the world.

7.3 Abundant Life

Between his brief sojourn in Egypt and his later settling in the Negev, Abraham spent some time moving around nomadically and found himself in the region of Bethel, ten miles or so (15 km) north of Jerusalem and 20 miles (30 km) west of the Jordan. Abraham's young nephew Lot, who had come with him from Mesopotamia, had been travelling with him, but the herds of the two men had begun to outgrow the capacity of their shared grazing lands in the Judean hills.

Their partnership was no longer sustainable and their servants were becoming increasingly hostile with each other. So in the interest of good family relations, Abraham suggested they part ways amicably. He encouraged Lot to consider which direction he would go.

Lot had an eye for agricultural potential and opportunity – and the nearby Jordan plain to the east caught his attention.

> Lot looked up and saw that the whole plain of the Jordan was well watered, like the garden of the LORD, like the land of Egypt, toward Zoar. This was before the LORD destroyed Sodom and Gomorrah.
> Genesis 13:10

The Jordan is a small river. But in ancient times it made a huge difference to an arid land: a steady supply of water, shade trees and verdant pasture land. Five cities grew affluent across its plain. It was lush 'like God's garden' – the Garden of Eden.

It is a mark of Abraham's character that he did not simply send his nephew off to seek his fortune in the world. Seniority has its privileges, but Abraham generously gave his junior first choice in selecting his preferred gazing lands. "So Lot chose for himself the whole plain of the Jordan and set out toward the east. The two men parted company" (Genesis 13:10-11).

This is a story about faith and economics; about natural resources and life choices. It's not that Abraham was naturally affable. In fact, he seems to have been suspicious and wary by nature. But he was learning to trust God. Rejecting the 'ideology of scarcity' that governs most of us, Abraham looked to God to supply his needs. Confident that he lived under God's good promise,[79] he worked hard, but resisted the impulse to grasp the best for himself. He dared to be generous.

Lot, on the other hand, was swayed primarily by self-interest; he looked to ensure his material prosperity. He chose what appeared to be the prime real estate for grazing herds and bringing them to market.

On the surface there is nothing wrong with Lot's dreams of affluence. The Jordan plain was 'lush like God's garden'– rich with God-given natural resources, water, trees and grazing land and all the potential they promise. But that allusion to the Garden of Eden also hints at the spiritual temptation implicit in Lot's dreams of success and the choice he faced. The reference in the next phrase to Sodom and Gomorrah, the two chief towns in the plain, suggests the disaster and tragedy that await Lot, who was oblivious to the destructive power of their influence.

Every gift life offers us and every choice we make, has implications. But Lot was blind to the toxic cultural pressures that awaited him in the cities of the richly resourced, well-watered plain where he eventually lost his entire family. His choice was shortsighted and tragic.

Lot and Abraham exemplify divergent life pathways. One followed the way of radical trust in a Living God; the other was blind to spiritual factors and made his choice based on what appeared socially and financially advantageous. One inherited God's blessing and a richly abundant life; the other became spiritually bankrupt.

I wonder ... in my outlook on life, if I am more like Abraham or Lot? And *I wonder* ... since I live in a lush, well-watered affluent region of the world, how can I leverage the privileges and opportunities I enjoy so others can experience God's goodness as well?

Prayer:
God of Abundance, since you have promised to meet all my needs, help me to trust you more fully today. From the fullness of your grace I have received one blessing after another (John 1:16), a life more abundant than I have ever even dreamed of (John 10:10). Help me to seek first your kingdom and your righteousness and to trust you for the material things I need for life in this world. Amen

7.4 Eastern Hospitality

It was hot in the desert sun, so Abraham was glad for the shade of his tent (Genesis 18). Looking up he spotted three strangers lingering a short distance away. With the vigor characteristic of middle-eastern hospitality, he hurried over to them and offered them a drink of water.

In the conventions of hospitality, you make the initial offer so small that to refuse would be an insult. Then, when the strangers respond, they become your guest and you give them more than you promised and keep them a little longer while you prepare the real meal.

So went Abraham's visit with the three visitors he eventually realized were manifestations of the Lord Yahweh. He started with water – a drink and refreshing footbath. Then he served milk and curds while he hurriedly selected a choice young calf and had it quickly slaughtered, butchered and barbequed in honor of his guests.

The Guest (now referred to in the singular) responded with a gift of his own – a promise no one on earth could fulfill. Long past her prime, Sarah would soon have the joy of a young woman; her infertility would give way and she and Abraham would become parents. Their world of barrenness will be shattered by a new possibility. Sarah laughed at the prospect. She had long since given up hope. But this is a God who renews life in unexpected ways.

Just as water brings life from barren ground, so Abraham's gesture of hospitality initiated a life-giving conversation and an unfolding destiny neither Abraham nor Sarah had believed possible. This is a story about transformation – and God usually starts with small things that show little evidence of potential. As Proverbs 11:25 says, 'those who refresh others, will themselves be refreshed' (NLT).

7.5 Hagar

Three chapters later, in Genesis 21, we see Abraham on the opposite side of the hospitality page. Family conflicts between his wife Sarah and her maid Hagar and their two sons had become so fierce; Abraham was forced to expel Hagar and her son Ishmael out of their home and into the desert.

> Abraham got up early the next morning, got some food together and a canteen of water for Hagar, put them on her back and sent her away with the child. She wandered off into the desert of Beersheba. When the water was gone, she left the child under a shrub and went off, fifty yards or so. She said, "I can't watch my son die." As she sat, she broke into sobs.
> Meanwhile, God heard the boy crying. The angel of God called from Heaven to Hagar, "What's wrong, Hagar? Don't be afraid. ... Just then God opened her eyes. She looked. She saw a well of water. She went to it and filled her canteen and gave the boy a long, cool drink.
> Genesis 21:14-19 MSG

But the desert sun has no mercy and what mercy Abraham showed in giving her water for the road was quickly used up. The desert of Beersheba is forbidding terrain, and a few miles after Ishmael swallowed the last of their drinking water, dehydration took its toll and he began to faint. He wailed for thirst, in fear and delirium. Hagar couldn't go another step. Like thousands of desert mothers before her – and since – she was desperate, but spent.

This story *will* end well, but not yet. She and her son will survive, but their story must be told so we can understand. Hagar is about to experience God and regain her footing in life, but the path to personal growth is often discovered through bewildering grief, loss, turmoil or despair.

Hagar was alone, desperate and afraid, but God meets us where we are. The Genesis narrator says that God called her by name, "Hagar, do not be afraid, ... and God opened her eyes and she saw a well of water" (Genesis 21:18-19). Exhausted though she was, her maternal instincts responded: 'water ... life ... Ishmael, drink!'

Mother and son were rescued by a Voice and a well of water – a Voice from above and water from below. There's something universal about this story. We all need these same critical resources. Without water we die –

and without the voice of God, we fill the silence with siren songs. Hagar recognized the Voice that called her. She had heard it years before when God had met her at another spring during an earlier crisis. She was fleeing from the tirades of Sarah her mistress when an angel of the Lord found her near a spring in the desert (Genesis 16:7-9) and instructed her to return home.

Rural springs and village wells are communal meeting places – and wells in the Bible are often places where God meets thirsty people and provides much more than water, because thirst comes in many forms. Just as wells bring to the surface a life-sustaining gift from the earth, so God surfaces spiritual needs and satisfies them. So it was with Hagar.

I read somewhere that this story is the only account in ancient Near Eastern literature where a deity calls a woman by name. Hagar is an outsider, but God knows her intimately and treats her like family. God becomes father to her orphaned son and, as the narrator says – for the first time in all of scripture, "God was with the boy" (Genesis 21:20) as he grew up in the desert.

Like the Samaritan woman of the New Testament, Hagar is an outsider in need of water – and of acceptance. Both women encounter God at a well and are surprised to discover the richness of God's awareness and grace. They drink deeply, astonished by God's empathy and acceptance, and they leave with renewed hope. Madeline L'Engle says that Hagar discovers a God who cannot fail, a God whose purposes in God's time will always be right.[80]

The story of Hagar reminds us that no one is outside Yahweh's span of attention. God provides for Hagar's young son Ishmael just as God will provide a rescue for Isaac in the next chapter. The parallels between the two stories in Genesis 21 and 22 are uncanny. Both tell of angel interventions and voices from heaven; in both stories, a parent is terrified at the impending death of their child; both parents look up and discover God's miraculous provision for their child. It's a critical observation about parenting, teaching and any work with youth. God is the ultimate provider, not us.

It is quite remarkable that the Biblical narrator of this incident puts the Arab patriarch Ishmael in such a positive light, given the deep animosity between Arabs and Jews in the ensuing generations, both biblical and contemporary.

This story also underscores how critical water is for physical survival in the real world. Without water, children die; without a source of water, parents have to watch their children shrivel and die. Hagar is the prototype of drought stricken mothers throughout history who agonize over the suffering of their offspring. Every day on our planet almost 5,000 children die from unsafe or unreachable water.

God is the ultimate provider who modeled consummate care for Hagar in her need. If Hagar's sobs evoked the response of God, perhaps it teaches us in our day to respond to the plight of millions of children and parents across the world who desperately need clean water to drink. No one is outside God's span of attention, but if we ignore them, we become as merciless as the desert sun.

On the other hand, how rewarding it is to be the hands and feet of God to put that water into the hands of thirsty strangers. Again we meet the proverb 'those who refresh others will themselves be refreshed' (Proverbs 11:25). You won't find a better example of this in all the Bible than a remarkable young woman named Rebekah, the wife of Isaac.

7.6 Rebekah

Rebekah knew a thing or two about wells – and about hospitality. Isaac's father Abraham had sent his servant to find a wife for Isaac. He had prayed for success in his search and for God's divine *hesed* – that rich Hebrew word that means kindness, loyalty and special favor – in particular for Isaac. And before he finished praying, this marvelous young woman showed up.

> The servant hurried to meet her and said, 'please give me a little water from your jar.' 'Drink, my lord', she said, and quickly lowered the jar to her hands and gave him a drink. After she had given him a drink, she said, 'I'll draw water for your camels too, until they have finished drinking'. So she quickly emptied her jar into the trough, ran back to the well to draw more water, and drew enough for all his camels (Genesis 24:17-20).

In a land where hospitality was king, Rebekah excelled. When the servant asked for water, she quickly lowered the jar to her hands and gave him a drink. Then she volunteered to water the visitor's camels. She emptied her jar, ran back to the well and didn't stop until the thirsty camels were satisfied.

If a matchmaker were looking for a 'get-the-job-done-with-a-cheerful-attitude' kind of woman, Rebekah was a stellar find. There was some haggling by the relatives before she was released to fulfill her destiny, but by the end of the chapter, she was Isaac's wife, comforting him after his mother's death.

Isaac's story is a tapestry of *hesed* and *hospitality,* prayer and hard work, God's gifts and human generosity. It focuses especially around wells and the gift of water, and the spacious living it makes possible.

But this gift hints as being something more than just the natural resource of water. It is symbolic of the universal human search for what ultimately satisfies, a search for beauty and meaning, for love, for God. Like Isaac, I can bear witness to the *hesed* of God in all these things.

7.7 Rehoboth

As his herds increased, so did Isaac's need for water. And when his crops flourished, the jealousy of his neighbors overflowed. Genesis 26 tells how they fouled his wells with rocks and dirt and eventually evicted him from the region.

In a day when revenge and dominance was a sign of strength lest your opponents sensed fear and weakness. Isaac showed remarkable restraint. He intuitively knew the proverb that a gentle answer can turn aside wrath (Proverbs 15:1).

Isaac left his crops and moved his herds elsewhere – to the Gerar valley where his father had dug wells and pastured flocks decades earlier. Local herdsmen had filled them in after the old man died, but Isaac re-excavated them and continued the family cattle business.

Prosperity makes enemies as well as friends – and the local herdsmen harassed the wealthy newcomer. When Isaac dug a new well, his neighbors claimed prior right to the resource. Isaac named the well "Argument" and walked away from it. They contested the next well, so Isaac named it "The Well of Anger" and abandoned it too (Genesis 26:19-21).

Patiently, Isaac outlasted his adversaries. He dug a third well over which no one fought. He named it "Rehoboth" – *Wide-Open Spaces* – in gratitude for the elbowroom it gave him and the opportunity to live peaceably among strangers – and to flourish together, sharing the natural resources. Space is not just legroom, but freedom from the encroaching demands of others.[81] Human beings need space, but we also need to learn to get along together.

The modern Israeli city of Rehovot was founded by Polish Jews in 1890 in the coastal plain about 40 miles (60 km) north of the original site. Israel Belkind, one of the founders of the settlement, proposed the name Rehovot based on Genesis 26:22 because "'now the Lord has made room for us and we shall be fruitful in the land.". Indeed the community did flourish. In 1908 immigrants from Yemen joined them, and together – Jews from two very different cultures – learned to live together, planting vineyards, almond orchards and citrus groves and working hard to overcome agricultural failures, plant diseases, and business challenges. Cooperation is one of the most crucial principles confronting water resource management in the contemporary world.

I wonder . . . what a difference it would make if the inhabitants around the Gerar valley today, Israelis and Palestinians, were to adopt the nonadversarial spirit and practice of Isaac? Sadly, harassment and contempt prevail on both sides as the *per capita* use of water in Israel is almost five-fold greater than what Israel allows to those in Palestine.

I'm convinced that this kind of injustice outrages heaven as much as it breeds frustration and anger on earth. Dr. Yosef Dreizin, deputy water commissioner for Israel recognizes the need to negotiate redistribution of natural water resources, and goes even further in calling for cooperation on the production of new water resources. Actualizing that vision would make partners out of enemies – and that is the secret Isaac teaches us at Rehoboth.

That is the spirit behind the song by Caedmon's Call, "Share the Well"

> Share the well, share with your brother
> Share the well, my friend
> It takes a deeper well to love one another
> Share the well, my friend.[82]

The Rehoboth story has personal significance for me because that's the name of my home. My wife Tiffany works as a hydrogeologist; wells are her métier. A few years ago, reading Isaac's story she was struck by his choice of a name that enshrined the values of freedom, space and harmonious relations with neighbors. She named her house "Rehoboth". A year later she welcomed me into her life, and now, together, we work to make our home a 'spacious place', a welcoming environment where even strangers might enjoy respite from the stresses of the world. We've learned as a couple that good communication, cooperation and giving each other enough space are some of the keys to harmonious marriage.

Another good example of cooperation is being developed by the European NGO 'EcoPeace / Friends of the Earth Middle East'. Their project called 'Good Water Neighbors' links together cross-border communities in Israel, Jordan and Palestine.[83] By focusing on the mutual dependence these people have on shared water resources they have created a platform for dialogue and cooperation which helps to build trust and understanding. And this initial trust can provide the basis for cooperative work beyond water issues such as land use, economic and tourist development.

Rehoboth is a reminder that if we work at it, human beings can live together amicably, and when we do, there is water enough for everyone. And there God speaks his blessing (Psalm 133:1-3).

7.8 Jacob's Second Kiss

It is only the second kiss mentioned in the Bible – and it happened beside a village well.

> Jacob said to the loitering shepherds, "the sun is still high; it is not time for the flocks to be gathered. Water the sheep and take them back to pasture."
>
> "We can't," they replied, "until all the flocks are gathered and the stone has been rolled away from the mouth of the well. Then we will water the sheep."
>
> While he was still talking with them, Rachel came with her father's sheep, for she was a shepherdess. When Jacob saw Rachel daughter of Laban, his mother's brother, and Laban's sheep, he went over and rolled the stone away from the mouth of the well and watered his uncle's sheep. Then Jacob kissed Rachel and began to weep aloud. He had told Rachel that he was a relative of her father and a son of Rebekah. So she ran and told her father (Genesis 29:7-12).

No doubt Rebekah told her son Jacob, how as a young woman she had watered a stranger's camels and gained a husband for her initiative. Now, twenty years later, Jacob himself stood by that same well.

The most breathtaking girl he had ever seen was leading her flock to water. Some dimwitted shepherds were loitering, waiting for help to move the large stone well cover so they could water their herds (and perhaps ogle or flirt with the girl). Jacob, a master of spontaneity, single-handedly hefted the massive stone away from the well mouth and drew water for the woman and her sheep.

The shepherds had told him she was the daughter of Laban, his uncle – which made the pretty one, his cousin. Each time he drew up a skin of water and poured it for the sheep, he glanced at the face of the comely shepherdess.

And when he finished, he did the most spontaneous, guileless thing he had ever done. He kissed her on the cheek and dissolved into tears. The virile stone mover, the energetic water carrier, the young man who had crossed a hundred miles of desert to find relatives – was home. He told the astonished girl that he was her cousin, the son of her legendary aunt, Rebekah.

Frederick Buechner says in his historical novel *Son of Laughter*, it was through the door of that kiss that Jacob entered the house of the years that followed.[84] Little did he know at that moment the hopes and heartbreak that awaited him in his life with this woman. It is worth the read in Genesis 29-35 – and it all started with Jacob uncovering that well.

There was more than water released in that act. Jacob's whole future opened up. Rachel became a wellspring of inspiration, joy and sadness in his life. But the years ahead also exposed the dark well of Jacob's soul, the murky recesses of his character.

That kiss by the well is the second kiss in the Genesis story of Jacob. Weeks earlier Jacob deceived his blind father Isaac with a kiss at the most sacred filial moment imaginable, when the old patriarch was passing on his fatherly blessing. Jacob lied, impersonated his older brother and stole the family blessing.

The first kiss violated family trust; the second began a new chapter in Jacob's life. Jacob embodies the duality in all of us. He is both scoundrel and man of destiny, and he will wrestle with God his whole life. Jacob's life teaches us about earthy spirituality downstream from Eden and a God who embraces us in all our shrewd duplicity, a God who rips off well covers, exposes his heart and kisses us with undeserved love.

7.9 Crossing the River

Jacob served Laban his father-in-law for twenty years, tending his flocks and bearing him a dozen grandchildren. But eventually Jacob grew tired of Laban's shabby treatment and deceptions. In a dream God told him it was time to leave and head back west to his home. With the consent of his two wives and without so much as a farewell note to Laban, Jacob headed west – he fled with all he had, and crossing the River, he headed for the hill country of Gilead (Genesis 31:21).

Crossing the River was a decisive step for Jacob, severing his dependence on Laban. Like Julius Caesar, crossing the Rubicon, it was an act of defiance. The die was cast, there was no returning.

In the year 49 BCE, Julius Caesar was camped north of the Rubicon River in northern Italy. Julius served as promagistrate with right of command over the province of Gaul. The Rubicon was the border between Gaul in the north and Italy proper in the south under the rule of Rome. Crossing into Roman territory with troops under his command would be an act of military treason. But on January 10, Julius led a thousand soldiers across the Rubicon deliberately defying the law of *imperium*. His swift action challenge terrified a large part of the Senate who fled Rome opening the door to his eventual victory and a change of regime in the Empire. The phrase 'crossing the Rubicon' has become proverbial to describe any risky or defiant act from which there is no turning back.

That's what crossing the River meant for Jacob and his wives Rachel and Leah. Risky and costly as their decision was, they chose to pass the point of no return.

The River they crossed was the Euphrates. Euphrates is really the Greek name which means 'beautiful'. The Hebrews simply called it Nahar, which means 'the river'. The word *nahar* occurs over 100 times in the text of the Old Testament, referring to various different rivers, but the Euphrates is the only significant river referred to as Nahar. The Nile and the Jordan are never called nahar; they are called by their proper names.

For Jacob the Nahar was a boundary that separated him forever from the dominance of Laban over his life. When Laban eventually tracked Jacob down, there was a testy confrontation, but Jacob stood up to his uncle/father-in-law as an equal. They warily signed a nonaggression pact and called on God as their witness that each would honor their pledge. It was not a happy parting of the ways, but it serves to remind us that in human relationships, including families, the drive to exploit people leads to dismal outcomes. God was working in Abraham's family line to show them a better way, a way of grace and truth, a way of mutual respect.

Crossing the River can be costly. It often means the end of an era, the loss of cherished connections with the past. Marriage is a kind of crossing the river, leaving father and mother in order to unite with a beloved and form a new family bond. We'll see later how baptism is another kind of 'crossing the river'. Jesus spelled out the decisive choice of discipleship in similar terms.

For Jacob and his wives and their children, a new world beckoned and the old life had to be jettisoned. This decisive initiative is the first of several such life-changing transitions in biblical history where God's people have 'crossed the river', breaking with the past to begin a new life. A contemporary term for this is 'liminality', the challenge of crossing a threshold between two situations, a transition that is often turbulent and fraught with danger, discomfort, uncertainty and opportunity.[85]

Cutting loose from the past is often harder than it seems. Anyone who has ever been baptized as an adult knows how quickly we can go from euphoric triumph to struggle and fear. The challenge is that despite your decision to part ways with the past, the old *you* still dogs your steps as you walk into the future. That was the reality Jacob had to face at the next boundary he had to cross.

Traveling west along the limestone cliffs of the narrow Jabbok valley towards the Jordan and home, Jacob had another fear. He knew that another part of his deceptive past would catch up to him in the form of his brother Esau, coming to meet him from the west. When he got news that Esau was approaching, Jacob sent his family across the stream – either to protect them from Esau or to protect himself, the text is not really clear. What is clear is that Jacob was afraid. In fact, he was frantic. His prayer to God is desperate –

> O God of my father Abraham, God of my father Isaac, O LORD, who said to me, 'Go back to your country and your relatives, and I will make you prosper,' I am unworthy of all the kindness and faithfulness you have shown your servant. I had only my staff when I [first] crossed this Jordan, but now I have become two groups. Save me, I pray, from the hand of my brother Esau, for I am afraid he will come and attack me, and also the mothers with their children. But you have said, 'I will surely make you prosper and will make your descendants like the sand of the sea, which cannot be counted'
> Genesis 32:9-12

Jacob recalled how greatly God had blessed him since he first crossed the Jordan twenty years earlier. Now he faced a threat potentially more sinister than Laban. He was urgent for God's protection. How very much like us Jacob appears in this moment. Often it takes a crisis of desperation before we realize how deeply we need God. What happened next is one of the great mystery events in the whole biblical text and one of the watershed moments in Jacob's journey with God.

That night Jacob was alone, but sometime during the night, a man grasped hold of him in the darkness and wrested him to the ground. Jacob fought back. His adversary was more wily and aggressive than his uncle Laban had ever been. The match seesawed back and forth until daybreak, when suddenly the surprise combatant wrenched Jacob's hip out of joint, a 'cheating' move that mirrored back to Jacob all his own shrewd and underhanded ways. Jacob suspected, rightly, that he was wrestling with God who was wrestling for Jacob's will and submission. "Let me go," the 'man' said to Jacob for it is daybreak."

> But Jacob replied, "I will not let you go unless you bless me."
>
> The man asked him, "What is your name?"
>
> "Jacob," he answered.
>
> Then the man said, "Your name will no longer be Jacob, but Israel, because you have struggled with God and with men and have overcome."

> Jacob said, "Please tell me your name." But he replied, "Why do you ask my name?" Then he blessed him there.
>
> So Jacob called the place Peniel, saying, "It is because I saw God face to face, and yet my life was spared" (Genesis 32:26-30).

This event redefined Jacob's relationship with God. He was humbled that God had confronted him but not forced him into compliance. He realized what an honor God had bestowed on him by giving him the right to resist. Some have said that this was a battle God could not win by force, because it was a battle for Jacob's character and will. In this arena God gives us the dignity of refusal.

Jacob showed that he was desperate for God's blessing; he held on for dear life to obtain it. And when asked his name, it seems to me that Jacob confessed to all his lowdown self-seeking scheming ways by which he had wrestled with others. In response God gave him a new name, in effect calling him to a new identity and a new way of being in the world.

The nation of Israel has always seen its relationship with God as a wrestling match with Yahweh. God has not been easy on his chosen people. Nor did God give Jesus a cakewalk in life[86]. Everyone God has ever entrusted with a great mission has had a Jabbok experience. They have had to wrestle with God. And if they prevail, God has given them the dignity of walking with a limp, scars that demonstrate what it cost them to accomplish something for God in a hostile world. John Walton says, "as always with God, one has to lose in order to win." And John Wimber once said, "Never trust a leader who doesn't have a limp."

7.10 Dreams and Nightmares

Joseph was famous for his dreams – but not always wise about sharing them – especially when they featured him as the center of attention. His father Jacob didn't help matters by treating him conspicuously as favorite son. His older brothers resented him and dreamed of a time when they might rid themselves of his annoying presence. One day opportunity knocked – and Joseph's nightmare began (Genesis 37:18).

Kidnapped by his brothers and sold to slave-traders en route to Egypt, Joseph was purchased by a high ranking army official. Things went well initially until his master's wife falsely charged him with sexual assault; he was imprisoned and eventually forgotten. Life had spiraled downwards for a man loaded with talent and ambition. It was his own worst nightmare. But along the way he had developed a knack of interpreting the night-dreams of others. And that eventually became his 'get out of jail free card'.

Turns out the Pharaoh had a nightmare that jolted him awake (Genesis 41). The king stood beside his beloved Nile as seven fat cows climbed out of the river and begin grazing along the bank. All was well until, ominously, seven scrawny cows came out of the same river, stalked the healthy cows and devoured them. Cannibal cows are a bad portent – something nasty was afoot on the banks of the sacred Nile. Pharaoh woke with a start.

The Nile is the lifeline of Egypt. Rising in the east African highlands it snakes its way northward 4,000 miles (6,000 kms) to the Mediterranean Sea, picking up natural nutrients and minerals and carrying them downstream. By the time it reaches the Egyptian flood plain, it is liquid fertilizer.

The annual flooding of the river refreshed and enriched the soil and flushed away the salt residue of previous floods. Egypt became one of the breadbaskets of the world – and with it, one of the cradles of civilization. Egypt also saw the river as an expression of divine favor and the Pharaoh as the embodiment of divine power and fertility.[87]

On the whole, this natural process served Egypt well; cows and people ate well. But the dream river could also be a nightmare. Some years the flooding wiped out the entire harvest; drought could be equally devastating – like scrawny cows.

Joseph was summoned from prison and interpreted Pharaoh's dream as a forecast of bumper crops, climate change and severe drought. He called for decisive leadership to alleviate the impact of the impending catastrophe – and was assigned by the Pharaoh to provide that leadership himself. His story is a case study for the ages about resource management and responsible stewardship. His shrewd planning saved the day for his family, and his gracious forgiveness of their cruelty is a highwater mark in Israel's experience of the ethical character of God. The narrator reminds us that God's presence with Joseph was the chief cause of his success.

But there was another sinister side to Joseph's work that is less obvious in the text. The Pharaoh's dream revealed that a time was coming when the stable prosperous empire would be destabilized.[88] Pharaoh was being invited into an alternate way of seeing his world – as a place of need, trouble and deprivation. This myth of Egypt's abundance and self-sufficiency was being challenged by the uninvited dream and Pharaoh felt helpless; it was a perspective that he had never considered.

Joseph was God's agent for a new understanding of empire – one that uses its resources to serve people and save lives. But in the course of his shrewd administration that saved the lives of many, Joseph also reinforced Pharaoh's oppression and exploitation. When Egypt's citizens were at their most desperate and vulnerable point, Joseph forced them to sell themselves as slaves to Pharaoh (Genesis 47:21). Nothing is said about it in Genesis, but this surely sowed the seeds of Egypt's national resentment against the Hebrews that flared up a few generations later.

Walter Brueggemann says, "Too bad that Joseph ceases to be an interpreter and becomes a manager for Pharaoh! By his "Egyptianization," he signs on to the task of stabilizing the regime that the dream had worked to destabilize.[89]

This first river story in the Bible, Genesis 41-46, reminds us that we have a very delicate relationship with our environment. Dreams can easily become nightmares with wide-ranging effects.

In the 1960's, after millennia of the Nile's erratic ebb and flow Egypt built the Aswan High Dam. This development increased effective farmland by 500% and provides electricity for hundreds of Egyptian towns and villages. But it has also had adverse impact on Egyptian fisheries, soil fertility, erosion and other concerns.

Stewarding nature is a complicated privilege. As an act of faith it requires courage and humility, initiative and patience, science and imagination, respect for creation, local counsel and collaboration and a sense of responsibility to fulfill creation's global purpose.

Pharaoh was very troubled by his mad cow dream. I wonder what he would find troubling in our world today. I wonder what aspects of our global development today God finds unnatural and nightmarish?

7.11 Joseph's Fruitful Vine

A remarkable evidence of God's grace is the way he transforms this scheming family-line into a source of blessing for the whole world. Before the old patriarch Jacob died, he gathered his sons around him and spoke his blessing over them in *Genesis 49*. Earlier he had given a private grandfatherly blessing to Joseph's two sons, but on this formal occasion, all the brothers listened as their father spoke to each of them in turn, describing how he envisioned their lives and future destiny.

At last he reached his two favorite sons, Joseph and Benjamin. Benjamin would become a ravenous wolf devouring his prey, a valiant warrior, dividing his plunder. Joseph on the other hand would be a giver of life, not a taker. Joseph will be "a fruitful vine, a fruitful vine near a spring, whose branches climb over a wall". (Genesis 49:22).

Joseph's great mission in life had been the preserving of life, but it had not been an easy mission. God had rescued him from a dry cistern in the desert, from the schemes of treacherous brothers and slave-traders, and from dark forgotten dungeons of Egypt. Joseph came into fame, fortune and economic power, but he used these not for private advantage, but to be the savior of his generation.

Indeed his branches grew beyond the wall of his family and blessed the entire nation and the world. God planted him in dry foreign soil and grew him into a very fruitful vine, fulfilling God's blessing to his great-grandfather Abraham in Genesis 17:6 "I will make you very fruitful".

Curiously, there is some ambiguity about the word *para* translated 'fruitful vine'. It is very similar to the word *pere* meaning *'wild donkey'* and some translators take that as the correct reading. The Message says, "Joseph is a wild donkey, a wild donkey by a spring" (Genesis 49:22 MSG). That makes more sense of the next verse "archers attacked him savagely, they shot at him and harassed him" (verse 23 NLT) – why would archers attack a fruitful vine? – "but he held steady under fire, his bow firm, his arms limber" (verse 24, MSG).

Whether we see Joseph as a vine or a wild donkey, he needs a steady source of water. Even blind old Jacob could see that Joseph's virtue and vitality were sustained not by Egypt's Nile or Pharaoh's treasury, but by an invisible spring of spiritual power. No one could endure the kind of hostility Joseph suffered without a strong sense of destiny and purpose. For Joseph, that was a strong conviction that Yahweh was at his side and that the deep purposes of Yahweh's covenant were being worked out in his life.

In the following verses of Jacob's blessing (Genesis 49:24-26) he described this divine fountain of grace with four vivid names for God – 'the Almighty', 'the Rock', 'the Shepherd', and 'your father's God'. He spoke of 'blessings of heaven above and the deep below' which suggest both abundant rain and never-failing wells. But this family's legacy went beyond material wealth and proven natural resources. They were sustained by the personal promise of the Great Shepherd, the Rock of Israel himself. The same Spring of Living Water that supported Abraham, Jacob and Joseph would continue to nourish the nation – and through them and the Savior who would one day come from them, be the Spring of water for the entire world!

It makes me wonder . . .

- how God might use any of us if we are willing to endure hardships and bloom where we're planted, even if the soil feels dry and hostile?
- What is *the spring within* that nourishes me?
- Do I have a sense of destiny and purpose sustaining me in adversity and the fog of doubt?
- Does the grace of God flourish in me and climb over the wall of my life to enrich others?

Chapter 8
Escape from Egypt

8.1 The Gifts of the Nile

"WHERE THE RIVER FLOWS, life abounds", says Ezekiel in Ezekiel 47:9(MSG). A NASA satellite image illustrates the vital importance of water in the Egyptian desert[90]. A long narrow band of green marks the flow of the Nile through a brown desert. From ancient times the civilizations of Egypt have depended on the Nile River for their agriculture and commerce. So vital was the water that ancient Egyptians deified the river. They called the Nile-god *'Hapi'*. Every year in late summer, Hapi's breasts overflowed with the surplus of the rains in the highlands to south. Hapi made Egypt wealthy and the affluent enjoyed security and sophistication. The gods seemed to smile on Egypt.

Israel saw the world differently. Yahweh was supreme above the gods and the Nile's fertility was a gift from Yahweh. Like rainfall and sunlight, the river delivered Yahweh's life-giving gifts to the Earth and all her people, demonstrating God as a merciful, faithful, generous provider for all.

The obvious response to such lavish goodness would be gratitude. "Give thanks to the Lord for he is good; his mercy endures forever" (Psalm 136:1), Israel sang. God's bounty gave Israel an ethical motivation to treat the world generously. God's abundant care inspires God's people to be generous to others. As Jesus said, "freely you have received, freely give" (Matthew 10:8).

But privilege can make people and nations proud and selfish, and so it was with Egypt. Egypt was a cradle of human civilization, but for Israel, it became a hostile cradle, a most uncivil civilization. Israel emerged from Egypt's tyranny with deep scars from injustice.

Rivers connect people – over 160 million people in the Nile River Basin. But rivers can also divide people – right bank from left bank; upstream from downstream, the haves from the can't-haves. The Nile Basin Initiative[91] has tremendous difficulty getting agreement on the rights of the various stakeholders among the ten nations that touch the Nile. Often the poor are the ones left out of the prosperity the river potentially provides for all.

Spurred on by their central government, various provinces in China that share the same river have negotiated compensation agreements. If the upstream province protects the quality of the water that flows through it and exceeds agreed-upon standards, the downstream region will compensate their resource-protecting neighbors; if the water quality falls below the standard, the upstream folks have to compensate the province below.

Rivers can make us very good or very bad neighbors, people who cooperate or who take advantage of our neighbors; people who deal fairly or who exploit others. No wonder the prophet Amos saw parallels between social justice and the flow of a reliable river – "Let justice flow like rivers and righteousness like a never-failing stream" (Amos 5:24).

8.2 Genocide and Hope

During a horrific 100 days in the spring of 1994, almost a million Tutsi and Hutu men, women and children were slaughtered and crudely dumped in Rwanda's Kagera River. The current carried their bodies – shot, hacked, clubbed or burned – over the waterfall down towards the quiet waters of Lake Victoria.

The history of genocide has deep roots in the rivers of Africa. The first chapter of The Book of Exodus tells how a cultured Pharaoh in the 18th or 19th dynasty, tried to obliterate the surging numbers of Hebrew people living in his land.

The Nile gave Pharaoh a natural vehicle for the extermination and disposal of his enemies – cheaper and cleaner than Hitler's death camps and equally effective. The life-giving river became a river of death, teeming with crocodiles who are not fussy eaters (Exodus 1:22).

Against the dark violence the story (Exodus 2:1-10) sparkles with human tenderness – parents who defied tyranny, hiding their infant for 3 months, water-proofing a papyrus basket in hopes of beating the crocodiles and Egyptian Gestapo, a big sister secretly watching her brother, a bathing princess (who my artistic granddaughter Tessa regards as the prima donna of the story) and a daycare arrangement so full of dramatic irony even a child can enjoy it.

So God brings good out of the worst human evil, life out of hate, and hope out of despair. God turns the perilous river into a river of hope.

But the Exodus text barely even mentions God in this part of the story. As so often in life, God works anonymously and God's presence is only discernible after the fact. The people in the story simply do what they have to do.

In desperate times people resort to desperate measures. This mother abandons her vulnerable baby, but she abandons him to God – which is what every parent eventually has to do, though some are more aware of it than others.

The future deliverer of Israel was left bobbing helplessly in a fragile basket on the river. How often God's salvation hangs in the balance on a very slender thread – like Esther risking all to visit the king . . . and Jesus being birthed in a stable!

And somewhere in the hills of Rwanda today, songs of forgiveness are being sung by Rwandan neighbors working side by side in the fields, neighbors formerly called Hutu and Tutsi who have learned that forgiveness and grace create a more promising future than the politics of hatred and revenge.[92]

8.3 Drawn Out of the Water

So God was at work as the unnamed infant floated precariously in a papyrus basket among the reeds along the Nile. He was condemned by imperial edict, guilty of being a 3-month-old Hebrew man-child. Miraculously, he was rescued by an Egyptian princess who named him 'Moses' meaning 'water-son' or 'drawn out of water' (Exodus 2:10).

He grew up to become liberator of the Hebrew slaves, but first he had to undergo his own rescue, his own exodus, experiencing on a personal scale the rescue-through-water which God would later accomplish through him for the whole nation at the Red Sea.[93]

Many commentators note the courageous women who are heroines of this story: the Egyptian midwives who defied the Pharaoh's edict, the mother and sister of Moses who risked their lives to protect him, the daughter of

Pharaoh who financed his daycare and gave him his name. They lived in a patriarchal world, but it's impossible to ignore the vital role these women played.

In *The Book of Negroes*, Aminato Diallo tells us that the word for *'mother'* in her West African tongue is the same as the word for *'river'*.[94] Like Moses, every person's life story begins in water. We were gestated in water and birthed by the breaking of water. Unless we were born by caesarian, a birth canal was our passageway into the world.

Our journey along this birthing river was risky and difficult for both our mothers and for us, but necessary for living a full human life. We are all 'drawn out of the water'. We passed through water to the *wonder* of a larger world, to all the heroics and hum-drum, the heart-breaks and hallelujahs of life.

Being birthed was our first exodus into life. It's also a rich metaphor for another gateway, rebirth into the astounding wonder of vibrant friendship with God.

That's why Jesus, our river companion a millennium after Moses, goes to John the Baptist at another river, the Jordan (Matthew 3:13-15), where John called to his compatriots to change their ways and renew themselves spiritually. Jesus tells John to baptize him in the Jordan, foreshadowing his plunge into the ultimate river of Death. Drawn out of that water he becomes liberator and Life-giver for all.

This symbolism lies behind every Christian's baptism since that day. The river represents all but certain Death, except that Someone braved those waters for us and rescued us from peril, drew us out of the water, gave us a new name and accompanies us in the great Adventure, a life of endless wonder and joy.

8.4 River of Blood

The first of the Ten Plagues (Exodus 7:14-25) exposed Egypt's vulnerability. The Nile was in extreme distress – and it wasn't pretty. The great River was bleeding and undrinkable. In a land with no rain, the people became desperate. It was an ecological disaster and it became even worse. There were no industries to blame – no oil spill or ruptured tailings ponds. This was a natural disaster with serious religious undertones.

Scientifically, there are various biological explanations. The Nile normally floods every year in late summer. If the annual flood were excessively high, it may have brought microorganisms such as *Pfiesteria piscicida* which could redden and poison the river and cause conditions that would kill the fish. Epidemiological theories and counter theories abound.[95]

The Bible simply ignores the question of natural causes. Instead it brings its ethical lens over this natural event and sees behind the blood red Nile the even bloodier hand of Pharaoh, his arrogant heart and supposed divinity, his scorn for slaves, his policies of injustice, his refusal to honor the supreme authority of Yahweh. The corrupt social and religious ecology of Egypt led to the ecological disaster of the bleeding river.

Social well-being in any community requires, (borrowing the words of Micah a thousand years later) justice, mercy and humility (Micah 6:8). Through Moses, Yahweh first gave Pharaoh the opportunity to act with justice and mercy and humbly release his Hebrew slaves. When Pharaoh refused, God upped the ante.

Pharaoh was believed to be responsible for the Nile's life-giving flood-season. The annual inundation was called 'the arrival of Hapi', the spirit or god of the Nile. No wonder that's where Yahweh began. Turning the Nile to blood meant that Yahweh was shedding Hapi's lifeblood.

The plague lasted a week followed by an infestation of frogs before Pharaoh pled for mercy. When Yahweh relented, Pharaoh reversed himself, and the showdown intensified. Through nine more rounds, strike after strike of 'shock and awe' that the Bible calls 'signs and wonders'. As 'signs' they pointed to the impotence of Pharaoh and his magicians and the whole pantheon of Egypt's gods. As 'wonders' they leave us shaking our heads at the sheer folly and stubborn pride of a king who refused to accept God's supreme authority and insistence on justice for all.

This ancient story of natural disaster resonates with timeless truth. As Lynn White Jr. wrote in *Science* in 1967, human ecology reflects our beliefs about our nature and our destiny. Our spiritual attitudes generate effects in the natural and social world. What we sow, we reap.[96] No wonder the Bible calls us to care for the whole of creation in a spirit of humility, gratitude and love.

8.5 Between a Rock and a Hard Place

It's a story for anyone who has ever been caught between danger and disaster, between a rock and a hard place. It's the ancient story of Exodus.

After centuries in Egypt and decades of slavery, after a harrowing contest with a despotic Pharaoh, now beyond their wildest dreams, a tribe of slaves found themselves free at last, heading east on the Desert Road towards their long promised home (Exodus 13:18-20). Two days later, camped by Yam Suph, the Sea of Reeds, they saw the dust of Pharaoh's army with 600 chariots bearing down on them. Yam Suph posed a formidable barrier – too wide to circumvent and too deep to cross; it blocked their only path of escape. If they were chosen people, they appeared chosen to die.

The traditional name for this site is the Red Sea and most modern Bible translators continue to use the traditional name. But the Hebrew text says Yam Suph, which means Sea of Reeds. This is how South African bishop Godfrey Ashby summarizes the historical data:

> It would seem most likely that the Hebrews escaped from Egypt via the marshy pans near the present town of El Qantara, where the Suez Canal is now, thereby avoiding the Egyptian garrisons that guarded the normal route for travelers from Africa to Asia. Their crossing would have been at the southern end of Lake Menzaleh, which is one of the shallow, seasonally fluctuating lakes in the isthmus. This route would be consistent with the wind that dried up or drove aside the shallow water but left mud to clog the pursuing chariots and put them at the mercy of the returning floods.[97]

Ashby also suggests that the Septuagint translators substituted the name Red Sea in order to make a theological point, that God had led Israel across the natural barrier between Africa and Asia and that Pharaoh and all the gods of Egypt could not recapture them.[98]

Yahweh's escape plan for Israel was ingenious and dramatic. That night, the story goes, a strong wind opened a path in the sea and Israel escaped on dry land. When the Egyptian cavalry followed, the waters returned and swallowed them up. They sank like stones. Israel was free.

8.6 Bastille Day

The day they crossed the Yam Suph became Israel's Bastille Day, their Fourth of July, their Day of Freedom! Jews have savored that moment ever since. It is an iconic motif of their national story – a resurrection from the verge of extinction to ecstatic freedom – and they have experienced it multiple times throughout history.

Israel's rescue at Yam Suph mirrors a universal reality. Death is the great enemy of every human being on the planet. Picture all of humanity on the shore of an un-crossable sea. Before the spectre of death, we're all doomed. Can anyone open up a way through this forbidding Ocean of Oblivion? The waters are frigid and dark and the tide is coming in. But wait! The wind blows and the waters part. There, striding down the dry newly opened path comes a solitary man. He has braved the waters ahead of us and forced the jaws of Death apart. He conquered death and opened up a way to Life, to God.

He summons us. *"Come with me. I am resurrection; I am Life. Follow me and live forever."* Jesus finds us between our rock and the hard place, and invites us to follow him into a new kind of life – a life of learning God's way, experiencing the freedom of God's reign.

8.7 Horse and Rider Thrown Into the Sea

In 1 Corinthians 10:1 St. Paul imagines Israel's crossing of the Red Sea as a baptism. The imagery is obvious – water, death resurrection, new life – a defining event that birthed Israel's national life as God's people. Today in churches, friends will often burst into applause when a friend is baptized. Is it any surprise that Israel erupted in spontaneous worship and celebration on the far side of the water?

The Sea would have meant certain death if God had not intervened. The promises of God and the hopes of the people would have disappeared into oblivion if God had not acted. But God did act, in mighty power, and that power reenergized everyone. They sang in jubilation –

> The LORD is my strength and my song;
> He has become my salvation.
> He is my God and I will praise him
> Exodus 15:2

There on the eastern shores of the Yam Suph, for the first time in the whole Bible we listen as Israel becomes a worshipping people.

> Who among the gods is like you, O LORD –

Majestic in holiness, awesome in glory
Working wonders!
Exodus 15:11

They celebrate God's power, but they also note the heart of love behind the power – God's 'hesed', unfailing love!

In your unfailing love you will lead the people you have redeemed.
In your strength you will guide them to your holy dwelling"
Exodus 15:13

Men and women celebrate as one. Miriam the prophetess[99], Aaron's sister, leads the women in a dance that embodies the joy of their new life and freedom.

Sing to the Lord for he is highly exalted
The horse and its rider he has hurled into the sea!
Exodus 15:1

The exodus of Israel was like the breakthrough of Easter. The astonishing and unprecedented pathway through the Red Sea foreshadowed Christ's shattering of death. And in the resurrection of Jesus we foresee the ultimate fulfillment of God's triumph over humanity's greatest foe.

Death has been swallowed up in victory.
Where, O death, is your victory?
Where, O death, is your sting?
1 Corinthians 15:54-55

My first course in Biblical Theology at Regent College was on The Book of Exodus, taught by Dr. Clark Pinnock. He quickly earned my respect for his intelligence and scholarship, but I was even more impressed by the vibrancy of his love for God and his joyful spirit. We called him 'the tambourine man' because, like Miriam, he helped lead worship with freshness and exuberance.

Throughout his whole life Dr. Pinnock embodied the great lesson of the exodus, that God set his people free so they could worship in the Spirit and live in the power and joy of the resurrection.

The vibrant power of the exodus and Miriam's song inspire me; the resurrection of Jesus gives me immense hope and assurance – and the example of people like Clark Pinnock inspire me to pray this prayer:

Prayer:
Lord of freedom and new life, you have broken the chains of death. Help me to live today in the newness of life – in the power of the resurrection. Let the vigor of your new creation fill my heart permeate my mind and energize every action and thought. May the joy of the world to come echo in my soul. Amen.

8.8 Writhing Waters.

Israel's miraculous liberation in the Exodus was seared into their national consciousness. That deliverance defined Israel as a free people – freed by God and for God. In later years whenever they faced crisis, they went back to their founding story to get their bearings.

Psalm 77 is one of those times. Life in the real world seems to bring one crisis after another. Friends turn hostile, disease threatens, money runs out and debts pile up, plans go south and family peace disintegrates overnight. Life can get really scary sometimes – and faith doesn't insulate anyone from distress.

Psalm 77 describes a time when not even prayer seemed to help.

> When I was in distress, I sought the Lord;
> at night I stretched out untiring hands
> and my soul refused to be comforted.
> I remembered you, O God, and I groaned;
> I mused, and my spirit grew faint.
> Psalm 77:2-3

This writer is in extreme distress – fearful, depressed, exhausted and full of questions. His heart is troubled beyond words and it seems that God is ignoring him. He is facing his own Red Sea trauma. The ancient national story parallels his own personal crisis and he is desperate for God's intervention.

He meditates on the story of the Exodus and imagines the convulsing waters of the Red Sea.

> The waters saw you, O God,

the waters saw you and writhed;
the very depths were convulsed.
The clouds poured down water,
the skies resounded with thunder;
your arrows flashed back and forth
Psalm 77:16-18

The 'writhing waters' of the sea echo the writhing spirit in the poet's own soul. He is unnerved by his ordeal. He shudders in the same way that nature shudders before the raw power of God. The poet sees God as a warrior hurling lightning bolts, roaring against Egypt, drenching his enemies, but opening a path for Israel.

He rhapsodizes about God's power exercised on behalf of his people and he longs for his own personal deliverance. He reminds himself of the infinite unrestricted power of God, untamed power, like Aslan's "of course he's not safe, but he's good."[100] And that power begins to secure his peace.

That's how our poet comes to terms with his own turbulence – by recalling a greater turbulence, a 'counter-turbulence'. He finds hope by trusting that this powerful God will once again be his ally and not his foe. His reeling world begins to stabilize. He recovers his footing; he writes a song to try and sort it all out, a song to recall in future turbulent times how God's power tames the most violent upheavals, not just for captive nations, but for ordinary frightened and confused individuals just like him.

And the great irony is that no one can bring peace to people writhing in the ragged turbulence of life like someone who has experienced similar upheaval and distress. It is through confusion and perseverance, through crisis and deliverance that we acquire the credibility that brings assurance to others. That's what turbulent waters are good for. That's why we need each other.

8.9 Unseen Footprints

The psalmist notes that God's path led *through* the sea, not around it or over it, but *through* it. I prefer to avoid obstacles; but apparently God does not. In v.19 reads –"Your path led *through* the sea, *through* the mighty waters, though your footprints were not seen" (Psalm 77:19).

Yahweh does not normally lead his people away from difficulties, but *through* them. One of the most vivid paintings of the Red Sea crossing I have seen was made by a 13-year old Haitian child.[101] Bright blue waves curl up on each side of the painting, towering over the head of Moses with his outstretched arms. Hundreds of black faces follow behind Moses. Haitians understand the concept of going *'through'*. Going through means everything is going on around you. There is nothing trivial about the ordeals God requires of his people, but the gigantic fact is that God remains present with us no matter how overwhelming they may seem to us.

In Isaiah 43:2 Yahweh promised,

> When you pass through the waters,
> I will be with you;
> and when you pass through the rivers,
> they will not sweep over you

God is always present with us – and that reality is celebrated in my favorite line in this entire psalm – "even though your footsteps were not seen" or as the New Living Translation says it, "a pathway no one knew was there" (verse 19).

God's footsteps may not be visible, and we may be completely baffled by our situation, but the psalm concludes with the words "You led your people like a flock, by the hand of Moses and Aaron" (verse 20).

I love that – God himself may not be visible, but Moses and Aaron were. With apologies to the popular poem about 'Footprints', God's presence is often evident to us in the form of human leaders and companions who 'just happen to be there' to accompany us through the difficult experiences of our lives.

Jesus is the ultimate expression of 'God with us', and he certainly didn't live a charmed or stress-free life. He embodies the reality of God present among us in the midst of the uproar and mayhem we call everyday life.

Prayer

Invisible God, thank you for all the ways you meet me in the turbulence of my life – and even though I cannot see anything as clearly as I would like, you open a pathway, not by making things simple and calm, but by sustaining me in the complexity and challenges of life. Draw near to all those who are experiencing desperate times today and open a pathway of hope for them – through your Son Jesus. Amen.

8.10 Desert Training

The Book of Exodus tells an epic story – the transformation of refugees from mud pit slaves to chosen people of God. But it's a roller-coaster odyssey, and they were slow learners!

After an astonishing deliverance at the Red Sea, these refugees trekked three days into the desert of Sinai without finding water. What a difference three days can make. Yahweh had promised to adopt them as family, to be their God and bring them to a land of safe haven. Now the parched desert seemed to mock the promises of the invisible God.

But there's more to the desert than meets the eye – and they were not to be the last refugees in history to be ravaged by thirst.

Greg Mortenson, author of *Three Cups of Tea,*[102] tells the story of thousands of Pakistani refugees during the 1999 India-Pakistan war stranded in desert land that nobody wanted. The closest water was the Indus River an hour's walk away.

The UN refused to assist them and their own local government had no resources to help. Against all odds, Mortenson and the refugee men created a settlement site out of barren desert in 8 weeks. They drilled a 120 foot (36 m) well, struck water and constructed a concrete tank capable of storing water for 5,000 people.

Five years later, it was a thriving community with rows and rows of mud block homes, some even equipped with satellite dishes, and a 5-room school where girls are learning to read. Nurtured by a deep aquifer, cherry trees grow thick and lush where the sand dunes used to stand. The desert blossoms because someone cared for people in need.

I wonder . . . if that's the reason Yahweh's chosen people had to endure the desert as refugees, ... so that empathy would be embedded deep in their collective psyche, so that, having survived their own ordeal with thirst, they would be the first to render help to others. As God's light to the Gentiles they would be relentless suppliers of water to those who for whatever reason find themselves searching in vain for the water they need.

In the library of Regent College in Vancouver there is a sculpture called 'The Font' by David Robinson. It shows a peasant water-carrier standing on a globe in a sea of water. To me this sculpture depicts Jesus as the ultimate bringer of living water; but equally it illustrates God's intention for all of God's people in a needy world – servants to the thirsty, fellow travelers with those in search of refuge.

I wonder . . . if my desert experiences have moved me in the direction of empathy or of self-preservation. Which of these responses is stronger in you?

8.11 Bitter Waters Become Sweet

Three days searching the parched desert for water – and then suddenly – the glint of a spring-fed pool! It was no mirage. Cheers of excitement filled the air.

But when the Exodus refugees finally reached the water (Exodus 15:22-26), it was undrinkable, brackish with mineral salts, bitter and foul to the taste. *Marah* – bitter waters! Frustration and disappointment overflowed in a torrent of anger and despair and the cruel sense of being betrayed by God.

As leader, Moses cried out to God and God showed him how to remediate the water so they could drink it. From aching thirst to soaring hopes to crashing disappointment and finally, refreshment! That's the surface story. But there's always an undercurrent of wonder flowing through these water stories.

First, we *wonder* why? Why do God's chosen people have to experience prolonged thirst and then brutal disappointment? Why does life have to be bitter? The text hints at an answer – "there Yahweh made a decree; there, at the bitter waters, Yahweh tested them" (paraphrased from Exodus 15:25). As absolute as our biological need for water, there is an equally compelling spiritual law that we need God. God proves good, but there is no way to develop that trust without suffering, without crisis, without wondering if God really can be trusted.

Wendell Berry writes

> It may be that when we no longer know what to do
> we have come to our real work, [...]
> The impeded stream is the one that sings.[103]

God seems to bring us to our real work when we can do nothing. That's when God's work in us begins to bear fruit. The test of character is how we respond to crisis. We can choose bitterness, resentment, suspicion, or we can learn the discipline of patience and trust. Jesus' wilderness testing at the outset of his public life illustrates this law of life.

The second wonder in this story is the miracle of transformation – bitter waters becoming sweet as "the Lord showed Moses some wood". Desert guides tell of barberry and other aromatic shrubs that can mask the acrid mineral taste of brackish water. Perhaps that's what Moses used. Instead of miraculously zapping the bad water, God may have told Moses to use natural means already at hand in the desert. But the 'miracle' is there all the same – the wonder of nature's healing powers.

The text is explicit that God is the healer even when intermediate means are used. It was the occasion for one of the remarkable self-revelations of God in the Old Testament, "I am Yahweh-Rapha, the Lord who heals you" (Exodus 15:26).

Whatever bitter waters, perplexity or disappointments you are facing today, let them deepen your trust in a God who heals; let them grow character and discipline in you. Let them draw you to wonder and lead you to joy.

8.12 Testing and Resting

Notwithstanding Israel's childish grumbling, Yahweh included respite in their itinerary: Then they came to an oasis, where there were twelve springs and seventy palm trees, and they camped there near the water (Exodus 15:27). Twelve springs in the desert – one for each tribe. Seventy palm trees – shade for every clan.

A few years ago my daughter Jennifer and I hiked in the Anza-Berraga desert near the Mexican border in California. Climbing a rugged dry riverbed it was hard to imagine the oasis that the brochures promised was awaiting us, but when we arrived, the shade and refreshment were welcome beyond words.

The water of an oasis mirrors the face of God as 'Shepherd' who refreshes weary travelers and the deep thirst of their hearts: "He leads me beside still waters; he restores my soul" (Psalm 23:2).

If the barren desert depicts the challenging journey of faith, an oasis illustrates God's sustaining grace even in harsh situations. Oasis is a metaphor for those occasions of spiritual renewal, refreshment and joy when God meets us in unexpected ways.

The life of faith is a rhythm of testing and resting, exercise and grace, fatigue and refreshment. Pilgrim people will never reach home by setting up residence at Elim Oasis, but it is a wonderful respite along the way. The Exodus story is about the balance of testing with resting.

Chapter 9

Enough Water to Get You Home

9.1 Water from the Rock

Deserts are relentless – and humans are not well-adapted to desert demands.

As the Israeli tribes travelled deeper into the wilderness of Sinai toward their promised home, their most urgent need was water. Once, when the need was especially acute, God told Moses to smack a nearby rock. To everyone's astonishment, water gushed out, satisfying the people's immediate need. The narrative reveals that God knows both the mapline of every underground aquifer and how to provide for his people.

Israel immortalized God's power in poetry and song:

> He split the rocks in the desert and gave them water as abundant as the seas;
> He brought streams out of a rocky crag and made water flow down like rivers.
> Psalm 78:15-16

The Invisible One who accompanied them in the desert was the very God of creation – One who makes "water as abundant as the seas" available to thirsty complaining pilgrims. The God of history and the God of our todays is the Source of all things. There is no limit to God's resources. Scarcity and barren geography are no impediment to Yahweh. As generations come and go, Yahweh is a faithful provider for Israel.

But song alone can't change character and Israel never seemed to pass the trust test, complaining constantly, testing God's patience, quarreling with God. Moses even named a couple of memorable landmarks Massah and

Meribah (*i.e. Testing* and *Quarreling*) to mark these low points in their spiritual odyssey.

9.2 Speak to the Rock

Towards the end of the Exodus journey, there was another occasion recorded in Numbers 20:2-13, when Moses used his staff as a cudgel to strike the rock and produce a flow of much needed water. It proved to be a fatal mistake. In the account of this story we read,

> The LORD said to Moses, "Take the staff, and you and your brother Aaron gather the assembly together. Speak to that rock before their eyes and it will pour out its water. You will bring water out of the rock for the community so they and their livestock can drink." So Moses took the staff from the Lord's presence, just as he commanded him. He and Aaron gathered the assembly together in front of the rock
> Numbers 20:7-10

Normally a mild-mannered individual, on this occasion, Moses exploded in front of the people.

> "Listen, you rebels," he railed, "must we bring you water out of this rock?" Then Moses raised his arm and struck the rock twice with his staff. Water gushed out, and the community and their livestock drank.
> Numbers 20:10-11

It was a miracle, but God was not pleased. The text says,

> But the LORD said to Moses and Aaron, "Because you did not trust in me enough to honor me as holy in the sight of the Israelites, you will not bring this community into the land I give them"
> Numbers 20:12

In some way Moses had disgraced God in front of his people. He failed in his leadership to uphold God's honor. The narrator does not explain exactly what Moses did wrong. Was it speaking to the people instead of the rock? Was it calling the people rebels? Taking credit personally for supplying the water, or losing his temper? Was it smacking the rock in anger instead of speaking to it as God had said? It's not at all clear, and for centuries Biblical scholars have debated the reason that Moses and Aaron were punished. But whatever it was, Moses' punishment was nonnegotiable. He forfeited the privilege of bringing his people into their long promised inheritance, the Promised Land.

Rabbi Shlomo Riskin has an explanation for God's dismay and disapproval. Riskin is the Chief Rabbi in the Israeli West Bank settlement of Efrat. After he emigrated from New York City to Israel in 1983, he worked hard to erase Palestinian refugee camps, to develop a joint medical clinic for Israeli and Palestinians and to supply the Palestinian villages with water from Efrat. He has helped pioneer the rights of women in the Jewish world, and is an advocate of respectful dialogue with the leaders of other religions to create better understanding and religious tolerance.

Rabbi Riskin says that Moses' tragic error was striking the rock when God told him to speak to it. He believes this story is a lesson in the power of speech.

> All relationships begin and end with proper communication. God said to the Jewish people when they were up against a rock, 'You've got to speak to the rock. And if you speak to it and you learn to speak properly, then water can even come out of a rock." [104]

Applying that lesson to the hostile politics in Israel, he says,

> You have to be willing to speak to those people who sometimes seem as hard-hearted to us as rocks. We've got to be willing to speak to anybody. Even to the rock. Even to the Hizballah."[105]

I like Riskin's insight on this issue. This is the way of shalom. Using the stick to smash the rock instead of using the power of words advances the cause of hate rather than respect, of violence rather than harmony, suspicion instead of dialogue and peaceful cooperation. As we read in the New Testament, "God's wisdom begins with a holy life and is characterized by getting along with others. It is gentle and reasonable, overflowing with mercy and blessings" (James 3:17 MSG).

Prayer:

Lord of the Spoken and Living Word, teach us to speak, to listen and to live in a way that upholds your honor and shalom in the world as Jesus did – and to wait for you to cause the water to flow. Amen

9.3 Learning to Trust – or Distrust

At the end of forty years, God told Moses that the years of Israel's deprivation in the desert had had a purpose. My design, God said, was "to humble you and test you in order to know what was in your heart" (Deuteronomy 8:2). "As a father disciplines his son, so the Lord your God disciplines you" (verse 5) "to do you good in the end" (verse 16).

Hunger and thirst are powerful tests, and God wanted Israel to internalize deep in their consciousness a conviction that they could trust their covenant Partner. Experiencing God's provision of water and food would lay a foundation of trust in other areas of life. But Israel never seemed to pass the trust test. They were habitual whiners, constantly accusing God, testing God's patience.

Moses named the memorable landmarks Massah (*i.e.* Testing) and Meribah (*i.e.* Quarreling) in order to mark indelibly these low-points in their spiritual odyssey, signaling later travelers, like us, to some of the prevalent dangers of the road.

Psalm 78, quoted earlier, is a long study of Israel's resistance against God, their suspicion that God was unable to meet their needs. "How often they rebelled against him in the desert, and grieved him in the wasteland," the psalmist laments in (verse 40). But God still "brought his people out like a flock; he led them like sheep through the desert" (verse 52).

In this context of Israel blaming God, we read about God's lavish generous response – "when Moses struck the rock, water gushed out and streams flowed abundantly" (verse 20). The psalmist seems to be amazed that God's grace towards a grumbling, dissatisfied and distrustful people is as lavish and abundant as the water streaming from the rock.

Other psalms also cite this event at 'the waters of Meribah' as a historic reminder of Israel's instinct to question and blame God rather than to trust God.[106]

> Do not harden your hearts as you did at Meribah,
> as you did that day at Massah in the desert,
> where your fathers tested and tried me,
> though they had seen what I did
> Psalm 95:8-9

The writer of Hebrews 3:6-19 picks up this challenge and applies it to believers in every age, lest we also allow our hearts to harden into distrust, lose our courage and confidence and fall short of the challenge to live by the high calling of faith.

But why did God test them? Surely the all-knowing God already knew what was in their hearts and had no need to test them to discover it. Perhaps it's closer to the truth that testing reveals to *us* what's in *our* hearts – our strengths and weaknesses – as a catalyst to our growth.

But don't difficult tests run the risk of harming us as much as growing us? It is possible that we can emerge through such tests gritty and hard and ascetic-like, but with a distorted relationship with God rather than with a deeper, richer relationship. Do we think of ourselves as God's cherished sons and daughters being groomed to better fulfill our destiny as bearers of God's glory to the world? Or are we more like Marine recruits in boot camp, who have to learn to suffer deprivation in order to survive in a mean and dangerous world? Maybe both – and maybe a lot more.

This doesn't fully explain the mystery of suffering or 'the problem of pain' as C. S. Lewis called it, but it helps me to find some sense of purpose in challenges I think I could do without.

If I start with the hypothesis of God's fatherly concern for me, I can interpret the harshness of the ordeals I have to face as opportunities to trust God rather than signs of a malicious, indifferent or demanding taskmaster. That does more to boost my sense of dignity and my motivation to grow than anything else.

Both testing and the human inclination to distrust God are virtually universal. We want our needs to be met on demand. We are impatient and restless when we have to wait. But there is no opportunity for faith and trust to grow without testing. And there is no oasis for our restless hearts unless we learn to rest in the ultimate Provider.

Also, small privations train us to face the big tests. I'm writing this on a Monday, which is my usual day of fasting. As I type these words, my stomach is growling. I'm hungry. Thankfully, I have food and drink in abundance, but I choose to discipline my appetites and curb my instinctive desire for good things so that my spirit and body can learn that I do not live by bread and drink alone, but by the words and grace of God. Fasting also links me sympathetically with millions of people in other places for whom hunger and thirst are not a choice, but their all-too-frequent experience. For me it's a simulated desert experience to practice and deepen the disciplines of trust – and I feel enriched by it beyond measure.

9.4 The Rock that Followed Them

So far we have looked at four of the five wonderful occasions in the exodus story when God supplied water for Israel and their flocks as they traversed the wilderness of Sinai: first, the bitter waters of Marah, then the sweet rest at the Elim oasis (Exodus 15), followed by the two occasions, Massah (Exodus 17) and Meribah (Numbers 20), where water flowed from the struck rock. The surprise well at Be'er (Numbers 21:6) is just ahead.

But beyond this handful of references the Bible tells us virtually nothing about how God provided Israel's water needs for forty years – and that leaves us with a very big question about logistics.

There was an oasis here and there, but how could they have survived a generation in that forbidding terrain without a regular supply of water? Moses summarizes the miraculous odyssey by saying, "the LORD your God, ... led you through the vast and dreadful desert, that thirsty and waterless land, with its venomous snakes and scorpions. He brought you water out of hard rock" (Deuteronomy 8:14-15).

In the absence of any further narrative or explanation, a legend developed in Judaism about a rock well that supposedly followed Israel throughout the desert for forty years, miraculously supplying abundant waters for both people and herds. It was called Miriam's Well, given to Israel because of Miriam's gracious character and piety. This source of strength and sustenance, however, dried up when Miriam died.

This legend was known at the time of Jesus and the apostles, and referenced in second century Jewish writings[107]. In the twelfth century, the Jewish commentator Rashi used this legend to explain the curious wording of Numbers 20 which says,

> the whole community of Israel . . . camped at Kadesh. While they were there, Miriam died and was buried. There was no water for the people to drink at that place, so they rebelled against Moses and Aaron.
> Numbers 20:1-2 NLT

Noticing the unusual juxtaposition of Miriam's death and the shortage of water, Rashi explained that God had provided for Israel throughout the forty years by means of Miriam's well. But the death of this mother of Israel and the loss of their miraculous source of water created a fresh crisis for Moses and Aaron.[108]

The legend affirms that Miriam's well continues to bless the world. Every Saturday night, at the end of Shabbat, its waters flow out into wells everywhere in the world.

As a well-read Jew, the apostle Paul knew this rabbinic tradition of Miriam's rock well. Commentators generally agree that Paul has this story in mind when he says in 1 Corinthians 10:4 "our forefathers all drank from the spiritual rock that accompanied them," but he radically reinterprets the rabbinic tradition, saying "and that rock was Christ."

Paul interprets the many Biblical references to Yahweh as the Rock of Israel's salvation[109] as referring to Jesus. This idea was not original with Paul. Jesus himself had made this connection at the Feast of Tabernacles in Jerusalem six months before his death, when he identified himself as the one the Scripture refers to as the source from whom streams of living water will flow (John 7:37). In Jesus, God continues to be not only the Rock of Israel, but also the source of salvation for the whole world.

Early Christians living in the Roman catacombs saw it the same way, painting the story of Moses striking the rock in the desert alongside Jesus raising the paralytic. According to New Testament scholar Raymond Brown, the rock in the desert, is the most frequently painted Old Testament theme in early Christian catacomb art.[110] They saw it allegorically as a prefiguring of the soldier piercing Jesus' body after his death releasing a flow of blood and water, symbolizing the salvation that flows to us from Christ.

This is saying that Jesus, the one who promised that thirsty people who come to him will be deeply satisfied, was the very same Creator God who repeatedly met Israel's water needs in the hot Sinai wilderness. That's pretty heady stuff! Jesus transcends time; his origins are ahistoric; he has tracked with humans all through history, and he will continue forever to be living water in the church. Bathe your brain and your heart in that notion for a few minutes!

9.5 Behind the Water

Imagine the scene moments after Moses struck the rock. If the water began as a trickle, there may have been just amazement. If the water burst out, imagine the initial fear that the water might suddenly engulf them all. However it happened, the first emotions soon gave way to joy and relief at the miraculous flow of water. Then the thirsty Israelites probably plunged right into the stream, lapping handfuls of water to their mouths before rushing off to return with their buckets, gourds and water jars. Gratitude and theological reflection often gets elbowed out by the insistent demands of survival. But behind all that water lay a miracle. The water from the rock revealed the nature and character of God – a powerful Creator God, a generous Provider and a merciful Savior. How much the Exodus refugees missed if all they did was to drink the water.

So I pause today to thank God for the physical *gift* of water and to pray for people living with desperate thirst – and dying for lack of water. Gratitude – don't take H_2O for granted. I also pause to reflect on the nature of God as the Giver of the gift and all that it makes possible in my life. I taste that water today and every day as the Holy Spirit pours the love of God into my life, as scripture comes alive, refreshing and feeding my mind and heart, as I study and admire the example of Jesus' life and seek to emulate him, and as I revel in the joy of knowing God's goodness in a thousand ways day after day.

9.6 Spring Up, O Well

Towards the end of Israel's 40-year migration we come across one more water supply story that is quite different from the others we've heard about. In Numbers 21:16, the people and their flocks were once again in dire need of water. God told Moses, "you assemble the people; I'll provide the water."

The next thing we know, the people are celebrating around a fresh flowing artesian spring. Imagine the *ooohs* and *ahhhs* of relief, the laughter and splashing, the cheers of thirsty, sun-weary souls enjoying fresh cold springwater.

Then everyone burst into a rousing rendition of an old folk-song, "*Spring up, O Well!*" In case we don't know the song, the writer quotes a couple of lines:

> Spring up, O well!
> Sing about it,
> about the well that the princes dug,

> that the nobles of the people sank—
> the nobles with scepters and staffs.
> Numbers 21:17-18.

It's a song about an unusual work project somewhere back in history, maybe during Isaac's time or maybe even before Abraham, a project where the nobility rolled up their sleeves, climbed down into the pit and dug until they found water.

When a mayor or queen plants a ceremonial tree or the president flips burgers at a summer BBQ, it's a photo op – the elite standing for a moment among the commoners, affirming the work of day laborers. But when celebs set aside privilege and immunity and get dirty and sweaty, scratched and bruised and weary, that's worth a song.

Sometime in the distant past something like this occurred – princes got involved using their ceremonial scepters as pry bars and pikes, digging a well. Chiefs didn't just commission the work; they engaged in it side by side with their people. They closed the status gap; they led by example and shared the prize at the end.

And a song was born – a song that entered Israel's psyche as an ideal – the notion that leadership involves hard work and that the rich would not enjoy privilege at the expense of those who worked for them. I wonder if that is why Yahweh told Moses to "gather the people together" (Numbers 21:16). As they prepared to enter settled society in a new land, God reminded them of his vision of a just and flourishing society.

This song foreshadows the example of Jesus who said, "kings like to lord it over their subjects and adopt prestigious titles. But don't be like them. The highest among you should be like the lowest; leaders among you must learn to serve, just as I have been a servant among you" (Luke 22:25 my translation), A society that lives like that will always be a wellspring of joy and hope.

What a timely reminder, on the threshold of their life in the new land, that water is both a social and a material resource. God provides the water from the sky above and the earth below, but people will need to collaborate to capture and harness it, to transport and utilize it, to share and steward it for the good of the community.

9.7 Signature Written in Water

John Hancock, was the first of the American patriots in 1776 to sign the Declaration of Independence. Today he is best remembered for his flamboyant and stylish signature, which, according to legend, he proudly wrote large and clearly enough that King George would be able to read it without his spectacles.

God, too, wrote his signature large and clear across the tyranny of Egypt. In a world of power politics, God wrote his signature firmly with water. Psalm 114 says,

> When Israel came out of Egypt,
> the house of Jacob from a foreign tongue, ...
> The sea looked and fled,
> the Jordan turned back . . .
> Psalm 114:1, 3.

The story of Israel's wilderness sojourn is framed by two natural boundaries, the Red Sea and the Jordan River, and both defer to the life-giving presence of God. In the poetic words of the psalm, the Red Sea took one look at Yahweh as Israel's champion – and fled away without a whimper of protest, yielding up a pathway instead of being a barrier to freedom.

Pharaoh had magicians, slave masters and military might, but at the Red Sea, Yahweh gave him a lesson in sacred governance. Instead of Pharaoh's cruel and abusive politics of raw power, God demonstrated a different way to exercise authority so that it bestowed life and hope to its subjects rather than intimidating and exploiting them as Pharaoh had done. Water was the primary instrument that illustrates God's formidable power directed to his people's well-being. God uses the weak things of this world to humble the mighty.

Across the wide desert, at the threshold to the new land, the Jordan surrendered its role as gatekeeper and guardian to the land, retreating like a chastened security guard complying with a directive from Yahweh, opening the road for Israel to march in.

At the outset of the exodus, the waters of imprisonment broke open, and a generation later at the end of the long ordeal, the 'No Trespassing' water boundary became a welcome mat to a nation in search of home.

The lyrics of Psalm 114 ask why such natural forces would so readily step aside.

> Why was it, O sea, that you fled,
> O Jordan, that you turned back?
> Tremble, O earth, at the presence of the Lord,
> at the presence of the God of Jacob,
> Who turned the rock into a pool,
> the hard rock into springs of water
> Psalm 114:5, 7-8

This psalm celebrates how completely the mere presence of Yahweh tames nature into trembling submission. When God wrote his name, the uncrossable sea and the unstoppable river instantly recognized that 'resistance is futile'. In literary terms Psalm 114 is called a 'taunt song'.

But with Yahweh, surrender does not mean humiliation or defeat; it means surrendering to Life. This is a God who chooses to befriend a man like Jacob, mentioned in v.1 and 7, that most unlikely candidate for grace. This God who turns hardhearted men like Jacob into reluctant saints, turns hard dolomite rock into flowing pools and causes flint stone to fracture and release artesian springs to flow out into desert sand (verse 8), daringly adopts a foolish and stubborn nation to showcase his grace.

Perhaps that is why, centuries after the Exodus, someone composed this psalm to remind Israel of God's wonderful purposes and continuing presence beyond the Red Sea, the River and water from the Rock. And perhaps that explains why Gentiles like me see our own story reflected in Israel's, and why we so proudly sign our name as devoted followers of Israel's God.

In Hebrew poetry, the sea means more than a mere body of water; it also mirrors the expanse of foreign nations, turbulent and unstable, restless and menacing, finally meeting their match. The river is every obstacle to God's shalom in Israel's geography and history and politics. The springs and wells are more than water; they are life itself flowing freely out of the most resistant circumstances. This song gives a foretaste of the new creation, when every corner of the universe will pulsate with the life-giving joy and purposes of God. This is the vision that God gave Israel to share with the world.

Walter Brueggemann calls Psalm 114, "an invitation for each new generation to participate in this world-transforming memory"[111]. In history Israel become God's home, God's sanctuary and domain; God became Israel's protector and her wellspring of life and joy. And Israel gained the privilege of mirroring to the world what it looks like in a human community for God to reign in their midst. Much of the unfolding story of the Old Testament tells of God's faithfulness despite Israel's dismal performance as God's ambassadors in the world.

Yahweh is a God who does not dominate, but who enables life to flow fully and freely. Here is a God worthy to reign over all.

9.8 Surprise Pathway

History repeats itself, they say; 'what goes around, comes around' and as we've seen, the Exodus motif is a recurring one in the Bible. But Isaiah says, 'don't limit your imagination to what has happened before. Keep looking ahead because God is as much a God of tomorrow as a God of yesterday. While God is consistent and faithful, God is also unpredictable. Yahweh is full of surprises.'

> This is what the LORD says—
> he who made a way through the sea, a path through the mighty waters,
> "Forget the former things; do not dwell on the past.
> See, I am doing a new thing!
> Now it springs up; do you not perceive it?
> I am making a way in the desert and streams in the wasteland."
> Isaiah 43:16-19

The ancient story of the Exodus was the identifying hallmark of Yahweh's covenant with Israel – and, Isaiah writes centuries later saying 'it's going to happen again' – but with a new twist! Once again the Lord of all the earth is about to rescue his people from oppression and bring them home. Centuries before in the exodus he had made a path through the sea, this time he would open a way through the desert that lay between Babylon and home.

As formidable as the oppression of Egypt and the resistance of Pharaoh had been, God's power was mightier. And so he still is. Even though Israel was captive to imperial Babylonian and Persian decree which blocked their return, yet God would again do the impossible and open a path. He would not only open the way, he would sustain his people in the most hostile and barren settings.

In my early twenties when I first read Isaiah seriously I was fascinated by this passage. It expressed the kind of hope filled vision and expectation that resonated with my youthful idealism. In addition, someone had recently coined the phrase 'do your own thing' that captured the free spirit of the late sixties – and here was God 'doing his thing' – a *new* thing, at that. For me it was an exciting biblical text urging a staid older generation to open the eyes of their imagination and allow God to do things in a new way.

Four decades later I can say that that has been God's hallmark in my life. When my son Jeff was born prematurely a thousand miles from home and God looked after us; when God turned my spiritual fatigue into a new vibrancy of life, when God opened up a sabbatical I never thought possible, when we had no funds and he supplied our needs, when the roof caved in on my work situation, when ministry burnout morphed into a restful spirit, when I was bereaved and longing for a new life and a life companion, God surprised me in ways I never anticipated.

I have learned that beyond any question, God delights in doing new things, unexpected things – good things. Sometimes they don't seem that good at first; sometimes God's unexpected is ecstasy, sometimes it is agony, but "in all things God works for the good of those who love him, who have been called according to his purpose" (Romans 8:28).

God opens up paths where you thought there was no path and supplies streams in the driest of ground. In the darkest moment of human history, Jesus did what no one alive expected – he rose from his grave, folded up his own death shroud and opened a surprise pathway for the rest of us through life's ultimate barrier. And that was just the beginning. I can't wait to see what other surprises await in his new creation.

Prayer:
Lord, when the present and future scare me, help me to remember your great deeds of the past – and to expect you to do the unexpected tomorrow and today. Amen.

9.9 Crossing Jordan / Coming Home

At last Israel came to the final frontier – the last barrier between them and their long-awaited long-promised home. According to Joshua 3:15, it was harvest season, which means the spring of the year, when the Jordan River runs at its highest level, swollen by melting snow and late winter rains. This was the season when God chose to lead Israel into the Promised Land, perhaps for two reasons. Pragmatically, it brought Israel into their new homeland in time for the abundance of the spring barley and wheat harvest. But more significantly, it provided a dramatic sign of God's amazing power for both Israel and the nations.

> Tell the priests who carry the ark of the covenant: 'When you reach the edge of the Jordan's waters, go and stand in the river.' And as soon as the priests who carry the ark of the LORD – the Lord of all the earth – set foot in the Jordan, its waters flowing downstream will be cut off and stand up in a heap (Joshua 3:8 and 13).

Seeing Israel's God stop the flow of the Jordan in full flood would terrify the inhabitants of the land. They would know that Yahweh, not Baal, was supreme Lord of the waters and of the land. This sign would also assure Israel that Yahweh was able to complete his redemptive work for them. If God could arrest the floodwaters of the Jordan, God could also drive out the current inhabitants who had 'defiled' the land by their abhorrent practices, such as child sacrifice. Twice in the story of the crossing, Joshua reminds them that Yahweh is "the Lord of all the earth" (Joshua 3:11 and 13).

So the momentous event began.

> Now the Jordan is at flood stage all during harvest. Yet as soon as the priests who carried the ark reached the Jordan and their feet touched the water's edge, the water from upstream stopped flowing. It piled up in a heap a great distance away, at a town called Adam in the vicinity of Zarethan, while the water flowing down to the Sea of the Arabah (the Salt Sea) was completely cut off. So the people crossed over opposite Jericho.
> Joshua 3:15-16

The crossing itself was dramatic – even ceremonial. The priests went halfway across carrying the Ark of the Covenant – twice called "the Ark of God of all the earth", underscoring his claim over the river, the land and all its inhabitants. Then the people followed, with delegates from each tribe picking up a large stone from mid-river for a monument on the west bank to commemorate their dramatic entry into the land.

The narrator gives us no hint as to what caused the river to suspend its flow just when the priests ventured into the river or why it resumed its flow when everyone had crossed over. An Arab historian tells of a landslide 2500 years later in AD 1266 which stopped the flow of the Jordan for 10 hours, and in 1927 an earthquake caused a blockage in the same place stopping the river's flow for 21 hours. But the Bible focuses more on the result than the cause.

The Jordan was a boundary that Israel finally crossed, opening the way into a new way of life. After four hundred years as refugees and then as slaves in Egypt, and the past forty years as nomads in the desert, now at last they had the opportunity to sink down their roots in their own newly acquired homeland. Crossing the Jordan marked a decisive transition point and a memorable milestone in their national history.

They understood that Yahweh had done this for them. As the narrator of Joshua says,

> The LORD your God did to the Jordan just what he had done to the Red Sea when he dried it up before us until we had crossed over. He did this so that all the peoples of the earth might know that the hand of the LORD is powerful and so that you might always fear the LORD your God.
> Joshua 4:23-24

9.10 Conclusion –

Water frames this amazing story of the Exodus. The waters parted at Yam Suph to show the way out of bondage into freedom. They parted again at the Jordan to show the way in to Rest and Joy. And the way through is marked by water spilling from the earth when least expected and most desperately needed, teaching us to trust in God's providence and care in the twists and turns of our life wanderings.

Israel's journey is more than history. It is also a metaphor of the journey we are always taking downstream from Eden into potentially deeper freedom and relationship with God. T. S. Eliot finishes his poem East Coker in *Four Quartets* saying,

We must be still and still moving
Into another intensity
For a further union, a deeper communion
Through the dark cold and the empty desolation,
The wave cry, the wind cry, the vast waters
Of the petrel and the porpoise. In my end is my beginning.[112]

Chapter 10
Where the Heavens Drop Dew

10.1 Dew from Heaven

A FEW WEEKS BEFORE the Israeli tribes crossed the Jordan, Moses stood on the plains of Moab, near Mount Nebo which overlooked the Promised Land. In keeping with the tradition of Middle eastern patriarchs, he pronounced God's blessing on each of the twelve tribes. The two longest blessings are for his own tribe of Levi and for the tribes of Joseph, whom he calls "the prince among his brothers." As part of his blessing upon Joseph, he prays,

> May the LORD bless his land with the precious dew from heaven above and with the deep waters that lie below; ... with the best gifts of the earth and its fullness and the favor of him who dwelt in the burning bush.
> Deuteronomy 33:13-16

A prayer for "precious dew" would mean a lot to people who have lived in the dry desert for 40 years. Add "the deep waters that lie below," the unseen wealth of aquifers, and you have the conditions for bountiful agricultural prosperity. Moses knew that the God who had led them through the wilderness was not stingy, and he was certain that God would prosper Joseph's tribes lavishly. Abundance, not scarcity is God's signature, though with an invisible anonymous hand.

Dew comes naturally from the moisture in the ground and air, but Moses called it the "dew of heaven". He looked ahead to "the choicest gifts of the ancient mountains and the fruitfulness of the everlasting hills", speaking of the spontaneous productivity of nature that had been evident since time immemorial, the best gifts of the earth and its fullness. Human eyes see the bounty of the land. Faith sees God's goodness in it all.

Moses' prediction of nature's bounty was balanced with a prayer for "the favor of him who dwelt in the burning bush". That bush was where God revealed himself to Moses as the 'I AM' God and where God's rescue of Israel began.

Centuries earlier this 'I AM' had rescued Joseph from oblivion in Egypt and established him as the food provider during a time of scarcity. This same God had now brought them out of Egypt and would continue to make his power and love evident to them in the fruitfulness of the land they were about to inherit.

Notice the contrast of "burning bush" and "precious dew", fire and water, opposites that complement each other. Two rich metaphors of the infinite resources of God, two very different ways God makes himself known to us – revelation and providence, nature and grace. As Elizabeth Barrett Browning noted,

> Earth is crammed with heaven,
> and every common bush is on fire with God;
> but only he who sees takes off his shoes;
> the rest sit around it and pluck blackberries.[113]

This ancient blessing might seem a world away from contemporary urban culture, but it is actually remarkably relevant. First, this vision inspires a spirit of generosity more than fear or greed, an outlook of provision rather than acquisition, of trust not fear. If God and nature have been lavish towards me, I should learn to practice an ethic of grace. As Jesus said, "freely you have received, freely give" (Matthew 10:8). This is certainly the lesson of Joseph's life. He lived as a giver and provider, whether it was grain or hospitality or forgiveness.

Secondly, Joseph cultivated his character in turbulent conditions and so was able to lead effectively in the public sphere when opportunity and need arose. He was "a man for turbulent times" as Gordon MacDonald calls him[114], times not unlike our own. Joseph's work as a public administrator in a time of scarcity serves as a model for leaders and consultants in every field in our day when population demands and economic slow-down and ecological pressures have put huge strains on the available natural and financial resources.

British journalist Fred Pearce writes, "as rivers run dry, underground water reserves are exhausted and fields are caked in salt", agriculture desperately needs a "blue-revolution", a fresh vision of how we steward the water resources we have.[115] And that is going to require innovative thinkers, policy-makers and educators. Joseph could be a great mentor for citizens of the 21st century. Moses' blessing of Joseph's descendents inspires me to pray for and try to stir up such leadership for the world my descendents will inherit.

Prayer:
Blazing God of the Burning Bush, thank you for providing me generously with some of the best gifts of the earth and its fullness. I have tasted the richness of material gifts and the abundant life of the Spirit. Let your fire within me warm those who are cold, let your dew flow through me to refresh those who are thirsty. Make me a channel of your abundance to those who do not know your name.

And just as you raised up Joseph to preserve his generation and Moses to deliver his, would you raise up leaders young and old around the world to launch a blue revolution, a ground-swell of environmental responsibility and innovation to cherish the waters we need to share. Amen

10.2 Flowing Streams

After leading his people across the desert to the threshold of the Promised Land, Moses gave them a glowing description of the land before them, with just a little extra dose of idealism: "The LORD is bringing you into a good land, a land with streams and pools of water, with springs flowing in the valleys and hills" (Deuteronomy 8:7). True, there are streams and springs here and there, but for the most part, Israel is a semiarid land, especially in the south, and access to water is a critical concern.

On another occasion Moses described it as "a land of mountains and valleys that drinks rain from heaven. It is a land the LORD your God cares for; the eyes of the LORD your God are continually on it" (Deuteronomy 11:11-12).

After forty years in the dry desert this must have sounded like paradise – rainwater, ground water and surface water in abundance, streams and pools and springs – a farmer's paradise for sure, and a hydrogeologist's dream!

The hills of Lebanon and upper Galilee get lots of rain which the earth absorbs and channels into underground aquifers. Some of this surfaces 30 miles (50 km) south in the Jezreel Valley – the famed Valley of Megiddo.

This is the region where Deborah and Barak defeated the Canaanite army when Sisera's chariots got mired in the bog (Judges 4:15). This is where, a generation later, Gideon's army lapped water from the stream (Judges 7:4-7).

The rainy season in Israel begins with the 'early rain' in October. This is crucial for softening up the sun-baked soil for the prime planting season in November. December to February are the heaviest months for rain, and farmers depend on the crucial 'latter rains' in May to plump the harvest. Sometimes the winter rains are torrential and the wadis become flashflood zones, but no rain falls at all during the four hottest months of the year. Underground cisterns are important reservoirs for retaining rainwater for the dry season. The invention of a waterproof mortar during the Bronze Age allowed cisterns to retain their water much longer than otherwise possible.

Different parts of Palestine receive different amounts of rainfall. The northern and central regions get an average of 60-70 cm annually. The south gets less than 5 cm with the Gaza Strip getting the least.

Without question, a land that drinks in rain is blessed, but Moses adds another key concept in his exhortation to the land's future inhabitants – "it is a land the LORD your God cares for; the eyes of the LORD your God are continually on it" (Deuteronomy 11:11-12).

Most of Israel's freshwater sources today are organized and managed by National Water Carrier (NWC), a network of pumping stations, reservoirs, canals and pipelines which transfers water throughout the country. Agricultural demands are heavy and the ever increasing population of both Israelis and Palestinians is straining the NWC's capacity. Equitable access to very scarce water is a key factor in the tense relations between these two people.[116]

Water is no respecter of borders; it is impartial and indifferent. But God is not indifferent. God watches with care over the land. "God's eyes are continually on it," Moses says. The spiritual implications of Moses' words are clear. The water belongs to the land and the land belongs to God. God intends that those who live in the land should share in its largess and steward it on behalf of their neighbors and descendents. There is no shalom without responsible ecology and compassionate justice.

When modern Jews began resettling the northern region in the late 1800's a lot of it was non-arable marshland due to deforestation, soil erosion and neglect. The settlers drained the swampland, constructed terraces, cleared rocky fields, reforested the hills to reverse soil erosion, and washed salty land. They developed a network of canals, harnessed the water for irrigation and tried to make it a fruitful breadbasket. More recently they have come to realize that they overdid it and are working hard to redress the loss of critically important marshlands.

The complexity of this sustainable ecological development is a great example of responsible earth care. It illustrates our human calling as stewards of creation, partnering with God for the full flourishing of society and the environment. This is what all creation groans for – when it will be "liberated from its bondage to decay and brought into the glorious freedom of God's new creation" as St. Paul puts it in Romans 8:21.

That glorious freedom also has political and personal dimensions as we can see in this next story.

10.3 A Town Called Lifta

In the suburbs of northwest Jerusalem, just off the edge of the busy Jerusalem-Jaffa highway, water flows from an ancient spring. It fills a small pool and then flows out into the Wadi-al-Shami. This spring has a rich and tragic story to tell. Millenia ago the water from this spring quenched the thirst of the early Canaanite inhabitants of the land. Across the centuries all manner of people have washed their faces and their laundry in its waters.

It is mentioned in Joshua 15:9 and 18:15 as "the spring of the waters of Nephtoah" at the time of the Israelite occupation. Nothing else is told about this landmark except that it helped to mark the border between the tribal territory of Benjamin and Judah. It was not assigned to one tribe or the other, but as a shared resource, giving both tribes equal access to the waters.

The Bible tells us nothing about how well they managed their joint access to the single spring of Nephtoah, but throughout history and around the world, sharing water resources has always been a challenge for human beings. Sharing water requires self-restraint and cooperation. How we respond makes us better neighbors – or worse.

The site has been populated since ancient times; in 1596 it was an Arab village of 400 people and in the mid-1940's, 2500, predominantly Muslim, but some Christians as well. Over the years, the name *'Nephtoah'* morphed into *'Lifta.'*

In 1948 the Israeli Defense Force occupied and forcibly 'depopulated' Lifta in order to protect Israeli military transit from Jerusalem to Tel Aviv. All Lifta's homes were destroyed and its Arab residents forced to find refuge in East Jerusalem and elsewhere. The town is still 'occupied' today – and the park around the pool that collects the waters of the spring is now a popular picnic and bathing spot for Israelis in Jerusalem.

American psychiatrist Tom Baskett visited Lifta in 2007. He was moved both by the beauty of the town and by its tragic history. He saw orthodox Jews bathing in the pool, using it as a mikveh, performing their rituals of purity. Baskett recalled how 60 years earlier, the Palestinian villagers had been expelled violently from their homes in Lifta and he wrote a poem about his ponderings. Here is an excerpt:

> . . . Screams, gunshots
> and shouted threats echo
> through the village and along
> the tree-shaded stream
> to the spring-fed pool.
>
> Two orthodox Jews, white shirted
> and broad-brimmed black-hatted
> casually stroll down the hill to bathe
> naked in the pool confident that their
> sins--racial, national, or merely
> personal-- will be washed away.
>
> Does the water run red on silent
> moonlit nights after all the people
> are gone and the stories return to
> the land from where they came?
> I imagine it is so. [117]

Water can be a powerful teacher if we are willing to learn.

Springs of water are always a sign of the generosity of the earth and our Creator. They stand as witness to undeserved grace – and in their quiet flowing waters they whisper a plea for people to love their neighbors as they love themselves and to return blessing for blessing.

10.4 Caleb's Daughter Acsah

When the Hebrew tribes invaded Canaan sometime around in the 12-14th century BCE, the city of Debir in the northern Negev proved a tough town to conquer. As the commander in charge of the southern campaign, Caleb offered an incentive to whoever successfully captured the city, his daughter Acsah's hand in marriage. Her cousin Othniel rose to the challenge and won both the battle and the bride (Joshua 15:15-17).

Offering a daughter as the prize for military victory hints at the position of women in that society, but this story also shows us the resourcefulness of this woman. She wasn't just a trophy wife. She understood the realities of life.

For her dowry, Acsah asked her father for farmland. She knew that marriage alone was not enough, that a young family needs some real estate as well as love to live on. While the men divided up the land, this woman was thinking about the practicalities of raising a family there. And she wasn't going to let the opportunity slip.

A thousand years later, the Greek translation of the Hebrew Bible interchanged the pronouns in the story. In this version it is Othniel who urged his wife to ask her father for a field. Perhaps this was to suggest more appropriate gender roles or perhaps simply to fit the flow of the story better, which it does. But in either scenario, Acsah was key to the family's real estate holdings – and probably for good reasons.

Her genealogy in 1 Chronicles 2:49 indicates that Acsah's mother Maacah was not Caleb's wife, but a concubine. Acsah may have learned from her mother that women have to speak up for themselves if they want to survive in a man's world. Acsah seems to have learned early how to exploit every advantage. Being the daughter of a national hero had its advantages – but Acsah didn't rely on privilege.

The Negev was not an easy place to farm, nor is it any easier today. Its name means 'dry country'. The Negev is hilly, if not mountainous, poor in rain and with few sources of underground water. What rain it does receive, drains to the east in narrow canyons and to the west along shallow wadis. Excavations in the 1960's revealed rock cut cisterns in the area around Debir, so we know there was both water and water shortages.

Acsah knew that without water to irrigate her fields, the land wasn't worth very much. So after inspecting her dowry, Acsah followed with an addendum: "since you have given me land in the Negev, give me also springs of water" (verse 19).

Caleb granted her request and gave her title to not just one spring, but two, an upper and lower spring, a rare double source of available water. A set of naturally occurring springs at different altitudes is a feature of the topography southeast of Hebron, and excavations there in 1968-69 turned up lots of material from the time of the conquest.

Acsah's story is much more than historic trivia and a vignette of family life. Her request is about necessity, not greed. The point of this story in the Hebrew Bible is that fair allocation of the land requires access to adequate water. Acsah's demand to her father represents the plea of the powerless crying for justice from the king. Justice is the lifeblood of society as water is life for the land.[118]

This story from Israel's first occupation of the land illustrates one of the critical factors afflicting Israel and many other countries today – the scarcity of water resources. One of the deep needs facing the Middle East peace process is for both sides to set aside political antagonism to ensure that everyone in the land, Israeli and Palestinian, has access to sufficient water. I wonder what would happen if government leaders there – and everywhere – were to commission the mothers and daughters of the land to resolve the scandalous disparities around access to water and to find equitable solutions that help family life to flourish?

Acsah's request could also illustrate the need for each generation to provide adequately for the generation following them, both material and spiritual resources they will need to succeed in life. I read somewhere that Dietrich Bonhoeffer reminded parents that they need to ground children in the scriptures as the spiritual spring that will sustain them forever, and that it is irresponsible to give them physical life without the spiritual nourishment that will enable them to prosper.

Acsah's husband Othniel went on to do exploits in Israel in later years. In Judges 3 we read that when the king of Aram subjugated them for eight years, "the Spirit of the Lord came upon Othniel" and he overpowered the Aramites. He became the first of a sequence of judges who governed Israel and delivered them from their overlords.

But behind every great man, they say, stands a capable woman, and Othniel's wife Acsah certainly shows the marks of competence.

10.5 Gideon's Dry Fleece

> *"Your doubts will evaporate like dew when the waiting is over."*
> Luci Shaw, *Water My Soul.*[119]

Call him a reluctant warrior. For seven years, according to Judges Chapter 6, God was silent while the marauding Midianites raided Israel's farms at harvest time at will. Year after year it was the same, so when Yahweh's messenger showed up and called Gideon a "mighty warrior" (verse 12) and told him that God was with him, the man was a tad skeptical. Waiting can do that to you.

It seemed to Gideon that God was more absent than active, more a god of legends than a God of the real world where thieves plundered crops with impunity. When the angel told Gideon to 'gird up his strength' and deliver Israel, he asked for a sign and received dramatic evidence of God's power. But it was not enough. Even with surges of heroic courage and moral outrage at the injustice he and his neighbors were suffering, Gideon hesitated to act. Could God please reassure him?

He placed a lamb's fleece on his threshing floor and asked God to drench it with dew in the morning while the ground around it remained dry. Presumably he hoped a dew free night would release him from any obligation to mount a risky campaign. But the morning light found the ground bone-dry and the fleece soaking wet, just as Gideon had asked.

It was a miracle – a sign! But the problem with 'proof by coincidence' is that you never know if you have proof or a coincidence. So Gideon tried it again the next day, reversing the terms – a dry fleece, please, on dew laden ground – which would be an even more extraordinary occurrence if it occurred. Wobbly faith seeks for signs just as Jesus said a perverse generation does. But once again God granted Gideon's request, proving that God does suffer fools gladly, or at least cuts them a fair bit of slack!

Just as dew reveals the presence of invisible moisture in the air, so Gideon's dew-drenched fleece was a tangible sign of God's invisible presence and power. It heralded a call to action which Gideon knew he must answer. His doubt evaporated like dew in the morning sun. The waiting was over. He mobilized his troops and drove the foe from the land.

In Gideon's fleece we see the signs of a vacillating man, hardly the marks of the hero God called him to be, but God never rebuked Gideon for his hesitancy and made a lion out of him. What patience and extravagance God shows!

Prayer:
God, my faith wavers like Gideon's. I, too, am doubtful of your power. I crave irrefutable signs, desire divination. Just as you did with Gideon, clothe me with your Spirit. Drench me with passion, enlarge my faith. Amen

10.6 Samuel's Water Ceremony

Things weren't going well for Israel. Politically they were fragmented; they were militarily impotent and economically depressed. For decades they had experimented with indigenous religious practices and were mired in idolatry. Somehow they were now at a breaking point, and breaking points can become turning points.

In their frustration they called out to God – which is often what it takes to get refocused. God sent Samuel into action. He urged the people to abandon their foreign gods. Then he convened a national conference to formalize their religious commitment renewal.

> Samuel said, "Assemble all Israel at Mizpah and I will intercede with the LORD for you." When they had assembled at Mizpah, they drew water and poured it out before the LORD. On that day they fasted and there they confessed, "We have sinned against the LORD."
> 1 Samuel 7:6

It was a dramatic exercise in confession and rededication. Part of the ceremony included a water ritual, but we don't know of another instance anywhere in the Bible where water was used in this way. There was no washing of the people's hands, no ritual bathing, no sacred drinking of the water. The water was simply drawn out of a well and then "poured out on the ground before the Lord". This ritual may have come from an ancient practice, or it may have been a spontaneous gesture by Samuel.

The most probable explanation is that it was a ritual of cleansing. Water is used that way in religious traditions everywhere. Or perhaps Samuel "poured it out before the Lord" as a visual reminder of the times Yahweh had delivered them by water – at the Red Sea, the Jordan, from rocks in the desert.

Perhaps it reminded them of their complete dependence on Yahweh as the provider of the simplest gifts of nature. Perhaps it was an act of confession of the folly, failure and waste of the squandered years. Perhaps it was a ritual of repentance, the abandoning of old practices or symbolic of a spirit of unreservedly pouring out their souls before the Lord in devotion to him.[120]

Water is such a common element with such a variety of uses and yet so vital to life that a water ritual could work symbolically in many ways. Some scholars suggest it may be the precursor of the water ritual that became a prominent feature of the Feast of Tabernacles celebration, which prompted Jesus to present himself as the water of life in John 7:37.

Samuel's water ministry here foreshadows that of John the Baptist a millennium later, calling the people to wash away the defiling past and start anew with God. This moment cemented Samuel's role as a "leader in Israel" (1 Samuel 7:6), but more significantly, it illustrates the character of Samuel's lifelong public ministry as a priest and intercessor. The young boy who learned to listen to God became one who "poured out his life" on behalf of others, bearing their burdens, bringing them to God. "He cried out to God on Israel's behalf, and the Lord answered him" (1 Samuel 7:9). And Samuel himself says, "far be it from me that I should sin against the LORD by failing to pray for you. And I will teach you the way that is good and right" (1 Samuel 12:23).

Try using Samuel's water prayer yourself in the next few days. Fill a glass with water and pour it out slowly before the Lord, praying as you pour. Let the action suggest ways to come clean with God and to express your desire to renew your life in God's ways. Do it again as you pray for others in your life.

Chapter 11

David – Thirsting After God

11.1 David and Goliath

This iconic story in 1 Samuel 17 celebrates the gutsy little guy taking on the giant and beating the odds. But between the unlikely hero and the big bully lay a small creek bed – and that creek holds the secret to what the fight was all about.

The valley of Elah was a strategic piece of real estate. It runs roughly east-west at a point where the western slope of the Judean hills drop down to the coastal plain inhabited by Philistines. The Philistines coveted the valley as a corridor to the agricultural interior of Israel. Pushing their way inland up the valley they posed a formidable threat to assert dominance over Israel.

The Israelite forces occupied a hill on the north to defend the valley and the two armies faced each other on opposite slopes of the valley. The Philistines had a significant technological advantage with Bronze Age weaponry. And with a hulking warrior the size of Goliath they had a huge propaganda edge.

Across the creek bed, the giant taunted and intimidated his foes. This battle was about access to water and agricultural land and the economic power they offered. It was also about national honor and whether Israel's God could be trusted.

David took Goliath's taunts not as a threat, but as an insult against his God, Yahweh. They aroused David's indignation and resolve. He would defend Israel's honor and security, not with the latest technology, but with a rural shepherd's sling. In full view of the armor bearing military machine on the other bank, David collected his ammunition from the creek, "five smooth stones" (1 Samuel 17:40), naturally crafted by the winter rains which tumble through this small channel every year. David simply used the resources at hand and trusted in the living God, the Lord Almighty, the one who kept covenant with Israel and one whom David has learned to trust.

The small stream seemed militarily insignificant, but it supplied the critical piece that felled the giant. The shepherd boy looked hugely outmatched against a towering trained warrior, but his faith in the power of an invisible God gave him vision, courage, ingenuity and chutzpah. "So David triumphed over the Philistine with a sling and a stone; without a sword in his hand he struck down the Philistine and killed him" 1 Samuel 17:50.

David himself was a smooth stone in the hands of Israel's Shepherd-God. He had been shaped by the river of circumstance in difficult family life and adolescent challenges in a hostile world. He had been polished smooth by the flow of God's faithfulness and grace around him and over him year after year. And then God used him strategically to protect others and further God's rule in the world.

And through him, the culture and faith of Israel grew stronger sinews of humility, trust and confidence in God.

11.2 The Bethlehem Water Caper

Hometown wells are always the sweetest, especially when you're far from home. David was a king-in-waiting – in hiding, actually, with a band of desperado friends. His native Bethlehem had recently fallen into Philistine hands and David was craving the best water in the world (2 Samuel 23:14-17).

"What I wouldn't give for a drink from the well in Bethlehem!" he sighed.

His daring friends secretly accepted the challenge, broke through enemy lines, filled a ewer of water and carried it back to David – an exploit full of bravado, bragging rights and esteem for their good friend and future king. No doubt they told in vivid detail how they had pulled off the caper under the noses of the sleeping Philistines.

But for David, the hazards his comrades had faced to get this water for him, made the water sacred. It was no longer a consumable commodity. Drinking it would have reduced it to mere water, when it represented his friends' lifeblood. Only God was worthy of such a sacrifice. So instead of drinking the water, David poured it out reverently before the Lord.

It's a timeless tale of friendship and heroic action and it shows how the most common thing like water can have meaning far deeper than the thing itself.

Many of Bethlehem's citizens today long for freedom the way David craved its water three millennia ago. As I write this in 2011, a monstrous security wall imprisons Bethlehem on three sides. Palestinian workers queue up in the dark for the 5:30 am opening of the gates so they can get to work in Jerusalem. It's a complex issue. The wall that suffocates Palestinian families makes Israel's life more secure. It is a vile and untenable standoff. But there are brave men and women, Israeli, Palestinian and international, laboring for an honorable sustainable peace in Bethlehem, Israel and Palestine. Like David's gutsy commandos, some of these people are hazarding their lives for others. We ought to pour out prayers on their behalf.

The greatest champion of peace, though, is the descendent of David who broke through enemy lines by being born in Bethlehem 2000 years ago, behind the siege, behind the 'security wall', in order to bring us the rarest, sweetest water in the world! No gesture of friendship has ever been so clear. No hazard or sacrifice has ever cost so much or achieved such wondrous rewards. He "became flesh and blood and moved into the neighborhood" (John 1:12 MSG) – to bring us the water of Life.

O come let us adore him, Christ the Lord.

11.3 Breakthrough

A few years later, David and all Israel experienced a memorable breakthrough event. David had just been acclaimed King of all Israel's tribes – and that was a signal to the Philistine occupiers of the land that he must be stopped before he could consolidate his kingdom. In 2 Samuel 5:17-25 we read that they went up in full force to search for him and then to take him on in battle in the Valley of Rephaim, west of Jerusalem.

The Philistine forces were formidable, so instead of direct assault, David retreated to the familiar deserts south and east of Jerusalem towards the Dead Sea, intending to use guerilla tactics at which he was so skilled. David prayed for God's counsel. With God's reassurance, David attacked and routed the Philistines decisively.

The Philistines regrouped and came back for another assault in exactly the same field of their recent humiliation. Once again, David prayed for guidance, and God told him,

> Do not go straight up, but circle around behind them and attack them in front of the balsam trees. As soon as you hear the sound of marching in the tops of the balsam trees, move quickly, because that will mean the LORD has gone out in front of you to strike the Philistine army. So David did as the LORD commanded him, and he struck down the Philistines all the way from Gibeon to Gezer.
> 2 Samuel 5:23-25

The victory was so dramatic that David renamed the battlefield, Baal-Perazim – which means 'The Lord who Bursts Through'. The Hebrew verb *paras* means to breach or break through. "The LORD did it!" David exclaimed. "He burst through my enemies like a raging flood!" (verse 20 NLT)

Old Testament scholar Joyce Baldwin says that for Israel this double victory "must have had all the emotional overtones that Trafalger has for the British".[121] Indeed it broke the back of the Philistine forces. It spelled the beginning of the end of their occupation of Israel and cemented David's position as king over Israel's fractured tribal confederacy.

Some time later David, the warrior poet, wrote a song commemorating God's victory, now recorded as Psalm 124.

> If the LORD had not been on our side-- let Israel say--
> if the LORD had not been on our side when men attacked us,
> when their anger flared against us, they would have swallowed us alive;
> the flood would have engulfed us, the torrent would have swept over us,
> the raging waters would have swept us away.
> Psalm 124:1-5

David was inspired by the picture of torrential waters that rip through the wadis of the Judean badlands during the winter rains, bursting their banks and sweeping away trees, flocks, homes, anything in their path. That was the threat of the enemy had presented, but God had out-flanked them. Yahweh was the ultimate flashflood.

This story shows David as a contrast to his predecessor Saul. Saul failed to obey God, but David was smart and humble enough to enquire of God and to follow the instructions of Yahweh implicitly. The sound of the wind in the trees that David was told to listen for (verse 24) was the sound of marching as Yahweh led the charge, signaling David to move at once. Baldwin comments that David had to move in sync with the Spirit of God if he was to fulfill God's purpose to defeat the enemy.[122]

We can see in this new king that wisdom had broken through into Israel's leadership. No wonder the nation rallied around David, and no wonder God used him so effectively. No wonder his spiritual influence continues through history to our own day!

11.4 All for One and One for all

It was the rallying cry of the heroes of Alexander Dumas' 1844 novel *The Three Musketeers* – "all for one and one for all!"

It is also the unofficial motto of Switzerland. In 1868, only 20 years after Switzerland ended civil war among its cantons and had become a federal state, officials had good occasion to use this phrase. In September and October of that year, storms caused extensive flooding in the Alps. Swiss officials launched an aid campaign, using the French, German and Italian versions of this unity slogan to evoke a sense of duty and solidarity that would promote national unity and address the flood recovery needs.

Psalm 133 is a lyric gem about harmony in families, societies and nations. It is attributed to David – and he may have written it early in his reign as a way of celebrating the support he received from all of Israel's tribes. It is a very short psalm, but full of wonder, realism and hope.

> How wonderful, how beautiful,
> when brothers and sisters get along!
> It's like costly anointing oil
> flowing down head and beard,
> Flowing down Aaron's beard,
> flowing down the collar of his priestly robes.
> Psalm 133:1-2 (MSG)

Harmony is a wonderful thing. When the whole family is getting along and enjoying each other, it's a great feeling. It's heaven on earth. At the consecration of a Jewish high priest, the nation gathered together as one. The ceremonial oil of consecration was poured over the priest's head in the name of all the tribes; it spilled down his face and drenched his robes. You could smell the fragrance, you could hear the cheering in unison, you could sense the joyful spirit of togetherness – one nation, one faith, one prayer of brotherhood. Oil flowing with exuberance – all for one and one for all.

Then the poem adds a metaphor from nature.

> It's like the dew on Mount Hermon
> flowing down the slopes of Zion.
> Yes, that's where God commands the blessing, ordains eternal life.
> Psalm 133:3 (MSG)

Dew is creation's daily anointing of the earth, its lavish outpouring of life-giving moisture, a gift out of thin air, mercy new every morning. In a dry land like Israel, unity would be like the well-watered north, Mount Hermon, sharing its abundance with the parched highlands of Judea. Such generosity, mutuality and collaboration as this – it's a rare experience, something you can only fanaticize about. Imagine if the dew of Hermon were to fall on Mount Zion – the drought would be over, it would be a foretaste of heaven!

As suggested earlier, imagine if the Israeli and Palestinian governments worked to earn each other's trust enough to ensure that everyone in the region received equal access to the limited water reserves, it would betoken a renewal as vibrant as the spring rains that burst the dry desert into bloom.

There's an irony hidden in the metaphors in Psalm 133, as pastor and author Mark Buchanan observes. Oil celebrates and dew refreshes, but these images also hint at how difficult unity can be to actually achieve. Oil and water don't mix so easily. Both have amazing properties, but try to blend them together, and you have impossible on your hands.[123]

It's our differences that make harmony such a gritty challenge, whether in families or nations. Differences test the true measure of our trust and truth telling, our humility and patience, our courage and grace. Harmony always costs something, but when we make the sacrifice, we discover its reward. Harmony hammered out on the anvil of tough human hearts is a monumental blessing for everyone – like life from the grave!

As this psalm concludes, "there the Lord commands his blessing – life forevermore."

Prayer

Drench me, God of the morning dew. Wherever there is harmony, bless the efforts of people to sustain it. Wherever there is friction, let the oil flow, let the dew rise afresh. Teach brothers and sisters, husbands and wives, how to anoint each other with grace, how to water each others' gardens with mercy new every day. Teach nations your path to peace. Pour your oil on the troubled waters of our world this day. Amen.

11.5 Rizpah

Suffering sometimes triggers good soul-searching. A three year drought set King David on a desperate search for answers – 2 Samuel 21:1-14. What he uncovered was a story of treachery and genocide that hadn't registered a flicker on the national conscience.

It involved one of Israel's tribal neighbors, the Gibeonites, who lived east of the Jordan. By ancient treaty (see Joshua 9), these people had enjoyed protection and immunity from attack by Israel. But David's predecessor, Saul, broke faith and attempted to annihilate them – and almost succeeded.

Years passed and no one called Israel to account, but Saul's act of treachery cried out to God from the ground, like the blood of Abel. Israel had an integrated view of the world, where human behavior affects the environment. It was as if nature itself had a moral conscience. A famine was like nature in mourning; famine is a kind of genocide on the land, stripping it bare, leaving it barren and hopeless. The drought called attention to the land's cry for justice.

When David learned how the Gibeonites had been violated, he summoned the survivors and found them hungry to exact revenge. They demanded seven descendents of Saul to be executed and exposed to humiliation. David acquiesced to their brutal request.

The timing was significant – it was the beginning of harvest, a meager harvest no doubt because of the drought. But the seven victims were slaughtered publicly to atone for their father's blood-guilt, and to satisfy the hatred of an abused people and the angry gods of revenge. Among the seven unfortunates were two sons of Rizpah, Saul's concubine.

Everyone hoped the curse had been broken, that the rains would come. But vengeance never rights ancient wrongs, and David showed abysmal leadership in this clumsy attempt at national atonement.

Rizpah, the bereaved mother, honored her sons and protected their corpses from disgrace. She mourned her loss and wailed her protest against their needless death. She enacted a prayer of lament. She spread her sackcloth of mourning and kept vigil over them day and night. For six months "from the beginning of the harvest until the rain poured down" (verse 10), all through the heat of the summer, Rizpah's maternal faithfulness proclaimed a virtue nobler than the king's.

When the rains finally fell, it was as if God was weeping with Rizpah. The text describes the rain like tears from heaven 'pouring down' on the bodies, not on the land as we would expect. God and Rizpah suffered and mourned together.[124] This public action of lament by God affirmed Rizpah's honor and her protest over the loss of life.

In the late 1800's Alfred Tennyson wrote a social justice poem called "Rizpah" about a Victorian era mother whose son fell afoul of the law and was executed for a petty crime. Like ancient Rizpah this nineteenth century mother defied convention to lament her pain and loss. Her devotion made an eloquent plea for a more compassionate society that empathized with the poor and the powerless, and Tennyson's wife often recited "Rizpah" at public gatherings.

The cry for justice never ends – and sometimes it is the mothers of the land who voice it best.

11.6 Waves of Death

On May 12, 2010, the *LA Times* carried a 'good news' story about a 30 ton gray whale that had become tangled in a thick snarl of fishing net. For two days it labored in a Southern California harbor until a marine rescue team was able to set it free. It took them four hours to soothe the distressed whale and cut away the ropes that had knotted around the whale's tail and head. It's hard to imagine such a huge majestic creature held prisoner to a braid of nylon cord. It's hard to imagine a 40-foot (12 m) whale helpless and drowning.

The Biblical words of a drowning man could equally be the anguished moans of a dying whale:

> Waves of death swirled about me;
> Torrents of destruction overwhelmed me.
> The cords of the grave coiled around me;
> The snares of death confronted me.
> 2 Samuel 22:5-7

This is a song of the poet-king David, describing a terrifying ordeal when his life was in peril. He was on the rocks, pounded relentlessly by "waves of death, torrents of destruction". Fear coiled its octopus tentacles around his neck, or as *The Message* puts it, "Hell's ropes cinched me tight." David was overwhelmed and exhausted.

I know that feeling. I can remember being so tangled in despair that I groaned in the morning that I hadn't died during the night. I felt completely alone in my nightmare, but stress and trauma are almost universal human experiences – and echoed in every area of nature. The world is out of kilter. This is why the psalms are so helpful. They give us words when our sense of crisis is beyond words.

This desperation fragment of song is not just the blues on steroids; it's actually a song of gratitude. David is looking back on a desperate time when God rescued him. This is another gift of the psalms – they offer hope. Not naïve hope, but a hope born out of suffering, disorientation and a real-life experience of God's rescue.

> In my distress I called to the LORD;
> I called out to my God.
> From his temple he heard my voice;
> my cry came to his ears.
> Psalm 18:6

David testifies that God doesn't exempt his chosen servants from pain and anguish. The Bible contains a gallery of these men and women of faith – Abraham and Jacob, Joseph and Moses, Hannah and Naomi, David, Job, Jonah, Daniel and Jeremiah, Mary and Peter, John and Paul. They experienced deep waters and anguish of soul on their way to maturity.

That's how God fashioned them into pure gold. They entered into the suffering of the world before they experienced glory.

Deep waters and strangling fear are not signs that God has abandoned us, though Jesus' cry on the cross tells us that it is normal to feel that. Deep waters can be a pathway to exuberant joy. As St. Paul wrote, "I consider that our present sufferings are not worth comparing with the glory that will be revealed in us" (Romans 8:18).

11.7 Going Under

Sometimes life gets crazy – everything happens at once and you feel yourself going under. A child gets intensely sick, a friend turns hostile, your wallet is empty, deadlines converge, you're losing your capacity to hold it all together. You're being sucked under, overwhelmed.

Several of Israel's songs express this kind of nightmare experience.

> Save me, O God, for the waters have come up to my neck.
> I sink in the miry depths, where there is no foothold.
> I have come into the deep waters; the floods engulf me.
> Psalm 69:1-2
>
> Rescue me from the mire, do not let me sink;
> deliver me from those who hate me, from the deep waters.
> Do not let the floodwaters engulf me or the depths swallow me up.
> Psalm 69:14-15

Water is wonderful, but in excess it becomes a flood. Overwhelming! When you're over your head in a torrent of circumstances, a sea of anxiety, your confidence shattered, what do you do? This singer calls out to God to rescue him, but God is silent. He scours the horizon, but there's no God in sight. God is far away and apparently unconcerned.

This song is called 'a David psalm' which means either that it was written by David or reflects David-like experience – in this case, desperation. David knew his share of life-threatening events, but even more overwhelming than those was his moral lapse, when adultery led to fraud, murder and cover up, when he felt himself sucked under by guilt and self-loathing.

What we learn from David's life and his songs is the art of desperate faith. When he was out of his depth, he called out to God. Having practiced his faith in calmer seasons, David instinctively knew how to pray in his extremity. But the ongoing silence of God completely unnerved him. His foothold became quicksand as he sank deeper into the abyss.

In Bunyan's *Pilgrim's Progress,* Christian nears the end of his hazardous life journey. As he crosses the final river, he loses his footing. His friend Hopeful feels the ground solid beneath him and tries to cheer him on, but we each have our own crossings and Christian flounders. He is overwhelmed.

Bunyan brilliantly catalogues the haunting fears and guilt that assail his hero on this final stage of his journey, almost drowning him in despair. Eventually Christian recalls God's promise, "when you pass through the waters I will be with you and when you pass through the rivers they shall not sweep over you."[125] He regains his footing and splashes through the rest of the river with ease.

Who can tell why some people find life easy and others are overwhelmed by it? Who can tell how vulnerable or afraid each of us will feel in the face of our own death?

Bunyan reminds us, like the psalmist, in our most desperate moments to trust God's ultimate goodness, to remember that Jesus Christ is no stranger to this overwhelming. He was engulfed by the horror of God-forsakenness and groaned to his sleeping friends, "My soul is overwhelmed with sorrow to the point of death" (Mark 14:34).

He knows the taste of our desperation. He has crossed our river and holds out his hand. He is the overcomer that meets us and sustains us in our overwhelming.

11.8 God, We're Thirsty!

The worst of times can inspire the most passionate songs:

> O God, you are my God,
> Earnestly I seek you;
> My soul thirsts for you,
> My body longs for you,
> in a dry and weary land where there is no water.
> Psalm 63:1

King David was fleeing for his life. His son had staged a revolt, overthrown the crown and was consolidating his power in Jerusalem. 2 Samuel 15:13

to 16:14 tells how David fled the city with a small band of supporters and headed east across the 20 km stretch of hills towards the Jordan.

David knew these hills well. He had grazed sheep there in his youth; these were the badlands where the crazed King Saul had hunted David as a young man. David knew the steep canyons, the hidden caves and bone-dry creek beds. It was a dangerous land – where the sun beat down and thirst stalked you relentlessly among all your other fears. The wilderness around him mirrored the landscape of David's soul. He was dry and bone weary, exhausted physically and emotionally.

There are few things more draining than thirst. But the anxiety in David's soul was not just a shortage of water, not just longing for personal safety and survival, but a deep soul thirst for God. He needed God's help, yes, but even more, he longed for God as a friend, he ached for the nearness of God as a lover longs to be in touch with his beloved. David's deepest craving was for God.

David's words about thirst express the universal human longing for God. Our thirst for knowledge, for pleasure, for justice, for belonging – these are echoes of the deepest thirst of the human heart – to see the face of God and to know God's touch. German theologian Dietrich Bonhoefffer describes the irony of this thirst every human being feels. He speaks of an indescribable thirst for life that seizes hold of Adam, but in his obsessive desire for life Adam has chosen the way of death. Adam has chosen to live out of his own resources instead of in dependence on God. He is estranged from God and centered on himself. This solitude "plunges Adam into an infinite thirst ... a desperate, an unquenchable, an eternal thirst that Adam feels for life. The more passionately Adam seeks after life, the more completely he is ensnared by death."[126] We will explore this thirst further in Chapter 21 when we consider Psalm 42.

David's years on the run in the Judean wilderness are part of a common pattern in the Biblical narrative. The delay David endured before receiving his 'inheritance' as king is parallel to Abraham's delay waiting for a son, Jacob's delay in winning his chosen bride, Joseph's detour into Egypt before coming to authority and influence. It parallels Israel's delay in possessing the Promised Land after escaping from Egypt. It seems that God uses chronological delay to deepen our thirst for what matters most in life.

Inevitably what we discover is that what our souls crave more than anything else is to know that we are deeply loved.

Keith Price was a friend of mine who shared David's intense desire for God. Keith wrote a book called *Thirsting After God* which expressed his lifelong ambition to know God better and to seek him earnestly every day of his life. Even with cancer wracking his body, he craved nothing more passionately than companionship with God. When he died in January 2001, they said of him at his funeral, "he thirsted after God and when he found Him, he drank from that bottomless ocean and never stopped craving for more."

11.9 Cleanse Me With Hyssop

David's passion for God was not the only appetite in his life. He was passionate for many things – justice and respect, victory in battle, and security from foes. He also had an eye for strong beautiful women – which provided the occasion for one of his most tragic failures. When he saw Bathsheba he desired her although she was another man's wife. He seduced her and then stealthily arranged for her husband's death. With lust, deceit and murder, he stumbled down a foul trail of self-indulgence. He was king; he felt entitled and invincible. Who knows how long this pretence might have lasted had his friend, the wise, courageous and wily prophet Nathan, not intervened.

Guilt is a terrible thing. But if there is something worse than guilt, its name would be Denial. Denial is the paralyzing refusal to come to terms with the monster that is destroying you. Shakespeare brilliantly illustrates the destructive power of repressed guilt in the sleepwalking in *Macbeth* as Lady Macbeth walks the halls of her castle with a candle, trying in vain to scour the damning blood-guilt from her hands.

> Yet here's a spot . . .
> Out, damned spot! Out, I say! . . .
> Who would have thought the old man
> to have had so much blood in him? . . .
> What, will these hands ne'er be clean? . . .
> Here's the smell of the blood still: All the perfumes
> of Arabia will not sweeten this little hand.
> Oh, oh, oh!
> Macbeth, Act V, Scene 1, 30-50.

Her façade is cracking; denial is hard to sustain. Her husband is even more tortured with guilt than she is. He moans to himself,

What hands are here?
Will all great Neptune's ocean wash this blood
Clean from my hand? No, this my hand will rather
The multitudinous seas incarnadine,
Making the green one red.
Macbeth, II. ii, 75.

Like his wife, Macbeth's hands are stained with the blood of the king he murdered. He realizes too late that all the oceans of the world can never purge his guilt. They themselves would turn scarlet before they could wash his hands or conscience clean.

Pontius Pilate was just as culpable as the Macbeths and lived even more in denial. But he is not nearly as heroic. Confronted by the most powerful innocence that ever stood before him, he nevertheless capitulated to political pressure and signed the execution decree of Jesus. As the crowning sign of his cowardice he poured water into a basin and publicly washed his hands of the injustice, claiming innocence.

But ceremonial washing can't absolve guilt. Character and integrity don't work that way.

King David also knew the gnawing pangs of a guilty conscience. He offers us a much better portrait of handling guilt in high places. Like Macbeth and Pilate, David followed his lust into violence, intrigue, bloodshed and denial. But the prophet Nathan, David's friend, unmasked him and urged him to end his cover-up, to come clean with his actions and shoulder his responsibility for what he had done. Tortured by his guilt, David contritely humbled himself before God and pled for mercy.

As a poet and songwriter, David worked through his anguish by composing a song that expressed the depths of his denial, his guilt and shame, his yearning for a clean heart and restored joy. Here is an excerpt:

Have mercy on me, O God,
Wash away all my iniquity
and cleanse me from my sin.
For I know my transgressions,
and my sin is always before me.

> Surely you desire truth in the inner parts;
> You teach me wisdom in the inmost place.
> Cleanse me with hyssop, and I will be clean;
> Wash me, and I will be whiter than snow.
> Psalm 51:2-7

No denial, no evasion. Honest confession ... and David's forgiving God washed him clean as snow and transformed tragedy into joy. Waves of guilt become an ocean of forgiveness for the foulest of sinners – and that spells hope for us all.

11.10 River of New Beginnings

When David's son Absalom usurped the throne and tried to unseat his father as king, intrigue and suspicion poisoned the atmosphere of Jerusalem. David fled for his life and escaped across the Jordan under cover of night (2 Samuel 17:22). He set up his headquarters-in-exile in the town of Mahanaim east of the Jordan River.

After Absalom's death (2 Samuel 18), David, the brokenhearted father and exiled king headed back home, but stopped short of crossing back over the Jordan. We read in 2 Samuel 19:15-40 that he waited until the leaders of Jerusalem came to greet him and swear allegiance. David needed to know that the conspiracy was over and that it was possible for a new era of trust and unity to begin. With a public sign of allegiance, they escorted David across the river and back to his throne in the Jerusalem. Like the crossing of the Jordan in Joshua's day, it marked the beginning of a new era, a new beginning for the king and his people.

Christian devotional literature has often interpreted the 'crossing of Jordan' as a metaphor of death, with Canaan as the promised land of heaven. But the Bible doesn't seem to interpret the Jordan that way. It seems rather to suggest a time of new beginnings.

A century and a half after David, Elisha accompanied his mentor Elijah eastward across the Jordan until a whirlwind and chariots of fire swoop the older prophet away (2 Kings 2). Crossing the Jordan in an easterly direction, leaving the land of promise, was the highway to heaven for Elijah. But when Elisha returned home, he smacked the Jordan waters with Elijah's robe, a keepsake from his heaven- bound mentor, and crossed the river on dry land. His reentry showed him to be a worthy successor to Elijah as spiritual leader of Israel, mirroring Joshua's succession to Moses. Like David's ceremonial reentry, Elisha's crossing symbolized the opportunity for a new beginning, a call to Israel to return to its covenant with Yahweh and start again.

As we will see in Chapter 14 the New Testament builds on these Old Testament narratives. It begins the story of Jesus by telling us about John the Baptist calling people to repentance through baptism in the Jordan River. Once again the waters of the Jordan will picture a spiritual new beginning, the nation and her people making a decisive break with past failure and entering by faith into the inheritance God had promised his people in the new covenant, the abundant life of Christ.

11.11 Leadership

The Arab Spring or Arab Awakening in 2011 was an extraordinary wave of demonstrations and revolutionary protests across the Arabic world, starting in December 2010. Human beings thirst for justice, fair laws, freedom and dignity. They boil over with anger and frustration when unjust leaders stifle their hopes. They dream of a better day; a new sunrise, springtime.

That's how King David describes the legacy of leaders who use their God-given power to serve their people.

> The one who rules righteously,
> Who rules in the fear of God
> Is like the light of morning at sunrise,
> Like a morning without clouds,
> Like the gleaming of the sun on new grass after rain.
> 2 Samuel 23:4 NLT

Rain and sunlight are gifts of nature that nourish the earth and brighten our lives. That's what visionary and virtuous leaders do too: they create vibrant communities, inspire creative participation, nourish productivity; they bring hope.

King David understood this. During his reign, Israel had endured times of famine, when natural drought converged with bad leadership decisions to create national crisis. David learned the hard way that good government is not just about shrewd politics and decisive action.

In the final song of his musical career, David cites 'the fear of the Lord' as the spiritual core of good governance. This is the principled beacon of those who resist the temptations of power and privilege, who refuse to be a rule unto themselves, but who understand that their authority is delegated by God. They protect the poor who are often victims of human injustice and, as God does, they temper justice with mercy. In other words, under God's direction, the Law is both humane and adapted to human frailty.

Leaders like this create a sunlit atmosphere of justice and shalom, a bright and hopeful future. Like rain and sunlight, good leaders help others to flourish. Whether business or community leaders, pastors, teachers, parents or coaches, people who influence the lives of others can either promote growth or stifle it. They create conditions that either foster or obstruct productive lives in those they lead.

Good leaders are visionary, they can see a better tomorrow and they inspire their people to imagine and contribute to a bright future. They are both decisive and compassionate.

11.12 Coronation Springs

Time was of the essence. The senile King David shivered in the hours before his death, but his scheming son kept his eye focused on his father's crown. Adonijah was handsome, shrewd and self-serving. Aware that the king favored Solomon as his heir, Adonijah moved quickly to grasp his advantage.

With a small bodyguard, he organized his own coronation. He invited all his royal brothers except Solomon to a lavish feast at the En-Rogel spring outside the southern walls of the city – a country barbeque – to celebrate his accession to the throne and, no doubt, to enlist their support.

News of his conspiracy leaked out and the prophet Nathan roused the dying king to act. David immediately named Solomon his successor and ordered Nathan to convene the official coronation of Solomon at the other spring – Gihon, a mile and a half (2 kms) north of En-Rogel. Nathan and Solomon set out with fanfare and a royal parade, a marching band of trumpets and flutes and public cheers of celebration which were said to make the earth shake – and which quickly dispelled Adonijah's conspiracy.

Why did both coronations – the true and the false – happen outside the city at a spring? The text doesn't say, but I suspect there was something symbolic about anointing the king at a spring. It may have implied that the king was as vital to his people as water is to life. Maybe it meant that the king himself needed divine power. Nature religions consider springs and wells as sacred sites where the powers of the earth come to the surface and can be accessed. Israel's faith saw a spring as a gift of life from the very hand of Yahweh, king of the Universe.

Being crowned near the spring signaled that the king's authority and power derived from God. It was a symbolic prayer that the spiritual vitality of God, the very powers of creation and God's abundance would flow through the king's reign, that his leadership would reflect the faithful provision of God evidenced in the flow of the spring.

Israel's coronation psalm, the psalm most quoted in the New Testament, Psalm 110 speaks of water as a dynamic life force that would sustain God's king through the passing years: "arrayed in holy majesty, from the womb of the dawn, you will receive the dew of your youth" (verse 3).

Another coronation psalm, Psalm 72, perhaps composed by Solomon for use on anniversaries of his coronation,[127] expands the king's vision beyond dew and springs saying "He shall have dominion also from sea to sea, and from the river unto the ends of the earth" (Psalm 72:8).

This text is especially meaningful for Canadians who call their country a 'dominion'. In 1867 when Canada became a nation, the fathers of confederation chose this text from Psalm 72 to express their vision that Canadians would recognize God's authority in the nation's laws and life together, and that the blessing of God would extend to every corner of the nation, from sea to sea to sea.

Today with oceans on three coasts, every July 1st, Canada proudly celebrates its national unity from coast to coast to coast. Canadians today take a more pluralistic approach to life than their founding leaders. Individuals and people groups from Atlantic to Pacific and from the Arctic to the Great Lakes make up a varied tapestry of opinions, values, hopes and dreams. It's hard to find consensus on many things – not impossible, but it's a challenge.

The ancient psalm with its sea-to-sea vision still stands as a challenging national dream. It is a kind of spiritual/social manifesto for the king, a prayer that the king (today we might say parliament or congress and the courts) would rule with justice, that people would enjoy prosperity, that children would thrive, that the weak and poor would not be marginalized, that agriculture and commerce would prosper, that international trade will flourish and the nation would be respected globally.

It envisions that the head of state will exert an influence as beneficial as rainfall watering the earth (verse 6). This echoes the thought in David's last song in 2 Samuel 23:4 about good leaders being like gleaming sunlight on fresh mown grass. What a dynamic vision of a government working hard in support of the best life has to offer. I don't think you'd have trouble finding agreement in any society around these goals, though you'd find differing suggestions, some passionately opposed to others, on how to go about achieving that vision. And I for one am happy to live in a nation with such divergent political perspectives, where there is freedom to express them boldly and pursue them with vigor.

There is one other plank in the spiritual/social manifesto of Psalm 72 that also deserves a shout-out – that across the land, from sea to sea, people would pray for their leaders and find reason to speak well of them (verse 15). Prayer is a way of uniting a nation from one border to the other, 'from Bonavista to Vancouver Island'[128] as Canadians say, coming together before God, asking for wisdom and courage and that the best of what makes us human will be protected and advanced in our day.

The Bible urges us to bathe leaders in prayer: "pray every way you know how ... especially for rulers and their governments to rule well so we can be quietly about our business" (1 Timothy 2:1-2 MSG).

Prayer enables us to participate in something beyond the borders of the nation. It engages us in the eternal reign of God – and that's something to celebrate every day of the year.

Prayer

Lord, let my prayers be coronation gifts to refresh and sustain the leaders you have appointed in my church, my community, my nation and world. Would you be in them a fountain of wisdom, a wellspring of hope, a stream of courage and creativity and life-giving purpose. And as I pray for them, let me find that same water springing up in my life. Amen.

Chapter 12
Prophets

12.1 The Big Elijah Rain Event

It had been a grim three years in Israel's northern region. Ahab was one of the bad kings – one of the worst. It was said that he "did more to provoke the LORD, the God of Israel, to anger than did all the kings of Israel before him" (1 Kings 16:33). One of his vices was his foreign wife Jezebel, daughter of the king of Sidon. She had a special fondness for the sexually explicit Baal cult which claimed that human orgies make for fertile field. Far and wide Ahab's people gave it a try. Jezebel's influence was pervasive; Asherah poles, Baal idols and hundreds of Baal priests filled the land.

So God sent the prophet Elijah with a message to Ahab: "as surely as the LORD, the God of Israel, lives – the God I serve – there will be no dew or rain during the next few years until I give the word!" (1 Kings 17:1 NLT) This was not good news. In that region of Israel rain is usually plentiful and agriculture flourishes. No rain or dew was a death sentence – for thousands of people. It was a serious ultimatum: abandon Baal worship or face catastrophic consequences.

If you were a nature worshipper in Ahab's day, you might have asked what the big deal was – what difference it makes whether you call the forces of nature Yahweh or Baal. Why not live and let live and let everyone practice their own spirituality according to their own inclinations?

It's a reasonable question for a twenty-first century reader. But, in fact, no one in ancient society would have asked such a question. Virtually all ancients assumed that they lived in a context of cosmic forces that could make life very bad for them if they violated the 'rules' that seemed very arbitrary. For this reason, socially approved norms – including religion – always trumped private inclination. Toleration of individual freedom in an area like religious practice would have been considered reckless and dangerous in a cosmic sense.

Nevertheless, on a global worldwide scale, tolerance was exactly the program God was carrying out. Nations and peoples were free to practice whatever religious and cultural norms emerged among them. What they sowed they reaped; they experienced the natural outcomes and consequences of their religion and ethics.

Israel was God's select group appointed to showcase to the world the social, cultural and economic benefits of following the way of Yahweh. But that experiment in comparative religions had been hijacked in Israel by the corrupt king and his foreign queen and their state sponsorship of the Baal cult – a form of religious practice that was rife with superstition, violence, sexual perversion and child sacrifice.[129] Yahweh's act of withdrawing the gifts of nature was a direct assault against the claims of Baal as the god of storm, rain and vegetation. It was designed to expose the barrenness (and the inherently destructive effects) of Baal-worship, to demonstrate Baal's impotence when Yahweh withholds the rain. Ahab refused to budge. He stubbornly stood his ground – and before long that ground was bone dry.

Elijah must have found it hard to step aside and leave the prophets of Baal to continue seducing the hearts of Israel away from Yahweh. But the nation was in God's hands and Elijah went into hiding in a ravine east of the Jordan where he was fed by ravens and drank from a brook flowing from the eastern hills. Soon, even that trickle dried up and Elijah had to move again. God sent him west to the coast, to Zarephath in Jezebel's home province, the heartland of Baal-worship, where he was public enemy number one.[130]

At Elijah's request, a woman in Zeraphath gave him hospitality even though she was both a foreigner and virtually destitute. But God supplied her needs – even resuscitating her son when he got sick and died. Elijah experienced the truth of Psalm 23:5 – God prepared a table before him in the presence of his enemies.

The drought grew more intolerable by the day. Streams ran dry; crops failed. The king was frantic for grazing land for his herds while peasants ached with hunger. Disaster stalked the land. Something had to break.

12.2 Showdown

In the third year of the drought, Elijah went to confront King Ahab. When they met, Ahab cursed Elijah. "You troublemaker" he sneered. "On the contrary", Elijah countered, "you and your family are Israel's troublemakers by abandoning the Lord's commands and following the Baals" (1 Kings 18:17-18 TNIV). Elijah called for a spiritual showdown on Mount Carmel, a sort of religious duel between Yahweh and Baal.

With a large crowd assembled from all over Israel, Elijah courageously faced down four hundred and fifty prophets of Baal. "How long will you waver between two opinions?" he challenged them. "If the LORD is God, follow him; but if Baal is God, follow him" (verse 20). Each side prepared bulls for sacrifice and competed to see which god could send lightening to ignite the sacrifice. All afternoon Elijah taunted the priests for Baal's failure to perform.

Finally, just to raise the bar impossibly high, Elijah had the Yahweh sacrifice drenched in water. Since the drought had been severe, this water was probably brought up from the sea. Then Elijah prayed, "O LORD, answer me, so these people will know that you are God, and that you are turning their hearts back again" (verse 37).

Then, as the Bible tells it, "the fire of the LORD fell and burned up the sacrifice, the wood, the stones and the soil, and also licked up the water in the trench. When all the people saw this, they fell prostrate and cried, The LORD – he is God! The LORD – he is God!" (1 Kings 18:38-9).

Elijah had the fraudulent priests rounded up and put to the sword. The influence of their vile practices was arrested for the moment and the nation had caught a glimpse of both Yahweh's power and Baal's impotence. Sadly, later kings adopted Baal worship again like an addiction, but for the moment, Yahweh was able to cut short the suffering of the drought.

Three years with no rain had left the land depleted and dry. Rain was desperately needed – and that was to be the next demonstration of the character of the true Rainmaker God. The showdown on Mount Carmel between Yahweh and Baal had confirmed which god deserved worship. Yahweh cared too much for the land and its people to leave the soil dusty and dead.

The sky did not look promising, but Elijah knew his God. He told Ahab that a major rainstorm was about to break. Why Elijah even gave this corrupt, spineless idolatrous king the time of day, I have no idea. Frankly, I'm baffled by God's patience and mercy towards him.

Elijah returned to the top of Carmel, bent to the ground and put his face between his knees and prayed for the desperately needed, long overdue rain. Later reflection on Elijah's life would focus on his being a model of perseverance in prayer (James 5:16-18).

Six times he sent his servant to look toward the sea for signs of rain, but each time the servant returned with the same message – 'nothing there'. But Elijah persevered, and the seventh time the servant reported, "a cloud as small as a man's hand is rising from the sea." That was all Elijah needed. "Go and tell Ahab, to hitch up his chariot and get home before the rain stops him," he said (1 Kings 18:44).

The sky grew black with clouds, the wind rose, and a heavy rain came on. The long wait was over; the drought was finished.

It's not apparent that Ahab learned anything about the extensive toll that moral and spiritual degeneracy takes on social, economic and environmental health of the land. But after three years Yahweh mercifully cut the suffering short.

> Mercy is falling is falling is falling
> Mercy it falls like a sweet spring rain[131].

The story closes with Elijah hiking up his pants and running for cover before the driving rains (verse 49). Or maybe he just ran in the rain for the sheer joy and relief of it all!

12.3 Salt of the Earth

Despite Elijah's public victory, Israel did not turf out the worship of Baal for another generation. New kings in turn took the place of Ahab, and a new prophet, Elisha, succeeded his mentor Elijah as the leading mouthpiece for God in the land. Many of the deeds of Elisha became legendary. These wonder stories of Elisha in 2 Kings 2-13, tell of Elisha's care for ordinary people. Four of them deserve our attention in a book about water.

A spring burbles to this day near the ancient ruins of Old Jericho, called Ain-es Sultan or Elisha's Fountain. The story associated with this spring is told in 2 Kings 2.

> The men of Jericho said to Elisha, "Look, our lord, this town is well situated, as you can see, but the water is bad and the land is unproductive." "Bring me a new bowl," he said, "and put salt in it." So they brought it to him. Then he went out to the spring and threw the salt into it, saying, "This is what the LORD says: 'I have healed this water. Never again will it cause death or make the land unproductive.'" And the water has remained wholesome to this day, according to the word Elisha had spoken.
> 2 Kings 2:19-22

This incident is so reminiscent of Moses' healing of the waters of Marah in Exodus 15:25, it is as though Elisha is demonstrating the ultimate prophetic credentials. Moses had promised that God would raise up another prophet like him – and the people had better listen carefully to him.

People everywhere depend on good sanitation and a consistent supply of clean water, but the citizens of Jericho had recently noticed their water becoming bad – really bad. Perhaps it just tasted bad, or perhaps people were getting sick. The fields had become less and less productive. All indicators pointed to the water, so they asked Elisha for help. Elisha poured a bowl of salt into the spring and announced that Yahweh had personally healed the waters. The proof was in the pudding – and wholesome water has flowed there ever since.

Interesting that Elisha credits God with the miracle, but used salt as an agent. We use salt in water softeners to replace calcium with sodium, but the problem in this town was not hard water. This water was contaminated. As my wife and her colleagues in hydrogeology know, the restoration of a contaminated aquifer normally takes a lot more than a bowl of salt. In fact, salt would be considered a contaminant. And there's lots of chemistry and technical know-how involved in the restoration, but when they get it right, remediation efforts are more than worthwhile. The outcome can have a transforming effect on a community. A prophet may use miraculous signs as the Chronicler tells us Elisha did, and a modern day hydrogeologist will use more technical methods, but both are doing the work of God in the world.

People who attend to a community's water supply, who work to resolve its problems and deficiencies and who safeguard this supply, are working as stewards of the earth and co-creators with God for the good of people. Their interventions make clean water flow and healthy communities and productivity possible. They belong to a noble profession with a good lineage!

But why did Elisha use salt? Perhaps because of salt's common usage as a preservative or disinfectant? Perhaps this story has more to teach us than just about clean water. Jesus describes his followers as salt agents in the world. "You're here to be salt-seasoning that brings out the God-flavors of this earth. If you lose your saltiness, how will people taste godliness?" (Matthew 5:13 MSG). Like Elisha and his fellow prophets in their superstitious world, we have a role to play in our world as agents of God. Perhaps some opportunity to bring the compassion and power of God to bear on a situation of human or environmental need is right under your nose. I wonder how God might want to use you today as an influence for good.

The next Elisha story displays the boundless generosity of God against a dark backdrop.

12.4 Thirsty in the Badlands

It was an ill-conceived military venture – Israel's kings marching out to exact revenge on their eastern neighbors, the Moabites, who had recently welched on their annual tribute obligations. This was economic thuggery, royal arrogance backed by military muscle and completely beyond the purposes of God. But this story in 2 Kings 3 showcases a God of grace who does far better for people than anyone deserves.

A seven-day roundabout march through the badlands south of the Dead Sea left the kings and their armies stranded at the frontier of Moab, without water. In desperation they consulted the prophet Elisha for an oracle from God. This is where the historian tips his hand. God was irrelevant to these kings until they get into trouble. Then they seek out Elisha as a kind of shaman who might magically help them through their dilemma.

The story becomes a kind of spiritual parable: their exhausted water supply mirrors the spiritual bankruptcy of these kings. Their leadership in Israel and the world is scandalous. Their militaristic adventurism is an ugly distortion of God's purpose for Israel, which was to be a light to the nations around them. And now they blame God for getting themselves into this mess.

God's grace shimmers and shines in this moral wasteland. Elisha chokes back his disdain and tells these God-disgracing kings to get shovels and carve out some space for God. "Fill the valley with trenches" he says, "and by morning they will be full of water. You are going to see the wonder of water where you least expect it – or deserve it. God will show up, not as a magic power, but as Israel's ultimate sustainer, providing water for you and your horses and all your provisioning livestock" (loosely paraphrased from 2 Kings 3:16-19).

So out into the searing sun they went, digging ditches in the bone-dry desert. And true to God's word, before morning, a flash flood filled the wadi and all the retaining ditches with water, saving the entire army. Not only that, but the Moab troops misinterpreted the red glint of the water in the sunrise and assumed their would-be attackers had massacred themselves; when they rushed in for the loot they were decimated.

I'm confounded by God's outrageous generosity to these self-serving kings. Water flows for the thirsty and the bloodthirsty alike. Even for people who are hellbent on folly, God often responds when they seek God's help. God meets us where we are. God's mercy creates space for us to learn God's ways. Those trenches of water glistening red in the sunrise illustrate the importance of making room for God in our lives, digging out resistance daily and creating receptive space even when we feel depleted and dry.

No matter how bleak and unpromising the landscape may be, God is capable of bringing transformation – and that is really Good News.

12.5 Naaman Takes the Plunge

Another foreigner who experienced God's transforming power through the hand of Elisha was the Syrian army general, Naaman, who suffered from a skin disease called leprosy.

A Jewish domestic maid lived in his home, an acquisition, we're told in *2 Kings 5*, from a recent raiding campaign south of the border. As she waited on Naaman's wife, she learned about the general's affliction and suggested a solution – the 'signs and wonders' miracle worker prophet in Samaria.

I love the political naïveté of this innocent young girl. A more cynical captive, might have thought, 'serves this imperialist right to have leprosy' or 'if this man were to show up in Samaria, the prophet would know he is our enemy and strike him blind or ignore his desperate plea'. But, no, this girl has a simple faith and a charming graciousness about her. She illustrates how God's people in exile, even nameless girls and women, can bless the nations and change the flow of history by their faith.

As general of the Syrian military, a big man in the echelons of Israel's eighth century enemy, Naaman was not enamored with the idea of going to Israel in search of a cure. But like many desperate pilgrims to Lourdes or the Ganges, the hot springs in Switzerland or the Mayo Clinic, he was willing to chase whatever offered the slightest glimmer of hope. When he arrived, Elisha told him to wash in the Jordan River seven times, and he would be healed. Naaman was offended. He wanted drama, lightning bolts from heaven befitting his noble standing, but all he got was the Jordan, a mediocre river, quite inferior to the rivers of his homeland. But in the end, through the urging of his servants, he humbled himself, plunged in, and the God of Israel healed him. His skin "became clean like that of a young boy" (2 Kings 5:14).

Eight or nine centuries later, Jesus cited this story in his sermon in Nazareth saying "there were many in Israel with leprosy in the time of Elisha the prophet, yet not one of them was cleansed--only Naaman the Syrian" (Luke 4:27) – a great Old Covenant illustration of God's lavish love flowing freely across borders.

12.6 The Floating Ax Head

The fourth story about Elisha stretches my credulity. The school of prophets which Elisha led was clearing trees in the Jordan River valley to build a larger place to live. Suddenly someone's ax head flew off and fell into the river. When a laborer loses a tool, it's bad, but even worse is losing a tool borrowed from someone else. So the poor man turned to the master and explained his plight.

The man of God asked, "Where did it fall?" When he showed him the place, Elisha cut a stick and threw it there, and made the iron float.

> "Lift it out," he said. Then the man reached out his hand and took it.
> 2 Kings 6:6

Is there anything this prophet can't do? Make iron float? My rational mind gropes for an explanation. Maybe Elisha thrust the pole into the water and was lucky enough to spear the ax head through the haft hole and lift it up. Why not? But I don't think that's what the text is intending to convey.

The story became legendary because something extraordinary happened, something not normally explainable. Iron by itself doesn't float on water, but somehow this iron came back to the surface. The narrator doesn't help us with an interpretation or lesson. He just tells the story of a poor, hardworking penniless religious worker – not the first or the last in history who couldn't afford to lose a borrowed tool – but who went to bed that night shaking his head at how God had somehow gotten him through his tough scrape.

These four Elisha water stories: the poisoned well, the ditches, Naaman, and the ax head, all illustrate both our need for water and the hazard that water can become. They all also point to a God who cares about people in crisis, little people and big, good people and bad, wealthy and poor. They show how God meets us not just in the sunshine seasons of life, but when we can't imagine how we will ever make it through.

We have no record of any sermons Elisha preached or prayers he prayed; his life story is a collection of deeds. He was a king-maker (2 Kings 9) and he responded to the plight of widows (2 Kings 4), but deep in his soul there was faith in a living God who could make a difference in ordinary people's lives. Perhaps that's one of the reasons the tide turned and the Baal cult was removed from Samaria in his day.[132] Somehow I think this is what the Chronicler of these stories wanted us to know.

When I read some of the other events the Chronicler recounts about Elisha's ministry, like raising to life a boy who had died of sunstroke (2 Kings 4:13-23), the amazing story of the ax head isn't so surprising.

12.7 Selling the Poor

A generation or so after Elisha, Amos was a rancher who thought hard and prayed hard. Ranchers generally take a pretty good read of the land – and when grazing lands grow dry they think hard about the implications.

In his day, two hundred years after David, Israel was a fractured nation, split into north and south. Both nations were prosperous; they practiced their religion with fervor and they credited God with their prosperity. But

Amos recognized that their religion had little effect on their ethics. While the wealthy were making money hand over fist, it was largely at the expense of the poor. They would "sell the needy for a pair of sandals" (Amos 2:6).

Exploitation justified in the name of religion, Eugene Peterson says, "is the most dangerous energy known to humankind."[133] Because the wealthy withheld justice, Yahweh withheld the rain.

Amos believed there was a connection between social ethics and climate change, between injustice and environmental disaster. Moses and Solomon had taught this in earlier generations. In our own century, Jared Diamond in *Guns, Germs and Steel,* and Ronald Wright in *A Short History of Progress,* both illustrate how the wellbeing of human societies and their land depends on restraint and respect. Unbridled greed, religious presumption and moral complacency inevitably lead to cultural and environmental disaster.

God wasn't about to let Israel self-destruct without warning. So his prophet Amos roared to the people of both north and south to repent of their callous indifference to the plight of their poor neighbors, to recognize that their religion was hypocrisy and a smear on the good name of God. He urged them to recognize the signs of their times, to see God's hand in the difficulties of their lives.

> "I gave you empty stomachs in every city
> and lack of bread in every town,
> yet you have not returned to me,"
> declares the LORD.
> "I also withheld rain from you
> when the harvest was still three months away.
> I sent rain on one town, but withheld it from another.
> One field had rain; another had none and dried up.
> People staggered from town to town for water
> but did not get enough to drink,
> Yet you have not returned to me," declares the LORD.
> Amos 4:6-8

Amos warned of worse judgments that would befall the land. He predicted earthquake and darkness – and, indeed, in June 763 BCE, an eclipse of the sun coincided with an earthquake, but even that brought no serious change of heart. Amos warned that the northern nation of Israel would fall to enemies and be sent into exile. But Israel's spiritual elite rejected Amos's warnings (Amos 7:12). Then Amos predicted a disaster of even more debilitating proportions – a famine, not of failed crops, but a spiritual famine.

12.8 Rock, Paper, Scissors

It's a game of trying to overpower your opponent, but you never quite know what form your opponent will take. Paper covers rock, scissors cut paper and rock breaks scissors. You just never know. But Isaiah knew how the powerful in his day were thinking. They were convinced that 'bigger was better' – and Isaiah could see that they were dead wrong.

In her superb book *Water Wars*, Diane Raines Ward shows how engineers, politicians and investors almost invariably choose massive, complex and expensive solutions to water management problems, rather than small, modest low-tech and low-cost solutions. Huge dams like the Hoover, Aswan or the gigantic Three Gorges Dam on the Yangtze are visually impressive; they cost billions of dollars to build and maintain, and they produce lots of electricity. They are designed to, and usually do, reduce destructive flooding downstream, but the cultural and environmental costs are enormous. Smaller, more modest schemes are available, but whether from hubris or the love of the challenge, the leaders in charge seem almost always to choose bigger.

Isaiah saw the same pattern in his day. The issue was not dams, but political allies. The powerful Assyrian empire loomed ominously on Israel's eastern horizon. Damascus and Samaria tried to force Jerusalem to join them in an anti-Assyrian alliance, but Isaiah urged Ahaz, Jerusalem's king, to trust Yahweh and not to rely on political alliances, especially with Rezin, King of Damascus and Pekah ben Remaliah, King of Israel.

In a vivid water metaphor, Isaiah prophesied how the Assyrians from Mesopotamia would sweep Israel away.

> Because this people [Israel's northern kingdom] has rejected the gently flowing waters of Shiloah [*i.e.* the spring waters of Jerusalem] and rejoices over Rezin and the son of Remaliah, therefore the Lord is about to bring against them the mighty flood waters of the River – the king of Assyria with all his pomp. It will overflow all its channels, run over all its banks and sweep on into Judah, swirling over it,

> passing through it and reaching up to the neck. Its outspread wings will cover the breadth of your land, O Immanuel!
> Isaiah 8:6-8

Isaiah called Judah 'Immanuel's land', because God was with them. 'Yahweh, our covenant God. is all the defense we need', he told them. But Ahaz lacked the courage or faith to trust God. He appealed directly to Assyria to come and save him (1 Kings 16:7). Isaiah foresaw the invading forces flooding right into the Judean heartland and up to the gates of Jerusalem.

Professor Alec Motyer in his commentary on Isaiah says

> The motif of the two rivers Shiloah (verse 6) and Euphrates (verse 7) offers a telling contrast between the seeming weakness of faith and the seeming power of the world. To the human eye the way of faith (Jerusalem and its vulnerable water supply) is full of insecurity and hazard, but the believer sees all this and says, 'He is faithful who has promised'(Hebrews 10:23). But to choose the world is to be overwhelmed by the world. [...] to choose a saviour other than the Lord is to find a destroyer, in some form or another.[134]

12.9 Storm Fury

Houses come in many styles and forms – hovels and mansions, temples and palaces. In affluent Samaria, a proud city on a hill, elegant homes crowned the hilltop like a beautiful garland. Chief among them was the magnificent palace of King Ahab (1 Kings 22:39). But Isaiah warned that without a moral foundation, both city and palace were doomed. Political alliances and religious pretence were futile defenses. God was about to send the powerful Assyrian army against Samaria; "like a mighty hailstorm and a torrential rain, they will burst upon it like a surging flood and smash it to the ground" (Isaiah 28:2).

Samaria's proud leaders scorned the Isaiah's warning as the ranting of a jealous southern prince. In reply Isaiah combined architectural and storm imagery:

> I will test you with the measuring line of justice
> and the plumb line of righteousness.
> Since your refuge is made of lies,
> a hailstorm will knock it down.
> Since it is made of deception,

> a flood will sweep it away. [...]
> When the terrible enemy sweeps through,
> you will be trampled into the ground.
> Again and again that flood will come,
> morning after morning,
> day and night,
> until you are carried away.
> Isaiah 28:17-19 NLT

In the midst of this storm, Isaiah sees God as architect of a new future. The plumb line of justice was a test Samaria failed which called for a sweeping away of moral debris and the erection of a cornerstone for a palace of righteousness:

> See, I'm laying a stone in Zion,
> a solid and tested foundation stone,
> a precious cornerstone.
> Adapted from Isaiah 28:16

Centuries later Peter interpreted this sound and solid foundation as the Messiah, Jesus himself who became the foundation of a new temple, which as Peter says, is comprised of every believer who anchors their life to Jesus (1 Peter 2:4-6). This is a spiritual house that will never be destroyed.

By contrast Samaria's foundation of moral deception was as unstable as sand. Enthusiasm without substance is hypocrisy; it's what we call 'living in denial'. As Socrates said at his trial, "the unexamined life is not worth living." Jesus said you can parrot words like 'Lord, Lord' all day long, but if you fail to live under his life-anchoring lordship, it is mere self-delusion.

Isaiah's doomsday warning against Samaria was fulfilled almost immediately. In 733 BCE, the Assyrian king Tiglath-Pileser captured Samaria and made it a vassal state (2 Kings 15:29). A decade later, in 721 BCE, a new Assyria king, Sargon II, decimated Samaria and deported more than 27,000 of its inhabitants to Assyria. Sargon rebuilt the city and populated it with refugees from other conquests (2 Kings 17:24).

A century after Isaiah, the prophet Ezekiel echoed Isaiah's storm imagery, ridiculing people who whitewash a flimsy wall in hopes that its superficial respectability will hold it up. But when torrential rain falls and hailstones are hurtling down and violent winds burst forth and the wall collapses, what's the good of the whitewash? (Ezekiel 13:10-15) I suspect that Jesus drew on both these faithful prophets when he told his parable of the wise and foolish builders (See Chapter 14.4).

Isaiah's earlier prophesy (Isaiah 8:6-8) about the Assyrian flood sweeping into Judah, occurred a few decades later in 688 BCE, when yet another king of Assyria was flexing his muscle. But first we need to look at the gentle waters of Shiloah at the beginning of Isaiah's words.

Prayer:
Living Christ, build your church around the world so it will withstand the onslaught of persecution. Help me to be authentic in my obedience and to be a faithful fellow builder with You. Amen.

12.10 The Gihon Spring

You would expect Jerusalem to be a dry city. With no river and very little rainfall how has it survived as a vital urban center for more than three millennia?

Since ancient times, Jerusalem has relied on two natural springs: En-Rogel in the Kidron Valley on the south side of the city, and the more important one, the Gihon spring on the east side of the hill of Jerusalem. The Gihon is a karst spring fed by groundwater that accumulates in a subterranean cave; whenever the space fills to the brim, it empties through cracks in the rock and is siphoned to the surface.[135]

Jerusalem's strategic advantage is its elevation, and getting the water up from the Gihon spring into the city has always been a challenge for Jerusalem both in peacetime and in war.

Early Bronze Age inhabitants of the city, perhaps 18th century BCE, before David captured Jerusalem, had widened a natural fissure in the rock into a shaft down to the spring. That structure is now called Warren's Shaft after Charles Warren, the British archaeologist who discovered it in 1867. The shaft is 6 feet (2m) wide and extends down 40 feet (12m) to the water surface of the pool. The top of the shaft opens to a horizontal tunnel that curves westward into the rock and gradually upward for 45 feet (14m) and then connects with a stepped tunnel up to the surface. Water carriers could descend from the city down to the top of the shaft and bring water up from the pool by buckets. Other cities in Israel such as Megiddo in the north had similar tunnels that were used for the same purpose.

Archaeology in 1961 confirmed that the ancient Jebusite inhabitants had enclosed the spring and its pool by building their city wall to encompass the spring. One popular theory, referencing 2 Samuel 5:6-9, says that David used this ancient water shaft to capture the city. However, there is evidence that the shaft was so heavily guarded by the Jebusites that, more likely, David captured the spring itself and forced the surrender of the city.

Before exploring the story of the Gihon further, I suggest that there is a life metaphor in this natural spring. I ask myself what springs irrigate my inner life? What are the sources of vitality that keep me alive on the inside? What threats make them vulnerable? What structures can I put in place to protect them?

During Solomon's reign in the ninth century BCE, another passage, the Siloam channel, was excavated, channeling Gihon water to the south of the city, but it was still outside the walls of the Jerusalem. Three centuries after Solomon, Jerusalem found itself in dire straits. The Assyrians, who had already defeated Israel's northern kingdom, were threatening the cities of Judah. King Hezekiah (715-687 BCE) understood that without a secure water source, Jerusalem could not withstand a long siege.

The Chronicler says that when Hezekiah saw that Sennacherib intended to make war on Jerusalem, "he consulted with his officials and military staff about blocking off the water from the springs outside the city. [...] A large force of men assembled, and they blocked all the springs and the stream that flowed through the land. "Why should the kings of Assyria come and find plenty of water?" they said (2 Chronicles 32:3-4).

So in 702 BCE, Hezekiah's engineers sealed the cave from which the waters of the Gihon flow so invaders could not access either the waters or the tunnel into the city. They also dug a new 600 yard (533m) long S-shaped tunnel to divert the water under the city into a pool they constructed at the south end in the lower city (2 Chronicles 32:.30).

Hezekiah was an activist. He proved his faith by his works, and his engineering initiatives helped save Jerusalem during Sennacherib's siege of the city. His entrepreneurship beautifully illustrates the necessary partnership between nature and human development. Nature provides springs, but engineers must cut tunnels and build infrastructure to move water to where it is needed. Every city, no matter how blessed it is with natural resources, needs both God's provision and human ingenuity working side by side. This partnership shows up in many areas of life where natural gifts must be supplemented by human effort.

Prayer:
God of groundwater, engineering and science, thank you for your lavish provision of water for our planet and for the consistent laws of nature which enable us to access it safely and easily. Forgive us for forgetting our responsibility to receive it as a gift, for failing to manage it with wisdom and moderation for ourselves, our neighbors and those who will inherit the planet after us. Remind us that what we do for you, we also do for them, and what we do for them, we also do for you. Amen.

Hezekiah's tunnel and the Siloam pool are still being used today. Tourists can walk the length of it and archeological excavations continue to uncover its marvels.[136] Centuries after Hezekiah, Jesus healed a blind man in Jerusalem by daubing his eyes with mud and sending him to wash in the pool of Siloam (John 9:6). We'll look at this story again in Chapter 14, but for now we note how it illustrates the blend of the human and the divine. God gives us revelation and sight, but God invites us, or rather requires us, to participate.

There is an art to stillness in life, being receptive and beholding with wonder and appreciation. There is another equally vital art, the art of initiative, the dynamic art of industry, strategy and technique, modifying things and achieving results. Civilization depends on both these arts. It is obvious in the field of water resource management – exploiting the supply, respecting its limits and ensuring its safety and replenishment for tomorrow. It takes a lot of wisdom to know which art to practice when.

Christian spirituality is rooted deeply in the free grace of God, the all-sufficiency of Jesus and the empowering of the Holy Spirit. Yet the Bible urges us to action, to "make every effort" to add virtues of character to our faith (2 Peter 1:3-5). Spiritual disciplines of engagement serve to stimulate and promote a healthy inner life; disciplines of abstinence help to curb the vices that easily pollute the spring within and rob us of joy and vitality.[137]

Like Hezekiah, we need to protect the wellspring of our lives if we want to sustain our souls. Because, let's face it, we're under siege every day. Forces and pressures around us will invade (or seep into) our hearts with greed, envy, discouragement, distorted vision and values, or just sheer fatigue. We have to protect the well. We need habits of the heart and of life that channel the water of the Spirit's spring to the quiet place where we can be nourished.

Church planter and consultant Jay Gurnett applies this insight to the tasks of evangelism. He notes the difference between natural meandering rivers and engineered canals and explores them as metaphors for two approaches in evangelism – things that we let just happen and things we initiate and intentionally organize in order to get the water of life out to the world. Prayer and planning, waiting and strategizing, faith and works – both are needed and both call for humility and wisdom.

Prayer:
Source of Living Water, help us to attend to the well within, to protect the wellspring of our hearts from which our words and attitudes flow, the decisions and actions that shape our character and the impact of our lives. Give us courage and creativity to join you in your initiatives and to initiate where you give us opportunity to bring your touch into our world. Amen.

12.11 One Foreign Well, Please

In his early years as king, Sennacherib built a palace in Nineveh that was, in his words, without rival. He built a stone lined canal and the world's first aqueduct to water his palace gardens, diverting water across a valley from a river 50 miles (80 kms) away.

With an effective military he sought to enforce his control of a far-flung empire, but the western frontier was proving restless. Sennacherib came west and thrashed Egypt for insubordination and captured scores of fortified towns in southern Israel. His siege of Lachish was celebrated in the famous Lachish reliefs, now on display in the British Museum.

Sennacherib accepted heavy tribute instead of surrender from Jerusalem's king Hezekiah (2 Kings 18:14-15). But a decade later, Hezekiah changed his mind and Sennacherib returned with a vengeance. In 688 BCE his army held the city of Jerusalem in a strangling siege. This was "the mighty flood waters of the River" that Isaiah had foreseen (Isaiah 8:7) that would almost drown Jerusalem.

Besides his state-of-the-art military, Sennacherib used a brazen propaganda campaign of taunts and threats to break the spirit of Jerusalem and her king, Hezekiah. Bragging about his far-flung exploits, he boasted that he could conquer any nation he targeted.

> I have dug wells in foreign lands
> and drunk the water there.
> With the soles of my feet
> I have dried up all the streams of Egypt.
> 2 Kings 19:24

Digging a well demonstrates control of the land (remember Abraham's argument in Genesis 21:30) – and Sennacherib regards the water resources of his vassal states as personal trophies, showing utter contempt for the people who depend on those wells and rivers.

Sennacherib never once imagined that Israel could keep its head above water or that Israel's God was tracking his every move and was about to crown his arrogant imperialism with humiliating defeat. The story is immortalized by Lord Byron's poem "The Destruction of Sennacherib":

> The Assyrian came down like the wolf on the fold,
> And his cohorts were gleaming in purple and gold.

Byron recounts how the whole formidable army, horses and riders, were struck down overnight as

> The Angel of Death spread his wings on the blast,
> And breathed in the face of the foe as he passed; . . .
> And the might of the Gentile, unsmote by the sword,
> Hath melted like snow in the glance of the Lord!

Sennacherib returned home to Nineveh a broken man and was assassinated by his son (2 Kings 19:36-37). Here was one foreign well the proud king failed to win. As both Old and New Testaments affirm, God opposes the proud, but gives grace to the humble (Proverbs 3:34 and 1 Peter 5:5).

By contrast, consider the international water passion of the American singing group Jars of Clay. They boast multiple platinum Grammy award winning songs and an international fan club, but they have leveraged their popularity to raise millions of dollars for wells in Africa to provide clean water to help combat HIV-AIDS.

Their "Blood:Mission" website and "Forty Days of Water"[138] are inspiring, and in May 2011 they celebrated the completion of 1000 wells in a blowout party called "Well: Done". I love it!

Capturing a well in a foreign country may feed a tyrant's ego, but helping to fund a well in a foreign land is a far more enduring way to build a personal legacy, advance God's shalom in the world, and promote international health and good will.

Prayer:
God, save us, the well-heeled and empowered of this world, from autonomy and pride. Help us learn humility and generosity by investing our capacity to provide water for those who need wells and whose pools and streams are undrinkable. Use such wells to make good neighbors across the world. Amen.

12.12 Jonah – Discovering God's Immensity

The strange story of Jonah is not just the tale of a runaway prophet and a very large fish. It is also an instructive parable with a provocative and global message.[139]

God refused to write off the city of Nineveh despite their vice and violence. God sent Jonah east to give them the word, but Jonah went west instead. He wasn't about to risk his life or reputation for such unworthy and improbable converts.

In truth, Jonah could see where God was going with this mission – and he refused to accept.

But God was relentless. The runaway preacher was plunged into a nightmare storm and then into the briny deep, tangled in seaweed and on the verge of drowning. Water is a good teacher, but God sent a fish to take Jonah even deeper. His three day confinement in the fish prison was a living death, a divine timeout so a willful child could realize the folly of his ways.

In a poem called "Reluctant Prophet" Luci Shaw notes that the fish was a more obedient and responsive servant than Jonah was:

> Both were dwellers
> in deep places (one

in the dark bowels
of ships and great fish
and wounded pride.
The other
in the silvery belly
of the seas.) Both
heard God saying
Go!
but the whale
did as he was told.
Luci Shaw[140]

Before Jonah could tell others about God, he first had to encounter his own defiance and ineptness as an ambassador of this God. He sank deep into the mire of religious pride and smug indifference to the brokenness of others. God let Jonah marinate (pun intended) in the stupidity of sin and the immense mercy of God. I wonder how long it took before he began to pray.

It was a severe mercy – and the story is only half done. The fish spat Jonah out and Jonah got a second chance to tell Nineveh about God. He saw them grasp mercy instead of death and he discovered depths to his own bitterness and resentment toward God.

Jonah's story is told with immensity – big storm, big sea, big fish, big city – all are immense! Jonah's folly, bigotry, terror, God's patience and mercy – also immense! It's a story about being engulfed by an infinite God whose love dwarfs our shallow imagination. When this God engages us as partners, it will shatter our pettiness; it will transform us and enlarge our horizon and our hearts.

I wonder how often my prejudice, fears and narrowness try to reduce God down to my scale? I wonder who I might be excluding from my world, who is already included in "for God so loved the world" (John 3:16).

No wonder Jesus used Jonah's story to illustrate his own mission in the world. It was the Ultimate Overwhelming! When Jesus carried out God's purpose of rescuing the nations and destroying death, there was no escaping the immense horror of the aloneness, the agony and the injustice of it.

But death did not undo him. Jesus overwhelmed Death, broke its tyranny over our race and transformed it into the doorway of Hope. Instead of judgment, we Ninevites got mercy, get mercy, and learn to give mercy. We Jonahs get grace and a second chance.

That's really immense!

Chapter 13
Exile

13.1 Lament

> Let your tears flow like a river day and night;
> give yourself no relief, your eyes no rest.
> Pour out your heart like water in the presence of the Lord.
> Lamentations 2:18-19

It was absolutely the darkest day in Israel's history – the ninth of Ab, in midsummer, 586 BCE. After an 18-month siege the invading Babylonian army had starved the people of Jerusalem almost to death. Finally the Babylonians breached the city walls, raped and terrorized the inhabitants, looted the temple, burned what remained of the city and smashed down the city walls. The king's sons were slaughtered before his eyes; then the invaders blinded him and led him off in shackles for execution in Babylon. 2 Kings 25 recounts the sad details.

Shock and shame overtook the nation; anger and bewilderment paralyzed them. God's covenant to protect them seemed a mockery. Later, in exile, survivors of this horrendous ordeal expressed their grief in an exquisite lament. Eight times in the course of the book of Lamentations, the poet or poets use water images to illustrate or describe their experience.

- their hearts are poured out like water – 2:11, 2:19.
- tears flow like a river – 2:18 and 3:48-49.
- their wound is as deep as the sea – 2:13.
- God's face is obscured like an overcast sky – 3:44.
- they're on the verge of drowning – 3:54.

- in disgrace they have to pay for drinking water – 5:4.

These metaphors are poignant and graphic. What measure better befits a nation's profound pain than the immeasurable depth of the sea? Where is the healer who can cure such a wound? The desperate fear of water 'closing in' over your head as you sink forever into the abyss, the anguish of feeling your heart and life draining away, of being poured out like a pitcher of water – these haunting descriptions capture the trauma the survivors knew all too well.

Perhaps such imagery helped them come to terms with their unspeakable experience. This was not just an exercise in morbid dirge writing. This lament helped keep alive the memory of the victims' and survivors' holocaust for their descendents, and they help us to grasp something of the horrendous suffering they endured.

We can imagine the disgrace of these prisoners-in-exile as they had to pay their captors for drinking water. Is there anything more degrading or demoralizing for a parent – in ancient or modern times – than to be too poor even to buy water for their children? Is there a more vivid symbol of powerlessness? Where was God during this ordeal? Perhaps the greatest pain of all was the sense that God had intentionally closed the door, hidden his face, wrapped himself in clouds so not a prayer could penetrate the overcast skies (Lamentations 3:44). Jesus was not the first to cry "My God, my God, why have you forsaken me?" (Matthew 27:46).

The two references to a river of tears (2:18 and 3:48-49) echo the words of the weeping prophet Jeremiah who wrote, "Oh, that my head were a spring of water and my eyes a fountain of tears! I would weep day and night for the slain of my people" (Jeremiah 9:1). Tears are a big theme in the Bible – over a hundred and ninety times we read of tears or weeping. Think of all the tears down through the history of the human race. In his book *The Jesus Way*, Eugene Peterson writes eloquently of all these tears,

> pooling into a great salt sea of sorrow: the tears of the tortured, the tears of the betrayed, the tears of the dying, the tears of the lonely, the tears of Rachel weeping for her children, the tears of [...] David weeping for Absalom, the tears of the Peter weeping outside the courts of Caiaphas, the tears of women on the Via Dolorosa, the tears of Jesus [...] Tears, tears, tears. We find ourselves swimming in

> a river of tears. […] every tear a prayer and not one unnoticed – "my tears are in your bottle" (Psalm 56:8).[141]

Jeremiah's tears and the Book of Lamentations foreshadow the heart-wrenching experience of Jesus six hundred years later. In fact, as Jesus entered Jerusalem for the last time, he seems to have entered imaginatively into this communal lament. Coming over the brow of the Mount of Olives and seeing the city that was about to reject and crucify him, and foreseeing its devastating overthrow by the Romans, Jesus wept over city, lamenting the suffering his people would once again experience (Luke 19:41).

It intrigues me that Jesus wept not for himself, but for his people. As happened a few weeks earlier at the grave of his friend Lazarus, Jesus' heart broke with compassion over the sorrow engulfing others. Perhaps this expression of empathy offers an answer to the haunting silence of the overcast heavens.

Where is God when it hurts? God walks incognito alongside the weeping victims in our violent world. He sits with the hungry and he suffers with those who cannot even buy water to assuage their thirst. He aches with their ocean-deep wounds. He is a man of sorrows, familiar with suffering and grief. In Jesus, we know for certain that God identifies with the brokenhearted. Because of him we can trust the promise that one day God will wipe away all tears from every face.

During a time of personal loss in my own life, someone gave me a copy of Nicholas Wolterstroff's *Lament for a Son*, written after the author's son died in a mountain-climbing accident. Wolterstorff writes,

> Through the prism of my tears I have seen a suffering God. It is said of God that no one can see his face and live. I always thought this meant that no one can see his splendor and live. A friend said perhaps this meant that no one could see his sorrow and live. Or perhaps his sorrow is his splendor."[142]

13.2 By the Rivers of Babylon

Israel's journey into exile brought them to the rivers of ancient Babylon, the mighty Tigris and Euphrates which define Mesopotamia, the huge fertile plain '*between the rivers*', one of the cradles of civilization. But despite its rivers of affluence and 'civilization', Israel experienced Babylon as a wasteland, a spiritual desert.

> By the rivers of Babylon we sat
> and wept when we remembered Zion.
> There on the poplars we hung our harps,
> for there our captors asked us for songs,
> our tormentors demanded songs of joy;
> they said, "Sing us one of the songs of Zion!"
> How can we sing the songs of the LORD while in a foreign land?
> Psalm 137:1-4

Psalm 137 describes the disorientation of Israel during the Exile. Israel asks "how can we sing the Lord's song in a strange land?" They're bereaved and confused. Babylon's armies had sacked Jerusalem mercilessly, captured her leading populace as trophies of war, and marched them to Babylon. No place could have felt more alien to the exiles than the banks of the Euphrates.

The memory of Zion, the city of spiritual shalom, brought them tears of homesickness and longing – and then of anger and revenge. Psalm 137 conveniently forgets Israel's own pattern of greed and injustice that had sold them down the river, the moral decadence and rampant injustice that led to the nation's collapse and exile (2 Chronicles 36:15-16). Nostalgia will do that, blurring the memory, but so does the ridicule of the arrogant and powerful.

Their Babylonian captors mocked the exiles, calling them to sing and dance the Hora, but jubilant songs are impossible when the spirit is crushed. So the poet weeps and asks God to do the remembering. "Remember, O LORD, what the Edomites did on the day Jerusalem fell" (verse 7). He asks God to remember the ferocious violence of the oppressors and to avenge the indignities of the prisoners. It identifies the cruelty that had been perpetrated against them and stands up in defiance of it and asks God to uphold their cause.

These ancient words have continued to serve Jews of the Diaspora down through time, camped beside other rivers and hearing the same taunts along the Volga during the Czar's pogroms of the nineteenth century and in the ghettos of Warsaw and Budapest in the mid-twentieth century.

Christians in the West today might well use this lament to express their bewilderment and sense of loss as they live as exiles in a post-Christian world facing similar disdain or ridicule for our faith. Psalm 137 voices the believer's sense of frustration with people's contempt for what we find precious. We wonder how we can sing the Lord's song in a foreign land. How can we gain respect among our tormenters?

Psalm 137 stands as part of the unfinished story of the Old Testament, awaiting the great dénouement revealed in the life of Jesus, the ultimate exile, who came to live along the banks of our spiritual Babylon. He is the one who teaches us a response of forgiveness that transcends the cry for justice of the exiles. He is also the one who validates this psalm, teaching both Israel and the Church that before we can forgive, we have to name evil for what it is.

As we noted earlier, there flows through our broken hurting world a wide river of tears: tears of regret, loss, loneliness, rejection, inequity, shame, homesickness, helplessness, confusion, injustice and despair. One reason psalms like this have endured is that they give voice to the tears, shed and unshed, in every generation.

Prayer:
Oh God of exiles, remember those who weep and comfort all who mourn. Through the presence of the exiled Christ bring freedom to all kinds of prisoners today. Amen.

13.3 Ezekiel at the Chebar River

Ezekiel was among the second wave of captives taken as prisoner of war to Babylon in the year 597 BCE. Daniel had been part of the first wave of prisoners eight years earlier in 605 and another wave was to come in another decade. Ezekiel had been trained as a priest, but the sacred temple in Jerusalem was left far behind, and a decade later when the final wave of exiles arrived in Babylon, they brought news of its scandalous desecration and destruction. But God used Ezekiel in a new way, to bring God's message to his people in exile.

As we've noted earlier, Babylon had lots of water. Ezekiel lived with other Jewish exiles in the vicinity of the Chebar (or Kebar) River, which is actually not a river, but a channel that flows out of the Euphrates near Babylon and returns to the river about 50 miles (80 km) further south. The Babylonians called it The Grand Canal. Nebuchadnezzar settled a colony of Jewish exiles on the banks of the Chebar, and archaeologists have found evidence of Jewish settlements at Nippur on the Chebar, but it is not clear whether Chebar was dug by the forced labor of the Jewish captives or not.

Eight times in his book, Ezekiel speaks of a vision he experienced by that river. He says that "the heavens were opened and I saw visions of God" (Ezekiel 1:1). What he actually saw looked like a storm cloud flashing with lightning, surrounded by a halo of brilliant light. In the centre he saw something that looked like four winged people, each with four faces – human, lion, ox and eagle. These creatures raced back and forth like lightning. Wheels sparkling like diamonds turned beside each creature as the foursome moved. Each wheel intersected with other wheels – like a gyroscope, wheels within wheels. The whole composite unit moved like a mobile platform, covered by an even more dazzling, shimmering dome. As it moved it reverberated like a pounding waterfall, "like the voice of the Almighty" (verse 24).

Above the dome was a throne, and sitting on the throne was a human-like figure blazing like molten metal rising out of fire. Ezekiel says that the whole effect struck him like the radiant brightness of a rainbow beaming through storm clouds on a rainy day. It was the glory of the Lord, and Ezekiel fell to his knees as he heard the voice of God speak to him. The Voice told him to stand to his feet. Then it commissioned him as prophet to his fellow exiles, to lead them out of their spiritual apathy and rebellion and to restore them to active trust in God despite their circumstances of exile.

What is most remarkable is that Ezekiel had these "visions of God" in such a place as this – at the river Chebar in the land of the Babylonians (Ezekiel 1:3). His compatriots were convinced that God's place of revelation was in the holy land, in Israel. But Ezekiel shows us that God is not border-bound. The river Chebar is as much hallowed ground as the Jordan River or the temple mount in Jerusalem.

Throughout his prophecy, Ezekiel returned to this vision. If God was able to reveal his glory through a storm cloud over the Chebar, it meant that God had not abandoned his people. God had stood with them in their shame and defeat, had travelled with them and was still actively their covenant God. He was now inviting his people to listen and begin their rehabilitation. Across the centuries this reminds us that no matter how badly we have failed, there is still hope. No matter how powerful the enemy is who opposes or belittles us, God is infinitely more powerful, like the roar of a waterfall. God is able to do, even in Babylon, things that will astonish both Israel and Babylon alike.

13.4 Drenched by Dew

Dew fell generously on the hanging gardens of Nebuchadnezzar. The emperor's palace and gardens were one of the wonders of the world and he took pride in his architectural achievements. But he was about to learn an important life lesson from the silent power of the dew.

As he tells his story in Daniel Chapter 4, Nebuchadnezzar was at home in his palace, prosperous and contented, when he had a dream that made him afraid. In fact, it terrified him. He dreamed of a magnificent tree cut down by a decree from heaven. The tree had a human mind, but it lost its sanity and lived for seven years exposed to the weather like an animal.

A palace advisor named Daniel interpreted the dream as a warning to the king,[143] and urged him to change his ways and begin to practice mercy and justice (4:27). But the king ignored Daniel's counsel until a year later when he was basking in his self-made grandeur – "Is not this the great Babylon I have built as the royal residence, by my mighty power and for the glory of my majesty?" (verse 30). The words were still on his lips when a voice from heaven announced that his warning time was up.

The proud king descended into a nightmare world of 'lycanthropy', a form of insanity where a person perceives himself to be an animal. Seven years the king lived this nightmare until eventually he regained his sanity and realized that God had humbled him and taught him that there is only one God – and it was not the king of Babylon.

Don't overlook the power of dew in this story. God uses the weak things of the world to shame the strong (1 Corinthians 1:27). Three times we hear of the king being 'drenched by dew': first in the dream, (Daniel 4:15), then in the interpretation in (verse 25), and again in the outcome (verse 33). The text says that the king was driven away from people and ate grass like cattle; his body was "drenched with the dew of heaven" until his sanity was restored. Three times (verse 15, 23, 25), always the same phrase, "drenched by the dew of heaven."

In the Bible, dew is almost universally a gift of life, one of the great silent blessings of nature in an arid world. But when the king lost the roof over his head and was exposed to the elements, the dew displaced his dignity. The story does not say that he was assaulted by wind and storm or even soaked by the dew of the ground. He was "drenched by the dew of heaven", as if God was pouring on him the kindness of a stern wake-up call. This threefold reference to heaven's drenching dew trumpets what the New Testament calls "the kindness and sternness of God" (Romans 11:32).

This pagan king who desecrated God's temple in Jerusalem and dragged Israel's finest citizens off in chains; this arrogant overlord who esteemed himself a self-made god, became the recipient of God's severe mercy, drenched by it, soaked in it until it seeped through his tough leathered pride and made him human again. Calvin says, "his deformity was so horrifying that his restitution could well be called a new creation."[144] He lived to thank God and gave testimony to the world of his recovery: 'Hi, my name is Nebuchadnezzar and I'm a recovering megalomaniac, a 'self-oholic'. Let me tell you about my higher power who is the ultimate authority in the world, and relentlessly a God of justice and mercy, a God of new beginnings.' That's a paraphrase; you can read the official text in Daniel 4:34-37.

This story reminds us that even while God's people were in exile, in the worst of times and the worst of places, God was still very much at work in the world, even in Babylon, behind the scenes, doing what others could not see. It reminds us that no one is beyond God's sphere of interest or redemption, not even the most arrogant and unlikely of respondents. And it shows how God can use his faithful servants like Daniel to influence the lives of the CEO's they report to.

13.5 New World Comin'

Ezekiel's message to the exiles of Israel closes with a stirring promise that there was a new world on the horizon. There in Israel's dark ordeal, in exile far from their homeland, the prophet to the exiles had a vision of history's ultimate outcome. He imagined himself touring the temple in Jerusalem. A river flowed from the temple of God across the desert hills towards the Jordan valley. An angel helped him to make sense of what he saw:

> This river flows east through the desert into the valley of the Dead Sea. The waters of this stream will make the salty waters of the Dead Sea fresh and pure. There will be swarms of living things wherever

> the water of this river flows. Fish will abound in the Dead Sea, for its waters will become fresh. Life will flourish wherever this water flows. . . .Fruit trees of all kinds will grow along both sides of the river. The leaves of these trees will never turn brown and fall, and there will always be fruit on their branches. There will be a new crop every month, for they are watered by the river flowing from the Temple. The fruit will be for food and the leaves for healing.
> Ezekiel 47:8-12 NLT

Talk about a transformation! Anyone who has visited the Dead Sea or seen photos of the region can hardly imagine such a reversal of the environment – the waste and barren landscape bursting with fishing and agriculture. It would be like discovering a rain forest on the moon.[145]

We can imagine Ezekiel telling this vision to his fellow exiles in Babylon. They probably took his parable as a promise that their Babylonian desert experience would soon be reversed and that they would be going home.

Yes, that was part of the meaning behind Ezekiel's vision, but I think just a small part. History tells us that against all odds Israel did return home, but the Dead Sea remained salty, and the religious life of Israel, though purged of fertility gods, became as sterile as before with even more exacting gods of religious purity, elitism and pride.

Meanwhile that life-giving river had a much bigger story to tell, a story that includes a Messiah who came to live in the desert and to change it into a place of life and joy, a river of vitality and hope that flows out of his death and resurrection. When that river flows through people and communities, they flourish and become a foretaste of the new creation transforming the old. Through Jesus, the entire creation is in for a makeover. 'Creation longs for what's in store.'[146]

The narrative of the Old Testament tells its own story and points ahead to the New. The story continues: decay and redemption continue to compete in lively deadly combat. The river of God's grace through Israel is about to widen and flow out into the whole world. That new chapter is what we move on to next.

Chapter 14
Living Water

14.1 Taking the Plunge

He is known everywhere simply as John the Baptizer. Each of the four Gospels tells us about this strange prophet who heralded the coming of God's new era by urging his people to get right with God and to make their action decisive in a ritual washing of repentance.

Religions all over the world and all through history have practiced ritual washing (and we'll look at this practice at in more detail in Chapter 21). Israel was no exception. Eight hundred years before John, the leprosy-scarred Syrian general Naaman was 'cleansed' and healed from his disease after a seven-plunge baptism in the Jordan River, a story that illustrates both the mercy of God and the prerequisite of humility before the blessings of transformation can flow into our lives.

John the Baptist called Israel to a similar humbling, a humbling of national repentance from a lifestyle that had become more pagan than covenantal. Baptism is a confession of need, an act of abandoning yourself to the water and embracing the purity, healing and renewal that the water represents. It calls for courage and resolve. Baptism says, 'forget decorum, to hell with face-saving, a new life beckons, it's time to answer the call'. Just as Elisha did with Naaman, John the Baptist called Israel to return to their spiritual entry point at the Jordan and to wash away their sins.

Jesus joined the crowds who heeded the words of John. It wasn't that he had personal sins to confess, but he chose to 'number himself with the transgressors', as Isaiah expressed it centuries before (Isaiah 53:12), to confess his love for God and his solidarity with Israel, to stand with a nation that needed to repent. Down to the Jordan he went, into the waters of death, the waters of judgment and mercy, drenched in obedience and sacrifice.

Here was the True Israel, giving himself for God's sake on behalf of others. As Jesus came up out of the river, foreshadowing his own future resurrection, the heavens seemed to split open. God's Spirit descended dovelike, and the Father's voice spoke, announcing that in this act of Jesus, God was plunging into the affairs of earth and that God couldn't be happier. The kingdom of God on earth was being unveiled.

This symbolic act of baptism launched Jesus on a journey to Jerusalem and eventual confrontation with the powers of darkness. His baptism prefigured his death and resurrection, the historic event from which a new humanity was born.

As the Anglican Prayer Book says, "to be a Christian is to be part of a new creation which rises from the dark waters of Christ's death into the dawn of his risen life. Christians are not just baptized individuals; they are a new humanity."[147]

That is why Jesus took the plunge. This is the great community we join and the great adventure we plunge into when we resolve to follow him. This is the great joy we miss when we plunge into lesser things. Baptism launches you into a new way of life.

14.2 New Birth

The Voyage of the Dawn Treader is the most water drenched of all C. S. Lewis' Narnia stories.

It tells about an obnoxious young boy named Eustace who took refuge from a rainstorm in a cave that turned out to be a dragon's lair. In the dim light of the cave he discovered hoards of gold, silver and jewelry. He filled his pockets and slipped a magnificent bracelet on his arm – and then fell asleep.

When he awoke, his arm throbbed because it had grown larger overnight and was covered with reptilian scales. Having fallen asleep "with greedy dragonish thoughts in his heart, he had become a dragon himself."[148] Greed will do that to you, I've learned. And as Eustace discovered, it is not that simple to shed our scales and become human again.

Eustace lived in this wretched state for days, aching for relief. Eventually a huge lion named Aslan found him and led him to a well of water – a large well, more like "a very big, round bath with marble steps going down into it."

As Eustace approached the pool for relief, the lion told him he had to undress first. So Eustace scraped off some of his dragon scales, only to discover more scales below. The more he scraped, the more he discovered layers of dragon skin below. Over and over he scraped at his hide to no avail. (I know that experience, too – the more you try to improve yourself, the more deeply ingrained your old ways seem to be.)

Eventually the lion told him, "you will have to let me undress you." Eustace cringed at the sight and touch of Aslan's claws which cut deep and peeled him like a willow branch. Aslan threw Eustace into the water which stung fiercely for a moment – until the refreshing coolness of the water soothed him because he had "turned into a boy again." He swam and splashed in the relief and joy of the healing waters.

That is the revolution expressed in the Christian ritual of baptism. It is a symbolic bath – a radical cleansing of our deepest self, washing away the moral grime of sin and greed and pride. It is a purging of the distorted identity that we adopt and hold on to as we organize our lives without God.[149]

In her book *Traveling Mercies*, Anne Lamott says, "most of what we do in worldly life is geared towards our staying dry, looking good, not going under. But in baptism, in lakes and rain and tanks and fonts, you agree to do something that's a little sloppy because at the same time it's also holy, and absurd. It's about surrender, giving in to all those things we can't control; it's a willingness to let go of balance and decorum and *get drenched*."[150] In the Christian experience of baptism, she says, you go under and come out maybe a little disoriented, but you know now that a new day is upon you.

Baptism expresses a desire to let Jesus do a clean-up job on us. And when Jesus cleanses us he doesn't just shiny up the broken, twisted distortions of our character, he does a deep radical makeover. He transforms our beastliness and humanizes us more deeply than we ever imagined possible – or necessary. He recreates us, renews us.

You might say we become born again. Plunging into water takes only moments; the transformation reveals its secrets over months and years. This is no doubt the truth Jesus had in mind when he told Nicodemus, "unless you are born of water and the Spirit, you cannot enter the Kingdom of God" (John 3:5). Nicodemus was well-taught in the ancient prophets. He would have recognized Jesus' allusion to the deep personal and national renewal God had promised in Ezekiel 36:

> I will sprinkle clean water on you, and you will be clean; I will cleanse you from all your impurities and from all your idols. I will give you a new heart and put a new spirit in you; I will remove from you your heart of stone and give you a heart of flesh. And I will put my Spirit in you and move you to follow my decrees and be careful to keep my laws.
> Ezekiel 36:25-27

14.3 Water Into Fine Wine

The week before visiting our local 'Make Your Own Wine' store, my wife and I spent hours scouring and cleaning a case full of old wine bottles in preparation for filling them. Water is a great cleaning agent, but water also has nobler roles, such as in the making of fine wine.

Winemaking is the first story in John's Gospel (Chapter 2) to introduce us to the amazing transformative work of Jesus.

It began as a wedding host's worst nightmare – and a bad omen for the marriage. At midpoint in a wedding reception, the wine ran out. The celebration sagged and the guests would soon have started leaving. It smacked of bad planning, embarrassing poverty or, worse, shabby hospitality.

Enter the mystery guest. Without fanfare, almost before anyone knew what had happened, Jesus replenished the depleted store of wine -- and not just one small glass per person! Jesus used the water of six very large (20-30 gallon/100-litre) stone jars. By our measure, that's 800 bottles of premium vintage wine.

The party really reignited when guests discovered that the new wine was much better than the earlier stuff. Dancing resumed and the bridegroom was the toast of the hall for saving the best wine for the finale, and for bringing out such a bountiful supply that everyone stayed on for a good long time.

No wonder the disciples said that they glimpsed the glory of God that day in Jesus. There for all who had eyes to see, Jesus embodied the generosity of God, the anonymity of God and God's penchant for transforming the ordinary into glory.

Jesus revealed the wonder of water – and of all created things. He didn't pull a rabbit out of a hat; he started with *water*. That's how the real world works. Everyday in gardens and vineyards around the world nature turns rainwater into grape juice, and vintners know how to turn that juice into fine delicate wines. With the Creator's prowess, Jesus compressed the natural process into nanoseconds. Water into wine – the miracle in the ordinary!

How fitting to do this at a wedding, because in almost every marriage eventually the wine runs out. Jesus came to enter our ordinary lives as living water, to transform our disappointment and poverty and embarrassments into glory and lasting joy, to fill our ordinary days with wonder!

Someone has said that Jesus "takes displaced, discouraged children and makes us Kings and Queens of Narnia. Then he invites us to open our eyes to the impossible, the unimaginable, and participate with him in his work in the world."[151]

Wine is a sign of God's presence in our everyday world in the presence of Jesus. Lifting a cup of gratitude in his name becomes a foretaste of the day when all our disappointments will shine with glory and "all our ecstasies and intimacies will be in God" (Matthew 22:30 MSG).

Prayer:
Jesus, the same way you participated in that wedding, I long for you to participate in my life. I don't want a stand-aloof God or a magician, but someone to turn the water of my life into sparkling wine. I welcome you to do this in me. Let me catch glimpses of your glory in the ordinary things of this day. Amen.

14.4 Advice from a Carpenter

Since 1994, the Darwin Awards have held up a mirror to human folly. Their tongue-in-cheek books and website[152] tell true stories of people who, as they say, 'live in the shallow end of the gene pool', people who 'show an astounding lack of judgment and cause their own demise'. 'Terminal stupidity' they call it, with lethal personal consequences. They cite these stories not to laugh at calamity, but as cautionary tales.

Jesus used a different metaphor in his story about the foolish carpenter and the raging river, but his insight into disastrous human stupidity is just as clear. As a carpenter Jesus knew the consequences of shoddy house building. He probably knew peasants in the hills around Nazareth who skimped on the foundations of hasty summer-built houses only to see their investment collapse in ruins when the winter rains fell and the wadis swelled with torrential floods that tore the earth away from their doorsteps.

So Jesus told a story about two builders. One built wisely, anchoring his house to bedrock. The other was a moron – yes, that is Jesus' exact word. Only a moron builds a house and ignores the foundation, because when raging water hits soft earth, a house had better have a solid underpinning or it will collapse like a sandcastle.

This 'cautionary tale' works because life storms happen to everyone. Misfortune rains down, sickness clobbers us, financial loss and broken friendships mock our well crafted stability; 'tsunamis of the soul' rock our world, often when we're least prepared. And never far away lurks the dark spectre of Death. Jesus was right. Storms happen; the river is rising as we speak. Is your foundation up to the test?

Jesus included in his story practical, down-to-earth directions for a well founded life. It wasn't a curriculum of religious rituals or secret mantras, but a way of life patterned after his own that can withstand the rigors of the storm. "Everyone who hears these words of mine and puts them into practice is like a wise man who built his house on the rock" (Matthew 7:24).

According to Jesus, the Darwin Award goes to men and women who hear his counsel for life but never put it into practice. They might even teach bible studies, but as the old Irish proverb says, "Nodding the head does not row the boat." A newer proverb says, "Just do it!" Dallas Willard urges us to 'apprentice ourselves to Jesus', actively doing what Jesus says. There's no greater tragedy in life, no greater folly, than walking away from Jesus.

When an earnest rich young seeker asked how he might inherit eternal life, Jesus told him to offload his extensive financial safety net, give it to the poor and then join Jesus in faith and service to God (Matthew 19:21). Ironically this upwardly mobile entrepreneur opted instead to build his life on the sand of his material wealth. We never hear from him again.

There was also a national horizon to Jesus' parable of the builders. Religious observance was a core feature of first century Jewish life. The Temple and the many practices associated with it were considered a rock solid tradition of moral and ethical virtue. Jesus saw through the pious façade of temple ritualism, its hypocrisy parading as love for God. He warned his listeners not to build their lives on these hollow traditions.

Eventually he took a whip to the mercenary practices of temple worship, and he warned everyone that the Temple's days were numbered, that it was sick beyond healing and ripe for judgment – for what Isaiah had called "an overwhelming scourge" (Isaiah 28:15-19). The temple was a house built on sand, doomed to be swept away within a generation. Jesus was actually retelling a story told by Isaiah 600 years earlier in Isaiah 28:15-19, warning Israel about her religious hypocrisy.

When you build the teachings of Jesus into the foundation of your life, you find yourself with a vibrant heart for God and neighbor, a grace that can forgive because it knows the joy of being forgiven. Other habits of the heart emerge with spiritual empowerment that stabilize you in the day of calamity and upheaval. We have Jesus' own assurance that we will survive the ultimate test of existence, the scrutiny and judgment of God.

Prayer:
Lord of down-to-earth spirituality, whenever I retreat into imagining that my beliefs are my reality, give my foundations a shake. Remind me that superficial discipleship will collapse. Help me to build my life consistently on the pattern of Jesus. Amen.

14.5 Healing Waters

Helen Keller was only seven years old, blind, deaf and without speech, when her teacher, Anne Sullivan, ran cool running water over one of Helen's hands while making motions on the palm of her other hand. That tangible lesson with water was the breakthrough moment, after a long frustrating isolation. It revealed to Helen the symbolism of words and opened up her ability to learn and to communicate with the outside world.

Jesus used water in a similar way in the remarkable healing of a man in Jerusalem who had been born blind (John 9). While others used him as a case study for the problem of suffering and sin, Jesus went to work on his healing.

> Jesus spit on the ground, made mud with the saliva, and spread the mud over the blind man's eyes. He told him, "Go wash yourself in

> the pool of Siloam" (Siloam means "sent"). So the man went and washed and came back seeing!
>
> When asked how this had happened, he replied, "The man they call Jesus made some mud and spread it on my eyes and told me 'Go to the pool of Siloam and wash yourself. So I went and washed, and now I could see."
> (John 9:6-7, 11 NLT)

We might wonder why Jesus didn't heal this man the way he healed other blind beggars, simply by the power of his word. Why use saliva and a plaster of mud and require him to go and wash?

Spitting in someone's face is a sign of vile contempt and, no doubt, like many beggars, this blind man had endured such insult from passersby. But Jesus, on at least two other occasions, used saliva as he healed people – a deaf mute in Decapolis (Mark 7:33) and a blind man in the Galilee area (Mark 8:23). With Jesus, it wasn't contempt, but compassion. These people had special needs, so Jesus spat on the ground and used his saliva as well as his touch and voice as a way to connect more deeply, intimately with them.

But why send the man with muddy face, groping his way to a public pool to wash?

The clue lies in the name of the pool – Siloam – which, we're told, means 'Sent', a name with a double meaning. First, the water originated from the Gihon spring on the east side of the city and was diverted or 'sent' by tunnel to the rock hewn pool inside the south walls of the city. Second, like all water, it was sent ultimately from the Creator for the blessing of the world.

In the same way, Jesus was sent from God to open the eyes of the blind, both the physically and spiritually blind. By sending the man to the pool Jesus drew attention to God's sending. The waters of Siloam didn't wash away this man's blindness any more than magical powers of Jesus' saliva did. Jesus used the elements of the natural world along with the man's faith to reveal the power of the Creator and to bring the gifts of heaven to earth.

John uses this story to show that Jesus is ultimately the light and life of the world. We are easily blinded by our gifts of sight and self-confidence and certainty; we are often unaware of how proud and wrong we are. Like

Helen Keller and the blind man in this story, we need someone to bring us the insight to help us connect reality with truth. This story shows us that the only way to correct our spiritual vision is through Jesus.

14.6 The Story of Grace Jacobson

"You never know who you'll meet at the water cooler.

I'd never seen him before. We could have been any two thirsty people coming for a drink. How could he have known that behind my mask I was forever searching for love in all the wrong places? Five times my dowry returned, I'd forgotten who I really am. I'd given up the formalities, and even worse, the hope of every finding my true love – or my true self. I came at noon to avoid the whispers of the gossips.

I could see right away that he was a Jew, and I braced for the sting of his slur. But he merely asked for a drink. "What, no racist epithet?" I asked. But he simply said that God is generous and that if I knew who was talking to me and asked him for a drink, he'd be more than willing to give me a drink. I stared at him. How he thought he'd collect water with his bare hands I had no idea.

I asked him if he thought he was better than old Yakov who gave us this water that has served our village and my ancestors for these past 18 centuries. (Isn't it great when you come up with the perfect comeback?)

"Oh," says he, "Yakov's water is fine as long as it lasts, but my water will satisfy your thirst the rest of your life. The water I give you will be an artesian spring within, gushing fountains of endless life."

Now he was talking my language. I didn't know if he meant solving my never-ending trips to fetch water or if he meant that other thirst that runs way deeper than the throat, deep down inside where your soul aches and sadness turns to sobbing sometimes. But I could use an 'artesian spring within'.

"I'd go for some of that," I said. "I'd love to never have to come back here for water." Then without even looking up he said it. I should have seen it coming, but I was so used to hiding my scars. He told me to bring my husband.

"Sorry, not married," I told him, but he just nodded and started reciting my marriage resumé back to me – the entire saga of my nightmare. Busted!

I had nowhere to hide. But I wasn't ready to surrender. So I asked him a question about religion. That's usually a safe place to hide your true heart. It makes you feel like you're being virtuous while you avoid being real.

He just said "you've been waiting forever for this moment, and it's finally come, when what you're called doesn't matter and where you worship doesn't either. It's who you are and the way you live that count before God." He said that God is a Father who is looking for people who are simply and honestly themselves before him in their worship.

Where he got all that from, I had no idea, but I told him that I would wait 'til the Messiah came and sorted everything out. To which he said *"I am He"*. That was it. *"I am He."*

I was completely overwhelmed – confused – elated and afraid all at the same time. I ran back to town – even left my pitcher behind. I had to tell the others about him. He found the woman behind the mask and offered me living water. How could he have known? He put his finger on the deepest pain in my life. He exposed my fear of being found out and my aching desire to be truly found.

He stayed with us for two days and we got to know him a lot better. And what he promised has been so true. He quenched that deep thirst inside me; he is a living spring of water in the very core of my being day after day. As a triple outsider – as a Samaritan, a woman and with a string of failed marriages behind me, he was the generosity of God to me."

You may have guessed that the name Grace Jacobson is a contrivance. Hearing her story in the first person helps us feel the intimacy of her encounter with Jesus recorded in John's Gospel, Chapter 4. As a descendent of the patriarch Jacob and one who drank deeply of God's grace, Grace Jacobson could well be her name. It is obvious that God's lavish and indiscriminate love flowed deep in Jacob's extended family. It flows just as deep in my family, and in yours.

14.7 Thirst-Quencher

One of the all-time high-water marks of the Bible's witness to water and the grace of God happened during the annual Jewish Festival of Tabernacles. This late summer festival looked back in history to Israel's exodus and God's provision of water in the desert, and it looked ahead to the dream of Israel's restored honor among the nations as predicted in Zechariah 14:16. Every year pilgrims came to Jerusalem from every direction in what Josephus called "a most holy and most eminent feast."[153]

Every day during this eight day festival, priests marched in solemn procession carrying water from the Pool of Siloam up to the temple and pouring it out at the base of the altar in remembrance of God's gift of water from the rock in the desert. On the highest day of the festival, the high priest poured out the water with a special prayer for rain, since the autumn rains are desperately needed to soften the soil for fall planting.

This water ceremony also recalled Zechariah's tantalizing prophecy that "living water will flow out from Jerusalem" (Zechariah 14:8) and "a fountain will be opened to [...] the inhabitants of Jerusalem" (Zechariah 13:1). The prophets Joel and Isaiah had made similar prophecies about life-giving rivers of blessing that will flow among God's people, depicting the abundance of God's salvation, forgiving sins and healing the scars of sin and misery. This was all implicit in the ritual that evolved for the Feast of Tabernacles.

Throughout the centuries people in every culture have created rituals and practices that respond to the thirst in their parched souls. Western consumer culture works as hard as any other to quench this inner thirst, just as the temple-obsessed Jews of the first century did. Where I live in Kitchener-Waterloo, Ontario, we celebrate Oktoberfest – surpassed only by Munich as the largest beer-fest in the world. Ostensibly Oktoberfest is a kind of German-Canadian harvest festival that indulges the desire to drink cheerfully and with impunity. Such is the spirit of the event. The reality is not always as jovial or innocent.

Jesus was deeply moved that year as he watched the water ritual unfold, knowing that he himself was God's gift of living water sent from heaven to quench our thirst. He held back until he could restrain himself no longer. Then he shouted at the top of his voice, "anyone who is thirsty, come to me and drink!" (John 7:37-38).

It sounds completely audacious that someone would claim that he personally is the answer to every human being's inner thirst. Audacious, yes, but through the centuries, millions have come to him and found his promise completely true. Ask Grace Jacobson, ask the former blind man dancing his way back from Siloam, ask the scarlet woman in this next story. Oh, yes, they'll tell you, Jesus is the great thirst quencher the whole world has been waiting for!

14.8 Tears of Joy

Here is a story for Valentine's Day, a story of great love and deep gratitude and the most exquisite water we know.

She was a woman who got invited to men's homes for only one reason. But she heard about another man who was different, a giver not a taker. He himself had a reputation for socializing with people like her and maybe she had met him somewhere – maybe overheard him telling another harlot that God heals the brokenhearted, washes away tears of shame and forgives debts long overdue.

How could she know for sure if this were true? And if true, how could she honor him, this man who looked past disgrace and saw worth in people that others couldn't see? How could she express the gratitude and affection welling up inside her?

She made her way to a dinner where he was the guest of honor. She stood behind him as he reclined at the table and she lost all composure. Her salt tears fell on him like rain and she bathed his feet with adoration. She kissed his feet and dried them with her hair and poured perfume over them. She could not contain her overflowing joy and gratefulness.

Jesus understood and explained to his host, "her many sins have been forgiven – that is why she shows such love. Those who have been forgiven deeply, love deeply, but those who are untouched by grace rarely feel gratitude" (paraphrased from Luke 7:47).

I think tears are the most exquisite form of water in human experience. We see them again in the most compact gem in the Gospel – "Jesus wept" (John 11:35). The Bible has 150 references to tears and weeping – tears of grief, sadness, shame and regret. But this is the only story I can recall about tears of gratitude and joy. Someone has said, "Our tears are sacred. They water the ground around our feet so that new things can grow."[154]

God's mercy to us is an undeserved feast – and Jesus is the host. Pondering this story makes me want to sit down and watch *Babette's Feast* again. If you're not familiar with this story, get yourself a copy of the book or movie.[155] Set in the rugged barren coast of Jutland, it shows how extravagant grace causes new things to grow. A small austere Lutheran flock experiences a gourmet dinner so exquisite they can hardly absorb it. They steel themselves against its intoxicating flavors and lavish abundance. But the generosity of the experience melts them; grace overwhelms them and begins to heal the resentments among them. The feast becomes an unexpected undeserved foretaste of heaven.

Prayer:
God of Amazing Grace, flood my heart with the tears Jesus wept over my brokenness. Let me know how deeply I have been loved and forgiven. Soften my heart, heal my wounds and clear away my dullness. Set my spirit free and release in me a river flow of joy and thankfulness. Amen.

Chapter 15
Working with Fishermen

In the pages of the four gospels we read about Jesus touching the lives of many people. Twelve men in particular spent an extraordinary amount of time with him. He invested his life in them and modeled before them what a God-energized life looked like up close and personal. These men came from various walks of life, but at least a third of them were fishermen. As a result, quite a number of their shared experiences happened in and around water.

15.1 Deep Sea Fishing

It was Simon's lucky day – but it hadn't started out that way (Luke 5:2-10). After a fruitless night of fishing, he had come home with an empty boat. For a professional fisherman that spelled failure, frustration, no income and the added burden of having to clean and repair your gear in hopes of a better outing tomorrow.

Simon had beached his boat and began untangling his twisted nets. The young rabbi Jesus, who a few weeks earlier had invited Simon to become his protégé, was talking with people on the beach. The crowd grew until Jesus was getting squeezed into the water. He climbed onto the prow of Simon's boat and asked him to anchor a few feet off-shore so he could better address the crowd.

As Simon worked on his frayed nets and frazzled nerves, Jesus talked about a new kind of world where justice and compassion thrived, a world where truth and honesty reigned and fear and greed were things of the past. He called it the reign of God, where the poor were no longer exploited, where neighbor watched out for neighbor and husbands were true to their wives, and where prayer was more like a heart-to-heart with God than a pious religious thing.

Simon watched people along the beach hanging on every word Jesus spoke; he admired the rabbi's sincerity and style; he thought how strange but rewarding rabbi work seemed to be, how significant and inspiring it was compared with all-night fishing and repairing sails and oars and nets all day. It never crossed Simon's mind that Jesus' work that day was possible largely because someone had made his boat available as a podium.

Jesus' teaching really did seem to inspire the crowd, though as Jesus said, some of them would walk away and forget it all; others would respond initially but be snared by the more compelling lure of wealth; others would adopt this vision of life until the going got tough and opposition mounted. "But for those of you who are serious," Jesus said, "the seeds of my teaching will multiply over and over in your life, twenty, fifty, a hundred times over; imagine your life rippling like waves of barley at harvest time" (Matthew 13:3-9)

Simon looked at the empty hold in his boat and tried to translate 'barley harvest' into fishing idiom – schools of fish leaping into the boat, nets bursting with trout. A nice fantasy, he thought, but too fanciful for a seasoned frustrated fisherman. Still, Simon hoped that the young rabbi would have something to show for his efforts when he went home that day.

Jesus urged his listeners to let his words echo in their ears. Then he turned to Simon and instead of saying "thanks for your help", he said "push out into deep water and let out your nets for a catch."

'What's the point in that?' Simon thought. 'I know fishing, and I know when it's time to accept defeat' – and he told Jesus as much. But there was something in Jesus' eye or in his voice that wasn't so much making a suggestion as giving a directive, so Simon added, "but if you say so, I'll let out the nets".

Pushing his boat farther out, Simon may have second guessed his decision. "Why am I doing this, I'm just going to foul up the nets again?" He looked at Jesus who was studying Simon's face and reading his mind.

"Here," said Jesus. "Throw your nets in here." Simon did as he was told – and as soon as his nets hit the water the lake erupted in thrashing fish and a haul so large his nets began to tear apart. His partners on the shore leapt to his aid and together they pulled in a catch that almost swamped both their boats.

When Simon grasped what Jesus had done, he instinctively fell to his knees. He was overwhelmed, stunned by Jesus' extravagance, mastery and authority. Simon was a veteran fisherman, but Jesus apparently knew the lake better than he did. Here was a paragon of humanity, one who could actually "rule over the fish of the sea" (Psalm 8:8). Simon also knew that Jesus was after bigger game than pickerel and trout. Jesus was trying to net Simon for his cause, and Simon was a reluctant fish. He felt completely inadequate. He told Jesus that he was just not made for the job; that he wasn't in Jesus' league; he wasn't holy enough. "Go away, Jesus; I'm a sinful man."

Behind Simon's reticence, Jesus saw a proud strong fisherman quaking in his sandals at the thought of throwing in his lot with Jesus. "Don't be afraid, Simon," Jesus said, "launch out into the deep – into this new venture with me. Yes, you'll be completely out of your depth, but we'll be there together, and the fishing will be beyond belief. From now on you'll be catching men and women, bringing them on board for life."

For the next few years, Jesus relentlessly took Simon into the deep waters of his own soul. Proverbs 20:5 says, "the purposes of the heart are deep waters." Jesus confronted Simon's motives and fears and gave him tasks that called forth courage and faith Simon didn't know he had. He gave Simon a new name, Peter – Rocky – and continued to deepen his rock solid character, transforming him into a renowned disciple and disciple maker. Simon accepted the challenge of Jesus' call; he didn't miss the opportunity to participate in a world that would last forever.

This is exactly the kind of thing Jesus has done in my life over and over again. He saw potential in me and asked to use the boat of my life as his podium; he called me to deep water adventures which I felt were beyond me, answered profound fears I hardly knew how to name, overlooked both my perceived and real inadequacies and showed his power through the work of my hands.

He has given me a new name, a sense of identity that affirms deep purposes he is drawing out of my life. I am a father, a husband, a brother, a grandfather, an uncle, a neighbor, a pastor, a teacher, a writer, a gardener, a friend and follower of Jesus – and in each of these roles, like Simon, I have known days of failure and disappointment, as well as nets bursting with life and undeserved grace.

There's nothing shallow about the way of Jesus. Deep-sea fishing with Jesus can be an astonishing ride. I wouldn't miss the opportunity for the world.

15.2 A Cup of Cold Water

Writing this book about water and the grace of God has been for me like drinking drafts from God's deep well and then trying to make each page a spillway of fresh cold water to share with you who are reading my words. So please lift a tall glass with me and repeat these words of Jesus – "If you give even a cup of cold water to one of the least of my followers, . . . you'll surely be rewarded" (Matthew 10:42 NLT).

That's one cool promise! Even the simplest gesture of kindness to the humblest follower of Christ will be rewarded. Jesus was emphatic about this, "I tell you the truth," he said, as if to say 'this may be counter-intuitive, but it's true!' Merely sharing water can get you a reward from God!

In a world where prestige and social status are respected and rewarded, Jesus announced an inverted social order. He was teaching his disciples that they may be despised or dismissed in high society, but they were highly esteemed in God's view. We may have trouble believing this is so, but this is absolutely true.

Jesus also inverts our notions of hospitality. Sumptuous banquets have their place, but a simple cup of cold water is an unmistakable sign of care and kindness. It is basic humanity. An ancient proverb says, "if your enemies are thirsty, give them water to drink; surprise them with goodness" (Proverbs 25:21-22 NLT and MSG).

Jesus said that a reward comes with the giving. He echoed another proverb that we've seen before: "those who refresh others will themselves be refreshed" (Proverbs 11:25 NLT).

It's an axiom of life that there's a rich reward in simply blessing others, whether it's sharing hot chocolate in December or iced tea in July. Acting like God, giver of rain and rivers, when we give water to others, we taste the joy of life, the joy of God flowing into us, through us, out of us.

But Jesus has even greater rewards in mind, the joy of an eternal kingdom. In his parable of the sheep and goats in Matthew 25:35 the king says "I was thirsty and you gave me a drink". You may not be aware that you are gladdening God's heart when you say a kind word, or bring an extra coffee for someone in your office, or send an e-mail telling a friend you're praying for them, but Jesus says he takes your kindness towards others as a kindness directly towards him.

I live in the Canadian province of Ontario whose name means 'sparkling waters'. We take water for granted. We forget that for millions of people, finding water is the first and last thought of the day – especially for women. In countless communities around the world, water is a scarce and crucial commodity.

Praying for them and providing funds for wells or clean water are practical ways of responding to their plight. Ignoring them is like ignoring Jesus in his thirst.

Eugene Peterson sees the words of Jesus as counsel on how to do simple acts of discipleship. He expresses Jesus' instructions to his followers this way:

> This is a large work I've called you into, but don't be overwhelmed by it. It's best to start small. Give a cool cup of water to someone who is thirsty, for instance. The smallest act of giving or receiving makes you a true apprentice. You won't lose out on a thing.
> Matthew 10:42 MSG

'Start small', he says. That's a good place to start today. So, raise your glass and share it with someone today. *Cheers!*

15.3 Storm Master

As lakes go, Galilee isn't very large – 13 miles long and 8 miles wide (21 km by 13 km), but violent storms can erupt very quickly as cool air rushes down from the adjacent mountains – the Arbel on the west and the Golan Heights 4000 feet (1200m) above the lake on the east. In March 1992, ten foot (3 m) waves crashed into downtown Tiberius on the western shore of Lake Galilee, causing significant damage.

The disciples were seasoned fisherman, familiar with the lake's turbulent ways. They knew how to handle her storms. On one occasion, Jesus was asleep in the boat when the winds erupted in a whopper storm like the classic described in Psalm 107:23-32 – "in their peril, their courage melted away; they reeled and staggered like drunken men; they were at their wits end." The rugged fishermen rowed for their lives as waves surged and broke with fury over the sides and threatened to swamp the boat. But all their rowing and bailing were a losing effort against the storm. They were in jeopardy and they knew it. They woke Jesus, shouting that they were about to go under.

Jesus stood and ordered the winds to be quiet and the waves to settle down. Within moments the sea was glass and the tattered sails hung limp on the mast. The disciples blinked in stunned disbelief. "Who is this man?" they asked each other; "even the wind and the waves obey his word?" (Mark 4:41).

We can discount this story as an exaggeration or reduce it to a metaphor. I regard it as the testimony of eyewitnesses who experienced something truly astonishing. All four Gospels tell the story , either this one or another similar one, or both – see Matthew 8, Matthew 14, Mark 4, Mark 6, Luke 8 and John 6.

The disciples faced a deathly terror – and then, suddenly, relief beyond words! They told their experience over and over again for the rest of their lives; something extraordinary had occurred that night! They had heard the Creator's voice; they had seen his power and authority over nature – and they called him "Prince of Peace", Master of Storms.

15.4 Water-Walker

On another occasion, a gale broke over them in the middle of the lake without warning and roared all night. For hours they strained at the oars, fighting the winds and the waves. They were seasoned veterans on this lake, but it was getting the best of them. The raging water was showing its legendary renown as the face of Chaos.

Suddenly they saw the unthinkable – the form of a man walking towards them across the water. '*Ghost*' was all they could imagine. But this 'ghost' was actually their very down-to-earth friend Jesus coming to them where they least expected him – but when they most needed his help. He called to them above the wind, "It's me. Don't be afraid!" (Matthew 14:27).

It was a night they never forgot. It was a voice that rang in their memory forever. Those men went on to face other storms. In the decades ahead, winds and waves of persecution engulfed the fledgling church. Political opposition and religious hostility were furious and relentless and the outlook was dark.

Cultural turbulence rocked them as they embraced people from the far corners of the world. Again and again, the disciples reached back into their memory and retold their experience of Jesus mastering the storms on Galilee. Nothing could shake their certainty. Even in the dark waters or fires of martyrdom they heard the voice of the Storm Master, and they knew his peace.

Three of the four Gospels tell this story and every generation of the church has needed to call it to mind. Being storm-tossed in this world is part of the collective experience of God's people – storms among us, between us and around us.

Each of us knows the storm of crisis in a personal way. Over and over again, the Water-Walker, the Storm Treader himself, comes to reassure struggling, bewildered, storm weary rowers that He is Lord, and the storm is not. He bolsters us with fresh courage and reassures us that we are not alone. The '*I Am*' is with us!

Take courage. Whatever storm you are facing today, don't be afraid!

15.5 Mere Mortals

Three Gospel writers – Matthew, Mark and John tell about Jesus walking on water in the midst of a wild storm, but only Matthew_tells us about Peter's wild response: "Jesus, if it really is you, tell me to come to you on the water." "Come" says Jesus (Matthew 14:28-29).

'Come' is one of Jesus' favorite words – part invitation, part summons – and always a call to do something that feels risky, to step out of our comfort zone and our places of pseudo-security and to trust him.

Walking on water is somewhat counterintuitive. 'Terra firma' is home for us. A boat is a constructed extension of home, canoes and kayaks give us both buoyancy and adventure, but stepping out alone onto the deep at the invitation of Jesus is an act of daring faith. Imagine the drama as Peter vaulted the gunwales to join Jesus out on the lake. Imagine the warnings of his friends – "Pete, you're an idiot!" "Don't be so reckless!" Imagine the shaking heads, the held breath, and then cheers as he stepped forward on solid water.

Peter mirrors us in our finest moments of courage and faith when we throw caution to the wind, when we take the plunge towards God, mere mortals attempting the impossible.

John Ortberg says in his fine book *If You Want to Walk on Water You Have to Get Out of the Boat,*

> There is more to life than sitting in the boat. You were made for something more than merely avoiding failure. There is something inside you that wants to walk on water – to leave the comfort of routine existence and abandon yourself to the high adventure of following God.[156]

He reminds us that discerning water walkers are not reckless, they respond to the summons of Jesus. He also reminds us how our fears often master our feeble faith. When Peter saw the wind, he froze in fear and began to sink. He was overwhelmed. He cried out to Jesus who immediately grasped his hand and lifted him up. "Why did you doubt?" Jesus asked. The beautiful truth is that Jesus does not turn his back on us when our faith falters. His purpose is to grow our capacity to trust him, and that involves us in a continual adventure of risk.

This reminds me of the incident in William Young's novel *The Shack,* where Jesus invites Mack to walk across the lake with him. Jesus takes off his shoes and steps out onto the water. Mack hesitantly follows and finds the water quite solid under his feet. Mack, of course, is drowning under a riptide of anger and doubt over the death of his daughter. But through his visit with Jesus and two others who reveal the nature of God to him, the chaos in his heart gradually calms, and he begins to trust the mystery of God's purposes, to walk with Jesus on the terra firma of faith.

Are you hearing Jesus call you to get your feet wet? Don't let the comfort of the boat or the fears within deprive you of the high adventure that awaits you.

15.6 Listen Up!

If only Peter could capture the magic of this moment. Jesus had brought them up on this mountain to give them new perspective – and what a sight opened up in front of them!

Peter had often seen Jesus deep in prayer, but this time, without explanation, Jesus' appearance began glistening with sunlight. Lightning flickered about his face, searing light. Ancient history came to life before their eyes as Moses and Elijah emerged out of thin air and joined the conversation.

Unaccustomed to paranormal things, Peter quivered with perplexity and dismay. He always felt more comfortable when he was at the center of things and influencing outcomes. Instinctively he grasped for something he could do or some way he could contribute to the discussion. His mind engineered tents of hospitality and he proposed his plan.

Nobody commented on his suggestion, but while he was still speaking, as if in reply, a cloud swept over the mountain and wrapped itself around them like a fatherly bear-hug. Out of the brightness of the cloud a voice spoke saying, "this is my Son, whom I love; listen to him" (Matthew 17:5).

Imagine God speaking out of a cloud! There were precedents like the storm clouds of Sinai when the law was given, and the bright cloud of glory that filled the tabernacle, the soaring cloud that led the way through the unmapped wilderness, and the wisp of cloud that foretold the coming of Elijah's monsoon rains, God's chariot-clouds (Psalm 104:3) revealing the mystery and radiance of God's glory. And here, on another cloud-wrapped mountain, God was showing up again with a fresh revelation for Jesus' slow witted disciples.

The disciples never forgot the voice that spoke to them from the cloud. It spoke of God's intimate affection for their friend Jesus and God's authoritative endorsement of him; it urged them, and us, to pay attention to him. In a word, listen. Listen to Jesus.

Jesus is God's chosen One, God's beloved, the One to listen to. He is the prophet, the Teacher, the Word, the One who communicates the mystery and magnificence of God to us. He embodies in his life and words the self-giving love of God.

When everything else around us is cloudy, Jesus is the Heart-whisperer and he invites us to listen to the still small voice of his Spirit. While Peter – and we – want to do something to validate ourselves, the cloud tells us to calm down, to shut up and listen!

15.7 Soaked and Soiled

In first century Palestine, it was courtesy to welcome guests to your home by washing their feet. Since most of the roads and laneways were unpaved, both in rainy seasons and dry, people's feet would quickly be caked with dust or mud. Simple hospitality required a host to arrange for a servant to wash the feet of the guests when they arrived. But as Jesus and his friends gathered to celebrate Passover, there were no servants to wait on them. Every disciple was jockeying for the right to sit closer to Jesus, each acutely focused on his prestige in the group. No one moved to initiate this basic lowly gesture of hospitality.

The meal was well underway, when Jesus got up and stripped down to the waist. He took up a towel, filled a basin with water and began to wash the feet of his disciples. You can imagine their faces as Jesus made his way around the circle. Glances across the table – 'What should we do?', 'What should I say?', 'Why didn't one of us do this?'

With each man, the water got a little bit dirtier, maybe a lot dirtier. No one could pretend it wasn't happening as Jesus went from one man to the next, bathing their feet and wiping them dry with the towel. The Great One who walked on water and silenced hurricanes was now humbly pouring water and bathing the feet of his status-obsessed disciples who had no idea how much they needed washing. They were oblivious to how deeply pride had fouled their souls.

But eventually they got it – transformed by the Cross and the resurrection and the power of the Holy Spirit, they learned the self-giving way of life that Jesus had modeled. They went out and bathed the feet of the world. They cared for lepers and widows, the homeless and the destitute; they rescued abandoned babies; they started hospitals and orphanages and asylums and schools. They welcomed into their gatherings all kinds of outsiders – slaves and publicans, harlots and soldiers, widows and orphans.

Christian history is rich in the stories of people like St. Francis and Wilberforce, Mother Theresa, Frank Laubach and Jackie Pullinger who changed the world by applying the love of Christ to the world's great need.

Water and dirt – Jesus didn't back away from either. He got soaked and soiled; he washes us clean and teaches us the cost of leadership and the joy of making others feel at home.

15.8 I Am Thirsty

The cross of Jesus is the greatest paradox in human history: the instrument of death opened the door to Life, the powerless One disarmed the powers of injustice and death, and the great Thirst-quencher himself completed his work in terrible physical thirst. The one who proclaimed himself as the Spring of living water, called out through parched lips, "I am thirsty."

> Knowing that all was now completed, and so that the Scripture would be fulfilled, Jesus said, 'I am thirsty'. A jar of wine vinegar was there, so they soaked a sponge in it, put the sponge on a stalk of the hyssop plant, and lifted it to Jesus' lips. When he had received the drink, Jesus said, 'It is finished' (John 19:28-30).

Jesus was physically exhausted from the ordeal of scourging and execution and wracked with pain. We're told that his cry of thirst was more than just a call for water; it was somehow a fulfillment of scripture, but what in the ancient record foretells this moment?

Psalm 22 comes to mind where the God-forsaken poet says, "I am poured out like water… my strength is dried up like a potsherd, my tongue sticks to the roof of my mouth" (Psalm 22:15).

But it goes deeper – Israel's journey to freedom led through "the vast and dreadful desert, that thirsty and waterless land." (Deuteronomy 8:15). Jesus was the true Israel, following God into the thirsty desert. His thirst for God was unquenchable. "O God, you are my God; earnestly I seek you, my soul thirsts for you as in a dry barren land" (Psalm 63:1). He thirsted to do God's will – and that meant sharing the suffering of thirsty people everywhere.

A bystander responded to Jesus' cry of thirst by giving him a sponge soaked in wine vinegar. It may have been a gesture of mercy, but the narrator saw it fulfilling scripture as the ultimate in human insults: "for my thirst they gave me vinegar to drink" (Psalm 69:21).

So there was Jesus, naked and parched, sharing the anguish of people throughout history, wretched and thirsting for justice, dignity and hope; children dying of thirst in drought and desert, a mother wilting in clinical depression, a gay son craving his father's acceptance, the parents of a prodigal aching for a phone call home that never comes, a refugee desperate for safety and vindication, an abuser riddled with guilt and regret, longing for forgiveness. Bearing the collective weight of all this human suffering in his body and soul, thirsting for God, Jesus called out on behalf of those with no voice of their own.

He drank the cup of thirst his father chose for him to drink. Yet the wonderful paradox is that as Jesus poured out his life, he released Life to the world. John tells us that after Jesus died, a soldier pierced his side with a spear "bringing a sudden flow of blood and water" (John 19:34). This image gave early Christians a graphic illustration of Jesus as the fulfillment of the ancient promise of a fountain of both cleansing and satisfaction. The emptying of the One fills the cup of us all; the Thirst-quencher was being drained to the bottom and in his thirst we find ours is relieved.

Hallelujah! What a Savior!

15.9 Beyond Fishing

When Jesus rose from death in Jerusalem, he surprised his friends by meeting them in various places: on country roads, in urban gardens, closed rooms and on mountain tops. John 21 tells us of one such meeting on the familiar shores of Galilee. It was inevitable, really. Most of Jesus' disciples hailed from Galilee as did Jesus, so it was only natural that he would reconnect with them back in their familiar haunts.

The angel in the tomb told the disciples Jesus would meet them in Galilee, so they left Jerusalem and went back north. One night eight of them went fishing, except that the fish didn't cooperate. It was a fruitless outing, and as dawn broke over the horizon, their nets were empty and their arms ached. No doubt they talked about the recent events and the puzzling whereabouts of Jesus. Their whole sense of mission seemed as vague and futile as this fishing venture.

A stranger on the shore suggested throwing their nets on the other side of the boat. Fishermen don't usually appreciate unsolicited advice – especially from folks on shore, but Peter and his friends did as suggested and, to their astonishment, netted a huge haul of fish. They figured out quickly that the stranger on the shore was Jesus. When they got to shore, they found that Jesus already had fish grilling for breakfast!

The whole event reminded Peter of a similar time three years earlier when Jesus first recruited him to join his mission. It had also been a fruitless night of fishing, similar instructions from Jesus and a net-ripping catch of fish that had scared Peter witless. "There's nothing to fear," Jesus told Peter, "from now on you'll be fishing for men and women."

'It's déjà vu all over again,' thought Peter as he counted his catch this time – over 150 large fish, and the nets untorn! But Peter once again knew Jesus had more in mind than a bonanza at the Galilee fish market.

After breakfast, Jesus took Peter for a walk and cleared away the debris in Peter's heart about his colossal collapse the night of Jesus' arrest. Jesus forgave him and reassured him. Three times Jesus asked Peter if he loved him (echoing his three denials) and three times Peter affirmed his commitment to Jesus. With each 'Yes!' Jesus recommissioned Peter to his mission.

There was a shift, however, in the way Jesus described Peter's new work, a change in metaphor that became a paradigm shift for Peter. No more 'you're going to fish for people'; now it was 'feed my sheep'. Jesus took a fisherman and retooled him into a sheepherder. His task would no longer be just to catch people for God; now he must nurture them into community. The Italian painter Raphael captured this transformation in his masterful tapestry "The Charge to Peter" with Peter's boat behind him and a flock of sheep on the other side of Jesus.[157]

The difference was massive. For the rest of his life, Peter continued netting people from the sea of humanity and drawing them to Jesus, but he was never content to merely *catch 'em* and *count 'em* as he used to do with fish. Peter spent the next 30 years, teaching young Christians the way of Christ so they would "grow in grace and the knowledge of Jesus" (2 Peter 3:18). He modeled for young leaders in the church how to "be a shepherd of God's flock that is under your care" (1 Peter 5:2).

The Lord of land and sea is still meeting people at the water – in our familiar habitats as well as our places of frustration or failure. He transforms visions, plunging you into a life of purpose with people and expanding your horizons to the whole of God's creation.

There were lots of events in Jesus' public and private life that had nothing to do with water, but seven water events that we have looked at are especially significant:

- He was baptized in the Jordan
- He turned water into wine
- He caused a miraculous catch of fish

- He wept tears of sorrow
- He walked on water and calmed the stormy sea
- He washed the disciples' feet
- He suffered thirst on the cross

These seven moments gave dramatic evidence to his disciples – and to us as readers of their stories – that Jesus was no ordinary man. Each of these water events had significance far deeper than the event itself, but together they signify something most profound. They paint a portrait of an authentic human person, deeply in touch with God, with people, and with the natural world. Life, vibrant and contagious, flowed through him and from him.

The authority of his character and the truth of his teaching about life-storms and washing, about rain and sharing cups of cold water, about himself as the water of life – these combined to form an ethical and spiritual foundation that people could build their lives on. When he rose from death, Jesus told his followers to spread his message to the whole world, baptizing them in his name, symbolically showing their adoption of his story and his way of life. The waters of baptism in which Jesus identified with us became the water by which we identify with him.

First, however, Jesus told his disciples to wait for the gift he had promised them: "in a few days you will be baptized with the Holy Spirit" (Acts 1:5). And so it happened a week and a half later that a handful of fishermen became a missionary team that began the saturation of the entire world with a life-giving story. That's the chapter of the story that we move on to next.

Chapter 16

The Rest of the Story

SEVEN WEEKS AFTER JESUS rose from death – fifty days to be exact – on the Jewish festival of Pentecost, the disciples of Jesus, empowered by the Holy Spirit, began to proclaim the story of Jesus with great vigor and conviction. Jesus was God's gift to the world, they said. He had mastered life and mastered death and was now offered to everyone as a new life source for all who embrace him.

16.1 Waters of Unity

In the first twenty years after the resurrection of Jesus, thousands of people welcomed this message and expressed their faith in Jesus through the water ritual of baptism. A dozen times in the Book of Acts we read about people being baptized. Three times we hear the story of Paul's radical conversion on the road to Damascus and his decisive act of baptism to 'wash away his sins'.

Baptism is laced with connotations of cleansing, forgiveness, repentance, resurrection and new life, but one early story of baptism adds another dimension that spoke eloquently into the social reality of the Roman Empire and equally into our fragmented globalized world today.

Acts 8:26-40 tells about an African government official who had been on a pilgrimage to Jerusalem and was now travelling home by chariot, reading the prophecy of Isaiah. By 'coincidence' he met a Christian named Philip who just happened to be on the same road. He offered Philip a ride and asked him about the text he was trying to decipher.

This official was intelligent and educated, responsible for the royal treasury for Candace, queen of Ethiopia, but he was having trouble grasping Isaiah's theology, especially his description of a "suffering servant" in Isaiah 53. Philip explained the puzzling text by telling him the good news about Jesus, who had been led like a lamb to slaughter, humiliated and denied justice, but whose wounds bring healing and peace to many.

When they passed by some water, the Ethiopian asked about baptism. Obviously, Philip's textual explanation convinced his companion to embrace Jesus in a deeply significant way. So they stopped the chariot; Philip and the official went down into the water, and Philip baptized him. The two men never met again, but the official continued home with great joy.

Luke tells this story to illustrate the spread of the Gospel, to show how eagerly people from every nation responded to Jesus and how naturally his message penetrated even the halls of power of the Mediterranean world.

There's more to this story than we might think. First, Luke calls this official a 'eunuch' which means he had been castrated, a common practice in those times for male officials working in close contact with women, such as the Queen. Jewish ritual law barred castrated men from entry into public worship (Deuteronomy 23:1). But in this story, the eunuch's baptism is a sign of his complete acceptance into the family of Christ.

Secondly, he's a Gentile and probably black skinned. But none of this mattered to Philip as he introduced him to Jesus. Clearly it didn't matter to Jesus, and the inclusion of this story in the narrative of Acts shows how significant this ethnic blindness was to the growing church around the Mediterranean.

In his letter to the Galatians, Paul describes baptism as a wide circle of acceptance, saying

> "all of you who were baptized into Christ have clothed yourselves with Christ. There is neither Jew nor Greek, slave nor free, male nor female; you are all one in Christ Jesus; you are all children of God because if you belong to Christ, you are Abraham's offspring, heirs of God's covenant promise" (Galatians 3:26-29).

Baptism is a ritual of inclusion that neutralizes every societal distinction that elevates people above one another – race, class, gender, wealth, education, achievements – everything. The picture of "Philip and the eunuch going down together into the water" (Acts 8:38) is a portrait of the radical unifying work of Jesus and the power of reconciliation that permeated the community of Jesus' followers.

Rome boasted that Caesar and the Pax Romana were the unifying force of the empire. But the militarism that enforced this 'peace' eventually crumpled before the power of the cross of Jesus and the waters of baptism that energized and united the fledgling communities of God's suffering servant.

The grace and inclusiveness of the Jesus Way are desperately needed in our fractured and fragmented world today, offering reconciliation and dignity for all. But the waters of unity also have a narrow aspect, calling us to stand with someone who was servant to all, insisting that we embrace his death as our lifeline and his resurrection as the dynamic by which we live.

16.2 Surviving Shipwreck

The Book of Acts finishes with a crackling good story of shipwreck. Since the time of Homer a thousand years before Jesus, Greek seafaring stories invariably included heroic adventures featuring the perils of sea travel. Such stories not only entertained well, but served also as metaphors of the challenge and uncertainties of human life, especially the precarious risk facing human beings pitted against nature and whatever divine powers, friendly or sinister, were thought to overlap with the natural world.

The Book of Acts takes its place alongside these stories. After telling of Paul's conversion to Christ, it traces a series of three missionary journeys that Paul took travelling by both land and sea to dozens of cities (Chapters 13-20). He is a well seasoned traveler by the time we reach Chapter 27 where we find him under military escort from Palestine to Rome to stand trial before Caesar.

The legal fiasco that led to this situation was a result of political opportunism by corrupt Roman officials Felix and Festus and the religious rivalry and hostility of Jewish temple authorities. Luke is at pains to show that Paul was an honorable Roman citizen and upright as a religious Jew. Paul was not merely a pawn or victim in the interplay of political adversaries. In fact, he was God's agent.

Paul stands out as a vivid contrast to the Jewish prophet Jonah a few centuries earlier. Both found themselves in furious mid-Mediterranean storms, the kind that strikes terror in the heart of veteran sailors. Jonah was running away from his mission, trying to escape God's calling to represent him in Nineveh. Paul, on the other hand couldn't wait to get to Rome to share Christ in the heart of the empire. When Jonah's storm hit, he was asleep and had to be awakened by a desperate crew. Paul was actively engaged with the crew helping to secure lines and stow tackle, bolstering their spirits when they grew desperate and intercepting crew on the verge of abandoning the ship. Instead of having his witness dragged reluctantly out of him like Jonah, Paul takes the initiative to tell his fellow travelers of his confidence in Jesus Christ. His faith, courage and poise in crisis reveal his deep and solid character.

Paul's Nor'easter raged relentlessly for two weeks eroding virtually all hope of survival. But when the wind and pounding surf and rocks finally destroyed the ship, Paul and all 276 on board made it safely to shore on planks and other debris. The shore turned out to be the island of Malta. It was cold and rainy, but miraculously everyone on board survived. New Testament scholar F. F. Bruce notes that "the supernatural promise made to Paul in their darkest hour had been fulfilled to the letter: the ship and its cargo were lost, but every life on board had been saved."[158]

Luke's description of the geography, the storm and the seamanship involved shows the marks of an astute eyewitness. The historicity of this account is unquestioned. But Luke has more in mind than just a riveting adventure story. Paul's near fatal shipwreck parallels Peter's miraculous escape from prison and execution in Chapter 12. These are 'stylized resurrections' echoing the resurrection of their Master Jesus[159] and demonstrating the dynamic power of God's Spirit who accompanies the message of Jesus as it makes its way across the world. Both Peter and Paul went on the face martyrdom as Jesus had, and both were absolutely certain that death was not the end of the journey for them.

Luke's story was written in part to assure the struggling church that the persecutions they faced, like the howling winds of the storm that assaulted Paul's ship voyage would not destroy them or the work of God around them. They would all make it safely to shore and one day "the entire earth will be filled with the knowledge of the Lord as the waters cover the sea" (Isaiah 11:9 and Habakkuk 2:14).

16.3 The Roar of a Waterfall

As the first century unfolded, Rome's imperial persecution of Christians intensified, and one by one the founding apostles of the church were martyred for their faith. John, the last surviving disciple of Jesus, became a political prisoner. The emperor and his regime feared the truth about Jesus and tried to silence John's witness by exiling him to the Aegean island prison of Patmos, their version of Alcatraz or Robben Island.

John was anxious about the church's capacity to survive both the assaults of persecution from without and the streams of heresy from within. In exile he was helpless to combat these dangers. As he sat alone one day, pondering and praying, suddenly a voice like a trumpet shattered his reverie. Whirling around to see who was speaking, John froze speechless before a dazzling vision of Jesus, alive and regal and speaking with a voice that thundered like ocean waves or the roar of a cataract.

Nothing quite rivals the sight and sound of a waterfall. Niagara Falls is the most powerful waterfall in North America and among the most impressive in the world. Four million cubic feet of water (110,000 m^3) plunge over the crest line every minute – more than 6 million (168,000 m^3) in high flow. Yet, according to the World Waterfalls Database, Niagara is only the tenth largest waterfall in the world by volume. Combine the two largest, both on the Congo River, and thirty-two Niagaras still don't equal their volume. That's the power of the voice that spoke to John that day.

Jesus was noted for the unparalleled wisdom and authority of his teaching. His words were gracious and life-giving; his questions were powerful and probing, his parables provocative. With a single word, he silenced storms, expelled demons and raised the dead. When he refused to answer his accusers, his silence was eloquent and deafening. No wonder John describes the voice of Jesus like a thundering waterfall.

When John heard that voice on his own personal Alcatraz, he was terrified, but Jesus reassured him and said, "Don't be afraid. I am the Living One. I was dead but now I am alive forever more" (Revelation 1:18). Ezekiel had heard that voice five hundred years earlier, a voice "like the roar of rushing waters" (Ezekiel 43:2), and it had given him a message of reassurance and hope for Israel's exiles.

John needed to hear that voice again. Maybe you do, too. It spoke peace into John's anxious heart and it can do the same for you today. Above the din of the world's rhetoric and propaganda, above the seductive clamor of advertising and the noise of your own fears, the words of Jesus still speak today with truth and authority. Disregard him and you might as well try to out-shout a waterfall. But he still invites us to choose; he extends freedom to listen or to ignore him, to cast our own vote. As Jesus regularly said, "anyone with ears to hear, should listen – really listen" (Matthew 13:9 adapted from MSG).

16.4 Thundering Hallelujahs

The 'waterfall' in the opening scene of Revelation was just the beginning. The powerful voice of the living Christ gave John a message of comfort and hope for his suffering church on earth. Then twice again as the Revelation unfolds, John tells us about the cascading roar of rushing water.

The sound and sight of water cascading down rocks or thundering over the lip of a precipice does something to you. It soothes and energizes at the same time. Water seems almost alive as it rushes forward and down, always down, almost like it was on a mission. Jesus, of course, is the ultimate waterfall, plunging headlong into the mission of salvation for the whole of God's creation, surrendering himself even to death on the cross to achieve resurrection for us all.

In Revelation 14:2 John hears a noise from heaven "like the roar of rushing waters and like a loud peal of thunder". Laced through the roar of the 'waterfall', he hears the fluid notes of an orchestra like a thousand harps, but, in fact, it was the voices of 144,000 followers of the Lamb.

This 'waterfall' resonates with the cataract in Chapter One. The Lamb's followers echo their Master. His words have become their words; they sing his praise and they bear witness to the truth he has taught them. The authority of his voice gives weight and substance to their voice. Their witness is compelling, with peals of thunder reverberating through their song. John understands from this vision that no matter how much rejection the church may have to endure on earth, their worship is welcomed and treasured in heaven.

Once again in Revelation 19, John hears the same majestic "roar of rushing waters", again with "loud peals of thunder". A huge choir of worshippers is singing a 'Hallelujah Chorus' – the original song from which Handel got his inspiration:

> Hallelujah! For our Lord God Almighty reigns.
> Let us rejoice and be glad and give him glory!
> For the wedding of the Lamb has come,
> and his bride has made herself ready.
> Revelation 19:6-7

This song reminds me not only of Handel's majestic oratorio, but also of Leonard Cohen's moving 'Hallelujah' with its beautiful haunting melody and melancholic stoicism.

> ... Even though it all went wrong
> I'll stand before the Lord of Song
> With nothing on my tongue but Hallelujah![160]

The 'Hallelujah' of Revelation, though, soars above Cohen's sadness and disillusionment, his 'cold and broken hallelujah'. The cataract song of Revelation is exuberant, joyous and forward-looking. It reverberates with adoration and love that overflows from the victory of Jesus, even when it is sung amid suffering. The Book of Revelation bursts into such song so many times, somebody should stage it as a musical. Augustine once said that 'a Christian is a jubilant hallelujah from head to toe'. This joy is the very heart of Christian worship, whether in our private prayers or public praise.

What amazes me is that the majestic cataract voice and teaching of Jesus does not drown out the praise of his people. He gives us voice and ignites within us hallelujahs that thunder around the world and will echo down throughout eternity like the flow of the majestic waters.

Do I hear you singing?

16.5 Desert, Torrent and Sea

Woven throughout the puzzling images of Revelation are the twin themes of victory and suffering. Halfway through the book John sees 'a great and wondrous sign' (Revelation 12:1) that illustrates this double truth. A pregnant woman is on the verge of giving birth, but a fierce red dragon stands in front of her ready to pounce on her infant the moment she delivers. It's a bizarre picture to be sure, but it is a symbolic portrait of the cosmic battle underlying the history of the human race.

The woman is a composite of Eve, the mother of all living, who was stalked by the serpent, and Mary, the mother of Jesus, who was stalked by Herod after Jesus was born. The newborn boy-child, we're told, "will rule all the nations with an iron scepter." So we know this vignette is about the reign of Jesus and the hostility of the evil one who seeks to destroy him. The child is no sooner born than he is "snatched up to God and to his throne" (Revelation 12:5). The story leaps from the birth of Jesus to his ascension to heaven.

When Jesus conquered death and 'escaped' to heaven, the dragon, who had hoped to destroy him in Bethlehem or in the wilderness or at Calvary, takes out his revenge against the woman and the rest of her offspring. Like Pharaoh racing into the desert to recapture Israel, this is nothing less than the vast campaign of spiritual warfare unleashed against God's people throughout history.

The whole earth is the battlefield for this conflict, but the woman is protected, just as ancient Israel was protected in the desert. God provides his people with the wings of an eagle (verse 14), which metaphorically is how God carried Israel out of Egypt (Exodus 19:4). These eagle wings picture the power of the Spirit that gives the church decisive advantage over the earthbound power of evil. But the church cannot entirely escape, any more than Jesus could escape.

The dragon stands on the shore of the sea, implying his vast earthly authority. He tries to drown the woman and her children by spewing out a river of water, a deadly torrent of ridicule, accusation and opposition, a "stream of lies, delusions, religious '-isms', philosophical falsehoods, political utopias, quasi-scientific dogmas,"[161] as well as outright persecution against the Church.

One scholar suggests that this flood of water spit out by the dragon is the counter-image to 'the river of the water of life' that flows from the throne of God and from the Lamb.[162] But the torrential river does not prevail. The earth sides with its Maker, not the intruder; it swallows the waters of persecution in the same way that Dutch people protected Jews from Hitler's death camps, and Roman citizenship protected Paul; the same way that righteous laws protect people from exploitation and modern civil laws of tolerance allow the church and other religions some reprieve from the deadly designs of evil. Creation simply will not allow untruth to prevail forever.

16.6 Queen of Many Waters

In Revelation 17, we meet another glittering woman. This woman is a prostitute who "sits on many waters" (verse 1). This description echoes Jeremiah's description of Babylon, the city surrounded by rivers and canals (Jeremiah 51:13) and shows her to be a formidable force. In the symbolism of Revelation, 'sitting on many waters' means that she has influence over "many peoples, multitudes, nations and languages" (17:15). This presents her as a parody of the Church, the bride of Christ, which is also comprised of people from many languages and nations. But this woman is a false bride, a harlot who seduces the whole world by her political power and economic clout, her deception and hollow promises. She is a queen of evil and corruption; she and the beast she rides on are the epitome of worldliness without God. They are agents and partners of the dragon who is continually assaulting the righteous woman in the desert.

Living in the desert means resisting the superficial allure of the 'many waters', the enticements of the world that would draw us away from our first love, our essential love for God. But the dragon, the seductress queen and the beast stalk us even in the desert. The warfare continues relentlessly, and all God's people are in the midst of it, but we are assured that God will bring us through. That is why the church can sing. The sea and its chaotic evil power, the river and its torrential hostility, the glitter and temptations of the woman of many waters cannot destroy the people of God. Those who keep God's commands and hold to the testimony of Jesus are 'more than conquerors through him who loves us' (Romans 8:37).

16.7 Sea of Glass and Fire

In between the portraits of these two women, the false and the true, John sees a crowd of people standing on the shore of a sea that looks like "glass mixed with fire" (Revelation 15:2). If we didn't know better this might appear to us as a glorious fiery sunset on the water. But in Revelation, as in common Old Testament imagery, the sea is the domain of evil and everything hostile against God. The Beast who assaults God's people rises from the sea. But this crowd stands triumphant beside the sea, not frightened in the least. The fire glistening on the water is a sign that the evil has been judged.

John describes the scene:

> I saw what looked like a sea of glass mixed with fire and, standing beside the sea, those who had been victorious over the beast and his image and over the number of his name. They held harps given them by God and sang the song of Moses the servant of God and the song of the Lamb" Revelation 15:2-3

When God redeemed Israel from Egypt and when Pharaoh's forces were destroyed in the Sea, Moses and Miriam led Israel in song and dance right there on the shores of the sea. They celebrated God's power with exuberant joy: "I will sing unto to the Lord for he has triumphed gloriously" (Exodus 15:21).

The crowd of people John sees in Revelation 15:1-4 are followers of Jesus who are victorious over the Beast. They too have been redeemed from slavery. They join with Israel and sing in celebration of the exodus they have experienced. They echo the song of Moses and they double it with praise to the Lamb who is their Passover redeemer.

Christians are redeemed men and women from every language and culture, every tribe and nation on earth. And just like Israel, we sing from the shores of every sea in this world, "in your unfailing love you will lead the people you have redeemed. In your strength you will guide them to your holy dwelling" (Exodus 15:13).

The writer of Hebrews reminds us that the journey of exodus people is always a journey of faith – "by faith the people passed through the Red Sea as on dry land; but when the Egyptians tried to do so, they were drowned" (Hebrews 11:29). The song of Moses describes Israel's pathway of faith in covenant relationship with her God. The entire history of Israel and the church is a saga of forgetting and relearning this need for faith.

Our song celebrates the great finale to the history-long human quest for justice:

> Great and marvelous are your deeds, Lord God Almighty.
> Just and true are your ways, King of the ages.
> Who will not fear you, O Lord, and bring glory to your name?"
> Revelation 15:3-4

This picture of God's exodus people is imprinted on the entire story of salvation. The One who brought Israel to birth, will bring the entire family of God safely home, rescuing us from every foe and teaching us to trust him all the way.

Prayer:
Lord Companion of the Way, when I feel caught between the devil and the deep blue, my first instinct is to panic and then to contrive a self-made solution. Teach me the path of faith. Help me not only to believe that Jesus conquered death, but also to live daily in the power and joy of his resurrection. Amen.

16.8 Never Again

I can't think of a better text to conclude our survey of the story of God's people on earth and their experience of God and water than this picture of the Lamb at the center of the throne of the universe:

> For the Lamb at the center of the throne will be their shepherd;
> he will lead them to springs of living water.
> And God will wipe away every tear from their eyes.
> Revelation 7:17

This Shepherd's primary function is to lead his people to springs of living water. This is the culmination of the needs and yearnings of human beings from the beginning to the end of the great story – Hagar and Jacob, Moses and Miriam, Acsah and David, and the Samaritan woman. The deepest needs of the human heart are met in the living water Jesus provides. What Jesus promised to the Samaritan woman is now given to men and women from every nation. This is the expansion of Psalm 23 from the personal to the global dimension, the shepherd leading his flock beside still waters.

But this Shepherd is none other than the sacrificial Lamb of God, who bore away the sins of the world. Jesus is both Lion and Lamb, suffering servant and triumphant Lord. He is both Lamb and Shepherd. His flock is both precisely numbered, sealed and secure (Revelation 7:1-8) and beyond numbering, comprised of people from every nation, people and language on earth (verse 9). They are the fulfillment of God's promise to Abraham that through him, all nations on earth will be blessed. They are also white robed like their Shepherd, having come out of deep suffering. They hold palm branches of victory and they will enjoy the security of the Father's home forever.

> Never again will they hunger; never again will they thirst.
> The sun will not beat upon them, nor any scorching heat.
> Revelation 7:16

Everything has changed. Their past is a story of suffering, but now God is wiping away every tear from their eyes. Their future is full of vibrant and joyful purpose, vigorously serving God, day and night in his temple. Suffering has given way to eternal satisfaction, not a static state of passive bliss, but a dynamic life in which the Good Shepherd will continue to lead them farther up and farther in, where springs of living water will flow to satisfy them and to stimulate ever greater thirst for the eternal joys that will never end.

Never again will they thirst! What a prospect! What a finale for the people of God!

This brings to completion our survey of the sweeping story of God's people and their experience of God through water – from the River flowing through Eden to the 'crystal sea' of Revelation and its springs of living water. Of course, it's a story that never ends. The waters continue to flow.

The next section of the book explores an array of water texts that describe the ways God intends for us to live life vibrantly – and the last chapter will eventually bring us back to the book of Revelation and the Grand Finale. Drink deep and Enjoy!

Part Three: WADE IN THE WATER:

Learning the Way of Life from Water.

Peace Like a River

Oh, that you had listened to my commands!

Then you would have had peace flowing like a gentle river

And righteousness rolling over you like waves in the sea.

Isaiah 48:18 NLT

THE FIRST TWO SECTIONS of this book looked at water as *Gift* and as *Story*, as the Feast and Festival of Creation's amazing gift of water, and the grand riverine narrative of Biblical stories that trace what people did with water and how they experienced water or the lack of it.

This final section is about the *Way*. It's an invitation to 'wade in the water' – and not just to 'wade', but to plunge decisively into a *way of life* that spells freedom.

The African-American spiritual "Wade in the Water" comes from the American Civil War era and the days of the Underground Railroad. This song helped to remind escaping slaves to wade in the ditches, creeks or streams so that tracking dogs could not follow their scent. Water was their path to freedom. Singing the song helped keep alive the dream of freedom in both those who were making their escape and those who were helping them to safety.

When Israel escaped to freedom through the waters of Yam Suph, they headed out into a hostile wilderness without hotel reservations, paved roads or a tour guide. They didn't have a single GPS device among them. Instead, we read that God went ahead of them in the form of a cloud. Normally you would never advise anyone to direct their lives by the clouds. But this was no ordinary cloud. This was their wise and compassionate God, Israel's ever-present companion and protector, leading them home, as Nehemiah reminded God:

> Because of your great compassion you did not abandon them in the desert. By day the pillar of cloud did not cease to guide them on their path, nor the pillar of fire by night to shine on the way they were to take.
> Nehemiah 9:19

All water comes to us first through the clouds. From there we encounter it in many other forms: in rain, ice and fog, in rivers, oceans and wells, in waterfalls, wash-pots and dripping roofs. Israel's wisdom writers, psalmists, prophets and apostles drew lessons from every form of water and applied their insights to a wide range of subjects from social ethics to personal spirituality, from love and sex to commerce and politics. Their writings don't just philosophize about life, they urge us to lap it up, to drink deep, to plunge in and follow the way to freedom and life, to 'wade in the water'.

The first followers of Jesus called themselves people of "The Way" (Acts 9:2 and 24:14). They had a conviction that despite opposition and ridicule, they had found their way home. They didn't pretend that it was Eden, but they chose to live by the principles of Eden, even against the currents of the day.

Qoheleth, the world-weary narrator of Ecclesiastes, often thought to be the voice of Solomon, Israel's sage king, looked on the phenomenon of rivers flowing to the sea and saw in them evidence of the tedium and futility of life.

> Rivers run into the sea, but the sea is never full.
> Then the water returns again to the rivers and flows out again to the sea.
> Everything is wearisome beyond description.
> Ecclesiastes 1:7-8 NLT

Qoheleth is right that water goes around and around, and, like water, some things seem never to change. Lots about life is downright tedious. Before we dismiss him as a hopelessly jaded philosopher, we should let his realism temper our delusions of grandeur. We human beings are inclined to overrate our capacity to change the world.

But we don't have to embrace Qoheleth's bleak interpretation of water and the earth's geography. Why not view the never-ending flow of rivers and rain instead as evidence of the generosity of nature, the endless gift of the sun to warm the sea without our efforts, lifting it to the clouds to water the earth and regenerate the rivers and forests of the world, the consistent cycle of water that has sustained the earth for millennia?

Ultimately the Bible's landscape is "a geography of hope," to use Wallace Stegner's wonderful phrase.[163] That hope flows from two great visions of the world – a creational vision, since the natural world is a breath-taking expression of God's wisdom, love and majestic glory, and a resurrection vision, a futuristic, eschatological vision of God's new creation through Jesus transforming all around us that is broken. Taken together, these two visions inspire and guide us in our task of earth-keeping and our task of living-out the principles of the reign of God, being the new humanity that Jesus inaugurated among us here in our very real world downstream from Eden.

As Brian McLaren says in *Naked Spirituality,* this is "the sea toward which all rivers run"[164]. This is the way of life that regenerates creation and community among people, a spirituality marked by love, gratitude, humility, sacrifice and joy! The next seven chapters you are about to read explore an array of water-related biblical insights into this way of life. The last chapter of this section, the final chapter of the book, unpacks half a dozen texts that envision a world beyond the one we know. There, water will fulfill its ultimate purpose and destiny – to nourish and refresh God's world and all God's creatures.

So, wade in. No, plunge in! Let's begin, where the human journey begins – in the Garden of Eden.

Chapter 17

Planted by Streams of Water

17.1 Garden of Delight

At the beginning of the Bible we read about the creation of the world, and a beautiful garden planted by God called the Garden of Eden. The second chapter of Genesis describes it as a landscape of sheer perfection, visually beautiful and biologically vibrant. One of the original meanings of the name Eden is the idea of *delight*,[165] and what a sense of delight it evokes! All kinds of trees grew in that Garden, trees 'pleasing to the eye and good for food', including one called the Tree of Life.

Eden is also a symbol of great fertility,[166] that was sustained by a river that watered the garden (Genesis 2:10). The garden and river come from a landscape artist who clearly loves life, beauty, form and function, and quite obviously, the people for whom the garden was designed. This is significant; the text is telling us that Nature is not primary. God is primary and nature derives from God. In the evenings, God would walk in the garden with Adam and Eve. It was a riverside garden of relationship – truly, a world of delight!

The word 'Eden' also carries the concept of abundance, and primarily, this refers to an abundant water supply.[167] In Israel's arid world, this would be an indicator of divine favor and blessing. The Eden river waters the garden and then flows in four streams out to diverse regions of the world.

Two of the streams are the great rivers of Mesopotamia, anchoring the story in the real world. The other two rivers, Pishon and Gihon are unknown. Biblical curiosity hunters knock themselves out trying to identify them and thus to determine the location of Eden. But its geographic location is not the point of the story of Eden. The significance of this river is how it nourishes the garden, and then flows out into the world.

The river is a sign of God's goodness as the source of everything that enriches life – all that delights us and makes us thrive. The river flows through – and *out of* Eden to show that God's gifts are not given just for our private enjoyment. The rest of the story of Genesis says nothing about this river, which leads some scholars to see this passage as an intrusion into the text. But I think it is significant that it refers to a larger world beyond the garden. God intends for that blessing to flow out to every corner of our world.

The Bible does not allow us to privatize our faith. Adam and Eve and their descendents were given the stewardship of the whole creation. Their work in the world was – and is – to flow, like the river, out into every sector of geography, society and culture in the world.

Imagine this: God designed us all to live in Eden, and for Eden to live in us! God's intention is that a river should flow through us, a stream of joy and purpose, of love and creativity, a stream that keeps us alive to God and to the world around us. This is the stream of human spirituality, what makes us truly human.

Out of each of our lives a river flows; we all influence others, for better or for worse. Every person and family, every city and nation, every school and industry has a direct effect on others. None of us lives to ourselves. This picture of a river-centered society proclaims interdependence as an axiom of human flourishing. This truth cuts across every self-serving culture.

There is a scene in the movie *Lawrence of Arabia*, which a friend of mine likes to recount. A sheik joyously shows Lawrence chests full of treasure. Then the wall of his tent is opened to reveal his people standing there. As his guards start handing out the treasure, the sheik says: "I am a river of blessing to my people". My friend is no sheik, but he has adopted that line as a motto for his life. He is generous and large-hearted and looks for opportunities to share what he has with others, whether money or time, ideas or inspiration.

Imagine . . . how social life on our planet might prosper if we all treated natural resources as if they belonged to God and as if God had mandated each of us to serve as trustees together of these assets! Imagine the impact if we all allowed God's generous spirit to flow through us to enrich the larger world!

Indian scholar and social reformer Vishal Mangalwadi, spent years in rural India trying to help the poor escape poverty. In his book *Truth and Transformation – a Manifesto for Ailing Nations*, he relates how a village of poor farmers was unable to overcome the repeated catastrophic flooding of their fields because they worship the river that destroys their livelihood. They never would have thought to create channels to divert the water. Instead of establishing dominion over the river, they have let the river, a god in their eyes, establish dominion over them.[168]

The liberating insight of the Hebrew scriptures allows us to harness the benefits and capabilities of nature. This gift is not given for our private advantage, but given so it might flow as God intended out to the larger world.

Sadly, the history of rivers in our world is often a story of degradation. Industries spew pollutants into the river and the river transports the poison to those who live downstream. Wendell Berry is quoted as saying "do unto those downstream as you would have those upstream do unto you."[169] History also shows how, with restraint and with concerted consistent effort, polluted dead rivers like the Thames and the Rhine can be revitalized so they can sustain life again.[170] Amazingly, the same can happen with people.

How fitting that the Bible begins its story with the river flowing from Eden and ends with a river flowing from the throne of God and of the Lamb. And flowing across all the intervening scenes of its story is the never-failing river of the water of life.

At Holy Wisdom Monastery in Wisconsin, a handful of Benedictine nuns are trying to implement that vision of heaven on the grounds of their campus. "Benedictine spirituality", writes author Joan Chittister, "requires all of us to go through life taking back one inch of the planet at a time until the Garden of Eden grows green again."[171] The sisters of Holy Wisdom have been quietly 'taking back one inch of the planet at a time', and partnering with volunteers and local organizations to restore the native prairie and glacial lakes on their land.[172] They are taking Jesus at his word when they pray, "May your will be done on earth as it is in heaven" (Matthew 6:10). I suspect Jesus finds their monastery grounds a garden of delight.

17.2 Tending the Garden

Before the Garden of Eden was planted, Genesis describes the world as barren and uncultivated: "neither wild plants nor grains were growing on the earth. For the Lord God had not yet sent rain to water the earth, and there were no people to cultivate the soil. Instead, springs came up from the ground and watered all the land" (Genesis 2:5-6 NLT).

Great potential was going to waste. Parts of the earth were dry from lack of rain and other parts were drenched by the inundation of streams but had not yet been cultivated because there was no one to harness the waters and apply them to any useful agriculture.[173] The world was obviously in need of some good farmers, so "the Lord God formed the man from the dust of the ground" (verse 7 NLT). In response to the need of the earth *(adamah)*, Yahweh fashioned *Adam* – an earthling. "Then the Lord God planted a garden in Eden in the east," (verse 8 NLT) and then placed the earthling in the Garden "to tend and watch over it" (verse 15 NLT).

This story beautifully illustrates our vocation in the world. Made from the earth, our first task is to care for the earth, the whole earth, tilling, irrigating, dredging, pruning. Curiously, the proportion of water in our bodies (about 60 percent) is not much different from the proportion of the Earth's surface that is covered by water (about 70 percent). The water is our domain as well as the earth, and the earliest civilizations grew out of mastery of both, using water and earth for both agriculture and animal husbandry.

The way the story unfolds reveals three vital elements of our calling. Our care for the earth is a form of partnership with God; it is priestly worship, and it involves protection of the environment entrusted to us.

First comes our *partnership* with God. The story illustrates how human beings were fashioned to serve the Creator as 'partners in residence'. The narrator notes two critical agents necessary for sustaining a fruitful landscape, the human and the divine, the gift of rain and the effort of groundskeepers: "the Lord God had not yet sent rain to water the earth, and there were no people to cultivate the soil" (Genesis 2:5). Ecology is a partnership in which the Creator initiates and the human creature responds, and both depend on the other. The Creator won't initiate the process until his partner is ready.

This Judeao-Christian world-view fosters human progress and prosperity. God has created an orderly universe that can be explored and understood. We are God's co-creators, endowed with reason, language and skill.

Civilization and culture, science, technology and commerce flow from these gifts. Through our use of these gifts, the resources of the world can benefit all humanity as well as the rest of creation. This enormous privilege brings with it a great responsibility.

In Genesis 1:28 God's charge to humanity was "fill the earth and subdue it. Rule over the fish of the sea and the birds of the air and over every living creature" (Genesis 1:28). The word 'subdue' in this mandate means "to make to serve, by force if necessary."[174] This keeps us from being too romantic about nature and our relationship with it. Make no mistake, the world will resist. Creation will not do our bidding easily. Our mandate is to bring creation into submission.

But we must ask, submission to what or to whom? Before we received this mandate of dominion, we were given a model for that work. We were fashioned in the image of God, in order to reflect and reveal God's character and purpose on the earth.[175] We are God's partners; our mandate of dominion is not a license to dominate or domineer. Marva Dawn suggests that the Hebrew "to rule over" could better be rendered "to rule with", that is, to rule in creation in a way that is consistent with the needs of every creature and the earth.[176] Our calling is to exercise mastery within the created world, not a ferocious self-serving mastery, but a reflection of a self-giving God, a mastery that will culminate in the crucifixion of Christ. That is the high privilege and deep purpose of our calling and task in the world.

C.S. Lewis wrote that "what we call man's power over nature turns out to be a power of some men over other men with nature as its instrument."[177] An essential component of our creation calling is to subdue the beast within, to restrain the vanity and warped pride and lust for dominance, to learn God's mastery over us and to extend that gracious love out into his world. Failure to do this has resulted in all kinds of grief, including massive degradation of the environment seen all over the world. No wonder Jesus says, "Take my yoke upon you and learn from me, for I am gentle and humble in heart, and you will find rest for your souls" (Matthew 11:29).

When Adam is placed in the primal garden "to work it and care for it" (Genesis 2:15), we naturally assume the task of farming, tending the trees and plants, caring for the ecology of the garden. The Hebrew word *abad* in verses 5 and 15 is a common word for agriculture and working a field, but in fact, it is more frequently used for the work of a priest.[178]

We should actually think of Adam first and foremost as a *priest,* caring for the sacred grounds of God. This portrays Adam as God's partner, maintaining order and keeping chaos at bay and sustaining the equilibrium that God had established in the cosmos,[179] as well as cultivating the earth to bring out its rich potential as a display of the Creator's wisdom and generosity. The farmer is actually a priest.

The implications of this picture are endless. It removes the artificial line between sacred and secular. Every kind of work, normal everyday, down-to-earth labor can be offered up to God as an act of service. Farming, cutting hair, plumbing pipes, forecasting weather, teaching third-graders and writing software are expressions of our innate humanness and creativity carried out for the glory of God. This perspective infuses our ordinary, mundane lives with the presence of God.[180]

Martin Luther King Jr. grasped this clearly. He frequently told his audiences,

> if it falls your lot to be a street sweeper, sweep streets like Michelangelo painted pictures, like Shakespeare wrote poetry, like Beethoven composed music; sweep streets so well that all the host of heaven and earth will have to pause and say, 'Here lived a great street sweeper, who swept his job well.'[181]

Just as Jesus turned water into wine, so our mundane daily work can reflect the glory of God, and ordinary people become what Peter in the New Testament called 'royal priests' (1 Peter 2:9).

Adam's priestly task also included a *protective* role. He was to 'tend' the garden and to 'watch over' it. Other translations say to 'keep' it or 'take care of' it.

The Hebrew word for 'keep', *samar,* is a military term. It is exactly the same word used in the next chapter when the angel with a flaming sword 'guards' the way to the tree of life against intruders; we meet it again in Chapter 4 in Cain's retort, "Am I my brother's keeper?" (Genesis 4:9). Adam and Eve were not just caretakers in Eden, they were guardians, tasked with protecting and preserving the garden and all its inhabitants from chaotic or destructive forces. This is part of the reason God brought all the animals to Adam to understand them and to name them.

Tony Campolo says that one of the most important aspects of our stewardship of creation is to sustain nature's worshipping capacity, protecting it so it can go on praising God and thrilling God's heart to the end of time.[182] This was part of humanity's original calling and purpose – and the need for this work has never been greater than it is today.

God's world needs to be guarded lest its rivers and air be polluted, its forests and minerals depleted, and its living creatures ruthlessly destroyed. Ecological responsibility is part of our God-given earth-keeping and culture-building mandate[183]. Genesis regards the work of human beings as vital for the ecosystem of the planet. It teaches us our vocation as stewards of creation, our fundamental responsibility for the environment and its resources entrusted to us.

In his book *Announcing the Kingdom,* Arthur Glasser notes that this creation mandate extends to every arena of human life – family and community, law and order, culture and civilization as well as ecological concern. As it continues to unfold through scripture, it widens and deepens as God's call to all who bear his image to fulfill their role as vice-regents over this world to participate responsibly in this task.[184]

Our gifting for this vocation opens us to great temptations. The gift of supremacy in stewarding creation can only be sustained by deep humility, by trust and by being rooted in a sense of partnership with God and one another.

Sadly, this is not how Genesis or the rest of human history unfolds. They tell a saga of distrust, deceit and greed, of rivalry, envy and violence; a story of fear and domination. Vibrant civilizations and many splendored cultures are also part of the human story, but all are tainted by the fruits of our twisted self-serving sense of privilege and entitlement. Today we find ourselves in a world of deepening ecologic crisis, economic inequity and global hostility. Our vocation today must be to begin to find a way out of this mess.

Water is one of the critical focal points of this challenge. In her book *Last Oasis,* Sandra Postel says, "water is the basis of life, and our stewardship of it will determine not only the quality but the staying power of human societies."[185] She argues that we need "a water ethic," a commitment to treating water not just as a commodity to be managed, but a resource that must be protected for the well-being of all people.

We have lost a sense of respect for the wild river, for the complex workings of a wetland, for the intricate web of life that water supports. Grasping the connection between our own destiny and that of the water world around us is integral to the challenge of meeting human needs while protecting the ecological functions that all life depends on.[186]

Postel urges us "to put as much human ingenuity into learning to live in balance with water as we have put into controlling and manipulating it."[187] This plea is part of what the Garden of Eden story intends to convey to us.

17.3 A Well-Watered Garden

Nobody admires a hypocrite, especially not God. But Jerusalem was crawling with hypocrisy. Isaiah 58:3 describes religiously observant people who practiced their sabbaths in a way that could best be called 'mal-practice', observing their fasts but living by their fists, acting humble on the outside, but inwardly proud, self-serving and exploitive. And God was sick and tired of the charade.

Instead of religious ritual, God challenged them to

> ... untie the cords of the yoke and set the oppressed free, to share your food with the hungry, shelter the homeless and clothe the naked. Spend yourselves on behalf of the hungry and work to satisfy the needs of the oppressed.
> Adapted from Isaiah 58:6-10

If you live this way, God said, with compassion and mercy, you will experience a deep renewal of both your inner and outer lives.

> The LORD will guide you always; he will satisfy your needs in a sun-scorched land and will strengthen your frame. You will be like a well-watered garden, like a spring whose waters never fail.
> Isaiah 58:11

A well-watered garden in a sun-scorched land! How does that happen? When mercy and compassion replace self-seeking, and whole communities are lifted out of misery by the initiative and generosity of those who have means and power, the desert bursts into life. This picture evokes the vitality of Eden, the world as fresh and vibrant as God intended it to be. This is what God wants for every one of us, no matter how far downstream we are.

This is what the new creation will be like. Isaiah spelled out as clearly and practically as he could how we can do begin to implement this new creation vision in the midst of the brokenness of the old.

Isaiah's vision arches across the centuries to our own day. People who experience God's well of joy just can't keep the pleasure for themselves, especially when they see the suffering of others. Paul Loney is one of those people. Paul is a Canadian water engineer. He and his wife Grace saw the heart wrenching effects of bad water in the Ethiopian village of Keraro, home to about 5,000 people. The only accessible source of water for these people, besides saline lakes, was a small creek at the bottom of a deep ravine. This water was used for both human and livestock consumption.

The women of the village would carry 10 gallon (35 l) jerry cans of water contaminated by animal waste to their homes. It was rarely boiled as firewood was a precious commodity. Children and adults were chronically sick, unproductive and poor.

Paul was told that the groundwater in the area would be good but "unusually deep" and just too expensive for the community to afford. Working with village leaders, Paul and Grace determined to raise the funds for a well along with a pumping, storage and distribution system.

Another of Isaiah's prophecies energized them: "with joy you will draw water from the wells of salvation" (Isaiah 12:3). Paul and Grace applied that to their Ethiopian friends. Their vision became 'with joy the people of Keraro will draw water from God's well of salvation'!

They shared their vision with others and watched God bring the funds together. Two years later they returned for the official 'opening' of the well which produced abundant clean clear water with a steady flow rate of 30 gallons a minute or 2 liters a second.

"There were speeches and feasting and gifts," Paul told me, "but for Grace and me the best gift was the radiant joy of people who now have clean water for drinking, cooking, washing and agricultural purposes."

> Canadians tend to take fresh water for granted, so it was utterly exhilarating for these two northerners to experience the jubilation of an African community over their new source of water! O once again,

the Biblical proverb was reaffirmed, "those who refresh others will themselves be refreshed" (Proverbs 11:25).

17.4 Investment

> Cast your bread upon the waters, for after many days you will find it again.
> Ecclesiastes 11:1.

Some proverbs were never meant to be understood literally. 'Casting your bread upon the waters' was a proverb in Israel about taking risks. On the surface, some ventures may look as foolish and ill-advised as taking good bread and throwing it in the river. But this proverb recognizes that you have to take some risks in life if you want to receive a good return. It's a basic law of investment: those who never take risks will never enjoy the rewards.

Farmers live by the truth of this proverb when they cast good grain seed on the land in sowing season. After a few weeks of rain and sunshine they see the promise of harvest. Then after more months of waiting and hard work, they receive the reward of their investment.

For millennia, camel caravans plied the deserts of the Middle East trafficking in spices, jewelry, exotic food and slaves. Then in more recent years, maritime trade routes began expanding markets; a wider array of consumer goods was becoming available. Solomon himself invested in a fleet of merchant ships, built with the help of Phoenician shipbuilders and manned by their experienced sailors (see 1 Kings 9:26-28). Maritime trade was a new horizon for Israel; it went against their cultural preference for life on dry land. Solomon's fleet was based in the south on the Red Sea and traded with Arabia and Africa and perhaps as far away as India, expanding their world and bringing enormous revenues into Solomon's coffers. The New Living Translation wording of this verse is probably close to the way Solomon thought: "Send your grain across the seas, and in time, profits will flow back to you" (NLT).

As a sidebar commentary on this proverb we should also look at Ezekiel 27:24-29 which is an extended reflection on the vulnerability of international maritime commerce. It ponders the massive profits the city of Tyre enjoyed, but it also warns her merchants not to trust in their uncertain riches.

In your marketplace they traded with you beautiful garments, blue fabric, embroidered work and multicolored rugs with cords twisted and tightly knotted.

> The ships of Tarshish serve as carriers for your wares.
> You are filled with heavy cargo in the heart of the sea.
> Your oarsmen take you out to the high seas.
> But the east wind will break you to pieces in the heart of the sea.
> Your wealth, merchandise and wares, your mariners, seamen and shipwrights,
> your merchants and all your soldiers,
> and everyone else on board will sink into the heart of the sea
> on the day of your shipwreck.
> The shorelands will quake when your seamen cry out.
> All who handle the oars will abandon their ships;
> the mariners and all the seamen will stand on the shore.
> Ezekiel 27:24-29

It's a sad and evocative lament, and Revelation 17 echoes a similar outlook. These warning texts are not indictments of capitalist ventures, but expressions of ethical realism. Even if greed doesn't cause you to overreach yourself, the east wind may still be your nemesis. There are two important variables in our proverb – water and time. Both are unpredictable. A few years after Solomon, another king saw his entire fleet of ships sink before they even sailed (1 Kings 22:48).

Casting your bread upon the water is a high risk venture and sometimes the water wins. But the writer of Ecclesiastes tells us to cast off restraint and do it anyway; he urges us to invest in tomorrow, to venture without guarantees, confident that risk will eventually result in reward.

This proverb is not an excuse for reckless behavior, but a call for responsible initiative. The Bible urges us to be lavish in our generosity, but it does not suggest that we should be careless or thoughtless in giving away the material gifts God has given us. Rather we should invest them and disperse them as stewards responsible for resources entrusted to us. Whenever a real need is evident, we should be as lavish in giving as we have received.

God's faithfulness to us allows us to risk being lavish, proactive, even serendipitous in our giving, not stingy or miserly, not giving with one hand while hoarding with the other, not giving in a grudging or self-protecting way. Our giving should be as natural as the clouds filled with water that rain down on the dry plains to sustain life far from their source.

Trust God to ensure your generosity is used to further God's work on earth with the knowledge that at some time in the future, perhaps when you yourself may require some help, it will be there for you. The NLT expresses this idea in an alternate reading of this proverb: "Give generously, for your gifts will return to you later."

17.5 Contentment

Investment can easily lead to greed – and it can probably be argued that Solomon was a victim of his own success. But at least he had the insight to recognize the power of insatiable appetite.

> There are three things that are never satisfied,
> four that never say, 'Enough!':
> the grave, the barren womb,
> land, which is never satisfied with water,
> and fire, which never says, 'Enough!'
> Proverbs 30:15-16

Think about these four places in nature where demand is fierce and insistent with an insatiable craving for more:

- Death has a voracious appetite. Graveyards may get crowded, but death itself has an infinite capacity for more.
- The deep longing of barren women is beyond words; nothing can satisfy their desire except to become pregnant and to give birth.
- Fire will burn forever as long as it has fuel.
- The ground will drink in water forever – especially in the Middle East. There may be temporary periods of flooding when the ground is saturated, but eventually gravity and evaporation will make the soil thirsty again.

These four signs of craving in nature serve as proverbs to sharpen our understanding of ourselves.[188] Human beings, too, have insatiable longings – for food, money, attention, power, fulfillment and love. We hunger for things we hope will satisfy, but often our cravings are a mask for deeper needs. Human restlessness and addictions come in many forms. God warns us in the Ten Commandments not to allow coveting to capture our hearts.

The four examples from nature, fire and death, thirsty land and maternal drive, are not perversions; they're part of the world as God designed it. The proverbs remind us how urgent these forces can be, both in nature and human nature. Whether our craving is for needful things or expressions of greed, we need to learn to recognize and acknowledge the intensity of our longings so they do not master us.

These proverbs call us to contentment, to rise above our natural instincts and drives. Learning to say 'Enough' is one of the tasks of growing into maturity. Weaning is one of the early disciplines infants have to master in order to move on to even more challenging exercises of restraint. Unless we learn over time to restrain ourselves we remain childish. Here is where voluntary fasting is a most profitable spiritual discipline. Fasting serves to harness our instinctive appetites and direct our attention to what satisfies most deeply. Happy are those who learn the secret of contentment.

17.6 Influence

Greed and covetousness will corrode your heart and soul if you're not careful. That's what happened in 8th century Israel BCE as wealthy landowners devoured their poor neighbors. Micah, a contemporary of Isaiah challenged them –

> Listen, leaders of Jacob, leaders of Israel.
> Don't you know anything of justice,
> Haters of good, lovers of evil?
> Micah 3:1 MSG

He accuses them of virtually cannibalizing their neighbors, stripping their flesh from their bones (verse 2-3) and he warns that God will avenge this injustice with dire judgment.

Micah also sees beyond the frightful horizon of judgment and exile to a ruler who will come forth from the same obscure village where King David was born (Micah 5:2). He will shepherd Israel like a flock, protecting them from both aggressors and from their own aggressiveness. They will be a 'remnant', "a purged and select company" (verse 7 MSG) who "will be in the midst of many peoples like dew from the LORD, like showers on the grass" (Micah 5:7).

Eugene Peterson calls Micah 'a master of metaphor'[189] and I love this picture of God's people living in the diaspora, 'among the nations', faithfully and mysteriously having an influence for good among them, like the morning dew and rain showers on the grass. What a metaphor of blessing! Dew and rain give themselves away, gifts from God for the benefit of others whether they deserve it or not. The exiles who would lose everything material that they owned, would be tempted to grasp for themselves as much as they could. But some of them, like Daniel and his friends, lived above that self-serving instinct. They saw their role as being "dew from the Lord" among their pagan overlords.

Tim Keller notes that as exiles, they could have tried to keep to themselves. Or they could have tried to infiltrate the government to take power.[190] Instead they expressed their faithfulness to God by serving the nation around them as best they could. They lived out the advice from Jeremiah who told the exiles to "seek the peace and prosperity of the city to which I have carried you into exile. Pray to the LORD for it, because if it prospers, you too will prosper" (Jeremiah 29:7). Keller goes on to say, "the route to gaining influence is not taking power. [...] If at the very heart of your worldview is a man dying for his enemies, then the way you're going to win influence in society is through service rather than power and control."[191]

On a misty September morning I was heading out for my early morning jog when I was arrested by an extraordinary beauty. During the night spiders had woven webs from every bush and railing they could find. All over the yard, dew laden nets sparkled like diamond necklaces in the sunrise. As I ran, I pondered nature's fragile beauty and Micah's imagery of dew.

It is no accident that Micah calls them the remnant of Jacob. Jacob lived in exile for twenty years, mastering the art of spiderlike deceit and self-serving. But God saw past his insecurity and greed. He patiently groomed Jacob to become a source of blessing to the nations through his son Joseph, and the vision of Jacob's remnant continues to this day. Gleason Archer in his commentary sees this remnant as those who bring showers of refreshment and blessing to the Gentile world through the liberating truths of Christ's gospel.[192]

Micah reminds us that no matter how spiritually dry and derelict we may become, God can renew us to his purposes and make us people of influence for a well-watered world.

Prayer:
God of Jacob, you intend your people to influence the world for good, but so often like Jacob and his sons, we are self-absorbed and self-serving. Purge our motives and purify our way of life so your church on earth may be like dew from God, a quiet refreshing influence.

Let us serve the world like rain, giving ourselves away, not pandering to the rich and famous or seeking to increase our stores, but showering mercy and truth, assuaging people's thirst for joy and restoring hope. Like dew and rain let us inspire the God-growth of people around us. Amen.

17.7 Polluted Well

Keeping water clean takes a lot of vigilance. Proverbs 25:26 says, "If the godly give in to the wicked, it's like polluting a fountain or muddying a spring."

Everybody who uses a spring or a well depends on the purity of the source. If a well shaft is not kept secure, things will fall into the water and pollute the well. If animals foul the ground around a spring, or if industries drain toxins into the ground nearby, the aquifer can be compromised and the water made undrinkable. In the same way, a leader who accepts a bribe wipes out trust and fouls the credibility of the workplace. An inspector who looks the other way, instead of being true to her duties, undermines whatever system she was supposed to protect.

The Hebrew verb *mot,* translated 'give in,' carries the idea of something slipping, wavering or shaking. Not big stuff, but it's the little stuff that can kill you. A small trickle of water in a rock fissure can crack stone apart, and it doesn't require a lot of bacteria to infect a water supply. Nor does it take a lot of bad behavior to corrupt a workplace, a schoolyard, a neighborhood, or a marriage. It is so very easy for good people to 'give in' or 'give way', to shade the truth, slip in with the crowd, cut corners. But as soon as the 'giving in' begins, the lines get fuzzier, and water gets muddier.

That's what happened in Walkerton, Ontario in May 2000. A deadly strain of E-coli bacteria leeched into the water table from nearby farms. The inspectors in charge of the Public Utility failed to adequately monitor the chlorine levels of the drinking water. Even when they knew the water was contaminated and people began to get sick, they failed to notify the community and nothing was done to protect the people. Within days, seven people died from drinking contaminated water. Hundreds more suffered from the symptoms of the disease, not knowing if they too would die. It was Canada's worst ever outbreak of E. coli contamination and cost millions of dollars to rectify.

What happens to wells can happen in any human enterprise. Let your vigilance slip and deterioration sets in. Fudge a little here, cover it up there, and it gets harder to resist next time. Principles blur, character gets eroded, standards and expectations slip. It happens gradually, imperceptibly, but each lapse gets easier to excuse and harder to reverse. The more we tolerate small wrongs and irregularities the easier it is for injustice and deceit to breed in the community.

Edmund Burke, the Irish political philosopher said, "all that is necessary for evil to triumph is for good men to do nothing". When those good men or women make overt choices that compromise the truth or that make them complicit in wrongdoing, the well gets polluted even faster.

Because water is such a vital resource to every community, this proverb couldn't be clearer in its appeal or more universal in its reach.

One of the motivating impulses behind Solomon's treatise on wisdom that we call the Book of Proverbs was the need for an ethically responsible workforce. As Israel's affluence grew, its monarchy needed competent administrators who were trained for responsible leadership, not just informed and technically competent, but discerning, principled and trustworthy, people who were upright, alert and teachable.

Even a little power can corrupt us – and the more power you have, the more opportunity you have to turn things to your own advantage. Solomon knew this as well as anyone.

17.8 River Director

In many parts of the world, small farmers irrigate their fields or rice paddies by means of small channels which divert water from a reservoir, stream, pond, or well. The farmer opens or shuts sluice gates to direct water where he or she wants it to go. In larger operations, a variety of irrigation systems are used to ensure that the crops that need water get it when they need it. Farmers meddle with nature to boost the productivity of their fields.

A Hebrew proverb draws a parallel between this agricultural practice and the influence of God on the practices of earthly rulers."The king's heart is in the hand of the LORD; he directs it like a watercourse wherever he pleases" (Proverbs 21:1). This proverb asserts that God takes great interest in how leaders lead. Their decisions and actions have an impact on the lives of many people, so what kings and rulers do matters to God. Perhaps that is why people of faith are urged to pray for "kings and all who are in authority so that we may enjoy peaceful and quiet lives" (1 Timothy 2:2 NLT).

What the proverb doesn't say is how God exerts this influence. Wouldn't you love to know that works? The word 'influence' is a river word – things 'flow' into a situation and exert a force upon it. Presumably God uses an array of means including the counsel of advisors, of friends and foes of the leader, the leader's personal experience, intuition and opportunity. Perhaps dreams, conscience and the strange interplay of ambition, circumstances, public pressure and available resources all play a part in this invisible influence on the actions of royalty, dictators, governors and bosses.

The proverb says that it's the king's *heart* that is in the Lord's hands – which implies some deep motivational influence. Yet God does not neutralize the king's personality or his free will. God told the Persian emperor Cyrus that divine influence had led him to determine policies that would unwittingly serve God's purposes. But God did not deprive Cyrus of exercising his own style of leadership.[193]

This picture of irrigation is probably the metaphor Solomon had in mind, since the word for 'watercourse' means a small stream or 'diverted water'.[194] But the proverb is equally well illustrated by a larger river.

Rivers are dynamic, always shaping and reshaping their channel, even migrating miles to one side or the other. The Brahmaputra changes channels every year under the pressure of the monsoon rains. The Mississippi has been trying for years to pour itself westward into the Atchafalaya River Basin. The Army Corps of Engineers invests enormous effort maintaining a series of dams, levees and spillways to limit the Mississippi's westward diversion to 30% and to force the remainder to stay in its channel lest industries that are located along the mighty Miss become beached far from the new course the river wants to adopt.[195] The point is that change is universal and rivers have a mind of their own. The same is true for political leadership.

The mind and heart of a king or president is in the Lord's hand, our proverb says, under an influence like the dynamic flow of the river. Wise leaders will recognize that they are not a law unto themselves; those who are truly wise will seek to partner with God in their leadership, seek God's counsel and apply God's wisdom to the problems and opportunities they face. But whether they recognize it or not, this text affirms the mystery of divine influence over their rule.

Clearly this proverb raises huge questions about God's willingness to allow brutal and foolish rulers to wreak havoc through their policies. Human history is rife with kings who chose to defy the call to justice, mercy and restraint. Equally, history records leaders who brought about great good through courageous and innovative initiatives. The potential for good or bad is present in every leadership domain. The proverb asserts a conviction about divine influence but does not resolve the ambiguity it raises. Life and hydrological engineering are full of such ambiguities.

Think of how much benefit or harm is possible by deliberately shifting watercourses: think of the consequences of carving out the Panama Canal, the Suez, or the St. Lawrence Seaway. Think of the incredible transportation facilitation that the European canal systems have achieved. On the other hand, consider the enormous ecological damage done to the Aral Sea through the reckless diversion of its inflowing rivers under Soviet rule (see Chapter 22). And consider the political blackmail that is implicit in discussions like the possible diversion of Great Lakes water into the Mississippi system. Hundreds of thousands of dams around the world create tremendous benefits – and often bring incalculable damage to communities and the environment.

My brother Ian, who ran for political office several times, sees this text as an assurance that no king or governor ever catches God by surprise; even the worst of them can continue only as long as God allows. Again, perhaps that is why God urges his people to pray.

Prayer:
God of Kings and Rivers, I affirm again today that you are king of kings and I am your loyal river subject. May your kingdom come; may your will be done in

me today. Gladly I submit to your direction; shape me by your boundaries. Let the gravity of your glory draw me toward what pleases you.

Keep me current with you for accomplishing your purposes. Let the course and direction of my life flow with the crystal clarity of Christ. May the spontaneity of the Spirit course through me with joy, justice and gentleness. Flow, River, flow in me. Amen.

17.9 Rooted by the Riverbank

I've always been impressed by the rugged roots of cedars growing along shale ravines. Those roots worry their way down through fissures in the rock searching out the waters below.

I love walking along woodland streams where gurgling waters keep plants alive and healthy despite the constant shade of the overhanging tree cover. Flowing streams provide continuous moisture and nutrients for the plants and animals that live along their banks.

The picture of a tree flourishing at the river's edge provides the classic metaphor for what the Bible calls an enviable life – a blessed life, a life of vibrant spirituality. The righteous are "like trees planted along the riverbank, bearing fruit each season. Their leaves never wither, and they prosper in all they do" (Psalm 1:3 NLT). As the seasons come and go, these trees, these people 'planted by streams of water', flourish. They survive calamity, storm and drought.

The river in this metaphor is what the Hebrews called *Torah,* the biblical story told by God and retold by God's people. Torah interweaves the stories of creation and redemption – or recreation.

Torah is a running stream of truth about God that never fails to ground us in reality; it tells us how to live wisely and well. Psalm 1 opens Israel's great Book of Praise with this metaphor, reminding us that we can't do any better than to root our lives in this never failing river of God.

Life can erupt into chaos; cynical and misleading voices clamor for our loyalty. But people who immerse themselves in the story and deeds of God live anchored and secure. They nourish their souls and their families with God's wisdom and absorb God's ways into their attitudes and actions. People who plant themselves by this river of God bear fruit in their character and speech. An impulse towards compassion and justice will motivate their interactions; they will exhibit the influence of God's heart in courage and contentment, in trustworthiness and generosity, in creativity and joy, in self-restraint and mercy.

In the jungles of Colombia, the Cano Cristales is called the world's most colorful river, 'the river that escaped from paradise'. During the wet season, the water flows fast and deep, and in the dry season there is not enough water to support the dazzling array of life in the river.

But during a brief span between the wet and dry seasons, when the water level is just right, many varieties of algae and moss bloom in a dazzling display of colors. Blotches of blue, green, black and red – and a thousand shades in between – festoon the river. Despite the extremes of their environment, these organisms survive and flourish year after year.

Translated into human terms, this is what I would call *riparian righteousness* – human goodness sustained along the riverbank of God.

17.10 Riparian Righteousness

The vivid riverbank imagery of Psalm 1 seems to have impressed itself on Israel's great weeping prophet. Jeremiah expanded the contrast of the river nourished life and preached it amid the political upheaval and moral decadence of his world.

> Cursed are those who put their trust in mere humans,
> who rely on human strength
> and turn their hearts away from the LORD.
> They are like stunted shrubs in the desert,
> with no hope for the future.
> They will live in the barren wilderness,
> in an uninhabited salty land.
>
> But blessed are those who trust in the LORD
> and have made the LORD their hope and confidence.
> They are like trees planted along a riverbank,
> with roots that reach deep into the water.
> Such trees are not bothered by the heat
> or worried by long months of drought.
> Their leaves stay green, and they never stop producing fruit.
> Jeremiah 17:5-8 NLT

Jeremiah saw clearly the alternatives facing his society. He lamented how everyone instinctively turned away from God and relied on their own virtues and efforts instead. With a large brush he painted a picture of the moral and social barrenness that marked the nation. He decried the spiritual denial that made people blind to their condition.

Echoing the call to worship in Psalm 1 Jeremiah called his people back to the riverbank, to a life nourished by confidence in God's goodness, a life that yields stability and assurance, a life that can stand up to the heat of drought and still produce fruit.

Jeremiah warns us that we can be either a thorn bush in the parched wasteland or a tree nourished by the stream of God, a tumbleweed or an olive tree. The choice we make determines whether we enjoy God's blessing or the curse.

No one in human history modeled this life of being rooted in God as richly as Jesus of Nazareth. He showed us how blessed it is to put our confidence in God and to nourish heart and mind in the stories of God's faithfulness. He embodied 'riparian righteousness' in the most creatively human life the world has ever witnessed. That's where you and I can nourish our souls as well.

17.11 Let Justice Roll Down

God's longing is not just multitudes of righteous individuals, but communities of people embodying righteousness in the very fabric of their culture. In his famous "I Have a Dream" speech at the Lincoln Memorial in Washington in 1963, Martin Luther King, Jr. quoted the Hebrew prophet Amos when he said "we will not be satisfied until justice rolls down like waters, and righteousness like a mighty stream."[196]

King and the ancient prophet both lived in prosperous nations that were proud of their religious heritage. Both were appalled at how religion so often masked hearts of greed and hostility.

Amos roared out God's disgust with religious piety:

> I hate, I despise your religious feasts;
> ...Away with the noise of your songs.
> But let justice roll on like a river,
> righteousness like a never-failing stream.
> Amos 5:21-24

Or as Peterson paraphrases God's longing,

I want justice—oceans of it
I want fairness—rivers of it.
Amos 5:24 MSG

Amos was a rancher in the arid south of Israel. He knew the value of a flowing stream and the challenges of hot dry grazing land in the deep summer. His spiritual burden was the ungodly lifestyle of his northern neighbors. They enjoyed abundant rains and the steady flow of the Jordan River coursing down from the highlands of Mount Hermon, but there was a dearth of social justice in their cities and towns. They trampled the poor in the mud, 'selling them for a pair of sandals' as we noted earlier (Amos 8:6).

Amos believed that justice was the lifeblood of society, as water is life for the land. Many streams in Israel are seasonal, rapid torrents in the rainy season, but bone dry the rest of the year. Some people's spirituality is like that – intermittent, seasonal at best. But God calls for a steady stream of righteousness, a 'never failing' stream, a system of justice people can depend on. The thunder of Amos' words still resonates today, challenging us to adopt a lifestyle marked by consistency of truth and right living.

John Perkins is one of my modern day heroes who understands Amos' call to justice. His biography, *Let Justice Roll Down,* enshrines Amos' words, just as his public career and private life embodied them. For fifty years, Perkins has practiced courageous faith, practical justice and righteousness in Mississippi and beyond.

Real-world righteousness is down-to-earth. It includes both social and ecological righteousness – doing right by the earth, extending God's peaceable kingdom, *shalom,* to the rivers and woodlands and oceans as well as to every person, especially those on the margins of society. Seeking justice, loving mercy and walking humbly with God is at the very core of being truly human. The time to do that is today.

To borrow another phrase from King's famous speech, there is "the fierce urgency of now. [...] Now is the time to lift our nation from the quick-sands of racial injustice to the solid rock of brotherhood. Now is the time to make justice a reality for all of God's children."[197]

Amos, Perkins and King call us to the kind of righteousness that honors God, builds healthy communities and makes us fully human.

17.12 Serenity

> "You have made us for yourself and our heart is restless until it rests in you."
> Augustine, 398 BCE [198]

The shepherd-poet David describes this God-given rest from anxiety and fear through the metaphor of sheep quietly grazing under the watchful care of the shepherd.

> He makes me lie down in green pastures,
> He leads me beside quiet waters,
> He restores my soul.
> Psalm 23:2-3

Pastures and streams provide the essentials for sheep: food and drink. After grazing in the meadow sheep lie down to ruminate, their appetite contented and their security protected by the vigilant shepherd. It's a picture of shalom. If the grass is dew laden in the early morning, the sheep have no need for streams, but the sun in Palestine can burn off the dew quickly and then sheep need additional water. The shepherd leads his flock to still waters where it is easy for them to drink. It's a picture of satisfaction, tranquility and peace.

This could easily be agrarian fantasy or social escapism, but, in fact, the song is very aware of the threats and dangers of life, and it goes on to speak of enemies and the shadow of death. Experience has taught David to trust the protective care of the Shepherd. He rests even in storms.

In the hectic demands of public life, Jesus too found quiet places in the early morning to breathe the calm of his Father's presence (Mark 1:35). Jesus coached his disciples to do the same. He knew the restorative power of the quiet place.

In his famous 1960 "Wilderness Letter", American writer and conservationist Wallace Stegner wrote about "the incomparable sanity the wilderness can bring to our insane lives, a geography of hope".[199]

Healthy life involves rhythms of public activity and solitude; intense pressure and restful space, action and prayer. The Shepherd leads his sheep from one to the other, and smart sheep trust the shepherd's timing; they let the shepherd lead.

We are restless sheep, achievement driven or pleasure obsessed; both modes exhaust our souls. God's quiet stream calms our spiritual restlessness. There, in stillness and silence we can hear the Spirit's whisper in our hearts. We will find sustained relief only through Jesus' rule in our lives. He says,

> Are you tired? Worn out? Burned out on religion? Come to me. Get away with me and you'll recover your life. I'll show you how to take a real rest. Walk with me and work with me—watch how I do it. Learn the unforced rhythms of grace.
> Matthew 11:28-29 MSG.

Chapter 18
The Well Within

In the opening section of this book we looked at the phenomenon of springs, openings in a hillside or valley that allow water to flow out of the ground. Three Hebrew words, *maqor, mayan* and *ayin* are used almost 65 times in the Bible to refer to this natural water feature that gives access to the underground aquatic treasure of the earth. In the second section we saw how important these springs were for Hagar, Acsah, David, for Israel in the desert, Hezekiah defending his city, and others who desperately needed or longed for water. Wells saved lives, restored strength, and revitalized people with joy and renewed hope. Wells also give us insight into other aspects of life, as we'll see in the following pages.

18.1 The Words of the Wise

The Psalms, Proverbs and prophets of Israel found springs and fountains to be parables of life. For example, Proverbs 10:11 says "the words of the godly are a life-giving fountain, but the mouth of the wicked conceals violence".

Our world is awash in words – tweets, blogs, books, whispers, broadcasts, advertizing, sermons, lectures. In the desert of empty and self-serving words or the warzone of words that hurt, poison or lie, the words of the righteous are a refreshing change. Like a life-giving spring, they flow with grace from speaker to hearer; they 'nourish' others (Proverbs 10:21) and bring joy to those who hear them. These words may not be witty or eloquent or even cheery; they may even be hard to speak or receive, but they are 'righteous', that is, they're virtuous, generous, relevant and true. They are "a fountain of wisdom" (verse 31 MSG).

Proverbs 18:4 adds more color to this picture: "Wise words are like deep waters; wisdom flows from the wise like a bubbling brook". Like the river in Ezekiel's vision, everything flourishes where this water flows (Ezekiel 47:9).

The last half of Proverbs 10:11 is a stark contrast to this life enriching speech; it says "but the mouth of the wicked conceals violence." These are insulting words, harsh, malicious, dishonest words that flow uncensored from polluted wells. The psalmist describes a foul-mouthed man who "wears cursing as his clothing" and who actually marinates in his own bitter words – his curses "enter into his body like water, into his bones like oil" (Psalm 109:18).

In the New Testament, James seems to have these proverbs in mind when he observes the irony and inconsistency of offensive language coming from the mouths of righteous people:

> With the tongue we praise our Lord and Father, and with it we curse human beings, who have been made in God's likeness. Out of the same mouth come praise and cursing. My brothers and sisters, this should not be. Can both fresh water and salt water flow from the same spring?
> James 3:9-11 TNIV

When wells become brackish or saline, they're useless. This is what happened after the tsunami in Banda Aceh, Indonesia. The day after Christmas 2004 when the tsunami struck the coast of Sumatra Island, large boats were hurled inland and thousands of people were washed out to sea – and some 30,000 shallow wells suddenly became saline.

Canadian water engineer Peter Gray traveled to Banda Aceh to help with damage assessment and consult on reconstruction. He told me how they repeatedly tried to pump out the saline wells with the hope of drawing fresh water into them from the surrounding ground. All efforts proved unsuccessful; the entire shallow aquifer had become saline. All the fresh water was gone and had been replaced with salty, putrid water unfit for human use. Wells that for decades had provided fresh water for drinking, cooking and bathing, now poured out seawater.

It happened in one hour. As the crest of the tsunami approached land, the water along the shoreline receded dramatically, exposing areas that were normally always submerged. Survivors reported an accompanying sucking sound as the trough of the massive wave literally sucked all the fresh water out of aquifers adjacent to the shore. The tsunami then inundated the low-lying shore line with saltwater and filled every crevice and well shaft.

Reestablishing a fresh water aquifer after the intrusion of salt water can take a very long time. It may never be restored again without an enormous rainfall sufficient to displace the sea water. That's the only way the villages outside of Banda Aceh will ever again have local wells for drinking water.

That's a metaphor for our hearts that have become unnaturally compromised; we're deeply sinful, more than we know, and from our lips and hearts flow streams of boasting, complaining, lies, exaggerations, insults and more. These all come so naturally, and flow out of the substrata of our hearts salty and bitter. Oh, many a kind and true word comes out as well; all is not poison; that's the subtlety of it. We're brackish when we've been designed to flow consistently fresh and refreshing.

The only thing that can reverse this condition is a massive counter-inundation of fresh clean water, a monsoon, like a reverse tsunami sufficient to displace the saline water or actually float above it as it refills the underground spaces with fresh water.

18.2 Wellspring

The Book of Proverbs is not only a collection of observations about life, but a passionate plea to adopt the best path for life. It urges us to consider our speech like a fountain, searching out what will recharge the aquifer within. It's easy to look at the public failures of other people and critique them for muddying the spring, but Solomon warns us not to ignore things closer to home. "Above all else," he says, "guard your heart, for it is the wellspring of life" (Proverbs 4:23).

The heart is a deep aquifer from which everything flows, motivation, speech, actions, passions and decisions. Whatever 'waters' flow out of my heart and through my mouth have the potential to refresh or to harm the people around me.

Both for the benefit of others and for my own good I need to guard my heart. The verses surrounding this challenge illustrate the larger anatomy of discipleship.[200] They speak of guarding ears (verse 20), eyes (verse 21, 25), lips (verse 24) and feet (verse 26-27), all of which express externally what the heart devises, flowing out into the world beyond which I have no control.

God is the ultimate fountain of life (Psalm 36:9). God is the One whose energy and vision gives us purpose, whose love and joy gives zest to our lives. All the gifts and vitality of life overflow and cascade down to us from God.

Learning this truth is Wisdom 101 and the first step in guarding our hearts from the seductive impulse towards autonomy.

Another proverb says "'the fear of the LORD is a fountain of life, turning a person from the snares of death" (Proverbs 14:27), or as *The Message* expresses it, "so you won't go off drinking from poisoned wells". If you counsel your heart and mind and soul at this well, inevitably you will grow wise. "Understanding is a fountain of life to those who have it" (Proverbs 16:22) and your speech will begin to exude the insight and understanding you have drunk in. Proverbs 13:14 says that "the teaching of the wise is a fountain of life" which, like the fear of the Lord, turns others from the snares of death. People who are wise in this way become a source of counsel and wisdom for others even without deliberate effort.

A community of God's people living out such a life, become energizing to others. People want to be part of such a community. The joy is contagious. This is what Psalm 87:7 is all about as singers and dancers celebrate Jerusalem, singing "all my fountains are in you!"

Prayer:
Dear God, let the wellspring of my life flow clean, clear and fresh today. Help me to guard the focus of my eyes, the effort of my hands, and the decisions of my heart, so that my character may be above reproach and my way of life may be a resource to many. May your people in this world become such a vibrant fountain of authentic love and joy that millions of thirsty people will find the waters they are searching for. Amen.

18.3 Deep Thoughts

> The words of the mouth are deep waters;
> but the fountain of wisdom is a rushing stream.
> Proverbs 18:4 TNIV

How are my words like deep waters? This proverb can be understood in different ways.

Perhaps the proverb is noting the depth of meaning hidden in the words we speak. Freud wasn't the first to observe the hidden depth of meaning in the words that come from our mouths. Jesus said, "out of the overflow of the heart the mouth speaks" (Matthew 12:34).

Some translations set the two halves of the proverb as contrast images. Solomon may be observing some people's endless capacity to talk "like rivers in flood" as Peterson expresses the first phrase of this proverb. By contrast, deep wisdom flows in more measured forms like a bubbling brook.

But Old Testament scholar David Hubbard sees the proverb not as a pair of contrasting ideas, but as a single metaphor of the profundity of wisdom and the ability of a wise person to "verbalize complex ideas and pose solutions to puzzling questions." This wise person is "knowledgeable, articulate and thoughtful." They are known for their "deep thoughts". There is integrity in their conversation and their listeners are refreshed.[201]

The second line of the proverb extends the metaphor of water with images of a flowing brook and an artesian well, images of life-giving blessing, refreshment and abundance. Their wisdom doesn't go dry. Hubbard says, "in a Palestinian setting there can be no higher tribute to helpful speech than to liken it to water, deep at its source, abundant and incessant in its flow."[202]

In *Paradise Regained,* John Milton described Socrates as "wisest of men; from whose mouth issued forth mellifluous streams that water'd all the schools of Academics old and new."[203]

The wise are not superficial or shallow in the comments they make or the advice they give. They know when to keep silent and when to speak up (Ecclesiastes 3:7). When they speak, their words inspire, refresh, encourage and help. By contrast, the learned friends of Job speak harsh clichés of conventional wisdom that taste like salt water to a man dying of thirst.

18.4 Consultants of the Deep

Aquifers, like clouds, glaciers, lakes and streams, are ingenious devices of nature for storing and distributing water. But unlike the others, the unique feature of aquifers is their invisibility. They lie deep below the surface, sometimes extremely deep, and we don't always know where to find them. Dowsers (or water diviners) have been around for centuries, but they have a very unreliable success rate.

Hydrogeology is the science that studies how aquifers work, how we can extract their riches without depleting them and how to protect them from contamination. It works on things below the surface. Aquifers are vital to nature's water supply system, but they are hidden from view. You could live right over an aquifer your whole life and still die of thirst. Aquifers can lay undiscovered for centuries, like the deep purposes of God. Proverbs 25:2 says, "it is the glory of God to conceal a matter; to search a matter out is the glory of kings."

Solomon observed that "the purposes of the heart are deep waters but a man of understanding draws them out" (Proverbs 20:5). Actually I think women are often more intuitive about such things than men, but this is still an astute insight into the psychology of human motivation. Why we do what we do is often a mystery to ourselves and others. But, says Solomon, an understanding person draws these reasons out. This is a proverb about good counsel, about drawing out deeply embedded realities.

The Hebrew word for 'purposes' is *'etsah'* which is from a root that means to advise, guide or resolve. Consultants and lawyers, journalists, accountants and doctors, psychologists and spiritual directors are people who know something about the complexity of their field; they have an understanding of the issues and they draw on that reservoir of knowledge and insight to give good counsel and relevant advice to others. Peterson says, "a wise person draws from the well within" (Proverbs 20:5).

Professor Beth Parker is an environmental engineer who researches the porosity and transmissivity of fractured bedrock, how water and contaminants diffuse into it or flow through it.[204] She's also a good teacher. As a nonscientist listening to her technical lecture, I not only understood that fractured rock absorbs and retains pollutants that seep into it,[205] I also got insights into the parallel task in my own profession of searching out the ways of the soul.

In some ways, our souls are like fractured porous rock. Children especially are like sponges that absorb what is poured out on them whether it is toxic or beneficial. But adults collect 'stuff' too. Over time the aquifer of our soul gets 'recharged' with positive memories and healthy attitudes or contaminated with toxic poisons – attitudes, resentments, suspicions that we absorb, hold on to and often unconsciously transmit to others.

All this happens 'under the surface', stored in the aquifer of the collective unconscious of our lives. This 'well within' shapes our outlook and behavior and affects the people around us. Families are silently formed by these hidden influences; communities are shaped by them. Societies become governed by these prevailing values and beliefs that are fused in the collective psyches by experiences and stories that become legendary and admired.

This proverb is a double insight. First, our actions and attitudes flow up out of a deep reservoir of purposes and motivation, whether in positive or dysfunctional ways. Second, perceptive people can bring the hidden waters up from caverns below.

I began my practice of journaling when I was 42 years old. I realized that I needed to work out the wisdom and the contradictions that were hidden within. I wanted and needed to examine the hidden motives of my behavior, I wanted to explore the hidden potential of my life; I needed to give more consideration to the significance of my activities and flashes of insight. As Socrates said, the unexamined life is not worth living. I wanted to be 'a man of understanding'. I wanted to be able to answer the question the angel asked Hagar, "where have you come from and where are you going?" (Genesis 16:8).

I continue this practice in order to hear God's voice speaking into the deep waters of my soul, bringing light and understanding, bringing out honest truth I'm otherwise too busy and noisy to hear. Taking time to write in my prayer journal twice a week helps me to do this. After more than 20 years, I have a shelf full of notebooks, and I can go back and trace the pathway not so much of my physical activities, but the journey of my heart.

There I discover that God has been tracking and tracing the deep places of my life long before I became aware of them. 1 Corinthians 2:10-11 asks who knows the thoughts of a person except the person themselves? But it also speaks of the Spirit of God who searches everything. I can't think of a better way to keep honest with my inner motives and aspirations than to invite God to search, examine and expose the things that I might otherwise repress or deny or overlook.

There is also another deep aquifer that I have found, that I have tapped into, that flows with the most pristine water and that inspires me afresh every day. I'm thinking of the vision and ideals and example of Jesus who described himself as a spring of flowing water. Jesus has become a 'well within' that refreshes and nourishes my heart. His words nourish my mind; his example critiques my lifestyle and graciously redirects me; his courage inspires me; his goodness motivates me; his forgiving spirit purges the pollutants that inevitably foul my own waters. This is why I find it so rewarding and energizing to pursue the deep purposes of his heart. His Spirit is the consultant within.

18.5 Groundwater and Rain

Life is a journey. Some people experience it as an exciting adventure, a whitewater raft ride. For others it's a plodding task, lonely and futile. For people of faith like the poet of Psalm 84, life is a pilgrimage, a journey towards God.

> Blessed are those [...] who set their hearts on pilgrimage.
> As they pass through the Valley of Baca,
> they make it a place of springs;
> the autumn rains also cover it with pools.
> Psalm 84:5-6

This song probably comes out of the experience of Israel's faithful who tried to attend the three big annual festivals held in Jerusalem every year, Unleavened Bread, Pentecost and Tabernacles, (Deuteronomy 16:6). Getting there was not easy.

The singers in Psalm 84 yearn to be in God's presence and can't wait to arrive at their destination, but their song is about the journey itself and the challenges along the road. This pilgrimage often has to cross valleys such as the Valley of Baca, meaning 'a thirsty valley' or the 'Valley of Weeping'. This depicts seasons in life when our feet get tired, the joy of the journey fades, friendships grow cold and our souls become dry, when we have to dig in search of water.

Pilgrims cannot skirt around this valley; they have to traverse it – it is the only way to God. We have to engage the challenges life brings. When the soul is dry, it is doubly hard work, but it is a requirement for growing faith.

In the allegorical book *Hind's Feet On High Places*, the shepherdess Much-Afraid has to travel through a desert on her way to the High Places where her Shepherd lives. She resists travelling through such desolate barren forbidding terrain, but as she journeys through it she discovers she is not alone, that the desert is full of people: Abraham, Sarah, Joseph and an endless procession of others. They hold out a hand to her and she finds herself part of a great chain of pilgrims. They reassure her that the desert is a place of promise as well as adversity. One day she notices a small yellow flower growing alone. Other than cacti, it is the only plant she has seen in the desert. There is a pipe connected to a water tank and a tiny hole in the pipe allows an occasional drop of water to leak out. As the drops fall, the flower grows. Much-Afraid bends to study the plant and asks its name. "Acceptance-with-Joy", the flower answers brightly.

In a letter to his parents in 1819, John Keats called the world "the vale of Soul-making", the place "where the heart must feel and suffer in a thousand diverse ways!" to become a true soul, fully alive.[206]

The psalmist notes that as pilgrims pass through this valley, they "make it a place of springs" (Psalm 84:5). The streams are underground, hidden from view and have to be searched out, but "faith dares to dig blessings out of hardships."[207] In fact, for those with "a heart set on pilgrimage" (verse 5) these times of drought actually strengthen their faith.

Other times God sends rain from above, unexpected and unsolicited showers of blessing and joy. "The autumn rains also cover it with pools" (verse 6). A life of pilgrimage includes both hardships and joys, and faithful pilgrims "go from strength to strength til each appears before God in Zion" (verse 7) or as *The Message* says, "These roads curve up the mountain, and at the last turn – Zion! God in full view!"

That's the pathway of faith – and what a prospect! Who knows what lies ahead for any of us on this journey, rainy seasons or dry? No doubt both, along with heat and cold, friends and foes, valleys and mountaintops! The well of God's grace becomes a living spring within and sustains us to the journey's end.

18.6 Learning to Pray with Theresa

One of the proven tools for thriving on the pilgrimage of faith is the practice of prayer. One of the best mentors in the life of prayer is a fiery sixteenth century Spanish nun by the name of Theresa of Avila.

A recent report calls Canada's groundwater reserves an "'invisible but vital resource.'"[208] That phrase perfectly describes Theresa's understanding of prayer. In her early years as a nun Theresa was bored with prayer and lukewarm towards God, yet she longed to be spiritually alive and to know God in the core of her soul. Eventually she came to a place of passionate love for God.

In her autobiography, *The Book of My Life*, she tells how she grew in her experience of prayer, how God's love became for her "an invisible but vital resource". Using the imagery of water, she illustrates four stages of this journey.[209]

1. Hoisting up a bucket
Our natural hearts are like a barren garden full of weeds. God helps us pull the weeds and plant good seeds. We can nourish the soil by focusing our thoughts on God, reciting psalms and other scriptures and meeting others for worship. These exercises water our interior garden so it doesn't wither. Theresa speaks of tears of repentance as another form of water, cleansing and refreshing our hearts in prayer. At first it takes a lot of effort to do all this. But the struggle yields reward; we taste God's love and are motivated for more. The more we persevere, the less laborious it becomes.

2. Using a pump
Unlike the effort required to hoist a bucket up the well shaft, Theresa's second level is like turning a crank or a water wheel. Being faithful in daily prayer, the bucket sometimes almost seems to fill itself. *Lectio divina* is the Latin term for slow prayerful reading of scripture. Here our hearts drink in the water of truth into our souls.

Beyond the reading of Scripture, prayer opens our eyes to God's presence in nature, in our bodies and in our interaction with other people. We begin to notice the divine in the ordinary around us. Our hearts are irrigated by a continuing awareness of God that permeates our lives.

Another thirst arises in our hearts that motivates us still further as we begin to realize how much others around us need this heavenly water that cleanses the soul and so deeply refreshes our hearts. This draws us into the prayer of intercession for them.

3. A bubbling stream
The third water is like a bubbling spring of love that cannot remain within the earth but flows into the hearts of those who draw near to God, erupting in praise to the God we adore.

4. Monsoon rains
The fourth water is pure grace, falling like rain from heaven, causing the whole garden to burst into bloom. Theresa observes that people who pray at this level experience love continually bubbling up in them. Their lives are

like the spring from which they drink; they are soaked with God and want others to drink of his love and join them in praising him.

At first I thought of these four stages as steps I could try to master, but in fact, there is only one step – bringing an empty bucket to the well of God, that Generous Abundance that sustains the human soul.

Prayer:
Oh God, grant me this grace. Keep me persevering in the school of prayer, watering my inner garden. Spring up, O Well! Amen.

Chapter 19
Marriage

19.1 Three Amazing Things – No, Make that Four!

Near the end of a book written to teach us wisdom, comes a profile of three things that can leave you in awe. No, make that four! Proverbs 30:18-19 says,

> There are three things that are too amazing for me,
> four that I do not understand:
> the way of an eagle in the sky, the way of a snake on a rock,
> the way of a ship on the high seas, and
> the way of a man with a maiden.

Each of these four subjects is a fascinating study in motion and direction. Each one moves with subtlety and grace that you could watch forever. The eagle soars with effortless power and majesty; the serpent glides with entrancing mystery, the ship makes its way masterfully against winds, waves and currents. But the crowning picture is the mystique of a man and woman in love.

Perhaps the writer has the elements in mind – earth, air, water and fire. Eagles, snakes and ships are perfectly suited to the first three, which leaves the young couple moving through fire. Fire is as fascinating and mesmerizing to watch as each of the other pictures, powerful forces at work, all perfectly natural and unpredictable. You never quite know which way they're going to move. Eagles and snakes amaze us with their elegance, ships fascinate with their vulnerable mastery on the high seas, but two human beings in love baffle us as they baffle themselves; they're equally warmed by the fire within and vulnerable to it. There's no telling which way this thing called love is going to move next.

In the fertile imagination of the medieval scholars these four images created a portrait of the church, the bride of Christ: like an eagle soaring in faith, stalked by serpent and tempted, like a ship tossed by storm, but preserved by the love of Jesus for his Bride.

Perhaps just as fancifully, I have used this as a wedding sermon text. I have urged couples to ride the updrafts of God's love in their marriage, to soar together on the wings of amazing grace. I've urged them to beware the beguiling fantasies that will glide silently into their minds and hearts; beware the cunning sense of entitlement that indulges in dishonesties, insults and offenses and that leads to competing instead of supporting.

Getting married is like launching your ship into uncharted waters. How can you successfully navigate life's challenges? I urge these couples to learn the ways of the sea, the currents of love, the winds of discouragement, so they will make progress in spite of storms that will blow in against them.

Above all, I tell them, 'do not underestimate the wonderful baffling complexity, even incomprehensibility, of the person you are marrying'. Men are from Mars, one book says, and Venus just can't comprehend why Martians act as they do. This is just one of the mysteries of marriage.

On top of that, love never stands still. A marriage is always a work in progress; it needs constant attention. The writer of this proverb is especially intrigued by the way each of these amazing masters move. The word is repeated with each one – the path, the direction, the mode of movement, the art of managing life itself.

Wise couples will find marriage mentors; will learn patiently how to hoist and trim their sails, pay attention to the rudder and keep their eyes fixed on the horizon.

19.2 Many Waters Cannot Quench Love

When Tiffany and I exchanged our vows of marriage, vows of lifelong devotion to each other, our ceremony included some powerful memorable words about water and love from the last chapter of Song of Solomon: "Many waters cannot quench love; neither can floods drown it" (Song of Solomon 8:6). Lots of water has streamed under our bridge since then, but it has not quenched the joy or love in our hearts.

When forest fires ravage the land, water bombers scoop massive gulps of lake water, 12-15,000 gallons (40-50,000 liters) at a time – and drop them across wide swaths of flame, a huge wet blanket. With enough passes, the fire eventually surrenders.

Sadly, that happens in too many marriages. There are rainstorms in life that do their best to douse love's flame; disappointments and distractions, jealousies and betrayals; rivers of grief and sorrow that often seem overwhelming. But mutual love has the power and motivation to face these many waters and not be overwhelmed. As it blazes in a marriage, it warms and comforts, it ignites laughter and joy, it renews and energizes the beloved.

This Song of Solomon celebrates such love and such a lover. The bride knows that no tsunami is any match for the intensity of her lover's faithfulness and devotion to her. She responds to him with the same energy of love she has received from him. This is responsive love, mutual reciprocal love, and nothing can quench it.

19.3 A Garden Fountain

Earlier, in the fourth chapter, the Song of Solomon uses the metaphor of a fountain in the midst of a garden to describe the couple's love. The Garden of Eden is the original biblical setting where a man and a woman first set eyes on each other, so it is entirely fitting that this song employs garden and water imagery to depict the intimacy and vibrancy of their love.

> Dear lover and friend, you're a secret garden,
> a private and pure fountain.
> Body and soul, you are paradise, [...]
> A garden fountain, sparkling and splashing,
> fed by spring waters from the Lebanon mountains.
> Song of Solomon 4:12-15 MSG

Don't let the exotic language of this song distract you; this metaphor is actually sexually implicit communication.[210] It is the couple's wedding night and the bridegroom is adoring his bride. When he tells her "you are a garden locked up, my sister, my bride" (verse 12), he is poetically praising her virginity: "you are a spring enclosed, a sealed fountain." Until now, she has 'kept the garden locked', preserving her purity as a gift for her husband, but now he is asking that she open the gates and give herself to him. He extols her as a luxuriant orchard, a pure paradise, rich with stimulating fragrances and flowing with water.

As his praise for his bride increases, his fountain imagery expands further. She was a 'sealed spring', but now he says "you are a garden fountain, … you are a well of flowing water, … you're a river streaming down from Lebanon" (verse 15). The river swells; the bridegroom is excited and ravished by his bride; his elation is overflowing. And she responds, "Oh, let my lover enter his garden! Yes, let him eat the fine, ripe fruits" (verse 16).

This is biblical water imagery at its most exotic. It is pure sensuality fused with spirituality, incarnated in passionate marital love. The waters of creation, the rains that end drought, the rivers of baptism, and the swells of the great deep all converge in this pure moment of rapturous ecstasy.

19.4 Dance With the One Who Brung Ya

It's not just Shania Twain who sings about staying with the one who brought her to the dance. The ancient wisdom of Israel also recognized the folly of infidelity.

> Drink water from your own cistern,
> running water from your own well.
> Should your springs overflow in the streets,
> your streams of water in the public squares?
> Let them be yours alone,
> never to be shared with strangers.
> Proverbs 5:15-17

This proverb knows how enticing other opportunities can be; it urges us to guard our hearts and marriage, to resist the enticing temptation to squander our sexual energies with strangers. Seeking intimacy outside your marriage is sure to ruin the dance.

In a land where rainfall is limited, cisterns and wells are crucial assets for farming and domestic life. Cisterns collect rain water and can store the overflow of spring-fed wells. They keep water local and accessible. Recently, even in water-rich areas, rain barrels are enjoying a comeback as tools of environmental stewardship. They're also a great metaphor for marriage. Like a rain barrel which serves a small garden, marriage is exactly right sized for two people. It nourishes and refreshes the hearts of lovers and helps keep the grass green close to home. Over time marriage becomes a reservoir of private memories and secrets, a setting for intimacy that helps to cement the bond of belonging.

Marriage is strengthened by bonds and boundaries, by both promises and prohibitions. A cistern is a family sized freshwater ocean, and just as the ocean shore protects the land from unruly seas, so the marriage cistern protects us from our reckless impulses. The voluntary limits and the solemn promises of marriage honor our creatureliness; they protect and sustain the commitments of our wedding vows. They foster restraint and respect; they deepen joy; they reduce confusion and regret; they stimulate creativity and delight. If these boundaries are neglected or compromised, crucial water reserves will leak away from the marriage. Faithfulness is a discipline that stares down the lure of other attractions and yields infinite rewards. Those who can say with confidence "I am my beloved's and my beloved is mine" (Song of Solomon 2:16) enjoy a rich sense of security and a restful rewarding sense of belonging.

When the dance floor gets crowded and other attractive faces start smiling your way, you're way better off if you continue dancing with the one who brung ya![211]

There's lots of water imagery in Sara Teasdale's poem *The Kiss*, but she will let nothing wash from her lips the memory of one who has kissed her heart of hearts.

> Before you kissed me only winds of heaven
> Had kissed me, and the tenderness of rain--
> Now you have come, how can I care for kisses
> Like theirs again?
>
> I sought the sea, she sent her winds to meet me,
> They surged about me singing of the south--
> I turned my head away to keep still holy
> Your kiss upon my mouth.
>
> And swift sweet rains of shining April weather
> Found not my lips where living kisses are;
> I bowed my head lest they put out my glory
> As rain puts out a star.

I am my love's and he is mine forever,
Sealed with a seal and safe forevermore--
Think you that I could let a beggar enter
Where a king stood before?[212]

19.5 Drip, Drip, Drip

That's not the sound of early morning coffee; it's the slow eroding of a marriage.

There's lots of ways to wreck a marriage – infidelity, anger, sloth and indifference are a few of the standard poisons, but the Book of Proverbs has a choice little evocative analogy for another form of domestic vice guaranteed to breed discontent: "a quarrelsome spouse is as annoying as a constant dripping on a rainy day" (Proverbs 27:15).

Drip, drip, drip – few things will grate on your nerves more than a drip you can't plug. The original proverb speaks of an ill-tempered and quarrelsome wife, but it is just as true of quarrelsome husbands. When people have no voice or power, they will do anything to assert their presence in some other way, by persistent questions, challenges, sniping, complaining. Drip, drip, drip, wear down the opposition by relentless annoyance.

This proverb is about something worse than the annoyance of nagging. It is about home-grown nastiness; not violence necessarily, but being a chronic contrarian, someone who is habitually critical, fault-finding and argumentative. A wife (or husband) who belittles their partner or who is cleverly sarcastic is often insecure and more deeply angry than they know or admit, even if their aggression is passive or covert. Their constant dripping makes life miserable for everyone around them; they're not happy until you're not happy, but there is no reasoning with them. The second part of the proverb expresses the futility of challenging their behavior – "restraining her/him is like restraining the wind or grasping oil with your hand" (Proverbs 27:16).

In the first occurrence of this proverb, in Proverbs 19:13-14, it is followed by a contrast with two much happier gifts of life: 'houses and wealth that are inherited from parents' and even better, 'a prudent wife that is a gift from the LORD'. It's as if saying, "marriage doesn't have to be this miserable!"

But three more times Proverbs warns against this angry miserable home –'better to live on a corner of the roof...' it says in 21:9 and again in 25:24 and then the third time it 'ups the ante' with "better to live in a desert than with a quarrelsome and ill-tempered wife" (Proverbs 21:19). It may be lonely in the desert, but at least there's no dripping to drive you crazy.

So today I wish you a drip-free day – and if you catch yourself sniping or nagging, give your tongue a strong twist and stop the leak.

19.6 Mirror, Mirror

Water is nature's first mirror. It reflects mountains, trees and sky to create some of creation's most evocative art – think of Mount Fuji reflected in Lake Kawaguchi or the moon shining on a mountain lake. Picture the Taj Mahal doubling its romantic glory in the reflecting pool in front of it. Every city on a river takes on a unique majesty at night when the city lights are mirrored in the water.

Water simply photocopies the reality around it and mirrors it back to us with fresh perspective and insight. It's physically impossible for me to look directly at my own face, but if I look into a pool of calm, perfectly still water, I'll see someone staring back at me.

In Aesop's fable, a dog with a bone sees his reflection in the river. Greedy for the bone in that other dog's mouth, the dog barks – and his bone drops into the river. That's not just a story about stupid dogs, it's a cautionary tale about human greed. Just as I can't see my own face, I often can't recognize my own greed until I see it in someone else.

The classics tell a myth about Narcissus who fell in love with his own image in water and became incapable of loving anyone else – a warning about the paralysis of vanity and self-absorption. But what is there in the external world that can mirror back to me the contours and colors of my own soul? In answer, the Book of Proverbs quotes an astute proverb about water reflection: "Just as water reflects the face, so one human heart reflects another" (Proverbs 27:19 NRSV).

There are two ways to interpret this proverb and they're virtually opposite ideas – one is relational and the other is solitary. Two verses earlier we read "as iron sharpens iron, so a friend sharpens the face of a friend" (verse 17). That's the relational idea – we sharpen each other by interacting, by confronting and challenging each other's perspectives and approach; by thrust and counterthrust two friends critique and wrestle with and test the merits of each other's position and posture and we whet each other's edge in the process. People rub off on each other through creative conflict, respectful confrontation and shared activity. Exploring the tension between opposing outlooks helps us to 'sharpen each other's face'.

Our water reflection proverb in v. 19 expands on the iron-against-iron metaphor. Friends serve each other and learn together not just by opposition, but by mirroring their inner souls to each other the way water does, by reflection not resistance. Talking, laughing, grieving together, sharing and echoing each other's ideas, values, questions, fears, doubts and hopes, the mutual conversation gives voice to each other's private thoughts. Patience and trust serve to draw out and reveal the sometimes unconscious inklings that lie too deep for words. Deep calls to deep in a still water face-to-face conversation; we discover our own heart through the words, questions and perspectives of a true friend.

Water and iron – contrasting materials, but these two proverbs set them virtually side by side; both speak of the face – the true interface between our inner and outer world. Both describe ways by which people influence each other, enrich each other's hearts, see beyond each other's face. Both remind us that we are made for community, that we really need each other.

There is another way to read this proverb – the solitary view. The words in v.19 simply say, 'water-face-face / heart-person-person'. The relational view assumes that these 'persons' are two friends who reflect one another's soul. But they could just as truly refer to the same person, meaning 'a person's heart reflects the person, just as water reflects their face'. Looking into the pool or mirror, I wonder, 'Who is this person staring back at me? What is he really like? What does she really want?' The answer to the Who question is easy – it is 'myself', but the answers to the other questions are more elusive.

This interpretation puts the emphasis, as Professor David Hubbard says, on introspection rather than on fellowship.[213] By carefully searching our own hearts and asking honest questions of ourselves, remembering forgotten ideals, exploring our dreams and the pain of our losses, we can begin to get a picture of our true motivation, desires and beliefs, a picture of our true self, a glimpse into the meaning we find in our own lives and what Parker Palmer call's "the heart's own imperatives."[214]

That requires a level of honesty and objectivity that eludes most of us. A host of forces around us and within us conspire to avoid this truth telling, but as Socrates said, the unexamined life is hardly worth living. I wonder why we resist taking time to listen to our hearts. I wonder if we fear the still small voice in which God whispers truth.

The moon is a mirror, reflecting only 'borrowed light', but few scenes are more majestic and serene, more stirring to the imagination than a full moon reflected on a calm lake. As a double reflection, the beauty of moonlight on water gives us a picture of the treasure that opens up to us when we ponder truth in the heart of a spouse or friend. What do you think?

19.7 Water, Love and Marriage

The New Testament gives us a strange but beautiful picture of a bride getting cleaned up for her wedding – and surprisingly, it's the bridegroom himself, at enormous personal cost and sacrifice, who bathes her and dresses her in dazzling silk.

> Christ loved the church and gave himself up for her to make her holy, cleansing her by the washing with water through the word. [...] so she might be unstained, without wrinkle or any other blemish.
> Ephesians 5:25-27

My good friend Glenn Smith who lives in Montreal, observes that Canadians have a hard time grasping the significance of this vibrant water metaphor. Canada has an abundance of water, seven percent of the world's renewable supply of freshwater and 20 percent of Earth's frozen freshwater locked in glaciers and the polar ice cap!

Glenn also visits Haiti frequently; it's like a second home to him. In Haiti water is scarce and precious; 70 percent of the population does not have access to clean drinking water. What he takes for granted in one place is a very precious commodity in the other. That scarcity of water makes Paul's words about love in Ephesians 5 leap to life for Glenn: "Look at those verbs," he says, "Christ loved... gave himself up... cleansed her... to make her holy... to present her to himself...."

His reflection on this text continues –

> Washing is routine in Canada. We hardly give it a second thought. But in Haiti, where fresh clean water is scarce, washing is a privilege, a costly event – a vivid metaphor of the extravagant love of Jesus.

> Washing is what baptism does for the Church. It makes visible that very costly work God did for us – and continues to do in us – through Jesus, cleansing us from all the muck of life, forgiving and restoring. Jesus also declares his love by his words and by inviting us to participate in his ongoing project in human history. What a gift!
>
> Then God tells me as a husband to echo this Jesus-modeled love in how I treat my wife Sandy. As I live out my baptism, I become a gift to Sandy and help her deal with the muck of life. Words help me to do that. Just as Jesus declared his unconditional love for me, I, too, help to cleanse Sandy by declaring every day, 'I love you!'

The way of a man and a maid is a complex picture – a ship venturing out on the high seas, fountains of ecstatic amourous delight and rain barrels of faithfulness, floods threatening to quench the fire of a couple's love, and rain dripping through the ceiling of a house of discord. But when we experience the face-to-face honesty that reflects the longings of our hearts in marriage, like moonlight on water, and when we speak gracious words that bathe our beloved in a love more pure and cleasing than our own, we begin to experience the fullness of love God intended marriage to be.

I wonder who in history ever demonstrated love like this more than Jesus Christ? His love stands firm against rivers of rejection, scorn and resistence. Nothing quenched – or quenches – his passionate love. It cost him dearly to pursue us, find us and share his life with us. The fire of his love not only warms the death chill in our souls, it evaporates the mists of doubt and disbelief; it purges our souls and reignites pure love for him. He is love incarnate, and he summons us to respond in flesh and blood to his devotion.

I know beyond any doubt that the love of Jesus Christ fuels the love that sustains my marriage every day.

Prayer:
Loving God, your passion and generosity blaze bright despite the drizzle of my common everyday affections. Help me learn from you what love really means, and how far it is willing to go. Amen

Chapter 20
Washing

I'll never forget attending the house blessing of my friend Norm. About fifteen of us had come over with housewarming gifts for Norm and his wife, and then we walked from room to room as Norm's pastor offered a prayer appropriate to each room. We prayed for the children in their bedroom, for the parents in theirs (amid hoots and chuckles and hearty best wishes). We thanked God for food in the kitchen and for friends and rest in the family room, but the prayer I remember best was for the bathroom.

We had all naturally walked right past the bathroom door, but the minister called us in. Fifteen people crowded into every available nook and cranny – someone even got to sit down – and we waited, wondering what kind of prayer befit that room. The minister began, "Lord, this is the room where each of the family will begin their day. As the outer person is cleansed in this place, we pray they will also remember that the inner life needs to be cleansed as well. As they look at their faces in the mirror, may they also know that you are not so much concerned with the outward appearance, as with the condition of their heart." I think we actually applauded at the end of that prayer!

Washing is a vitally important part of human life. If the first function of water is for human survival, for drinking, cooking and irrigating the crops we need to eat, the second function of water is for washing. Many substances dissolve in water, so it is commonly referred to as the universal solvent. Indeed this is one of the unique properties of water that make it so vital to life on earth.[215] Washing is not only hygienic and pleasing to the senses, but symbolic of inner cleansing, purifying of the spirit.

20.1 Laver – God's Purity

The laws of Moses were scrupulous about purity, and a large bronze washing vessel was placed near the entrance to the tabernacle. For the priests who worked there, ritual washing was both a practical necessity when working around butchered animals, and also symbolic of moral issues, recognizing that evil pollutes our lives as surely and as continuously as filth of every kind contaminates our bodies.

Washing wasn't optional. It was enshrined in Israel's code of worship:

> Place [the bronze stand] for washing between the Tent of Meeting and the altar, and put water in it. Aaron and his sons are to wash their hands and feet with water from it. Whenever they enter the Tent of Meeting, they shall wash with water so that they will not die.
> Exodus 30:18-20

The use of the laver illustrates the spiritual need for inner cleansing and the discipline of confession. In Chapter 11 we looked at the anguish and denial of a guilty conscience. We saw Lady Macbeth scrubbing at her hands and Pilate trying to absolve himself (Matthew 27:24). We heard King David's penitential prayer in Psalm 51, "wash away all my iniquity and cleanse me from my sin" (verse 2). David knew he needed cleansing and a renewal that penetrated deep inside him.

> Surely you desire truth in the inner parts;
> you teach me wisdom in the inmost place.
> Cleanse me with hyssop, and I will be clean;
> wash me, and I will be whiter than snow.
> Psalm 51:6-7

Centuries later, when David's son Solomon replaced the tabernacle with a magnificent temple, he had a huge water reservoir built to serve as the laver for the purification for the priests (1 Kings 7:23 and 2 Chronicles 4:2-6). It is so large, 45 feet (13.5 m) across and holding 11,000 gallons (44,000 liters), that it is called a 'Sea'. This grandiose symbolic ocean illustrated the infinite dimension of God's grace and forgiveness.

It also added another level of meaning. Since the sea for Israel represented the chaotic forces of evil opposed to God, this artifact probably also symbolized "the forces of chaos that had been subdued and brought to order by the Lord who is creator of the world."[216] Yahweh was supreme over the Canaanite deities Yam and Baal, gods of sea and storm. In a troubled and tumultuous world, Solomon was saying, 'Yahweh is a God of serenity and peace'.

Solomon's symbolism is echoed in John's vision of heaven in Revelation where "before the throne there was what looked like a sea of glass, clear as crystal" (4:6). If there was ever a symbol of God's infinitely forgiving heart, it is this ocean of crystal water, as is eloquently expressed in the hymn "The Love of God":

> Could we with ink the ocean fill
> And were the skies of parchment made,
> Were every stalk on earth a quill
> And everyone a scribe by trade,
> To write the love of God above
> Would drain the ocean dry,
> Nor could the scroll contain the whole
> Though stretched from sky to sky![217]

There are hundreds of references in the Bible to human sin and failure – words like evil, guilt, unrighteousness, transgressions, etc.; each brings its own nuance and color to the general concept of moral failure. Then add all the other words that identify particular forms of sin like lust, pride, greed, idolatry, sloth, and deceit – the Bible is very candid about a huge toxic flow running across the human landscape, as foul and harmful to God's creation as all the oil spills the world has ever seen. It's not a pretty picture – and we're all contaminated by it.

Against this terrible condition, our human condition, flows an enormous divine grace, a crystal clear and crimson tide that flows to wash us clean. The prevalence of water in the Bible, exceeding 2,000 references – more than matches the extent and depth of human sin. The river of God's grace is sufficient to expunge the whole filthy mess, to purge the poison from the earth. As an old hymn exclaimed, "who is a pardoning God like thee, or who has grace so rich and free?"

20.2 Holy Water

Ashes and *water* combined to form a sacred part of ancient Israel's purity code. Not just any water. It had to be fresh spring water, called 'living water'. Not just ashes from any old fire, but the ashes of a special sacrifice.

This sacrificial animal had to be a red heifer, free of blemishes, one that had never calved and been put under the yoke. To make the ashes perfectly, the heifer had to be slaughtered and burned with great ceremony with three red 'seasonings', cedar wood, hyssop and scarlet wool until it was reduced to ash. Then the ash had to be ceremoniously carried to a sacred place and stored there until it was mixed with the spring water to make the holy 'purification water'.

Israel had a strong taboo against touching dead bodies. This did two good things: it made for good hygiene and it increased reverence for life.

Numbers 19 spells out all the regulations governing this taboo. Anyone touching a dead body was ritually unclean for a week and had to be purified with the sacred ash/spring water, sprinkled on them with hyssop, a spicy grass, in order to resume life in the community. Skipping the ritual was forbidden. Israel reverenced both life and purity very highly.

To me this curious ash/water ritual symbolizes the intertwining of life and death. The ashes speak of death with a lot of redness – think blood – in its origins. Blood is the fluid of life. The ashes of death are mixed with living spring water. The text is clear, it must be '*living*' water. The Hebrew word is *chai* – as in *L'chaim – to life!* Buried deep in this ritual are the convictions that natural life is precious, death is a travesty, purity is easily lost, but God has provided a way back.

Centuries after Moses and Sinai, the entire nation needed 'a way back'. During the exile, Israel suffered the humiliation of having lost her homeland, but God promised them,

> I will gather you from all the countries and bring you back into your own land. I will sprinkle clean water on you, and you will be clean; I will cleanse you from your impurities and from all your idols. I will give you a new heart and put a new spirit in you; I will remove your heart of stone and give you a heart of flesh. And I will put my Spirit in you and move you to follow my decrees and be careful to keep my laws.
> Ezekiel 36:24-27

An early Christian writer takes this transformation a step further, reflecting on Israel's ancient purification ceremony in light of the sacrifice of Jesus:

> The blood of goats and bulls and the ashes of a heifer sprinkled on those who are ceremonially unclean sanctify them so that they are outwardly clean. How much more, then, will the blood of Christ,

> who through the eternal Spirit offered himself unblemished to God, cleanse our consciences from acts that lead to death, so that we may serve the living God!
> Hebrews 9:13-14

I am writing these words on Ash Wednesday. This is a day when Christians remember their mortality and the spiritual contamination of their sin. We are marked with ashes in honesty and humility. We receive these ashes in the shape of a cross as reminder that a sacrifice has been made on our behalf, and that Christ's blood purifies us forever. Living water flows into our hearts by God's Holy Spirit.

That deserves another heartfelt *Hallelujah!*

Being marked by ashes, whether in ancient Hebrew ritual or in contemporary Christian practice, is a sign that we, the living and sinful, are the walking dead, dead in trespasses and sins, condemned for our misdeeds, but, amazingly, privileged by God to live on in the land of the living. The living water that combined with the ash in Israel's Red Heifer ritual, assured the guilty or tainted that a God of Grace was extending their life.

In today's context, it reminds me that the resurrection of Jesus guarantees my own eventual resurrection. The Church that teaches this truth, helps to create what one writer calls "a culture of resurrection." [218]

20.3 CSI – Ancient Palestine

What should you do when you discover a corpse, but your basic detective work cannot identify a killer? The question was not hypothetical in ancient times and Deuteronomy 21 provided an ancient water ritual so that cold cases don't just suffer the indignity of civil neglect.

If a man is found slain lying in a field, and it is not known who killed him, your elders and judges shall go out and measure the distance from the body to the neighboring towns. Then the elders of the town nearest the body shall take a heifer that has never been worked and has never worn a yoke and lead her down to a valley that has not been plowed or planted and *where there is a flowing stream.* There in the valley they are to break the heifer's neck. The priests, the sons of Levi, shall step forward, for the LORD your God has chosen them to minister and to pronounce blessings in the name of the LORD and to decide all cases of dispute and assault.

Then all the elders of the town nearest the body shall *wash their hands* over the heifer whose neck was broken in the valley, and they shall declare:

> "Our hands did not shed this blood, nor did our eyes see it done. Accept this atonement for your people Israel, whom you have redeemed, O LORD, and do not hold your people guilty of the blood of an innocent man."
> And the bloodshed will be atoned for. So you will purge from yourselves the guilt of shedding innocent blood, since you have done what is right in the eyes of the LORD.
> Deuteronomy 21:1-9

This civic ritual of responsibility intrigues me because it implies a communal burden of guilt for the death of an innocent person in their neighborhood. It implies that everyone is their brothers' and sisters' keeper. Everyone has a right to hospitality and security of the person. The community owes that to locals and visitors alike. If someone should fall victim to foul play, the community cannot plead 'not guilty', even though nobody saw the crime perpetrated and no one knows anything about who committed it. It's a community code that treats everyone as family, or at least neighbors.

When the crime is discovered, an investigation ensues. The land is desecrated and justice cannot rest until the offense is put right. If no perpetrator is found, the neighbors have an ethical obligation to address the bloodshed of this innocent person. Failing to do so breaks the bond between society and the land. The victim is as sacred a person as the living, so the local elders must take responsibility for the unresolved guilt in their region. The crime must be purged and they have to pay a price.

Six elements are involved in the ritual – the elders of the community, a significant location for renewal, a sacrificial animal, a washing ceremony, a confession and prayer for forgiveness, and a blessing of absolution.

First, all the elders of the town must join in the ritual to show full public ownership of the problem concerning what has occurred and the full community's need for atonement. Second, the ritual must take place in a virgin valley, never plowed or planted, with a stream running through it, perhaps as a symbol of a new beginning.

Third, a heifer is selected that has never pulled a plow, perhaps in recognition of the innocence and the lost employment of the fellow citizen who has died. The heifer is taken to the stream in the valley and its neck has to be broken symbolizing the seriousness of the crime that has recently occurred. The sacrificial animal dies in place of the guilty murderer who remains at large, and in place of the townspeople who otherwise carry the burden of guilt for the unresolved crime.

The heifer is slaughtered either in the river or beside it, because the sacrifice and the cleansing water are symbolically linked together. In the fourth element of the ritual, the elders wash their hands over the body of the heifer in the flowing stream. As they wash their hands, figuratively the stream carries away the guilt of the community and purges their land.

The fifth element is a declaration and prayer which the elders recite declaring their innocence and asking God to lift the pall of offence that hangs over their town. This declaration recognizes that Yahweh is a redeeming God who takes the value of human life very seriously, even the life of strangers, but who opens a way for renewal and cleansing when the people and their land have been defiled in some way. The sacrifice and prayer of atonement preserve the sacredness of the bond between God, the people, and the land. If this bond is broken and not restored, the whole land suffers. Hosea describes the environmental degradation that follows when a society ignores this holistic integration of people and land.

> The LORD has a charge to bring against you who live in the land:
> There is no faithfulness, no love,
> no acknowledgment of God in the land.
> There is only cursing, lying and murder, stealing and adultery;
> they break all bounds, and
> bloodshed follows bloodshed.
> Because of this the land mourns,
> and all who live in it waste away;
> the beasts of the field and the birds of the air
> and the fish of the sea are dying.
> Hosea 4:1-3

That is why each element of this ritual mattered – and why the final element was especially vital: the visiting priests fulfill their God-given task of blessing the townspeople by pronouncing the spiritual 'all clear' and assuring them that they have done the right thing before God and the world.

Prayer:
God of flowing grace, forbid that I should excuse myself, washing my hands of responsibility for ways in which my community fails to protect the vulnerable. Keep me from polluting my neighborhood by neglecting people. Thank you for your forgiving grace where I can wash my hands and purify my heart so that my actions and motives are clear before you and open before others. Amen.

20.4 Clean Hands, Pure Heart

When I was a child growing up, my mother used to signal suppertime with an announcement and a double command: "Supper's ready; wash your hands and come to the table."

Every family and culture has its customs of cleanliness, and every religion has its rituals of ablution and ceremonial cleansing. Shinto worshippers in Japan seek cleansing under waterfalls. Hindus plunge into the Ganges and bathe in its sacred waters in spite of its horrible pollution. Despite the toxic quality of the water, they believe the sacredness of the river will purify the worshipper. Orthodox Jews use a mikvah to represent a flowing stream.

Cherokee in the southern U.S. have a going to water ceremony; other indigenous people believe the body's own sweat purifies them, The Qur'an tells the faithful to wash before prayers and if water isn't available, they can 'wash' their hands in sand or earth (Surah 5:6). As we have seen, the Israelites also had a complex system of washings, and the rabbis of the Second Temple period around the time of Christ had mastered the art of complex washings.

In the Bible, washing your hands became a symbol of living the righteous life in purity. Psalm 24 says that only those with clean hands and a pure heart may ascend the hill of the Lord (Psalm 24:3). Two psalms later we read,

> I have led a blameless life;
> I have trusted in the LORD without wavering.

> I wash my hands in innocence,
> and go about your altar, O LORD,
> proclaiming aloud your praise.
> Psalm 26: 1, 6-7

Another psalmist in a spiritual slump laments "surely in vain have I kept my heart pure; in vain have I washed my hands in innocence" (Psalm 73:13).

In the New Testament, James thunders, "wash your hands, you sinners, and purify your hearts, you double-minded" (James 4:8). Outward cleanliness does not necessarily equate with godliness. Rituals can be richly symbolic, but they can also become a superficial substitute for what they are supposed to symbolize. Jesus challenged the superficiality of ritual washing that ignored the need for heart-cleansing:

> The words you speak come from the heart—that's what defiles you. For from the heart come evil thoughts, murder, adultery, all sexual immorality, theft, lying, and slander. These are what defile you. Eating with unwashed hands will never defile you.
> Matthew 15:18-20 NLT

On another occasion he chided the Pharisees: "you clean the outside of the cup and dish, but inside you are full of greed and wickedness. [...] But give what is inside the dish to the poor, and everything will be clean for you (Luke 11:39-41).

That's a great concept – you can become clean by opening your heart to the poor.

Baptism is frequently seen in the New Testament as an act of inner cleansing, "not the removal of dirt from the body, but the pledge of a good conscience toward God" (1 Peter 3:21). The New Testament reflects on the significance of baptism in various ways: initiation, death and resurrection, unity, but for the first three centuries of the church the most common understanding of baptism was the idea of washing.

This idea derived from a variety of Old Testament texts including Ezekiel 36:25 with its promise of being sprinkled with clean water that we noted earlier. Isaiah was insistent both on our need for cleansing and God's readiness to cleanse. "Your hands are full of blood," he said; "wash and make yourselves clean. Take your evil deeds out of my sight! [...] Come now, let us reason together," says the LORD. "Though your sins are like scarlet, they shall be as white as snow; though they are red as crimson, they shall be like wool" (Isaiah 1:15-18). God promised in Zechariah 13:1 that "a fountain will be opened to the house of David and the inhabitants of Jerusalem, to cleanse them from sin and impurity."

As we saw in Chapter 15, the blood and water that gushed from Jesus' side after his death made vivid in the minds of early Christians the conviction that Jesus was the fulfillment and embodiment of these prophecies, the long promised fountain of cleansing from sin and impurity. The writer to the Hebrews sees Jesus as the new and living way and urges us therefore to "'draw near to God with a sincere heart in full assurance of faith, having our hearts sprinkled to cleanse us from a guilty conscience and having our bodies washed with pure water" (Hebrews 10:22).

This is wonderfully expressed in the rich the water imagery in the Anglican Baptismal Prayer:

20.5 Baptismal Prayer

> "We give you thanks, almighty God and Father, for by the gift of water you nourish and sustain all living things.
>
> "We give you thanks that through the waters of the Red Sea, you led your people out of slavery to freedom in the promised land.
>
> "We give you thanks for sending your Son Jesus. For us he was baptized by John in the river Jordan. For us he was anointed as Christ by your Holy Spirit. For us he suffered the baptism of his own death and resurrection, setting us free from the bondage of sin and death, and opening to us the joy and freedom of everlasting life.
>
> "We give you thanks for your Holy Spirit who teaches us and leads us into all truth, filling us with his gifts so that we might proclaim the gospel to all nations and serve you as a royal priesthood. We give

you thanks for you have called us to new life through the waters of baptism.

"Now sanctify this water, that your servants who are washed in it may be made one with Christ in his death and resurrection, to be cleansed and delivered from all sin. Anoint them with your Holy Spirit and bring them to new birth in the family of your Church, that they may become inheritors of your glorious kingdom.

"We give you praise and honour and worship through your Son Jesus Christ our Lord, in the unity of the Holy Spirit, now and forever. Amen."[219]

Chapter 21
Deep Calls to Deep

Out of the depths I cry to you, O LORD;
O Lord, hear my voice.
Psalm 130:1-2

Though you have made me see troubles, many and bitter,
you will restore my life again;
From the depths of the earth you will again bring me up.
Psalm 71:20

21.1 Deep Thirst

Picture a peaceful meadow on the edge of a woodland: a doe and fawn are grazing near a stream. The foraging is good, the forest cover makes it safe and their thirst is quenched at will. It's the epitome of the good life for a deer. This is the picture often evoked when worship leaders sing the opening words of Psalm 42 –

As the deer pants for the water
so my soul longs after you.
You alone are my heart's desire
and I long to worship you.[220]

These words are the testimony of someone who has a deep longing to know God. In Chapter 11, we talked about King David's thirst for God when he was in the Desert of Judah: "O God, you are my God, earnestly I seek you; my soul thirsts for you, my body longs for you, in a dry and weary land where there is no water" (Psalm 63:1).

But a careful reading of Psalm 42 actually paints a very different picture. Here the deer is panting desperately for water, but the stream bed is bone dry. It is not an idyllic woodland scene with a flowing stream, but a drought stricken place where the water has dried up. It is a fierce drought situation like the scenario described by the prophet Joel,

> where the animals moan with hunger! Herds mill about confused because they have no pasture; flocks of sheep and goats bleat in misery. Even the wild animals cry out to you because the streams have dried up and fire has consumed the wilderness pastures.
> Joel 1:18-20 NLT

In Psalm 42, the focus is not so much on the writer's desire for God, though it is real and deep; the emphasis is on the distress that comes from that desire being unfulfilled. His desire is intense, but the greater intensity is the anguish of disappointment.

> My soul thirsts for God, for the living God.
> When can I go and meet with God?
> My tears have been my food day and night.
> Psalm 42:3

This psalm is the lament of a parched soul. As we read between the lines we find that the writer feels not only spiritually dry, but very distant from God, both geographically and emotionally. This ordeal has been going on for a long time with no end in sight. Critics and foes taunt him – "where is this God of yours?" (verse 3) These jabs echo the doubts ringing in his own mind – '*Where is God?*'

His faith vacillates between trust and confusion. He is bewildered. He wants to hold on to the spiritual fervor he knew in earlier days, but he can't shake his doubts. Part of his mind urges him to keep trusting God, encouraging him that this dark night of the soul will soon be over and that songs of praise will flow again in the morning. The harsh reality is that he is in a spiritual wilderness, a time of inner drought.

What do you do when you thirst for God, but find the well dry? This is the genius of the lament psalms. This is why they have proven so useful to worshipping people for a hundred generations – because they allow us to be honest with God. They invite us to name our emotional state and bring it before God. It seems to us a pretty shabby offering, but God so values the gut-wrenching honesty that it is a sweet fragrant offering. So true-to-life is this experience of spiritual drought that over the centuries the faithful have come to know that this psalm was inspired by the Spirit of God.

The poet's thirst is intensified by two more factors. First, people around him are aware of his pain and are happily making it worse. They taunt him constantly, asking where his God is, why God doesn't answer his prayers. Their questions jab his heart like thorns, expressing a nagging fear that God actually has gone AWOL.

Secondly, he is tormented by nostalgia. He remembers how sweet it used to be back in the day when he led crowds of worshippers into the temple with shouts of joy, when he was on a spiritual high, when the river flowed with the refreshing vibrancy of God. But now these memories mock him as he pours out his heart to God and hears nothing in reply. He wonders if perhaps his faith was much ado about nothing.

In verse 5 he argues with himself.

> Why am I discouraged?
> Why is my heart so sad?
> I will put my hope in God!
> I will praise him again—
> my Savior and my God!
> Psalm 42:5 NLT

One side of his brain challenges this spiritual funk, asking what reason he has to feel so sad and why he should allow this time of doubt to rock him so severely. The other side knows the dull painful truth that he is spiritually 'downcast' – and he says so. This honest recognition of the inner condition of the heart opens the way for more reflection, because the troubled soul is not easily restored.

In verse 6 he says, 'I will remember you even though I am far away from the temple'. In the northern region of Mount Hermon, far from Jerusalem, the singer intentionally turns his thoughts to God. He still feels far away, doubts overshadow his faith, but his imagination allows him to connect with God, to 'rehearse everything he knows about God' from better days (verse 6 MSG).

21.2 Whitewater

Psalm 42 is an eloquent proof that faith and confusion can coexist if we are honest with God. We see further evidence of this inner confusion in verse 7 when the metaphor changes radically from the dry stream of verse 1 to a raging torrent: "deep calls to deep in the roar of your waterfalls; all your waves and breakers have swept over me" (Psalm 42:7). From 'parched soul' to 'deluge' in less than a minute.

Turbulent water can knock you off your feet, all right. Every year all around the world we hear tragic stories of people being swept away by the current of rivers. But what prompts the psalmist to shift so radically from thirsting to drowning?

The metaphors he uses match both his psychological and geographical situation. He is homesick, far from home and stranded in northern Israel where the Jordan River originates. The headwaters of the Jordan flow down from the highlands of Mount Mizar and Mount Hermon, the highest points in the region. At 9232 feet (2814m) elevation, Hermon is twice the altitude of Banff – and the skiing is superb.

Winter rains and summer snowmelt cascade down from this mountain range. The magnificent Hatachana waterfall and the river flowing through the steep canyons below it are loud and tumultuous, especially in the spring. But the writer has no interest in skiing or sightseeing. The crashing of the water echoes his inner turmoil and sense of being overwhelmed.

Don't think the words 'deep calls to deep' as just a touch of local color. To a Hebrew writer the word 'deep' carried connotations of the chaos of Genesis 1:2 before creation. It echoed the flood story where the abyss broke in on the world. 'Deep' suggests everything chaotic and evil asserting itself against life. 'All hell' was breaking loose. *The Message* says "Chaos calls to chaos", as if the powers of evil were conspiring to overthrow the world as the writer knew it. Out of the depths he calls to God. It's a cry of desperation. He's overwhelmed, he's lost his footing and can't hold on! It all seems so pointless and hopeless.

Have you ever been there? Overwhelmed by the current of circumstances, feeling alone and hopeless? That's where the psalms help us. They speak for us to God with honesty and echo the distress of our hearts. They assure us that we're not alone and we're not wicked to feel this way. Someone has been there ahead of us and given us words to express that we can hardly say for ourselves. Though we can't appreciate it in the present, this time of perplexity is actually deepening our capacity for faith, teaching us to trust God in the dark.

It's fascinating how the words of this psalm express the experience of Jesus when he plunged into the raging current of human injustice and sin – "all your waves and breakers have swept over me" (verse 7). There's nothing shallow about that kind of suffering or the reassurance his resurrection gives us. In fact, it's deeper than we'll ever know.

21.3 When Courage Melts Away

My daughter Joanna and her family live in Gloucester, Massachusetts, a fishing town on Cape Ann, north of Boston, made famous by the movie *The Perfect Storm*, the tragic story of the *Andrea Gail* that sank in furious seas in 1991. Over the 360 years of its sea-faring history, Gloucester has lost over 10,000 sailors and fishermen to the waters of the Atlantic. Today a large bronze memorial along the sea-walk records many of their names. Even more haunting is a nearby sculpture by the Fishermen's Wives Association[221] of a mother and two small children scanning the horizon for a glimpse of a boat they long to see, but that will never return.

The waters off Cape Ann are no more dangerous than most fishing harbors. It's just that fishing and sailing have always been hazardous occupations, taking people into an environment better designed for whales and seagulls.

The ancient Hebrew poet of Psalm 107 described the anxiety of sailors caught in the jaws of a fierce sea-storm –

> Others went out on the sea in ships;
> they were merchants on the mighty waters.
> They saw the works of the LORD,
> his wonderful deeds in the deep.
> For he spoke and stirred up a tempest
> that lifted high the waves.
> They mounted up to the heavens and went down to the depths;
> in their peril their courage melted away.
> They reeled and staggered like drunken men;
> they were at their wits' end.
>
> Then they cried out to the LORD in their trouble,

and he brought them out of their distress.
He stilled the storm to a whisper;
the waves of the sea were hushed.
They were glad when it grew calm,
and he guided them to their desired haven.
Let them give thanks to the LORD for his unfailing love
and his wonderful deeds for men.
Psalm 107:23-31

Every seasoned sailor can identify with the emotions of this psalm – being thrashed about in the waves, at your wits end, on the verge of terror, and then the enormous relief when all is calm again.

This poetic vignette brings to mind the terrifying storm of Jonah, the Galilee gale that raged around the disciples, and Paul's typhoon driven ship-wreck. Each of these experienced God's 'wonderful deeds in the deep'; they all came through their distress 'to their desired haven'. But not every storm ends in relief and joy, as the evocative Fishermen's Wives Memorial sculpture in Gloucester reminds us with such sad silence.

21.4 Engulfed

Psalm 88 is the darkest psalm in the Bible, anguished from start to finish. God is hidden and silent; the singer is terrified, abandoned and engulfed by despair.

Your terrors have paralyzed me.
They swirl around me like floodwaters all day long
They have engulfed me completely.
You have taken away my companions and loved ones.
Darkness is my closest friend.
Psalm 88:16-18 NLT

Like being lost at sea in thick fog, these deepwater terrors describe clinical depression, an ordeal of extreme mental suffering and hopelessness. We might wonder what a poem like this is doing in a book of faith like the Bible.

I think it is a tribute to the honesty of the Hebrew people that they accepted and preserved such uncensored expression of spiritual pain. It reveals a listening community that was willing to hear the anguish of its suffering members and a belief that honest doubt can be a vital part of the journey of faith. It teaches us that even in our worst moments, when we can find no answer for our suffering we can voice our outbursts of agony to God.

Reading a psalm like this when you're not in trauma yourself is an invitation to empathy, to stand alongside those who are engulfed in deep crisis, to express solidarity with the depressed, the prisoner, the terminally ill. The very existence of such expressions shows a community that understands.

It is important to say this, because darkness and unspeakable horror can also suffocate faith. The unspeakable horrors of Auschwitz did that for Elie Wiesel, whose book *Night* describes the evaporating of his childhood faith. But faith doesn't have to die when God is silent and when suffering continues unabated.

I vividly remember touring in Jerusalem and visiting the site that archaeologists believe was the house of Caiaphas. Some of our group crowded into a small dungeon, quite possibly the prison where Jesus was held between his late-night arrest in Gethsemane and his early morning Sanhedrin trial (Luke 22:63).

We read the whole of Psalm 88 in that dungeon. Here are some excerpts:

> My soul is full of trouble and my life draws near the grave. [...]
> You have put me in the lowest pit, in the darkest depths.
> Your wrath lies heavily upon me;
> you have overwhelmed me with all your waves.
> You have taken from me my closest friends [...]
> I am confined and cannot escape; [...]
> Why, O LORD, do you reject me and hide your face from me?
> [...] Darkness is my closest friend.
> Psalm 88:3, 6-8, 14, 18.

I was profoundly moved to imagine Jesus throughout that long night literally engulfed by evil and injustice, feeling abandoned by God and alone in the darkness, the terror of being swallowed up by a flood. It was probably the closest I have come to feeling something of the horror of what he endured. That brief experience of empathy with Jesus continues to fuel my adoration and commitment to him.

21.5 Buried Alive – Almost!

For twenty-two hours in October 2010, millions of people around the world were riveted to their televisions, laptops and cell phones, as thirty-three Chilean miners were being rescued. As one man after another emerged from a shaft in the dark earth and embraced his loved ones, we all choked back tears of joy.

Trapped under 2000 feet (650m) of bedrock for sixty-nine days, and then, against all hope, being plucked from the grave – it must have seemed to them like being resurrected from death. On the back of the t-shirts that the rescued miners wore were the Spanish words of the biblical text "In his hand are the depths of the earth, and the mountain peaks belong to Him" (Psalm 95:4). I suspect that conviction sustained their hearts as they waited for rescue.

"Deep calls to deep", the poet wrote in Psalm 42:7. Something deep within us connected us to these men and their families – the drama of rescue, the relief of not being buried alive. But there is something more. The human soul is deep and mysterious like a goldmine or a deepwater aquifer. Hidden from view, deep below the surface, an aquifer stores an enormous volume of water, just like the deep purposes in the human heart.

Why we do what we do is often a mystery to ourselves and others. Deeply embedded purposes and beliefs, values, memories and fears shape our outlook and actions, our creativity, our decisions, our words, sometime to great benefit and sometimes in ways that sting or wound or block others or ourselves.

Again we meet Solomon's observation, "the purposes of the heart are deep waters, but a wise person draws them out" (Proverbs 20:5). Our motives run deep, but a wise person tunes in to these hidden impulses, probes them, digs them out and brings them to the surface. God does not waste our experiences, positive or painful. They influence us but they need not bury us alive as victims. God transforms painful wounds, our failures and tragedies or the falsehoods we easily embrace. God's healing goes deep if we are honest with God.

The thirty-three miners escaped from a profoundly harrowing experience. We watched them step out of their rescue cage like the phoenix into the sunlight. But what no one could see, still buried deep inside them – but very alive – were memories, regrets, triumphs and deep resolves that influenced their newly minted lives.

In the days, weeks and months afterwards, the deep waters they went through shaped the way they made decisions, how they related to their family, what they dreamed for. They can't just shake off such 'deep' memories and return to normal. Post-traumatic stress hangs like a darkness over many of them; nightmare flashbacks stalked them. We can hope some are able to mine the mother lode of their ordeal, to explore the deep places of their soul and live freely in God's wide earth.

21.6 Erosion

One of the effects of water and wind is the magnificent reshaping of landscape we call erosion. Rain, waves, current and cold conspire with wind and gravity and the natural process of weathering to re-contour rocks and riverbanks into new forms. Erosion can be devastating like a tsunami, but it can also produce magnificent scenery like the beautiful Garden of the Gods in Colorado, the Grand Canyon and the White Cliffs of Dover.

We understand, more or less, the mechanics and chemistry that cause erosion, but as Luci Shaw observes, it still strikes us a riddle, "the way water, in its softness knuckles holes in granite."[222] Erosion and the chemical process of dissolution that carves out hollows, coves and caves all over the world are expressions of the universal law of attrition. Nature wears things down. The word *'erosion'* has the same Latin root as *'rodent'* – nature and time gnaw away at us. Whether gradually or ferociously, everything moves from order to disorder.

But something in the human heart resists that law. Job 14:18-19 says, "as a mountain erodes and crumbles [...] as water wears away stone and torrents wash away the soil, so you destroy a person's hope." Job was not just lamenting the law of natural attrition. He protested against it! Ultimately, he says, we end up with nowhere to stand!

Like the mountains, we are creatures of time, but we are not granite. We feel pain in a way that mountains don't. We are creatures of hope, but we don't stand a chance against the onslaught of time. As *The Message* puts it, "you relentlessly grind down our hope" (Job 14:19). Job writhes against this futility, despair and the hopelessness of hoping.

E. J. Pratt is one of Newfoundland's best-known poets. Much of his poetry examines humanity's struggle with nature. As the son of a Methodist minister, he sometimes accompanied his father as he delivered tragic news to a surviving family member.

On one occasion he recalled seeing the change on a woman's face as she heard that her husband's ship had gone down, "the pallor and the furrow on her face as the desolating news sank in". His poem *Erosion* bears witness to the powerful impact of the sea on the land and the faces of those who experience its power. After telling how it took the sea a thousand years to carve the face of a granite cliff, he says, by contrast,

> It took the sea an hour one night,
> An hour of storm to place
> The sculpture of these granite seams
> Upon a woman's face.[223]

Talk about a fearful wonder of water! Tragedy truly defaces our humanity. We are all of us weather-beaten. I think Job would have resonated with Pratt's poem.

Yet in the fullness of time, God did something to reverse the soul-eroding, life-destroying process that tears things down. In Jesus, God came to live among us to bear our tragedy with us and to restore our dignity. The powerful flow of Jesus' life erodes and tears away all kinds of evil from our hearts and leaves unique beautiful formations on the landscape of our lives. Ultimately Jesus transforms erosion into new creation!

21.7 Fearless at the Cliff Edge

On a stormy winter night in 1639, the residents of Dunluce Castle on the coast of Northern Ireland were entertaining neighbors. Dunluce is Gaelic for *strong fort,* and doubly strong it appeared to be even as the raging sea clawed at the basalt cliff on which the 12th century castle was built. The surf pounded the rock that night until without warning, the cliff face crumbled and the kitchen wing of the castle collapsed into the sea, plunging servants to their death. Despite the grandeur of the castle and its impressive view – a must-see for tourists visiting the Antrim coast –, the mistress of the house, Lady Catherine MacDonnell, lost her nerve and refused to live there after that night.

> We stand fearless at the cliff edge of doom

courageous in sea-storm and earthquake,
Before the rush and roar of oceans,
the tremors that shift mountains.
Psalm 46:2-3 MSG

Israel's Psalm 46 describes God as an unshakable fortress for his people, a strong refuge that gives us the utmost confidence. For this reason, the song continues, we have nothing to fear even if the earth gives way or mountains collapse into the sea (verse 2).

Make no mistake, storms assault us a hundred different ways. Calamities creep or crash upon us, but his psalm sings above the roar of circumstance. Surging waves can shatter our world, but God's presence and God's strength are unshakeable and enduring realities.

German Christians in the 16th century rallied around Martin Luther as he faced papal outrage and fury. Luther's hymn based on Psalm 46, *A Mighty Fortress is Our God,* became a marching song of the burgeoning protestant movement.

In November 1942, Japanese troops captured the Christian mission School in Chefoo, China, with its teachers and students – including the famous Eric Liddell of *Chariots of Fire* fame. As they marched towards the concentration camps, and as they lived there in appalling conditions for the next five years, they sang the words of this psalm which became a favorite of the China Inland Mission and the Overseas Missionary Fellowship that followed it, "God is our refuge, our refuge and our strength; In trouble, in trouble, a very present help."[224]

21.8 City of Joy

Psalm 46 is a study in contrasts. It begins with mountains collapsing into violent seas and then quickly changes to a cityscape graced by a peaceful river.

Let the oceans roar and foam.
Let the mountains tremble as the waters surge!
Interlude
A river brings joy to the city of our God,
the sacred home of the Most High.
God dwells in that city; it cannot be destroyed.
Psalm 46:3-5 NLT

Many cities are defined by a river – think of the Thames in London, the Seine flowing through Paris, New York's Hudson, or Montreal on the St. Lawrence – impressive cities, impressive waterways, natural beauty and economic engines. Jerusalem, however, has no river. The only naturally occurring water Jerusalem enjoys, besides occasional rain, is a couple of springs, primarily the Gihon spring on the east and the tiny conduit that carries its water into the city to the pool of Siloam. It's barely a stream, how could such a 'river' be a source of joy, how can it 'gladden the city of God'?

What makes this city impressive is not its natural assets but its spiritual resource. God is there – "within the city". God is the river that refreshes this city and invigorates her people with confidence. The way of faith seems so feeble, but God makes the faithful invincible.

This psalm gives us a new lens to view the world. 'Look' it says. 'Open your eyes.' Powerful armies and economies storm the world like raging seas. They surge and roar and overthrow each other, but God will have the last word. Wars will end; God will shatter spears and burn the chariots. God's river of grace will prevail. It's an impressive geopolitical vision – either complete naiveté or a worldview that could transform us all.

The crescendo line in the psalm says, "Be still, and know that I am God!" (verse 10) That's an interruptive command. It's a summons to nations to cease their arrogant aggression, and it's a personal corrective to our restless souls when knotted with anxiety. Daily life brings constant demands; pressure is relentless. We fret and fume and work furiously until the psalm roars to us above the din – "Stop! Return to the river. Find your joy and rest in God.'

Two dynamic expressions of water – pounding surf and the quiet river – both bid to control our hearts. This psalm show us where to find our joy and peace.

Prayer:
Rock solid God, wherever people today feel their world is reeling and on the verge of collapse, let them know your peace as a powerful counterforce in their life. May the pounding surf subside and may the calm river of your presence gladden their hearts today. Amen.

21.9 Presence
One of the most memorable lines in all of Isaiah's prophecy is this –

> When you pass through the waters, I will be with you;
> and when you pass through the rivers, they will not sweep over you.
> Isaiah 43:2

These words occur in the part of Isaiah that speaks about Israel's eventual release from exile and return home, but Professor Alec Motyer says that these words are actually God's promise to sustain Israel through the ordeal of exile. It was truly a deep water trauma. Many Jews doubtless lost whatever faith they had. It seemed that God had abandoned them and broken covenant with them. In fact it was Israel who had broken covenant, and the astonishing thing is that God resolved not to abandon his rebellious people, but to accompany them into the floodwaters of judgment, to preserve them, just as he preserved Noah, and to bring them home.[225]

We glanced at this text briefly in Chapter 11.7 in the context of David's overwhelming experience and Bunyan's story of Christian crossing the final river of death. And I considered discussing it in Chapter 13 as we surveyed the story of Israel's exile, since this passage reflects that historic experience. But I've placed it here, because the poetry in this promise transcends the ordeal of exile and the experience of Israel. It speaks of every kind of situation that we find dangerous or overwhelming. It speaks first of floodwaters and raging rivers and then about fire – "when you walk through the fire, you will not be burned; the flames will not set you ablaze" (Isaiah 43:2).

Water and fire are opposites that cover the entire spectrum of dangers that we might encounter on our journey. Surrounding the words of promise, God reminds us of his identity as Creator, Redeemer and Savior –

> This is what the LORD says—
> he who created you, O Jacob,
> he who formed you, O Israel:
> "Fear not, for I have redeemed you;
> I have summoned you by name; you are mine.
> When you pass through the waters, I will be with you; [...]
> For I am the LORD, your God,
> the Holy One of Israel, your Savior.
> Isaiah 43:1-3

The stabilizing power that promises to carry us through the most profound and crippling crisis moments in life is not our self-reliance. It's not good luck or our reputation or achievements. It's the presence of a God who created us, crafted us in his image, who calls us by name; a God who calls himself Savior and summons us to know him and trust him and to experience his redeeming of our failures and his power in our lives.

Chapter 22
Drought

22.1 Climate Change

Sometime in the 4th century BCE, it would seem, a plague of locusts descended on the land of the Bible. Locust plagues were not uncommon, but this one brought wave after wave of devastation. The opening chapter of Joel describes the ordeal. I include it in this book about water for two reasons. First, life was already grim due to a severe lack of rain; the locusts simply made a serious situation even more critical – or perhaps it was the other way around; it's not clear which calamity came first. Secondly, the way Joel describes the resulting crisis seems to me to echo the concerns in our day about the impact of climate change. This chapter is not comfortable reading, but as long as any part of our planet or any sector of the human family finds themselves suffering, it is important for us to read, to empathize and to pray.

Read the words of the following text and imagine some area of today's world that you know from recent news reports to be a drought stricken zone:

> The fields are ruined, the ground is dried up;
> the grain is destroyed, the new wine is dried up,
> the oil fails.
> Despair, you farmers, wail, you vine growers;
> grieve for the wheat and the barley,
> because the harvest of the field is destroyed.
> The vine is dried up and the fig tree is withered;
> the pomegranate, the palm and the apple tree—
> all the trees of the field--are dried up
> Joel 1:10-12

Agriculture in many places in our world is under severe stress. Often this distress correlates with the level of poverty in the population who are the most vulnerable before the changing fortunes of weather. If you can't pay for imported food, drought and famine become even more desperate.

> Has not the food been cut off before our very eyes, –
> joy and gladness from the house of our God?
> The seeds are shriveled beneath the clods.
> The storehouses are in ruins,
> the granaries have been broken down,
> for the grain has dried up.
> How the cattle moan!
> The herds mill about because they have no pasture;
> even the flocks of sheep are suffering.
> Joel 1:16-18

In his extremity the prophet calls out to God. As you read the following words, join the writer in praying for God's mercy and intervention.

> To you, O LORD, I call,
> for fire has devoured the open pastures
> and flames have burned up all the trees of the field.
> Even the wild animals pant for you;
> the streams of water have dried up.
> Joel 1:19-20

Prayer:
Lord of the scorched earth, we pray on behalf of those who are the most deeply affected by the severe impact of our changing climate. For those whose crops lie shriveled and dry, we pray for rain; for those whose fields remain waterlogged from lingering floods, we pray for relief; for those whose fish stocks have disappeared we pray for alternate harvests and for wise stewardship to prevail.

We pray for humility to reverse our wasteful ways and for wisdom and courage to find better ways to live in partnership with our environment. We ask for your mercy and for your strong saving hand for ourselves and others. Amen.

22.2 The Sound of Silence

Amos had grown hoarse pleading with the wealthy farmers in the north of Israel to translate their religious faith into compassion and fair dealings with the poor. Otherwise, he said, it was completely fraudulent. He warned his hearers that if they wouldn't listen to God's words, God would eventually give them the silent treatment – and that silence would not be golden for very long.

> The days are coming," declares the Sovereign LORD, "when I will send a famine through the land – not a famine of food or a thirst for water, but a famine of hearing the words of the LORD.
> Amos 8:11

Echoing everyone's frantic search for water during the dry season, Amos said people would "stagger from sea to sea and wander from north to east, searching for the word of the LORD, but they will not find it" (verse 12).

Nelson Mandela says that when he was imprisoned on Robben Island, "newspapers were more valuable to political prisoners than gold or diamonds, more hungered for than food or tobacco; they were the most precious contraband on Robben Island. News was the intellectual raw materials of the struggle. We were not allowed any news at all, and we craved it."[226] Amos foresees a similar drought about to engulf his northern neighbors. Drought in the soul of the nation is a terrible thing. People cannot live without spiritual resources, without answers for the questions of life. Their fears mount and they search desperately for direction.

Forty years later, in 722 BCE, Samaria, the capital fell to the Assyrians and 20-30,000 northerners were marched east into exile, never to return to their ancestral home. No prophets rose up among them to counsel and encourage them in Assyria as Ezekiel and Daniel did 170 years later when the southern nation of Judah was exiled to Babylon.

Poets of the twentieth described their own time in a similar way, a spiritual wasteland, a period when there seemed to be no word from the darkness. We continue to live in an age that is suspicious of religious messages but that is still searching for signs. Jesus said that hypocrites search for signs but are unwilling to heed them (Matthew 16:1-3). If we won't listen, how will we hear God speak?

In their 1964 hit song *The Sound of Silence*, Simon and Garfunkel lament the tragic emptiness of "people talking without speaking; people hearing without listening." In another stanza they plead to no avail,

Hear my words that I might teach you
Take my arms that I might reach you"
But my words, like silent raindrops fell
And echoed in the wells of silence.[227]

T.S. Eliot's *Gerontion* describes "an old man in a dry month [...] waiting for rain." He is looking back on his uninspired life, regretting that he had not lived or loved more passionately. He goes on to say,

Signs are taken for wonders. "We would see a sign!"
The word within a word, unable to speak a word,
Swaddled with darkness. In the juvescence of the year
Came Christ the Tiger.[228]

When the vitality and potency of Christ is ignored or shrouded in religious ritual, the Word remains infant – which literally means 'unable to speak'. When we tame the Tiger, there is no other life-giving, youth renewing word for our generation, the years run out and the silence remains. No wonder Jesus said that if we have ears, we really should listen (Matthew 11:15 and 13:9).

22.3 Double Fault

In 1126 C.E. a well was drilled in the province of Artois in northwest France. Free flowing water poured out of the ground. In later centuries similar wells across Europe came to be known as wells of Artois, or 'artesian wells'. An artesian well is one where underground pressure on a source of water causes the water to rise above the ground. No pumping is required to draw the water out.

In his book *Simply Christian*, N.T. Wright describes a similar phenomenon, a hidden spring that bubbles up irrepressibly within human hearts and human societies, the deep subterranean yearning we call spirituality.[229]

In our day, many people are wary of the religious expression of this impulse, but we cannot deny the indefinable thirst, the longing for springs of living refreshing water to bathe in, delight in and drink to the full. Wright says that this deep spring of spirituality is strong evidence, along with our instinctive quest for justice, our craving to connect in relationship and our yearning for beauty, evidence that we are made for something more than just physical existence.

Jeremiah and other writers in the Bible assert that God is the ultimate spring of living water for which our soul's thirst. God is the unique source and satisfaction of our deepest need, the love and dignity, the belonging and beauty, the mercy and music and purpose that we long for. Jeremiah noted that his society had by and large forsaken this exquisite wellspring of joy, empowerment and life that they craved. "My people have committed two sins: they have forsaken me, the spring of living water, and have dug their own cisterns, broken cisterns that cannot hold water" (Jeremiah 2:13).

The invention of waterproof mortar during the Bronze Age, allowed cisterns to retain their collected water much longer than would otherwise be possible. Cracked and broken cisterns were no doubt the result of local seismic shocks which shattered the limestone so that the water stored for the emergency of summer drought leaked out.[230]

Despite God's pledge of faithfulness, Israel deserted God in favor of more exotic deities and rituals. As Jeremiah saw it, that's a poor trade every time, exchanging 'glory' – that which gives us dignity and honor – for third-rate substitutes. Why would anyone abandon a freshwater spring for stale water cisterns that require laborious effort to dig and which ultimately leak badly? Ironically, though, it's a choice people commonly make. Our substitute solutions often intensify the problems they were chosen to solve, or they create new and more serious problems.[231]

Some people deliberately avoid God; for others it may be simple neglect, assuming that life will work fine without God – or without very much of God. But inevitably we have to satisfy our thirst one way or another, and every substitute god ultimately disappoints.

Prayer

Irrepressible God, Artesian well of life, why do other things so easily seduce me? You are the source of my deepest joy, you are the lifter of my head; you crown me with dignity and honor. Forgive me for grasping after straw when you provide sterling. Let me drink deep your promise never to abandon me; let me bathe in the fountain of your forgiveness and love; let me delight in your refreshing truth and joy. Amen.

22.4 Desperate Drought

Droughts are a common occurrence in the Middle East, but every time they hit, they bring a feeling of impending doom. Their impact runs deep and no one knows when the dire situation will end. Jeremiah wrote about a fierce drought that raged in his day. Rich and poor were equally frantic trying to fill empty water jars. Cisterns were bone-dry; farmers were helpless and dismayed; the ground cracked under the heat of the sun and the next generation of wildlife hung in the balance.

> Even the doe in the field deserts her newborn fawn
> because there is no grass.
> Wild donkeys stand on the barren heights and pant like jackals;
> Jeremiah 14:5-6

In the face of such life sapping drought, Jeremiah pleaded with God, "do something – for God's sake" (verse 7). He addressed God as Israel's only hope, "our Savior in times of distress" (verse 8) and then he pummeled God with a series of sharp questions (verse 8-9) –

- Why are you acting like you don't know us?
- Are you like an overnight traveler indifferent to the folks who live here?
- Has our distress caught you by surprise?
- Are you a helpless warrior?

Desperate circumstances provoke desperate language in prayer, and Jeremiah interceded with the desperation he saw in his neighbors' eyes. But God told Jeremiah to stop interceding for them because God was actually bringing upon them the natural consequences of their evil ways (verse 11).

Drought does not always equate with human sin, but in this instance there was a connection. The barren fields mirrored a barren society that was no longer rooted in their promises to God. Moral backsliding brings spiritual dryness and spreads outward.

American photographer and environmentalist Ed Firmage Jr. notes the link between social ethics and the land when he says, "drought takes on something of the character of the society it keeps. If that society lives on the edge, then drought shows up as the grim reaper."[232]

Jeremiah saw the drought as an indictment and pleaded guilty on behalf of the nation. But he also appealed to God's mercy in hopes that the anguish would be a moral corrective for his people. He wept for his people

(Jeremiah 14:17) and appealed to God to keep covenant even though Israel had broken it.

> Do any of the worthless idols of the nations bring rain?
> Do the skies themselves send down showers?
> No, it is you, O Lord our God.
> Therefore our hope is in you.
> Jeremiah 14:22

Jeremiah refused to accept his compatriots' superstitions that idolatry might bring the needed rain. He also refused the option that many in the twenty-first century hold to, the belief that there is no link between rain and righteousness, the myth that we live amid impersonal natural forces. Jeremiah believed that God was an active covenant-partner with Israel and vitally involved in their national well-being, including their weather. So he urged God to defend his own honor and to act decisively to help the nation in need, evil though they are. "Although our sins testify against us, O LORD, do something for the sake of your name" (Jeremiah 14:7).

Today as I write, the evening news brings word of the latest severe drought in Africa. Climate change, civil war and corrupt government have all contributed to this crisis. It would be easy to dismiss it as a perennial and hopeless situation. But Jeremiah mentors me to pray today for God's mercy for the parents and children, for the refugees from conflict and for the barren fields.

Prayer
Merciful God, we pray for all who are suffering today. In places of drought and famine we pray that you will send rain. Where lives are in crisis or danger, we pray for your peace. Where government is chaotic or unjust, we pray that competent and wise leaders will rise up with integrity and lead – and that your shalom will fill the earth as the waters cover the sea. Amen.

22.5 At the Scent of Water

The Aral Sea stands as one of the monstrous environmental catastrophes of the 20th century. Before 1960, it was the world's fourth largest inland sea, surpassed by only the Caspian Sea, Lake Superior and Lake Victoria. With an area of 26,300 sq. miles (68,000 km^2), it had a vibrant fishing industry employing 40,000 people. Today discarded fishing boats lie on the sand miles from shore.

In the 1950's and 60's Soviet engineers began diverting its two major inflowing rivers to irrigate cotton fields. As a result, Uzbekistan has become one of the world's major cotton producers. The cost of that productivity was the disastrous loss of the Aral's source waters. As a result, the Aral Sea began shrinking – and shrank steadily until, in 2004 it was only 25% of its original surface area, and by 2007 it had declined to 10% of its original size. The collapse of the fishing industry and the degradation of the land brought unemployment and economic hardship. The retreat of the sea has reportedly also caused local climate change, with summers becoming hotter and drier, and winters colder and longer.

There is now an ongoing effort in Kazakhstan to save and replenish what remains of the northern part of the Aral Sea (called the Small Aral). A dam project completed in 2005 has raised the water level of this lake. Salinity has dropped and fish are again found in sufficient numbers for some fishing to be viable. The outlook for the much larger southern part of the sea (the Large Aral), however, remains bleak.

It is no exaggeration to describe the destruction of this once-magnificent sea as a kind of ecological death. Job used such an analogy to protest the tragedy of a human life.

> As water evaporates from a lake
> and a river disappears in drought,
> people are laid to rest and do not rise again.
> Job 14:11-12 NLT

A journalist for *The Economist* in 2010 came to the sad conclusion that the entire Aral region is doomed. "It comes as a shock to be persuaded that human folly and hubris on this monstrous a scale has, in just my lifetime, devastated such a big chunk of Asia. Now only nature and time, probably on a geological scale, have any hope of redeeming it."[233]

One of the signs of global climate change is that many places in the world are becoming drier by the year, though not always as a result of decisions as reckless as with the Aral Sea. Climate change is taking its toll, and desertification is encroaching on many communities around the world.

It's not just happening in Africa, Texas and California. Climatologists and meteorologists in central Europe have said that the region is seeing more and more extreme weather, including long periods of dry and hot weather in the summer, severe flooding and bitter winters.

A 2011 report claimed that the Czech Republic had become one of the driest countries in Europe. The region experienced the effects of climate change in more frequent extreme weather events and changes in biodiversity. Half the Czech population relies on crucial underground water supplies, but these were drying up. With the drying of the landscape, drier periods get longer and are followed by bursts of intense rainfall which the dry soil cannot absorb, resulting in less recharge to the aquifers.[234]

This could make us very pessimistic, and the beleaguered wise man Job has a knack for nailing the bleakest of prospects. Job observes that desertification doesn't just happen in geography. It's part of the human condition. In Job 14:2-12 Job laments the brevity and frailty of human life. Using a string of similes, he ponders our human mortality – we're like flowers that wither (verse 2), fleeting shadows (verse 2), we're like day laborers, here today, gone tomorrow (verse 6); then, as we read earlier, "as water evaporates from a lake and a river disappears in drought, people are laid to rest and do not rise again" (verse 11-12). Then he adds an exclamation point to underscore the finality of death:

> Until the heavens are no more, they will not wake up
> nor be roused from their sleep.
> Job 14:12 NLT

We're like the wadis of Africa and the Middle East that run fast and full in flood-time but quickly become parched and dry. In a similar way, once-vibrant human beings "breathe their last and are no more" (verse 10). Sometimes without warning, sometimes painfully slowly, but eventually we all evaporate as surely as water under the summer sun, and there's nothing we can do about it. Job protests this irrefutable gloom that hangs over human life. He doesn't want to just lay down and die. Like Dylan Thomas, he would "rage, rage against the dying of the light."

But knotted into this string of death images is the intriguing thing called hope. Job grasps at a straw from biology, from botany. Is it a mirage? Is it a false dream, a futile longing that our lives have meaning and significance? Or does the world contain hints that point to a reality bigger than death?

> At least there is hope for a tree:
> If it is cut down, it will sprout again,
> and its new shoots will not fail.
> Its roots may grow old in the ground
> and its stump die in the soil,
> yet at the scent of water it will bud
> and put forth shoots like a plant
> Job 14:7-9

Nature gives lots of evidence that mortality gets the last word – we erode like mountains; given enough time we disintegrate. But nature also gives hints in the other direction. When a tree is felled, its roots don't necessarily rot in the ground. Sometimes 'at the scent of water' they sprout again.

Water can kill you; torrential floods can rip apart a riverbank, but water is also life-inducing. The faintest trace of water is enough to animate the roots of a felled tree and bring renewal. Why can't human beings revive like trees do and have another go at life? But the hints don't add up to a proof. Hope remains elusive. For every story of human redemption there were (and are) anguished stories of loss.

I love Job's steadfastness and the resilience of his faith. If there is hope for trees, maybe there is hope for human beings, too. Job isn't naïve or sentimental; he has unflinching courage and penetrating honesty; he eloquently expresses the anguish of his soul and the injustice of his suffering. Yet, in the face of his physical pain and spiritual bewilderment and the mystery of God's silence, he maintains his trust in God. "Though he slay me, yet I will hope in him" (Job 13:15).

Job's convictions do not shrivel in the heat; his faith does not evaporate despite the intensity of his suffering. His soul, though parched and dry, is sustained. Somehow the scent of water, hints of God's reality, perhaps his earlier experience of God's goodness and trustworthiness, kept Job rooted and alive in drought.

So for centuries we pondered Job's riddle and re-worked his questions – until a breakthrough nobody expected. In the resurrection of Jesus, hope gained new evidence. The failed disciple Peter, shocked and shame-ridden for abandoning his friend Jesus, was restored and reinvigorated with hope through Jesus' resurrection. His story has been repeated a million times.

Violence and death still run rampant in the world, but life and hope prevail. At the scent of that living water, the roots of hope sprout new life all over the world. Glandion Carney says "nature is always on the brink of rebirth." [235]

Wellspring International is a ministry that works for the release and renewal of women trapped in the sex-trade and children in serious at-risk environments. In her book *The Scent of Water – Grace for Every Kind of Broken,* Wellspring director Naomi Zacharias tells moving stories of the liberating power of love and hope from her own and other women's lives.

"Wells of Hope" is another example of hope blossoming in communities that desperately need water, work and other basics of life. The owners of Niagara's Stony Ridge Winery were so inspired by Jesus' miracle of transforming water into wine, that they decided to 'turn wine into water' by taking a portion of every wine-bottle purchase to finance wells and clean water for villages in the hills of Guatamala, freeing women and girls in those communities from hours of water-hauling every day. That's hope made real and practical, the dream elusive no longer.

Job's heart-wrenching questions reveal how universal is our search for hope. Programs like Wellspring and Wells for Hope give evidence that compassion, love and sacrifice can win the day over degradation and despair. The resurrection of Jesus became the living hope, the scent of water that gives hope new life.

22.6 Egyptian Reversal

The political pundits of his day wrote him off as simplistic and out of touch, but Isaiah foresaw the unthinkable. The mighty Nile, longest river in the world, he said, was drying up like a wadi in the desert. In shocking metaphor, Isaiah depicts the economic demise of one of the world powers of his day.

In the late seventh century BCE, with Assyrian armies threatening from the east, Israel's leaders kept eyeing Egypt as a hopeful ally. The Nile was a powerful natural resource, an engine of economic prowess. But Isaiah warned them that Egypt was not the answer. As prosperous and healthy as Egypt appeared, Isaiah foresaw that Egypt was heading into irreversible decline. What better symbol to illustrate Egypt's collapse than the evaporation of the Nile River!

> The waters of the Nile will dry up,
> and the riverbed will be parched and dry.

The streams of Egypt will dwindle and dry up.
The reeds and rushes will wither,
Every sown field along the Nile will become parched,
The fishermen will groan and lament,
Those who work with combed flax will despair,
and all the wage earners will be sick at heart.
Isaiah 19:5-10

The Nile has always been the economic backbone of Egypt's prosperity; if it were to collapse, the whole of Egyptian society would go down. This is precisely what Isaiah foresaw and foretold in Isaiah 19 – civil infighting, community breakdown, national morale melting away. The economy will flounder and people will resort to superstitious handwringing instead of industrious and commercial initiatives. When that happens, it will be as if the Nile itself no longer flows through their land.

The irrigation system will fail to function; fields will become saline; agriculture that depends on the river will become infertile and unproductive. Fishing on the river will dwindle, the textile industry that depends on the flax crop will lose its supply chain; workers will quit showing up for work; investor confidence will withdraw; employee morale will plunge and the entire workforce will slip into recession. Politicians will propose reckless and foolish strategies, and Egypt will descend helplessly into ruin.

What a graphic vision! In literal terms, the Nile has never evaporated the way this poem expresses it, but Isaiah's prophetic hyperbole was designed to warn Israel not to enter into military alliance with Egypt. Isaiah saw Egypt as a dry stick, a spent force. The never failing Nile was doomed to fail, because human society was never meant to function apart from God. Like the tower of Babel, Egypt would become impotent, a symbol of what happens to a culture that tries to solve its own problems and operate without God. God would intervene by releasing forces that bewilder and undermine the culture.

22.7 Egypt's Finest Hour

Isaiah's shocking prediction of Egypt's economic demise is echoed at the end of the Bible in the book of Revelation when John sees collapse of a world-class city and the maritime commerce that made her wealthy. Global investors are distraught and lament –

> In one hour such great wealth has been brought to ruin!
> Every sea captain, and all who travel by ship,
> the sailors, and all who earn their living from the sea, will stand far off.
> When they see the smoke of her burning, they will exclaim,
> 'Was there ever a city like this great city?'
> Revelation 18:17-19

Isaiah's prophecy was ominous, but, like John's Revelation, it was not merely a doomsday tirade. Like John, Isaiah was a prophet of hope. In a way unforeseen by any other Hebrew writer, Isaiah perceived that God had a national destiny in store for Egypt that would astonish even the most imaginative zealot in Israel – or the church today. Isaiah foresaw a day when God will open Egypt's heart, not to foolish superstitions, but to the worship of Yahweh. Egyptians will become passionate Yahweh worshippers and Yahweh will become Egypt's savior (verse 20).

A highway of commerce and communication will open from Egypt to Assyria, linking Israel's ancient oppressors in a covenant of loyalty, not simply with Israel, but with Israel's God. Egyptians and Assyrians will worship Yahweh together (verse 23). The doomed Nile will become a river of blessing to the whole world, like the rivers of Ezekiel and St. John.

Who could have foreseen such a paradigm-bursting turn-around, such a river of blessing from such a cursed source? Who would have imagined that –

> In that day Israel will be the third, along with Egypt and Assyria, a blessing on the earth. The LORD Almighty will bless them, saying, "Blessed be Egypt my people, Assyria my handiwork, and Israel my inheritance.
> Isaiah 19:24-25

Such a promise as this gives hope to Egyptian Christians today. Through centuries of harassment, they have seen how God uses adversity to strengthen his church. The Bible Society of Egypt, for example, is actively engaged in the mission of "flooding Egypt with God's Word". What the Nile does for Egypt's agriculture, they believe the Bible can do for the soul of their people, especially in this extraordinary time of change in Egyptian history.

Prayer

God of rivers, revenue and righteousness, your words today remind me that the flow of wealth in this world is not automatic. The river of your favor flows in channels of justice and truth. You have ordained a law for all nations that industry and mercy must flow together or they will eventually shrivel and die. You have promised that if we pay attention to your commands, our peace and prosperity will flow like a river, our "righteousness like the waves of the sea." (Isaiah 48:18).

May your mercy flow today into every country drained and watered by the mighty Nile – Tanzania, Rwanda, Kenya, Uganda, Ethiopia, Sudan and Egypt. And, may the good news of Jesus flow like a river through these nations and cause them to flourish in ways we can hardly imagine. Amen.

Chapter 23
Restoration

Isaiah's promise of renewal and restoration discussed in the last chapter, is just one of many springs of hope that gush out of the text of the Bible to assure us in every way possible that God is passionate about bringing us into a flourishing tomorrow. As God told Israel in the dark dry days of the exile, "I know the plans I have for you, plans to prosper you and not to harm you, plans to give you hope and a future" (Jeremiah 29:11).

Restoration is the fulfillment of Job's wistful longing, "there is hope for a tree if it is cut down, yet at the scent of water it may sprout again" (Job 14:7-9). We catch that scent of life renewing water in a variety of texts.

In his poem "Water", Conservationist Wendell Berry tells us how the scent and flavor of water and the sweet sound of rain rouses his spirits after seasons of dry heat. Having been born in a drought year, all his life he has dreaded the return of drought. He calls himself now "the faithful husband of the rain":

> I love the water of wells and springs
> and the taste of roofs in the water of cisterns. [...]
> My sweetness is to wake in the night
> after days of dry heat, hearing the rain.[236]

23.1 Faithful Husband of the Rain

The fear of drought haunts not only the dreams of farmers between seeding and harvest, but the hearts of people everywhere who know the thirst of longings that are beyond our power to fulfill. We thirst and wait and sometimes learn wisdom. Nature is a relentless teacher and wise farmers learn patience – the art of waiting expectantly, of watchfulness without worry, of anticipation without presumption.

James draws a wonderful analogy between the patient farmer and the patience of believers who long for the reign of God to appear.

> Be patient, then, brothers and sisters, until the Lord's coming. See how the farmer waits for the land to yield its valuable crop and how patient he is for the autumn and spring rains. You too, be patient and stand firm, because the Lord's coming is near.
> James 5:7-8

We live often in the delusion that everything depends on us. Waiting, longing and persevering are disciplines that rebuke our assumption of self-reliance, our impatient fretting, our annoyance towards others. Waiting for the rains to arrive is a reminder to pray for the coming of Christ, that his kingdom will come in us and around us, as well as through us.

23.2 Restoring the Years the Locusts Devoured

Joel, we recall from the last chapter, was desperate for God's intervention. The shock and awe of devastating drought in Joel 1 ended with the haunting words, "how the cattle moan. [...] Even the wild animals pant for you; the streams of water have dried up and fire has devoured the open pastures" (Joel 1:18-20). But Joel was not paralyzed by the crisis. He called the nation and its leaders to a fast of weeping and penitence (Joel 2:12-15). He was convinced that the drought and locust plague were caused in part by moral collapse that could only be reversed by personal and national repentance.

His spiritual initiative bore fruit and God answered with a resounding promise of new life – "Be glad, O people of Zion, rejoice in the LORD your God, for he has given you the autumn rains in righteousness. He sends you abundant showers, both autumn and spring rains, as before" (Joel 2:23).

People who have never known the desperation of dry earth cracking under their feet, can hardly imagine the ecstasy that promise must have brought to the people. It was like a death row reprieve – and the promise was not given in a muted whisper! When English speakers want to emphasize a word, if we really, *really* want people to get it, we double the word. That's what Joel does here. The Hebrew text of v.23 reads literally '*moreh moreh, malqosh malqosh*' for the autumn and spring rains. Joel was saying 'Count on it, people, this rainfall is gonna set records! Our God of abundance is going to give us crops that will more than make up for all that the drought and locusts destroyed.'

Besides doubling the words of promise, Joel plays with the rain words another way, as an English speaker might play with the words 'rain' and 'reign'. The word *moreh* can mean both rain showers and 'teacher' or 'teaching'. So while many translations say, "He has given you the autumn rains in righteousness; He sends you abundant showers",[237] others, like *The Message* say,

> He's giving you a teacher to train you how to live right —
> teaching, like rain out of heaven, showers of words
> to refresh and nourish your soul.
> Joel 2:23 MSG

Commentators suggest the pun is intentional, meaning that the rains are an eloquent communication of God's mercy. If you think about it, that makes a lot of sense. If we listen, the rains are both a gift of nature and a message of grace, teaching us the way of righteousness. Rain restores life and megaphones God's message to our contrite God-hungry hearts, "I am the Lord Your God. I will repay you for the years that the locusts have eaten" (Joel 2:25).

Many people look back on a bleak period of their life as months or years lost to the locusts. But instead of leaving us in deserts of regret, God specializes in restoring wasted years, healing our backsliding, renewing dignity and purpose to our lives, restoring us to fruitfulness and joy. That was the spiritual renewal Joel could foresee pictured in the greening fields and the breakthrough of new life on the hills of Israel. In the very next verses God adds, "and afterward, I will pour out my Spirit on all people. Your sons and daughters will prophesy, your old men will dream dreams, your young men will see visions" (Joel 2:28).

It was at Pentecost, Israel's traditional harvest festival, centuries after Joel preached and wrote, that his promise had its dramatic fulfillment. That is when God rained down his Spirit in a monsoon. It fell, not as we might expect, on Israel's privileged elite or even on Jesus' favored twelve apostles (Acts 2). No, this baptism of joy drenched the whole rag-tag collection of Christ's followers, young and old, women and men, slaves and land-owners – and before long, Jews and Gentiles. It fused them into a multi-national egalitarian charismatic community. That's when Joel's drought really came to an end. The flourishing of the church in the centuries since then has confirmed the presence of God's Spirit among us. This, despite our many sins, both personal and corporate, that could easily discredit our being the temple of God on earth.

The Pentecostal and charismatic movements in the twentieth century have highlighted the truth that this out-pouring of God's Spirit was not simply a once-for-all historic event that occurred and ended at Pentecost, but an on-going reality. The promise continues to be fulfilled whenever someone experiences a fresh infusion of God's grace and love by the Spirit of God. Some call it the second blessing or a second level of salvation. But any Christian who has gone through a barren sterile stretch in their spiritual life and then experienced a renewed joy and desire for God and a resurgence of love for others, knows that it feels like a renewed personal Pentecost. We become more alive to the presence of the Spirit and our hearts sprout with fresh hope and joy –and Joel's promise dovetails with Isaiah's: when God pours his Spirit out upon us, the desert becomes a fertile field and the fertile field grows thick as a forest (my own paraphrase of Isaiah 32:15).

There's another sense in which this prophecy awaits further fulfillment. Messianic Jews would say that their compatriots are still in a spiritual drought or desert. Having spurned their Messiah, their God-sent teacher of righteousness, Israel continues to suffer deep spiritual hardness of heart. But one day, it is promised, they will discover their error, admit their desperate need and embrace their Messiah; God will "restore the fortunes of Judah" as Joel 3:1 says. Such a turn-around says Paul, would be like "life from the dead" (Romans 11:15). That's when humanity's drought really, really will come to an end!

23.3 Fresh Rain

It's every teacher's dream – her students soaking up her inspired teaching like thirsty grass. Parents and poets and preachers have the same hope and dream. Nothing sweeter or more satisfying than hungry minds feasting on your words – that's why we talk and write.

Moses was such a teacher. He spent a lifetime walking with God, decades after his burning bush experience, not just talking his faith, but living it, modeling it in the rough and tumble of unfolding history. Now as a farewell gift to his people, he wrote a song as his legacy, Deuteronomy 32, about the timeless ways and love of God. It was not just a swan song; it summarized his convictions about God's unconditional commitment to Israel despite their habitual unfaithfulness. It urged every new generation to embrace the truth he had discovered about their God and to live in the light of that grace.

> Let my teaching fall like rain
> and my words descend like dew,
> like showers on new grass,
> like abundant rain on tender plants.
> Deuteronomy 32:2

Like rainfall, God's truth comes from above; it is freely given. Like dew, it is gentle, gracious and refreshing. It is not something human beings can originate or control. No wonder Moses says at the end of the song, "these are not just idle words for you – they are your life" (32:47). To an agrarian society, the images of rain and dew conveyed how vitally important it was to receive the words of life Moses gave them about the character of God.

They urge us too, to welcome God's truth into our lives as eagerly as we imagine seedlings drinking in the nourishing spring rains. We need repeated doses, all season long, if we are to stay fresh and vibrant and our spiritual lives are to prosper.

Jesus told a story about the way different kinds of ground under the same sun and rain can produce very different yields. Everything depends on how deeply we embrace the seed that is sown. 'If you have ears,' he said, 'listen, really listen' (Matthew 13:9 MSG). The writer of Hebrews has the same thought in mind when he writes "when the ground soaks up the falling rain and bears a good crop for the farmer, it has God's blessing. But if a field bears thorns and thistles, it is useless. The farmer will soon condemn that field and burn it" Hebrews 6:7-8 NLT). He wrote this parable confident that his readers were the kind of soil that would welcomed God's word and put it into practice; he was confident that they would inherit God's promises because of their faith and endurance.

> Word of God, speak.
> Let it pour down like rain
> Washing my eyes to see
> Your majesty.[238]

23.4 Spring Rain – Restoration

A tough thing happened to me on March 23 one year. The calendar said 'Spring' two days earlier, but nature had a mind of its own and treated us overnight to a cruel dump of unwelcome snow. The day before, I had taken pictures of crocus shoots triumphantly announcing the new season. The next day they were buried in white.

But having endured 5 months of winter, I wasn't about to let a spring blizzard get me down. I knew what was coming. I'm Canadian. I'm a man of hope. Still, by the end of March I'm tired of winter and itching to get my hands dirty in the soil again, to participate in the annual miracle.

The 14th century poet Geoffrey Chaucer used this image in the opening lines of the Prologue to the *Canterbury Tales.*

> When that April with his showers soote
> The droughte of March hath pierced to the roote
> And bathed every veine in swich licour
> Of which vertu engendred is the flowr . . .

Or to put it in modern parlance, 'April showers bring May flowers.'

In the land of the Bible, the spring rains are vital for bringing the winter growing season to its climax. The 'early rain' falls in late October and softens the summer hardened soil for planting. January brings the peak rainfall, but most vital is the spring rain, also called 'the latter rain', just ahead of the heat that plumps the harvest. No rains, no harvest.

Hosea uses this annual phenomenon as a metaphor for our life with God. Just as the spring rains bring renewal to the earth, Hosea says, God longs to bring renewal to our lives. There are winter seasons in the soul when we desperately need renewal, when love grows cold, vision goes dormant and songs go silent; when you're in a slump, devitalized and dry, and doubt settles on you like snow.

Hosea knew the humiliation of personal winter. After three children, his wife froze him out, abandoned him and returned to her earlier career as a prostitute. Numb with rejection and grief, Hosea drilled deep into the faithfulness of God and found the courage and grace to seek out his wife and woo her back. He paid off her pimps and renewed her honor and dignity. Together they discovered the essence of spring – the depth of God's love and the healing of their own fragile marriage.

Hosea sang to her,

> Come, let us return to the LORD.

He has torn us to pieces but he will heal us;
he will bind up our wounds.
Hosea 6:1

His song reverberated to his whole community. As a pastor and prophet Hosea saw how estranged his whole society was from God and he urged them to renew their vows, to acknowledge Yahweh again:

Oh, that we might know the Lord!
Let us press on to know him.
He will respond to us as surely as the arrival of dawn
or the coming of rains in early spring.
Hosea 6:3 NLT

God comes to us faithfully as the seasons, faithful as the dawn. Count on it, says Hosea, God longs to revitalize your hope, your vision, your faith like the spring rain. Your marriage can be renewed; your faith can be revived. But it doesn't just happen.

I find myself often being passive, hoping I'll intuitively get to know God better one day. But love never grows passively. Hosea says "come, let us return to the LORD. He has torn us to pieces; now he will heal us. (Hosea 6:1 NLT)." Allow God's initiative to rouse your response. Pursue him; press into that quest like a hunter pursues prey, the way golfers pursue excellence (or at least par), the way lovers pursue their beloved.

The warming sun and spring rains eventually thaw the frozen ground. The earth passively absorbs the rain that falls on it, but the rain activates the living things – roots, seeds and bulbs lying in the dark earth. Roused to life, they exert themselves with prodigious vigor to be all they were made to be.

As Jesus said, you are worth more to God than they are (Luke 12:24). That's the alluring promise of God and the invitation of Hosea to us no matter what the weather feels like and whatever date the calendar says.

23.5 Like Streams in the Negev

On July 9, 2011, a new African nation was born. During my visit to South Sudan three years before, I saw the ruins of schools and churches destroyed thirty years earlier at the hands of their own government. I met young people born in refugee camps and listened as grandparents spoke of their dreams of rebuilding their nation. Against all odds, and thanks to enormous international efforts and a landslide referendum in support of independence, 2011 brought them a fresh opportunity for peace and growth.

When Israel's refugees returned to their land after exile in Babylon, someone wrote a song about their dreams. It became Psalm 126 in Israel's Book of Psalms. It is a psalm of great joy and hope, but it is realistic about the challenges of nation building. It bears the painful memories of past oppression, but it also dances with near delirium at the gift of freedom.

> When the LORD brought back his exiles to Zion,
> it was like a dream!
> We were filled with laughter, and we sang for joy.
> And the other nations said,
> "What amazing things the LORD has done for them."
> Yes, the LORD has done amazing things for us!
> What joy!
> Psalm 126:1-3 NLT

At the heart of this song is a vibrant water image that fits the context perfectly,

> Restore our fortunes, LORD, as streams renew the desert.
> Those who plant in tears will harvest with shouts of joy.
> They weep as they go to plant their seed,
> but they sing as they return with the harvest.
> Psalm 126:4-6 NLT

The dry inhospitable Negev serves as a mirror of the national ordeal of exile. The summer sun bakes the earth hard, but when it rains the dry ravines rapidly fill with water. Astonishingly the desert blossoms with wildflowers. "With such suddenness long years of barren waiting are interrupted by God's invasion of grace into our lives."[239]

In his book *Tending to Eden*, Scott Sabin highlights a wonderful passage from Isaiah that anticipates the great reversal and joyful restoration that Psalm 126 celebrates:

> When the poor and needy search for water and there is none,
> and their tongues are parched from thirst,
> then I, the LORD, will answer them.

> I, the God of Israel, will never abandon them.
> I will open up rivers for them on the high plateaus.
> I will give them fountains of water in the valleys.
> I will fill the desert with pools of water.
> Rivers fed by springs will flow across the parched ground.
> I will plant trees in the barren desert—
> cedar, acacia, myrtle, olive, cypress, fir, and pine.
> I am doing this so all who see this miracle
> will understand what it means—
> that it is the LORD who has done this,
> the Holy One of Israel who created it.
> Isaiah 41:17-20 NLT

In the reforestation ministry he leads, called 'Planting with Purpose' Sabin often uses this text to illustrate God's passionate response to the poor and the correlation between water and woodlands. Water makes forests possible, but forests also enhance the watersheds that sustain them. Trees provide soil stability and shade that reduces evaporation and helps water infiltrate into the soil. This Isaiah text bursts with biodiversity – seven kinds of trees – as an expression of God's abundance and creativity. Such a variegated woodland would also provide cover for animals and other organisms.[240]

In Isaiah's day this text served as a visionary promise lifting the eyes of the exiles to a more hope-filled future and to their God, Yahweh, who promised to redeem the barren years and restore Israel's fortunes. In the 21st century this same text speaks in practical ways to peasant farmers in the developing world, giving them a similarly hopeful and realistic vision that God can make even barren hills blossom with abundance. It also paints a landscape-of-the-heart of someone who has experienced God's restorative touch on their life, transforming barrenness and devastation into scenes of vibrant new life. Restoration is one of God's specialties!

The day my friends in South Sudan achieved their independence, I prayed the words of Psalm 126 for them. The images of water bringing life to the desert and of farmers planting seed in an insecure future, guided my prayers that God would prosper their efforts at nation-building and restore the fortunes of this war ravaged people.

War clouds still hang over this young nation, but I prayed – and pray – that they will be protected from their enemies, that tribal prejudice will be turned towards neighborly peace, that a commitment to integrity and public service will displace the corruption which poisons so much of Africa, that agriculture will adapt to the realities of drought and a changing climate with the best of new technologies, that schools and hospitals will be built and staffed well, that nutrition will improve, that wells will be dug and clean water will abound, that women will rise in dignity and that commerce will flourish, and that a degraded ecology will be restored.

Above all I prayed – and pray still – that the Living Water, the good news of Jesus Christ, will flow like rivers across South Sudan and win the hearts of millions.

23.6 Wells of Joy

In 1938, after a seven year search, the Jewish settlers at Kibbutz Na'an in Palestine finally found water. Their joy was ecstatic. Among them was a dancer named Else Dublin who choreographed a simple dance to celebrate the event. Later that year they performed the song and dance at a folk festival in Galilee and it became an immediate hit. Today it is one of the most popular Israeli folk dances – *Mayim, Mayim* – 'Water, Water'.

Mayim, Mayim is a circle dance, so it is easy to imagine dancing around a well. The words of the song come directly from Isaiah 12. Even though Kibbutz Na'an is proudly unreligious, the words of Isaiah seemed the perfect expression of their joy, 'Water, water, water. With joy you shall draw water from the wells of salvation!' (from Isaiah 12:3).

The Jewish tradition of dancing their joy goes back to the days of Miriam and Moses. With the Red Sea and their slavery in Egypt behind them, Israel burst into spontaneous song –

> Yahweh is my salvation;
> Yahweh, my strength and song"
> Exodus 15:2.

Miriam led the women in a dance, tambourine in hand and the joy was palpable. Then they headed out across the hot wilds of Sinai. Sometimes the water they found was brackish and undrinkable, but by various means, their saving God supplied their needs: remediated wells, water bursting from rocks, an oasis with springs and palm trees.

Five hundred years after Moses, Isaiah foresaw doom and exile for Israel, but beyond the gloom . . . hope: God's deliverance, a new exodus, a resurgence of life. Isaiah drew on exodus language and imagery and wrote a song to brace Israel for the ordeal ahead, to focus their faith in Yahweh.

> The LORD, the LORD, is my strength and my song;
> He has become my salvation. [...]
> With joy you will draw water from the wells of salvation.
> Give thanks to the LORD [...]
> Sing to the LORD, for he has done glorious things;
> Let this be known to all the world.
> Isaiah 12:2-5

Notice that Isaiah sees salvation not just for Israel. He sees a global exodus, nations set free by Yahweh! The vision was still misty for Isaiah as it was for Moses and Miriam. But today the good news of Jesus invites us from every nation to drink deeply from God's wells, the boundless depths of grace from a desert God who provides water for thirsty tongues and joy for burned-out spirits, forgiveness for hard hearts and fresh hope for discouraged souls.

Fresh clean water is a gift of endless wonder! An even greater wonder is the living water of God's salvation well. Leap to your feet and do a circle dance – alone or with a friend – to the One who gives these gifts and who pours out joy without restraint.

23.7 The Wild Kisses of a Lion

In the last chapter of *The Silver Chair,* Jill and Eustace stood beside a beautiful fresh-flowing stream in bright sunshine. The only sound was heartbreaking funeral music from a faraway world. Aslan and the two children gazed into the water.

There on the golden gravel of the bed of the stream, lay the king, dead, with the water flowing over him like liquid glass. His long white beard swayed in it like water-weed. And all three stood and wept.[241]

Like Jesus weeping at the tomb of Lazarus, "even Aslan wept – great Lion-tears." If you've ever lost a loved one, you know the sadness that is deeper than words. The river of death is the inevitable end of every person's life, but Lewis shows us that death does not have the last word.

Aslan told Eustace to bring a rapier-sharp thorn and pierce his lion's paw. A great drop of blood, "redder than all redness you have ever seen," splashed into the stream over the dead body of the king – and a transformation began. The funeral music stopped. The king's white beard turned fresh and then vanished. His sunken cheeks became round and red. His wrinkled face brightened until the king leapt out of the water with boyish laughter and flung his arms around the Lion. "He gave Aslan the strong kisses of a King, and Aslan gave him the wild kisses of a Lion."

There, on the Mountain of Aslan, "beyond the end of the world" Eustace and Jill watched as Aslan welcomed the king home into resurrected Life on the far side of Death. He wasn't a ghost; he was real, transformed by the sacrifice of the Lion, by the deep magic of Narnia. In *The Lion the Witch and the Wardrobe,* Aslan explained that when a willing victim who had committed no treachery was killed in a traitor's stead, Death itself would crack and "start working backwards."

The thorn that pierced Aslan echoes the curse in the Garden of Eden. Aslan's pierced paw echoes the ancient Genesis prophecy about the crushed foe wounding the rescuer's heel (Genesis 3:15). The crimson blood of Aslan's self-giving is the greening of death, transforming its sting into laughter and joy. Best wonder of all, this is not just a fiction of Narnia. In our own world, that very thing actually occurred. And one day the wild kisses of the Lion will welcome us home!

This story really sets us up for the grand *Finale,* which is the theme of the next chapter.

Chapter 24
Finale

Water figured prominently in the creation of the world, as a *gift* uniquely fitted to the needs of living things. It continues to be a vital resource in sustaining every ecosystem on the planet. In surveying the *story* of Israel and of Jesus and his church on earth, we saw how often water served as the physical setting for important personal and family and national experiences. We have seen how water affects the *way* we live and how it illustrates principles of God's pattern for human life.

In this final chapter we're about to pull back the curtain to glimpse the Bible's vista on the ultimate horizon of human life. We will see that water continues to be God's gift to us, a key indicator of God's purposes for us, God's response to us, and his invitation to us to partner with him on behalf of his creation.

24.1 Fire and Ice

How do you think the world is going to end? Poet Robert Frost posed the question this way:

> Some say the world will end in fire,
> Some say in ice.
> From what I've tasted of desire
> I hold with those who favor fire.[242]

Frost recognized the potential of human ambition, greed and passion to lead to hostility and violence. He wrote this poem in 1920 after the great 'war to end all wars' which was followed 20 years later by another equally horrendous global conflict. Frost was right; fire is deadly. But Frost goes on to speak of icy attitudes of hate that freeze out one's foes, of indifference, apathy and scorn that are equally destructive and lead to death by isolation and loneliness. Frost is right on both scores. Love and hate; violence and apathy. Both can destroy the world.

There is a widespread feeling – call it fantasy or dread – that the world is in for a gigantic meltdown. 'Armageddon' has become synonymous with notions of a violent end of the world. From the 1950's to the 90's people tended to fear a nuclear holocaust. Since then, apocalyptic warnings have shifted to scenarios of environmental collapse.

Early in the Bible's story God purged the evil of the world with a great flood and then made a covenant promise, "never again will all life be cut off by the waters of a flood; never again will there be a flood to destroy the earth" (Genesis 9:11). Was this a blanket pledge of protection for the created world, or did God simply preclude flooding by water while holding open the option to destroy the world some other way?

In 2 Peter 3:10-13 we read about the universe disintegrating in a meltdown expressed especially vividly in *The Message*:

The sky will collapse with a thunderous bang, everything disintegrating in a huge conflagration, earth and all its works exposed to the scrutiny of Judgment. Since everything here today might well be gone tomorrow, do you see how essential it is to live a holy life? Daily expect the Day of God, eager for its arrival. The galaxies will burn up and the elements melt down that day—but we'll hardly notice. We'll be looking the other way, ready for the promised new heavens and the promised new earth, all landscaped with righteousness.

A literal interpretation of this text foresees the disintegration of the physical universe, a cosmic fireball, and out of the smoke and ashes, a pristine new heaven and earth. Jesus did say that heaven and earth will pass away (Matthew 24:35), but did he mean a literal material disintegration?

Another interpretation regards Peter's description as apocalyptic language, graphically overstated in order to shock and astonish us, indicating how completely God will transform the world as we know it. When he says, "the elements will be destroyed" (2Peter 3:10) the 'elements' (in Greek '*stoichia*') that will melt away are not the elements of the periodic table, the atomic building blocks of the physical cosmos, but the fundamental spiritual and social structures that keep the world running as it does, political leaders, religious traditions, economies and politics.[243] Everything about the way the human world functions will be radically transformed. Everything that is not needed for the new creation and everything that is unworthy of it will evaporate, and a radically purged renewed creation will emerge. Since the physical environment resonates with the moral environment we can expect radical changes and transformation in the physical landscape, the kind that Ezekiel describes as the river from God's temple renewed the environs of the Dead Sea.

24.2 Sea of Tranquility

Back in Chapter 16 we explored some of the water-related experiences and visions of John the Divine on the island of Patmos. In Revelation 4, John is invited into a vision of heaven, and the drama of Revelation bursts into life as John sees and listens to four living creatures around God's throne praising God as creator and leading God's people in worship – "You are worthy, our Lord and God, to receive glory and honor and power, for you created all things, and by your will they were created and have their being" (4:11).

The eye widening images in John's vision are deep with meaning. The four living creatures symbolize the four winds, the four corners of the earth, the whole of the created cosmos.[244] A rainbow encircles God's throne as vivid witness to God's character and faithfulness as a covenant keeper towards his creation. In front of the throne of God and these four dramatic creatures John sees a 'sea of glass, clear as crystal" (verse 6).

To the Hebrew mind, the sea symbolized the restlessness of humanity in revolt against God. But this 'crystal sea' is not raging. It is a sea of tranquility, unperturbed by the restless wickedness of earth. Like Solomon's 'bronze sea' that we looked at in Chapter 20, John's crystal sea pictures God's infinite purity and his infinitely purifying grace. It also proclaims the peace that surrounds God's throne. God's shalom is not ignorant of earth's turbulence; it is not indifferent to the anguish and struggles of people, but it speaks of God's peace that is supreme. Our prayers and praise are offered – and our faith is lived out, sometimes falteringly – in a world where evil lurks and threatens to engulf us, where life often feels chaotic and random. But that danger is not the defining horizon of our life.

This heavenly vision reminds us of the ultimate reality – that God reigns and that chaos and evil will not prevail. Darrell Johnson notes[245] that because of this heavenly assurance, God's people here on earth can sing as Israel sang in Psalm 89:8-9,

O LORD God Almighty,
who is like you?
You are mighty, O LORD,
and your faithfulness surrounds you.
You rule over the surging sea;
when its waves mount up, you still them.

24.3 The Whole Creation Groans

Then in the next chapter we hear even more waves of worship to the Lamb that climax in a song which "every creature in heaven and on earth and under the earth and on the sea (Revelation 5:13), sings to God and to the Lamb. The focus is on Jesus as Redeemer and Lord of creation. These visions of a creation tuned to praise its Lord anticipates the outcome of the saving work of God and Christ when the new creation finally emerges.[246]

Until the new creation breaks fully upon the world like a sunrise, the powers of darkness continue to prowl the earth, raging against God's purposes and fouling the landscape of God's creation. Rivers run dark with industrial arsenic and PCB's and other poisoned elements, shorelines are smudged with leaked crude oil, whales become trapped in vast nylon nets, rain forests are mowed down by chainsaws and bulldozers, and giant bluefin tuna are hunted to extinction.

The whole creation groans as in the pains of childbirth, longing to be liberated from its bondage to decay (Romans 8:20-22). When that transformed world comes, it will be worth the wait, but in the meantime, the ordeal of birth pangs is long and intense. Revelation uses graphic imagery to describe those painful convulsions of nature in its suffering state. Three successive waves or cycles unfold. In Revelation 6 we see four horsemen: evil, war, famine and death as they gallop across the earth.

Then in Revelation 8 a second cycle of judgments follows – seven trumpets that announce the dire consequences that follow the refusal of earthlings to stop their carnage upon the earth and their defiance of God. After only four trumpet blasts the devastation is horrific. A third of the earth and its trees and grass are burned away, the sea turns to blood destroying a third of all fish and sea life and a third of ship traffic; a third of the rivers and aquifers are poisoned and many people die from drinking the contaminated 'bitter' waters. The atmosphere darkens, diminishing sunlight, moonlight and starlight by a third.

It's not hard to read the story of contemporary environmental degradation in this apocalyptic scenario. The impact of global warming, pollution of the ocean and reckless harvesting of its bounty, the contamination of rivers and groundwater from industrial and agricultural pollution, the impact of excessive dams, mining and forestry practices and the fouling of the air, are loud trumpet blasts from the world of nature – wake-up calls – the silence of the canaries in the mine that foretell doom if nothing is done.

Biblical prophecies are warnings, not doomsday predictions; they are divine appeals to human conscience and moral choice. Whenever nature unleashes its fury in tornadoes and earthquakes, tsunamis and cyclones, volcanoes and hurricanes, hailstorms and locust plagues, there is nothing unnatural about what occurs – volcanoes erupt; tectonic plates shift; catastrophes happen. Fortunately, most of the time nature is more hospitable, but when catastrophic natural events occur, they dwarf us, humble us and remind us that there are laws beyond us that we must reckon with. And behind nature's laws stands nature's God and ours, the ultimate lawgiver. When we ignore or defy God, we destroy our own world.

Notice that the trumpet-announced destruction in Revelation 8 is not total. In this trumpet cycle of judgments, only a third of each sector of creation is stricken. A third is large enough to get our attention, but God restricts the scope of the judgment to give us time to repent. Sadly in the story of Revelation, as in so much of human history, the trumpets are ignored, and the cry of nature is shrugged off.

So a third cycle of judgments ensues. Revelation 16 tells of the outpouring of seven bowls of poisonous fury even more intense and bloody than the seven trumpets. The sea turns to blood and everything in it dies (verse 3). The rivers and aquifers become blood (verse 4) – a horrific picture, echoing the Exodus judgment on the Nile. Then, just as we are feeling repulsed by the gruesomeness of the assault, we hear a voice calling out over the agony. The 'angel of the waters' announces that this action of judgment is completely justified. The angel says to God, "You are just in these judgments, ... for they have shed the blood of your saints and prophets, and you have given them blood to drink as they deserve." (16:5-6)

As Macbeth lamented, 'blood will have blood' (*Macbeth*, III, iv, 121). Violence begets violence; the society that sheds innocent blood will be given blood to drink. Toxic social behavior overflows into the environment and eventually all nature is poisoned. Over and over, God has restrained and limited the intensity of the judgment in hopes of a change in our behavior, but in the end God allows our reckless defiant humanity to reap the results of its own folly.

24.4 Angel of the Waters

Who is this angel of the waters? The Bible talks in various places about angelic guardians of cities, nations and churches, and angelic authorities concerned with various natural elements; we read about angels controlling wind, fire, and here water.[247] The Bible says virtually nothing about these assignments. One suggestion is that they personify the ethos of a city, a nation, an institution or the essence of the natural elements. They appear to be active agents or forces in the world and they reveal that there is far more going on around us than meets the eye.

We know how CNN, the BBC and other media networks disperse their reporters across the globe to observe and report on the interplay of economic and political events, cultural trends, weather and personal activities, informing us and shaping how we might think about these activities. Imagine in a parallel way a vast network of unseen angelic observers – and perhaps interveners – tracking the progress of God's mission in the world. Imagine the reporting that goes on in heaven concerning all the ways water is used to advance or to frustrate God's purposes.

Add to this picture Paul's concept of evil spiritual forces plying the unseen world and you get a glimpse of a vast cosmic battle raging behind the scenes of the observable world. Every one of us is much more complicit in the conflict than we can imagine. Though we may not be aware of it, the angel of the waters reminds us that God is deeply concerned with how we treat the creation God entrusted to us.

In Revelation 10, a huge angel stands like a colossus with one foot on the seas and the other on the land. He roars like a lion and seven thunders echo ominously across the sky. But this angel is not a messenger of doom. He wears a rainbow above his head, raises his hand solemnly to heaven and swears "by him who lives for ever and ever, who created the heavens and all that is in them, the earth and all that is in it, and the sea and all that is in it" (Revelation 10:6) and announces that there will be no delay in carrying out God's ultimate purposes for his creation.

The angel's exaltation of God as creator assures us that God's purposes are ultimately protective, not destructive.[248] This angel's words echo the praises sung by the four living creatures before the throne in Revelation 4 and the chorus of the entire creation in Revelation 5:13. He further extends the mercy of God towards creation which we saw in the restraint of the trumpets. He assures us that God will bring justice to the earth by "destroying those who destroy the earth" (Revelation 11:18). In other words, far from treating the material world as something disposable, God declares himself to be creation's ultimate protector and defender.

G.B. Caird, says, "it is a travesty of Christian belief to suppose that God has no purpose for creation as a whole. [...] John believes that the redemptive work of God, achieved through the death of Christ and the martyrdom of his followers will bring the created universe to its proper goal, for though the present heaven and earth must pass away, whatever in them is worth saving will find a place in the new heaven and earth that follow."[249]

The story of Revelation assures us that after the judgment there is peace. John hears a voice saying "I am making everything new" (Revelation 21:5). But how will God renew the world? With fire ... or ice ... or something more like resurrection?

24.5 Resurrection

Reading these stories of judgment should impel us to strip off our shoes, because the place where we're standing is holy ground. Continue standing barefoot in the grass, as we move on to brighter features of this finale of God's love and grace. In the morning on a summer day, I like to take off my shoes and get my feet soaked walking in the grass – not from rain or puddles, but from dew – sweet cool refreshing delicious dew! There are more than thirty references to dew in the Bible. But far and away my favorite is Isaiah 26:19:

> Your dead will live; their bodies will rise.
> You who dwell in the dust,
> wake up and shout for joy.
> Your dew is like the dew of the morning;
> the earth will give birth to her dead.

Isaiah saw the morning dew as a foreshadowing, a sign from the earth that can't keep its secret, a hint to anyone who is listening between the lines, a promise of resurrection.

Many Biblical scholars maintain that Israel had no theology of life beyond death until shortly before the time of Christ, but Isaiah had this vision eight hundred years earlier. Perhaps he simply foresaw the restoration of Israel after her exile in Babylon. But I have a hunch there was more. In an earlier vision he saw the shroud of death unraveling:

> The LORD Almighty will destroy
> the shroud that enfolds all peoples;
> he will swallow up death forever,
> and wipe away the tears from all faces.
> Isaiah 25:7-8

Isaiah had an intuition: if God is almighty, death and disgrace will not have the final word. If God is good and faithful, the unanswered prayers of the righteous who call out to God in their distress, literally those who "could barely whisper a prayer" (Isaiah 26:16), will eventually be heard. God will listen and the earth will surely "give birth to her dead." It's a vision that the dead will rise dew-drenched in the freshness of a resurrection morning.[250]

Jesus was the first tremor of this new creation, slipping out of his shroud with the sunrise that first Easter. Then a trainload of us, stretching farther than the horizon, people who have tasted the fresh dew of new life even in mortal bodies, who live by the code of Christ, awaiting the ultimate awakening, will rise to life!

What a prospect! Shuffle through the early morning grass in a cemetery and the earth will soak your sandals with its secret. The whole creation groans with anticipation of that morning when life will triumph over death. Better still, live in the joy of a dew-kissed day today. Best of all, pray something like this:

Prayer
Lord of resurrection and life, drench me today in the promise of new life. When I barely have the strength to whisper a prayer to you, energize me with hope. Infuse me with the prospect of your ultimate day of transformation and joy. Amen.

24.6 Where Did the Sea Go?

As the dust and smoke of Judgment Day clear away and the dew of sunrise soaks our feet, our attention shifts as John, the writer of Revelation, gazes on another dazzling sight – a new heaven and a new earth, "for the first heaven and the first earth had passed away" (Revelation 21:1). A city decked out like a bride comes into view and a loud voice declares that God has come to live among his human family. All the sad vestiges of life on planet earth are transformed into joy; tears, grief, hunger, violence, disease and death will be eradicated as God says, "I am making everything new!" (Revelation 21:5).

That is going to be some transformation! Everyone will be happy to see tears and cancer wiped out, hurricanes, divorce and hostage-taking finished forever. What a prospect! But two details of John's portrait of the new creation strike me as peculiar. The last words of the first verse say, "there was no longer any sea" (21:1) and in two later verses we're told "'there was no night there" (21:25 and 22:5). If that's the case, the new creation is going to be deprived of some pretty spectacular beauty. If the Milky Way suddenly disappeared today from the night sky, and if the Caribbean and South Pacific dropped out of sight, our world would be much poorer for their loss. Why does Revelation celebrate the removal of these two features of the world as we know it?

First, we need to know that the new creation will out-dazzle our wildest dreams and imagination. It will surpass our present order of things the way digital technology surpasses cave wall drawing. We will look back on the world we knew and marvel at its transformation. To be honest, I have trouble anticipating a world without seas and oceans, but if I wrestle my wits a little, I can imagine some other water distribution system. Maybe the new world will miss the oceans the way a fetus misses its umbilical cord after birth. Maybe life will flourish with a vastly superior nutrient delivery and sanitation system, better suited to our new mode of life. Perhaps we'll adapt to a world without night the same way we outgrew an afternoon nap, training wheels and a night light. Perhaps the new creation will have rhythms of rest and recuperation that work better than sunset and sunrise.

As Paul says, paraphrasing Isaiah, "No eye has seen, no ear has heard, no mind has conceived what God has prepared for those who love him" (Isaiah 64:4 and 1 Corinthians 2:9). But more likely, I suspect, we need to read the story more carefully. Revelation is written using highly graphic 'apocalyptic' language which is cryptic by design to convey ideas by inference and connotation rather than by literal meanings. If we read it in a wooden literal way, we misread it, and our conclusions will actually obscure or distort what the writer is trying to tell us.

For example, at one point John sees a drunken prostitute riding a ten-headed monster "sitting on many waters" (Revelation 17:1). That sounds like she's riding a dragon on the high seas, but an angel interprets the waters as "peoples, multitudes, nations and languages" (Revelation 17:15). 'Water' doesn't mean 'water' at all, but the vast sea of humanity that pools its resources in defiance of God. It is cryptic language symbolizing a stormy, dark and menacing social network as untamable as the sea and profoundly resistant to God.

In the same way, the language about night makes sense as a symbol rather than literal night. The New Testament often speaks of night to convey the darkness of sin and ignorance and defiance against God, a condition of the heart rather than degrees of sunlight. When John says, "there was no night there" (Revelation 21:25), he wants us to understand that the darkness of sin and death will have no place in God's new Jerusalem.

This gives us a strong clue for understanding that the absent sea has nothing to do with the physical geography of the new heavens and new earth. It is describing the new creation in moral and theological terms. Eugene Peterson explains that just as Hebrews used the one word 'heaven' for both the physical sky and God's dwelling, even though two realities were in mind, so the *sea* refers to both the oceans of the world and the abyss, the domain of evil; "whichever sense is at the fore, the other is whispering in the background."[251]

Darrell Johnson says, "the sea represents the forces of chaos which seek to suck the world back into the void of nothingness."[252] The sea is an all-inclusive term for the whole range of evil that will be excluded from the new creation. John is assuring us that the powers at work in the universe that threaten to undo us have been defeated and will be gone forever.[253] The forces of chaos will be undone, no more Vesuvius eruptions, no more earthquakes, hijackings, fraudulent Ponzi schemes, oil spills, or ecological degradation. Parabolically speaking there will no longer be any sea.

24.7 Harbinger of Hope

This transformation, or what Jesus called "the renewal of all things" (Matthew 19:28), will be the fulfillment of a host of hints and clues that God has scattered through the story of the world – the way seeds transform into oak trees and caterpillars become monarch butterflies, the way washed-up sinners become lively followers of Jesus, experiencing what Jesus called 'a new birth'.

The miracles of Jesus were signs of the wonder and promise of the new creation that invaded the old world with his first coming. Changing water into wine, opening blind eyes and deaf ears, giving cripples the power to walk, multiplying bread, silencing demons and restoring dead sons and daughters back to their families – these were foretastes of the coming reign of God in the new creation. Jesus overrode the standard laws of physics by walking on water in the old creation, giving a brief glimpse of how different things will be in the new.

Jesus himself became the harbinger of that new creation when he rose from death, the first fruits of millions more whom he will raise from death (1 Corinthians 15:20). His resurrection reveals the kind of continuity and discontinuity that the new creation will display – a recognizable carry-over from the past, but something radically new.

It's absurd to try to explain the new creation in terms of the physics of our time-strapped, entropy driven world. You might as well describe the wonders of airborne flight to caterpillars or ask acorns to imagine the wind crashing through their branches. But these examples are hints within the present order of the great metamorphosis that awaits the whole of creation and that will deliver up something beyond imagining. The makeover will be dramatic as the world emerges from its pupa stage and takes flight with capacities of freedom and wonder it never knew were latent within it. The curse will lift and wonder will leap to life. Rivers will clap their hands (Psalm 98:8).

Death will be swallowed up in victory. Life will emerge, robust and radiant and I'm convinced that the song of blue whales will not be missing, the vitality of tidal pools will flourish, the fragile beauty of coral will be on display, the dance of sea horses and octopus, the playful energy of dolphins, porpoise and sea otters will grace the new creation every bit as much as it does the oceans of the present world, but without the threat of extinction, without the burden of the curse that blocks and frustrates the ecology of nature in the old order. Every form of water will fulfill its destiny and purpose.

Eyes have not seen nor have ears heard what glories God has prepared. Like the Queen of Sheba in Solomon's court, we will be overwhelmed (1 Kings

10:4-7) and 'lost in wonder, love and praise.' Personally, I wouldn't miss that opportunity for the world.

However, I don't believe that this vision is given to us solely to whet our appetites for the future. Biblical visions reveal to us something of the nature and heart of God in order to activate our imagination and prayers and obedience. If this is God's vision for God's new creation, what can I do today to bear witness to such a God even in the old tired decaying order of things?

24.8 Urban River

In March 2011, the theme of the United Nations annual World Water Day focused on Water for Cities. A thousand delegates gathered in Cape Town, South Africa, to address concerns related to water, poverty, politics and urban issues.

The Bible begins with a river flowing through the Garden of Eden and ends with a river flowing through a city. The final chapter of Revelation describes a magnificent urban river scene – a sparkling river with crystal clear water flowing down the middle of a great avenue. John tells us,

> the angel showed me the river of the water of life, as clear as crystal, flowing from the throne of God and of the Lamb down the middle of the great street of the city. On each side of the river stood the tree of life, bearing twelve crops of fruit, yielding its fruit every month. And the leaves of the tree are for the healing of the nations.
> Revelation 22:1-2

Of course, John was not the first to envisage this healing river of life flowing from a life-giving, life-renewing God. Ezekiel was John's Old Testament counterpart as an exile writing to sustain the faith of fellow exiles. John was familiar with Ezekiel's vision of a river transforming the environment. The trees along John's river serve to heal the nations just as the trees in Ezekiel's vision (Ezekiel 47).

A few centuries earlier, Joel and Isaiah had had similar visions – "in that day the mountains will drip new wine, and the hills will flow with milk; all the ravines of Judah will run with water. A fountain will flow out of the Lord's house and will water the valley of acacias" (Joel 3:17-18). Isaiah sings about God as the owner of a fruitful vineyard who tends his vines with great care: "I, the LORD, watch over it; I water it continually. I guard it day and night so that no one may harm it. [...] In days to come Jacob will take root, Israel will bud and blossom and fill all the world with fruit" (Isaiah 27: 2-6).

John's final vision is especially relevant for us today in a world that is becoming increasingly urbanized. John translates the pastoral context of ancient Israel into an urban setting. The river flows from the throne right into the core of the city, showing us that God loves the city and sustains it as a place of refuge and safety and where its citizens are being spiritually renewed and nourished.[254] Jesus is the spring of living water for the thirst and cleansing of the world.

Flowing down the center of the main avenue, I picture the Thames in London or the Seine in Paris, but you could imagine a hundred cities where a river is the centerpiece of city life. People sit in cafés or parks along the river or look out office windows to enjoy the scenery below. The river reflects the importance of water for everyone who calls the city home. With the river flowing through their neighborhood, everyone has access to clean water for drinking, washing and sanitation; central location implies equitable access for everyone.

But for 800 million people in our world today, many in urban slums, this is only a dream – an impossible dream – unless we let this vision of a God-designed, God-nourished city instruct us how to pray and work in the world today so that urban people in every city on earth may enjoy these amenities that God intends for human life.

In addition to proximity to fresh water, another vital feature of this river city is its vibrant green space. Fruit trees grow all along the riverbank with a year-round variety of fruits. Human beings have a deep affinity with nature and we grow sick when we are nature deprived.[255] The Creator who planted Eden for our first parents fills this city with green, teaching us to pursue similar greening efforts so that our cities may more accurately reflect God's purpose and example.

The leaves of these trees are "for the healing of the nations" (Revelation 22:2). Imagine a world free of disease because everyone has clean water. Imagine a richly cosmopolitan city where ethnic enclaves no longer breed fear and hostility. Think of the river-nourished trees as God's people serving as agents of reconciliation. Wherever discord reigns, they are active in pursuing reconciliation and peace for the wellbeing of the whole city. The writer does not explain why healing would be needed in this new paradise

– perhaps like the healing of memories and grief in this world, the world to come will include on-going ever-deepening experiences of healing, renewal and creativity. Whatever the nature and scope of this transformation, the source of it is the life-giving river that flows from God's throne into the community around it.

This vision is both the promise of God and the mandate of God's new creation people. God's original assignment to Adam was to steward the world's resources and to bring them to their full potential. Now that Jesus has become the savior and master of all creation, his followers are sent to share this good news with all creation and to summon everyone and everything to plunge into this life renewing river.

If I had had the opportunity to address that strategic group of delegates in Cape Town I would have read them this biblical vision from Ezekiel and Revelation to paint the picture of an urban world no longer afflicted by the old curse. I would point them to Jesus as the wellspring of life for all nations. And then I would invite them to discuss how to implement this vision in the daily life of the city – its politics, economy, arts, education, health care and faith life, so that no sector of life was written off. Ezekiel's river vision explicitly mentions the transformation of water resources, industry, social development, medicine, law and faith.

The practical problems of implementing such a lofty vision are myriad and complex, but they deserve our best efforts. It would be a tragic mistake for Christians and other people of faith in this world to regard these challenges as merely secular concerns. This vision reveals God's heart for his cherished creation. As Kuyper said, "there is not a square inch of the entire creation over which Jesus Christ does not declare "This is mine."

This is what it means to live under the life changing, life giving lordship of Jesus. This is a vision that guides me; it's where I want to live out my days.

Seeking to live out John's vision of the river and city has great potential for reshaping the church's sense of mission. This is what it would look like if God were dwelling among his people in this world. This is the challenge of everyone who weeps over their city like Jesus did in Luke 19:41 because of the river missing from its heart.

24.9 A Free Gift

These last chapters of the Bible take us 'farther up and farther in' towards the world God has prepared for all his creation. They show us a world healed from the indifference and injustice that infect our cities today. We glimpse a world where God dwells among his people, and through them, is reshaping the world. In this God-bathed world Jesus calls out in a clarion voice, "I am the Alpha and the Omega, the Beginning and the End. To all who are thirsty I will give freely from the springs of the water of life" (Revelation 21:6 NLT).

As John's vision comes to an end, he tells us "The Spirit and the bride say, 'Come!' Let anyone who hears this say, 'Come!' Let everyone who is thirsty come. Let anyone who desires drink freely from the water of life" (Revelation 22:17 NLT).

In the Beatitudes, Jesus had promised that all who hunger for a just world will be satisfied, that those who thirst for righteousness in their own lives will be blessed. Jesus, who embodies God's justice, radiant with compassion and truth, is himself this spring of flowing water. Jesus promises priceless satisfaction for those who have nothing but "an emptiness ready to be filled"[256]. "It's free, it's free," John cries to his readers.

Free? The water of life free for the taking? Rain comes to us tax-free, but the economics of water in our world are very complex. Rainwater has to be collected and stored; cities have to access it, purify it, store it, transport it, and distribute it. Engineers and consultants have to be paid, and governments have to tax us to recover their investment in our water. It's a costly business. Even in the developing world, the boy who delivers water by donkey charges the villagers for his services and in some communities water is controlled by mafia-style gangs and thugs. Water is never free.

But in this final vision of the water of life in the closing words of the Bible we are assured that this most fundamental resource is available to everyone at no cost. That is the first and last word on water in the Bible. God gives it freely. Both in its fluid form as rain and snow and dew – and in the metaphor of which they speak – the words of God that refresh our souls and the Spirit of God that energizes our lives.

Isaiah had caught a glimpse of this free gift and sang out –

> Come, all you who are thirsty,
> come to the waters;

and you who have no money,
come, buy and eat!
Isaiah 55:1

Now Revelation takes up the theme – "drink freely," the Alpha and Omega call out. The Spirit prompts the Bride to echo that good news offer to the ends of the earth. "Come! (Revelation 22:17) The water is all yours! Come and receive! Jesus is the one you have been searching for all your life." He is the answer to Hagar's search and David's thirst. He answers the thirst of the Samaritan woman. To Jeremiah he is the spring of living water that will never go dry.

How can he do it? He is the one who cried "I thirst", who parched his own soul, who embraced the anguish of unslaked longing on the thirsty Cross. By the power of the eternal Spirit flowing within, he broke through the desolation of death to bring the water of life that the whole race was panting for.

Early in Lewis' story about Jill Pole in *The Silver Chair*, Jill finds herself desperately thirsty but afraid to go to a nearby stream for a drink because a huge lion lies between her and the stream.

> "Are you not thirsty?" asked the Lion.
> "I'm dying of thirst," said Jill.
> "Then drink," said the Lion.
> "May I – could I – would you mind going away while I do?" said Jill.
> The Lion answered this only by a look and a very low growl. [...]
> "Do you eat girls? she said.
> "I have swallowed up girls and boys, women and men, kings and emperors, [...]" said the Lion.
> "I daren't come and drink," said Jill.
> "Then you'll die of thirst," said the Lion.
> "Oh dear!" said Jill, coming another step nearer. "I suppose I must go and look for another stream then."
> "There is no other stream," said the Lion.

When Jill knelt down and began to drink, she found it "the coldest most refreshing water she had ever tasted. You didn't need to drink much of it, for it quenched your thirst at once."[257]

Lewis gives us a similar picture near the end of *The Voyage of the Dawn Treader*. The ship is sailing east across an immense calm sea, bathed in extraordinary sunlight. Reepicheep the mouse discovers that the sea is not salt, but sweet. "That's real water, that," declared the king Caspian, and Lucy calls it "the loveliest thing I've ever tasted." They drew buckets of dazzling water from the sea and drank deep draughts of it, finding it "stronger than wine and somehow wetter, more liquid than ordinary water". Some of the older sailors who drank it "began to grow younger every day and everyone on board was filled with joy and excitement."[258]

This is Lewis' metaphor for the living water which Jesus promised to all who embrace him with all their heart. The 19th century American Anne Ross Cousin expressed it this way:

> O Christ, He is the fountain, the deep, sweet well of love.
> The streams of earth I've tasted; more deep I'll drink above.
> There to an ocean fullness, His mercy doth expand,
> And glory, glory dwelleth in Immanuel's land.[259]

24.10 The River and the Spring

These closing words of the Bible about free water are not just a utopian dream. They are God's invitation, God's promise that just as the rain falls and the dew rises as gifts of creation, so God will quench our soul-thirst freely with his gifts of mercy, forgiveness, hope and welcome. Jesus meets our deepest thirst, but he doesn't stop there. He gives us a model for responding to prisoners of poverty and despair across the world.

If physical rainfall and spiritual grace express the hospitality of God, our challenge is to steward creation's gifts and share them with the same sense of hospitality we have been given. Here is where our economic policies and practices are tested – along with our love of neighbor, our creativity, leadership and willingness to sacrifice and work together.

On July 28, 2010, the United Nations declared water to be a universal human right. Obviously every human being – and every living thing – needs water to survive and flourish, but it not nearly so obvious how to fulfill that need. There is great debate among governments and NGO's, among business and environmental interests about what is just and what strategies will most effectively meet the urgent water needs of the world in the decades ahead. How do we protect the common treasure? How do we share it fairly? Who should pay for it?

Water continues to be very unevenly distributed. Even with prodigious efforts such as the drive to achieve the Millenium Development Goals[260], the poorest of the poor in the slums of Nairobi, Manila and Rio de Janeiro will receive short shrift. In the last chapters of the Bible, though, we glimpse a better world, beyond injustice and indifference.

These two biblical glimpses, the spring of free grace and the river of God's abundant bounty, are designed to energize our imagination and our actions as we pray that "God's will might be done on earth as it is in heaven" (Matthew 6:10). They are not just archetypal fantasies, but concrete expressions of God's intentions for his creation.

24.11 Let the Sea Resound

> Shout for joy to the LORD, all the earth,
> burst into jubilant song with music;
> Let the sea resound, and everything in it,
> the world, and all who live in it.
> Let the rivers clap their hands,
> let the mountains sing together for joy.
> Psalm 98:4-8

Resounding seas, hand clapping rivers, mountain valleys echoing with music and all creation pulsating with joy – what a vision for our world! Psalm 98 is an ancient Hebrew song that summons the earth to shout for joy to God and burst into jubilant song because God is on the move! It calls on the sea to thunder its encore and rivers to add their applause in a rousing symphony that celebrates or anticipates the arrival of God's wise and righteous rule over the earth.

What a symphony that would be! Imagine the roar of waves crashing all along the entire 534,000 miles (860,000 km) of global coastline – the equivalent of 21 times around the globe. Add whale songs and gull calls, the bark of sea-lions and the squeal of otters, the splash of breaching marlin and porpoises, of diving cormorants and pelicans. It's a raucous concerto!

Add the applause of rivers – the 25 longest in the world combine to 63,000 miles (more than 100,000 km) – with thousands more rivers and streams – every one of them flowing, surging, swishing, and gurgling. And don't forget the thunder of waterfalls and cataracts. What a resounding Ode to Joy! Nature strains and aches to praise its creator, but there's a jarring discord in this orchestra.

Conservationist Carl Safina's *Song for the Blue Ocean,* is a landmark study of the majestic bluefin tuna and other marvels of the sea – an extended community of nature, he calls it, of which humans are a vital part. Safina explores the impact of human beings in this community: our greed, ignorance and deceit that imperil the earth and its oceans and our protective initiatives to care for them. Safina wonders which way it will go – towards deeper degradation or recovery – it's hard to tell which way our actions will tilt the precarious balance.[261] Safina is hopeful, but more than a little cautious.

The psalms echo the great creation theme that nature itself will not come into its own until human beings come under the rule of God's righteousness and truth.[262] Perhaps this is the truth that inspired Isaac Watts in 1719 to translate Psalm 98 as the great Christmas hymn *Joy to the World.* While there's nothing in the psalm about a baby or manger, about shepherds or angels, Watts saw the coming of Jesus as God's response to the creation's great need – "He comes to make his blessings flow far as the curse is found."

In his birth, Jesus joined the harsh realities of our beautiful and blighted world. In his life he showed that God's reign comes through worship and serving. Through his sacrifice and resurrection creation's curse was shattered and reversed. Hope burst on the earth like a sunrise. Nature still waits for the finale, but already it bursts into jubilant song.

This psalm invokes our imagination to anticipate the day when the whole world enjoys the reign of God, when God's saving love is experienced among all nations of people and where all of nature responds in a stupendous chorus of joy. Whether Christmas is approaching or a long way off, raise your voice today and echo the crash of distant waves. Join in as heaven and nature sing. Clap your hands and help the mountains, the marlins and the moonlight to repeat the sounding joy!

This 'Ode to Joy' of Psalm 98 provides a great 'Finale' for our study of water. It celebrates the *gift* of water and brings the *story* to a crescendo. It also reminds us to pay attention to the *way* God intends for vibrant human life to resonate in harmony with the rest of creation. It's proclamation, celebration and exhortation all rolled into one, for the sea will never rest until "the earth is filled with the knowledge of the glory of the Lord as the waters cover the sea" (Isaiah 11:9). On that day, the sea will neither be restless nor motionless. It will pulsate with the rhythms of the fluttering dove, trembling with a joy and creativity that will continue forever, for, as *The Message* expresses it so vividly,

> The whole earth will be brimming with knowing God-Alive,
> a living knowledge of God ocean-deep, ocean-wide.
> Isaiah 11:9 MSG.

Manifesto for Action:

Ten Disciplines for Living Downstream from Eden

Proposal for a Personal and Global Water Ethic

1. The Discipline of Reverence, Worship and Awe

Rivers, waterfalls, rain and the night sky – the entire creation reveals to us magnificence and power beyond our comprehension. Every feature of the created world from glaciers to hummingbirds, from geysers to gemstones is a lens in which we glimpse the wisdom, power and beauty of God. There's a mystery in nature that humbles us, a grandeur and majesty that ennobles us with the sheer privilege of sharing the world with them. Surrounded by such wonder, we can grow so accustomed to it that we forget its significance. It takes discipline not to lose the wonder, and double discipline to turn wonder into worship and adoration towards God as the source and creator of our radiant world. Worship, reverence and awe reorient us to the world and to God. We do not worship nature, but we love her and cherish her; we can learn from her and treat her with deepest respect.

2. The Discipline of Gratitude

The gifts of water – rain, dew, rivers, aquifers and springs are bequeathed to us freely – as are the assets of earth, sun, oxygen and life itself. Since we neither created nor earned these gifts, we should not take them for granted. Embracing the richness of nature as expressions of God's generosity and joy, we respond with gratitude for both for the gifts themselves and for the love of the Giver. Many thoughtful people are grateful, but those who trust God as the giver, know the 'someone' to whom they can direct their thanks.

Gratitude opens our eyes to observation; it expands our joy and deepens our appreciation of the value of these gifts. If we exercise it, gratitude gives us voice to translate vague feelings of privilege into creative expressions of thanks. Gratitude changes our attitude towards the creation, erodes our notions of entitlement, increases our sense of privilege and teaches us to not waste or degrade the world, but rather to search out ways to protect and preserve it.

3. The Discipline of Responsive Stewardship.

Partnering with God in God's creation initiative is one of the high privileges of being human. God has given us extraordinary capabilities so that we will cherish and protect the created world on God's behalf and bring it to its full potential. We show respect and reverence for God as Earth-maker by treating our environment with care. We should be as focused in caring for the earth as God was in creating it and giving it dignity. Our vision is to see the whole earth enjoying the shalom of God.

Each generation has their own challenges and their own opportunities to respond to the changing needs of the world. Melting glaciers, dying rivers, species declining towards extinction, lost woodlands and wetlands, and changing climate all cry out for responsive stewardship and for balancing the needs of both people and the environment today with the needs of future generations. Restraint is an important discipline in the conservation and enhancement of creation. Restraint curtails our impulse to plunder creation and exploit its treasury for selfish or short-term gain.

4. The Discipline of Generosity

Generosity is the responsive overflow of people who have experienced the extravagance of God. Psalm 145 celebrates God's generosity and compassion towards all creation. We are not instinctively self-giving, but if God and nature have been lavish towards us, we should learn to practice an ethic of generous response – even, as Jesus said, with our enemies!

5. The Discipline of Community

Water brings people together, whether it is around a village well or a local flood, a shared river, waterfront or family baptism. Sharing water can bring out the best or the worst in us, our instincts to neighborliness or a mean-spirited underside, cooperation and self-restraint or competitive hostility. We're all in it together when it comes to water.

Both Old and New Testaments picture God's people on earth as a city in order to exhibit the neighborliness of love, and the creativity and sacrifice it requires. A community that works together for common goals, that sacrifices to enrich others, that washes one another's feet, models the heart of God for the world. It offers an alternative to the pride, selfishness, insecurity and greed that characterizes so much of urban life in our world. As urbanization increases in the 21st century, millions of the world's poor gather in vast slums and barrios with no adequate water supply or sanitation. Those who take to heart Jesus' promise to all who thirst, should be leading the way to bring the hope of that promise into such demoralized humanized places.

6. The Discipline of Seeking Justice

The prophet Amos calls out for 'justice to flow like a river, righteousness like a never-failing stream!' He spoke for God but it could equally be the voice of the powerless and the poor. God intends that all people should share in the largess of the earth and steward its resources on behalf of their neighbors and descendents. There is no shalom without responsible ecology, compassion and justice.

Justice is a community-building exercise, not something anyone can achieve single-handedly. It requires respectful listening, serving and sacrifice. Water is a universal human need and while it may be impossible to legislate it adequately as a right, when we see the plight of people without the basic necessities of water and sanitation, we recognize the injustice that needs to be addressed and resolved.

7. The Discipline of Compassion

Tears are perhaps the most exquisite form of water in the world. And the frequency of tears in the Bible is a clarion call to compassion. Yahweh's nature is "gracious and compassionate, slow to anger and rich in love", so those who reflect God's image must respond with empathy and energy on behalf of those who suffer. Henri Nouwen says, "Compassion asks us to go where it hurts, to enter into places of pain, to share in brokenness." Compassion and mercy are at the root of Jesus' instruction to wash one another's feet, to creatively and tangibly fulfill the Old Covenant directive to "act justly, love mercy and to walk humbly with God" (Micah 6:8).

8. The Discipline of Protecting Children

The Bible has a bias towards children. Its first story of water scarcity records the cry of a child dying of thirst and that cry echoes down through history. Nine thousand people die every day from water-borne disease – more than half of these are small children. The Bible's mandate that children must be protected and cared for is not a soft sentiment. It is part of God's deep concern for the weak and powerless. Children are the living embodiment of our continuity with the past and the future and of our need to invest in the next generation.

9. The Discipline of Repentance and Renewal

Everyone gets soiled. The daily washing of food, clothes and our bodies reminds us of the need for personal hygiene, both physical and moral. From Noah to John the Baptist, the Bible flows with stories about repentance and renewal. Living 'downstream from Eden' in an ethical way requires that we admit our private and public sins, our failure to live up to our human potential and divine calling, our failure to care for the earth and each other, and our failure to give honor to God. The call to repentance is always seeking us out, beckoning to us, not rubbing our nose in our failure, but announcing the redemptive opportunity that opens the door to new beginnings.

10. The Discipline of Spiritual Thirst

Millions of people suffer with severe water scarcity; their need is physical and very real. It is also a mirror of the spiritual thirst deep in human souls and communities not only in drought-stricken deserts and ghettos, but in affluent suburbs and tropical resorts. People everywhere are thirsting for God. The Bible names this deep yearning in the soul and urges us to embrace Jesus as the ultimate source of living water and to nourish our souls in his grace. Acknowledging and assuaging our own thirst takes humility and courage; recognizing and responding to the thirst of others requires a discipline of evangelism every bit as vital as deeds of mercy and love.

Reading and Discussion Questions:

From the following, select a few questions that will help you explore what your group feels are the more important issues in the book.

1. What do you make of the title of the book? What does "downstream from Eden" suggest to you? If the title refers to the real world of today, how does the memory or ideal of Eden affect your view of the world or your thoughts about God?

2. The first section of the book (Chapters 1-4) explores the role of water within the natural world. Does the author's description of creation expand your perspective? What insights into water and the environment piqued your interest? How did this section of the book affect your sense of ecological responsibility or concern?

3. Chapter 6 is an extended reflection on the story of Noah's Ark. Do you resonate with the author's view of God and the flood? Have you ever experienced catastrophe and recovery in your life? Does anything in this story echo your experience? What can you apply from this iconic story to other kinds of natural catastrophes in our world?

4. Some of the water stories of the Jewish people (Chapters 7 to 13) are well-known. Which stories were new for you? What did you find inspiring or intriguing in them? What significant role does water play in these stories?

5. The author frequently points out how water focuses our attention on social justice, citing situations where children, women, the poor or the powerless are denied dignity, power or equal access to water or other resources. How did reading this book raise your awareness

of justice as an important issue? Does the book offer practical strategies for promoting justice? Can you suggest others?

6. How did the three chapters on Jesus and the early church (Chapters 14-16), affect your understanding of Jesus? How does water help to 'tell the story' of Jesus more vividly? What aspect of Jesus' life in these chapters would you like to see more consistently in your life – or in the lives of people who call themselves Christians?

7. The writer is obviously zealous about Jesus but says he has tried to be fair in his interpretations. Would you say he succeeded in balancing his enthusiasm with sound reasoning? Is his enthusiasm contagious or off-putting to you?

8. The last section of the book is called "Wade in the Water", *i.e.*, responding to the moral and relational challenges that the Bible presents through various reflections on water. What examples in the units on marriage (19), purity (20), crisis (21), drought (22) and renewal (23) connected with you? How does the water imagery in these texts bring fresh perspective?

9. The author argues that social and religious 'malpractice' leads to environmental degradation. Do you agree with this, or do such connections seem improbable to you?

10. The last two chapters of the book deal with restoration and renewal. Do you share the author's sense of hope and optimism or would you say your outlook on the world is more bleak?

11. Which of the ten themes or disciplines in the Afterword stand out for you? What do you wish you could do to engage more people to adopt this way of 'living downstream from Eden'?

12. How has this book changed or expanded your thinking about water? How do you think it will have an impact on how you live your life?

Index of Biblical References

Each chapter of *Downstream from Eden* has several sub-units. The numbers to the right of the scripture references below identify the sub-unit where this scripture is cited or referred to.

Proverbs

Ecclesiastes

Song of Solomon

Isaiah

Mark

Luke

John

Acts

Romans

Bibliography

Adams, Douglas. *So Long, and Thanks for All the Fish*, in *The Hitch Hiker's Guide to the Galaxy: A Trilogy in Four Parts*. London: William Heinemann Ltd. 1986.

'Ali, 'Abdullah Yusef, *The Meaning of the Holy Qur'an*. Brentwood, MD: Amana Corporation, 1991.

Anderson, Bernhard W. *Creation versus Chaos*. Philadelphia: Fortress Press, 1987.

----. *Understanding the Old Testament*. Third Edition. Englewood Cliffs, NJ: Prentice-Hall, 1957, 1975.

Anderson, Francis. *Job* [Tyndale Old Testament Commentaries]. Downers Grove: InterVarsity Press, 1974.

Augustine. *Saint Augustine's Confessions*. [translated by Henry Chadwick], Oxford: Oxford University Press, 1991.

Anglican Church of Canada. *The Book of Alternate Services of the Anglican Church of Canada*. Toronto: Anglican Book Centre, 1985.

Arnold, Bill and Bryan Beyer. *Encountering the Old Testament*. Grand Rapids, Baker Books, 1999.

Ashby, Godfrey. *Go Out and Meet God – A Commentary on the Book of Exodus*. International Theological Commentary, Grand Rapids, Eerdmans, 1998.

Baldwin, Joyce. *1 & 2 Samuel* [Tyndale Old Testament Commentary]. Leicester: Inter-Varsity Press, 1988.

Berry, Wendell. "Christianity and the Survival of Creation" in *Sex, Economy, Freedom, and Community*. New York: Pantheon Books, 1994.

----. "Water" in *Farming: A Handbook*. Berkeley: Counterpoint, 1971.

----. "The Real Work" in *Collected Poems*. Berkeley: North Point Press, 1987.

Bloucher, Henri. *In the Beginning*. Downers Grove: IVP Books, 1984.

Bonhoeffer, Dietrich. *Creation and Fall*. Minneapolis: Fortress Press, 2004.

Borgman, Paul. *Genesis: The Story We Haven't Heard*. Downers Grove: InterVarsity Press, 2001.

Bowen, John. *The Spirituality of Narnia*. Vancouver: Regent College Publishing, 2007.

Bright, John. *A History of Israel*. Third Edition, Philadelphia: Westminster Press, 1981.

Brodfuehrer, Ross. *H20 A Journey of Faith*. Nashville: Thomas Nelson, 2009.

Brown, Raymond E. *The Gospel according to John*. Vol 1. Garden City: Doubleday, 1966, 1970.

Bruce, F. F. *The Book of Acts. [The New International Commentary on the New Testament]*. Grand Rapids: Eerdmans, 1979.

Brueggemann, Walter. *Genesis* [Interpretation]. Atlanta: John Knox Press, 1982.

----. *The Message of the Psalms*. Minneapolis: Augsburg Publishing House, 1984.

Bryson, Bill. *A Short History of Nearly Everything*. Toronto: Anchor Canada, 2004.

Buechner, Frederick. *Secrets in the Dark: A Life in Sermons*. New York: HarperSanFrancisco, 2006.

----. *The Son of Laughter*. New York: HarperSanFranciso, 1993.

Bunyan, John. *The Pilgrim's Progress* in L. Edward Hazelbaker's *The Pilgrim's Progress in Modern English*, Gainesville, FL: Bridge-Logos, 1998.

Burge, Gary M. *The NIV Application Commentary: John*. Grand Rapids: Zondervan, 2000.

Cahill, Thomas. *The Gifts of the Jews*, New York: Doubleday, 1998.

Caird, G. B. *The Revelation of Saint John the Divine*. Second Edition. London: A & C Black, 1984.

Campolo, Tony. *How to Rescue the Earth Without Worshiping Nature*. Nashville: Thomas Nelson Publishers, 1992.

Capon, Robert Farrar. *The Third Peacock*. Garden City: Image Books, Doubleday, 1972.

Carson, Don. *The Gospel According to John*. Grand Rapids: Eerdmans, 1991.

Chapelle, Francis H. *The Hidden Sea, Groundwater, Springs and Wells*. Westerville, OH: National Ground Water Association, 2000.

Couture, Pauline. *Ice: Beauty, Danger, History*. Toronto: McArthur & Company, 2004.

Covey, Stephen R. *The Seven Habits of Highly Effective People*. New York: Simon & Schuster, 1989.

Davis, Wade. *The Wayfinders: Why Ancient Wisdom Matters in the Modern World*. CBC Massey Lectures, Toronto: House of Anansi Press, Inc., 2009.

Dawn, Marva J. *In the Beginning, God: Creation, Culture and the Spiritual Life*. Downers Grove, IVP Books, 2009.

Denton, Michael J. *Nature's Destiny: How the Laws of Biology Reveal Purpose in the Universe*. New York: The Free Press, 1998.

de Villiers, Marc. *Water*. Toronto: Stoddart, 1999.

Diamond, Jared. *Guns, Germs, and Steel: The Fates of Human Societies*. New York: W.W. Norton & Company, 1999.

Dillard, Annie. *Pilgrim at Tinker Creek*. New York: Harper Perennial, 1974.

Dinesen, Isak. *Babette's Feast and Other Anecdotes of Destiny*. New York: Random House, 1988.

Eliot, T. S. *Four Quartets*. London: Faber, 1954.

----. "Gerontion" in *Poems*. New York: Knopf, 1920.

Fernhout, Harry. *Of Kings and Prophets*. Toronto: The Joy in Learning and Curriculum Development and Training Centre, 1979.

Ford, David F. *The Shape of Living: Spiritual Directions for Everyday Life. Grand Rapids: Baker Books, 1997.*

Foster, Richard. ed. *The Renovaré Spiritual Formation Bible*. New York: HarperSanFrancisco, 2005.

Fox, Everett. *The Five Books of Moses*. Dallas: Schocken Books Inc., 1995.

Fox, Michael V. *A Time to Tear Down & A Time to Build Up, A Reading of Ecclesiastes*. Grand Rapids: Eerdmans, 1999.

Frankel, Ellen. *The Five Books of Miriam: A Woman's Commentary on the Torah*. New York: HarperSanFrancisco, 1996.

Freeze, R. Allan and John A. Cherry. *Groundwater*. Englewood Cliffs, NJ: Prentice-Hall, 1979.

Fritz, Maureena. *The Exodus Experience: A Journey in Prayer, Winona, MN: Saint Mary's Press, 1989.*

Frost, Michael and Alan Hirsch. *The Faith of Leap: Embracing a Theology of Risk, Adventure and Courage*, Baker Books, 2011.

Frost, Robert. "Fire and Ice" and "Once By the Pacific" in *A Little Treasury of Modern Poetry*. [Oscar Williams, ed.] Third Edition. New York: Charles Scribner's Sons, 1970.

Glasser, Arthur F. *Announcing the Kingdom*. Grand Rapids: Baker Academic, 2003.

Gleick, Peter H. "Water Resources" in *Encyclopedia of Climate and Weather* [S. H. Schneider, ed.], Vol 2. Oxford: Oxford University Press, 1996.

Gibler, Linda. *From the Beginning to Baptism: Scientific and Sacred Stories of Water, Oil and Fire*. Collegeville, MN: Liturgical Press, 2010.

Glickman, S. Craig. *A Song for Lovers*, Downers Grove: IVPress, 1977.

Goldingay, John. *Songs from a Strange Land: Psalms 42-51*. Downers Grove: InterVarsity Press, 1978.

Gopnik, Adam. *Winter: Five Windows On the Season*. CBC Massey Lectures, Toronto: House of Anansi Press, Inc., 2011.

Goudzwaard, Bob. *Idols of Our Time*. Sioux Center, Iowa: Dordt College Press, 1989.

Grahame, Kenneth. *The Wind in the Willows*. New York: Aladdin Paperbacks, 1999.

Green, Thomas SJ. *When the Well Runs Dry*. Notre Dame: Ave Maria Press, 1979.

Guthrie, Donald et al. *The New Bible Commentary Revised*, London: Inter-Varsity Press, 1970.

Hamlin, E John. *Inheriting the Land: A Commentary on the Book of Joshua*, Grand Rapids: Eerdmans, 1983.

Harris, Laird, Gleason Archer, and Bruce Waltke (eds.). *Theological Wordbook of the Old Testament*. Chicago: Moody Press, 1980.

Helevi, Yossi Klein. *At the Entrance to the Garden of Eden*. New York: Perennial, 2002.

Hendriksen, William. *More Than Conquerors*. Grand Rapids: Baker Book House, 1940, 1994.

Heschel, Abraham, (Susannah Heschel, ed.). *Abraham Joshua Heschel: Essential Writings*. Maryknoll, NY: Orbis Books, 2011.

Hill, Lawrence. *The Book of Negroes*. Toronto: HarperCollins; 2007. Published in the USA, Australia and New Zealand as *Someone Knows My Name*.

Hubbard, David. *The Preacher's Commentary – Proverbs*. Nashville: Thomas Nelson Publishers, 1989.

Hurnard, Hannah. *Hind's Feet on High Places*. Eastbourne, UK: Christian Literature Crusade, 1955.

Johnson, Darrell. *Discipleship on the Edge*. Vancouver: Regent college Publishing, 2004.

Josephus, Falvius. *Josephus – Complete Works*. Grand Rapids: Kregal Publications, 1960.

Keller, Timothy. *Kings Cross*, New York: Dutton, 2011.

Kidner, Derek. *Psalms*. Downers Grove: InterVarsity Press, 1979.

Koester, Craig. *Revelation and the End of All Things*. Grand Rapids: Eerdmans, 2001.

Lapin, Daniel. *The Gathering Storm – Decoding the Secrets of Noah*. (*Genesis Journeys*, Volume 2). Lifecodex Media Publishing; 1ST edition, 2007.

Lamott, Anne. *Traveling Mercies: Some Thoughts on Faith*. New York: Random House, 1999.

L'Engle, Madeline. *And It Was Good*. Wheaton: Harold Shaw Publishers, 1983.

Lewis, C. S. *Reflections on the Psalms*. London: Fontana Books, 1958.

----. *The Abolition of Man*. (1944). New York: HarperCollins, 2001.

----. *The Last Battle*. New York: Penguin Books, 1956.

----. *The Silver Chair*. New York: Penguin Books, 1953.

----. *The Voyage of the Dawn Treader*. New York: Penguin Books, 1952.

Lloyd-Jones, Sally. *The Jesus Storybook Bible*. Grand Rapids: Zondervan, 2007.

Longman III, Tremper. *How to Read Genesis*. Downers Grove: InterVarsity Press, 2005.

Louv, Richard. *Last Child in the Woods*. Chapel Hill: Algonquin Books of Chapel Hill, 2005, 2008.

MacDonald, Gordon. *Facing Turbulent Times*. Wheaton: Tyndale House Publishers, Inc. 1981.

Mandela, Nelson. *Long Walk to Freedom*. Boston: Little, Brown and Company, 1994.

Mangalwadi, Vishal. *Truth and Transformation – A Manifesto for Ailing Nations*. Seattle: YWAM Publishing, 2009.

Mason, Bill. *Canoescapes*. Erin, Ontario: The Boston Mills Press (affiliated with Stoddard Publishing, Toronto), 1995.

McGilloway, Olly. *McGilloway's Ireland*. Belfast: The Blackstaff Press, 1994.

McGrath, Alister E. *A Fine-Tuned Universe: The Quest for God in Science and Theology*. Louisville: Westminster John Knox Press, 2009.

----. *Glimpsing the Face of God*. Grand Rapids: Eerdmans, 2002.

McLaren, Brian D. *Naked Spirituality: A Life with God in 12 Simple Words*. New York: Harper-One, 2011.

Melville, Herman. *Moby Dick* (1851). Signet Classics, New York: The New American Library, 1961.

Moll, Rob. "A Culture of Resurrection – How the Church Can Help its People Die Well" in *Christianity Today*, July 6, 2010. http://www.christianitytoday.com/ct/2010/june/5.35.html?start=3 Accessed Sept 2, 2011.

Mortenson, Greg. *Three Cups of Tea*. New York: Penguin Books, 2006.

Motyer, J. Alec. *The Prophecy of Isaiah*. Downers Grove: Inter Varsity Press, 1993.

Newbigin, Lesslie. *The Light Has Come: An Exposition of the Fourth Gospel*. Grand Rapids: Eerdmans, 1982.

----. *The Open Secret*. Grand Rapids: Eerdmans, 1982.

Norris, Kathleen. *The Cloister Walk*. New York: Riverhead Books, 1996.

Ortberg, John. *If You Want to Walk on Water, You Have to Get Out of the Boat*. Grand Rapids: Zondervan, 2001.

Palmer, Earl. *The Intimate Gospel*. Dallas: Word Inc., 1978.

Palmer, Parker. "The Politics of the Brokenhearted: On Holding the Tensions of Democracy." Fetzer Institute, 2005.

Parker, Bruce. *The Power of the Sea: Tsunamis, Storm Surges, Rogue Waves and Our Quest to Predict Disasters*. New York: Palgrave Macmillan, 2010.

Pearce, Fred. *When the Rivers Run Dry*. Toronto, Key Porter Books, 2006.

Peterson, Eugene. *A Long Obedience in the Same Direction*. Downers Grove: IVPress, 1980.

----. *Reversed Thunder*, San Francisco: Harper & Row Publishers, 1988.

----. *The Jesus Way*. Grand Rapids: Eerdmans, 2007.

----. *The Message Remix*, Colorado Springs, CO: NavPress Publishing Group, 2003.

Poivan, Iain. *1 and 2 Kings*. New International Biblical Commentary. Peabody, MA: Hendickson Publishers, 1995.

Poivan, Iain, V. Philips Long and Tremper Longman III. *A Biblical History of Israel*. Louisville: Westminster John Knox Press, 2003.

Postel, Sandra, *Last Oasis: Facing Water Scarcity*. New York: W.W. Norton & Company, 1992.

Postel, Sandra and Brian Richter. *Rivers for Life, Managing Water for People and Nature*. Washington D. C.: Island Press, 2003.

Price, Keith. *Thirsting After God*. Camp Hill, PA: Christian Publications, 2000.

Ross, Hugh. *"Genesis One: A Scientific Perspective"*. Revised edition, Reasons To Believe, Inc.; 1979.

Reynolds, David K. *Water Bears No Scars: Japanese Pathways for Personal Growth*. New York: William Morrow, 1987.

Sabin, Scott. *Tending to Eden: Environmental Stewardship for God's People.* Valley Forge, PA: Judson Press, 2010.

Safina, Carl. *Song for the Blue Ocean*. New York: Henry Holt & Company, 1997.

Sanguin, Bruce. *Darwin, Divinity and the Dance of the Cosmos: An Ecological Christianity.* Kelowna B.C.: Copperhouse/Wood Lake Publishing, 2007.

Shaw, Lucy. *Polishing the Petoskey Stone.* Vancouver: Regent College Publishing, 2003.

----. *The Green Earth*. Grand Rapids, Eerdmans, 2002.

----. *Water Lines*, Grand Rapids, Eerdmans, 2003.

----. *Water My Soul*. Vancouver: Regent College Publishing, 1998.

----. *Writing the River*, Colorado Springs: Pinion Press, 1994.

Silf, Margaret. *At Sea With God: A Spiritual Guide to the Heart and Soul.* Notre Dame: Sorin Books, 2003.

Stegner, Wallace. *The Sound of Mountain Water.* New York: Penguin Books, 1946, 1980.

Stott, John R. W. *The Spirit, The Church and the World: The Message of Acts.* Downers Grove: InterVarsity Press, 1990.

Svoboda, Melannie SND. *When the Rain Speaks: Celebrating God's Presence in Nature*. New London, CT: Twenty-Third Publications, 2008.

Tal, Alon and Alfred Abed Rabbo (eds.). *Water Wisdom*. New Brunswick, NJ: Rutgers University Press, 2010.

Tasker, R.V.C. *The Gospel According to St. John*. London: Tyndale Press, 1960.

Tsumura, David Toshio. *The Earth and the Waters in Genesis 1 and 2.* Continuum International Publishing Group, 1989.

Veith, Gene E. *God at Work: Your Christian Vocation in All of Life*. Crossway Books, 2002.

Walker-Jones, Arthur. *The Green Psalter: Resources for an Ecological Spirituality*. Minneaplolis: Fortress Press, 2009.

Wallach, John and Janet. *Still Small Voices*. San Diego, Harcourt Brace Jovanovich, Publishers, 1989.

Waltke, Bruce. "The Literary Genre of Genesis, Chapter One" *CRUX* 27:4 December, 1991.

Walton, John H. *The Lost World of Genesis One*. Downers Grove: IVPress Academic, 2009.

----. *The NIV Application Commentary: Genesis*. Grand Rapids: Zondervan, 2001.

Wilkinson, Loren. *Earthkeeping in the '90s: Stewardship of Creation*. Grand Rapids: Eerdmans, 1980.

Willard, Dallas. *The Spirit of the Disciplines*. New York: HarperCollins, 1988.

Wolterstorff, Nicholas. *Lament for a Son*. Grand Rapids: Eerdmans, 1987.

Wright, N. T. *Simply Christian. New York: HarperSan Francisco, 2006.*

Wright, Ronald. *A Short History of Progress*. CBC Massey Lectures, Toronto: House of Anansi Press, Inc., 2004.

Yancey, Philip. *What's So Amazing About Grace?* Grand Rapids: Zondervan, 1997.

Endnotes

1. Bill Mason, *Canoescapes* (Erin, Ontario: The Boston Mills Press, 1995), p. 15.

2. Data collected from <www.chemcraft.net/wbody.html> and Wikipedia at <http://en.wikipedia.org/wiki/Body_water>.

3. Michael J. Denton, *Nature's Destiny: How the Laws of Biology Reveal Purpose in the Universe* (New York: The Free Press, 1998), p. 19.

4. Francis of Assisi, "Canticle of the Sun" in *Eerdmans' Book of Famous Prayers*, (Grand Rapids: Eerdmans, 1984), p.28.

5. Millenium Development Goals, Target 7C is to "halve, by 2015, the proportion of the population without sustainable access to safe drinking water and basic sanitation." See <www.un.org/milleniumgoals/> - especially Goal 7 - Environmental Sustainability.

6. The phrase "Send my roots rain" comes from Gerard Manly Hopkins' poem "Thou art Indeed Just, Lord" and expresses a longing for greater spiritual vitality.

7. Abraham Heschel, quoted by John Dear SJ in his blog <http://ncronline.org/blogs/road-peace/Abraham-heschels-prophetic-judaism>. in which he reviews *Abraham Joshua Heschel: Essential Writings* [Susannah Heschel. ed.] (New York: Orbis Books, 2011).

8. This concept comes from Dietrich Bonhoeffer, *Creation and Fall*, (Minneapolis: Fortress Press, 2004), p.131, where he says, "Adam is upheld alive between curse and promise."

9. This phrase is shamelessly taken from the book title *A River Runs Through It* by Norman Maclean and the 1992 movie by the same name, though I haven't told even a single fly-fishing story in my entire book.

10. Mary Oliver's fine phrase from her poem "The Summer Day" in *House of Light* (Boston: Beacon Press, 1990).

11. Wendell Berry, "Christianity and the Survival of Creation" in *Sex, Economy, Freedom, and Community* (New York: Pantheon Books, 1994), p.13. Or see <www.crosscurrents.org/berry.htm> Accessed December 15, 2011.

12. Alister E. McGrath, *A Fine-Tuned Universe: The Quest for God in Science and Theology* (Louisville: Westminster John Knox Press, 2009), p. 147.

13. Ibid.

14. Space.com Saturday, July 23, 2011. See <http://news.yahoo.com/astronomers-largest-oldest-mass-water-universe152702637.html?utm_source=Circle+of+Blue+WaterNews+%26+Alerts&utm_campaign=68bea78ee6-RSS_EMAIL_CAMPAIGN&utm_medium=email> Accessed on September 28, 2011.

15. Old Testament scholar David Hubbard says that this poem about Wisdom "rises from the pages of Proverbs like the Jungfrau over Interlaken or Rainier above Puget Sound. It is the summit of Old Testament discipleship." *The Preacher's Commentary - Proverbs* (Nashville: Thomas Nelson Publishers, 1989), p. 118.

16. McGrath, p. 3.

17. Hubbard, p. 126.

18. Source unknown. For another wonderful analogy of the creation process, see Robert Farrar Capon's *The Third Peacock* (Garden City: Image Books, Doubleday, 1972, p. 11-12.

19. Marva J Dawn, *In the Beginning, God: Creation, Culture and the Spiritual Life* (Downers Grove, IVP Books, 2009), p. 22.

20. See Bruce Waltke, "The Literary Genre of Genesis, Chapter One" *CRUX*, December 1991 27:4. Waltke argues that Genesis One is a polemic against the entire Near-eastern pantheon of gods and astral deities, with each successive day debunking the claims of another of the various pretender-gods worshipped by surrounding nations, and assuring Israel that Yahweh, not any of the rival gods, is indeed the God of all the earth.

21. This is cogently argued by John H. Walton in *The Lost World of Genesis One* (Downers Grove: IVPress Academic, 2009).

22. Hugh Ross, "Genesis One: A Scientific Perspective", Revised edition, 1979, p. 7. Check out <www.reaons.org. for more information on Dr. Ross and the work of *Reasons to Believe*.

23. Paul Borgman, *Genesis: The Story We Haven't Heard* (Downers Grove: InterVarsity Press, 2001), p. 23.

24. Henri Bloucher, *In the Beginning* (Downers Grove: IVP Books, 1984), p. 32.

25. Dawn, p. 25.

26. See Bruce Parker, *The Power of the Sea: Tsunamis, Storm Surges, Rogue Waves and Our Quest to Predict Disasters* (New York: Palgrave Macmillan, 2010).

27. Robert Frost, "Once by the Pacific" (1928) in *A Little Treasury of Modern Poetry*, Third Edition (New York: Charles Scribner's Sons, 1970), p. 175.

28. Alfred, Lord Tennyson, "Ulysses", 1842.

29. Stephen R Covey, *The Seven Habits of Highly Effective People* (New York: Simon & Schuster, 1989), p. 33.

30. Derek Kidner, *Psalms 1-72*, Tyndale Old Testament Commentary, (Leicester: Inter-Varsity Press, 1973), p. 137.

31. Victor P Hamilton, "shabat" in *Theological Wordbook of the Old Testament* (TWOT) (Chicago: Moody Press, 1980), Vol 2, p. 903.

32. Peter H. Gleick, Water Resources" in *Encyclopedia of Climate and Weather*, [ed. S. H. Schneider] Vol 2, (Oxford: Oxford University Press, 1996), p. 817-823. See U.S. Geological Survey Water Science for Schools web site <http://ga.water.usgs.gov/edu/waterdistribution.html> Retrieved October 19.

33. Ibid.

34. *A Rocha* is one of many organizations that are deeply committed to the protection of such homes and habitats. *A Rocha* is "inspired by God's love to carry out research, to educate and to foster practical initiatives to conserve habitats". Check out the *A Rocha* web-site at <http://www.arocha.org/int-en>

35. C. S. Lewis, *The Last Battle* (New York: Penguin Books, 1956), p. 165.

36. Fred Pearce, *When the Rivers Run Dry* (Toronto, Key Porter Books, 2006), p. 43. Pearce gives the annual global evaporation volume as roughly 500,000 km^3.

37. Ann Voskamp, "when food's a hallowed thing" July 29, 2011 blog-post in "A Holy Experience" at <http://www.aholyexperience.com/2011/07/dinner-guests-when-food-becomes-holy>

38. A Rocha, ibid.

39. See especially chapters 2, 3 and 4 in *Tending to Eden* (Valley Forge PA: Judson Press, 2010.

40. See <http://www.tropical-rainforest-animals.com/Tropical-Rain-Forests.html

41. Wade Davis, *The Wayfinders: Why Ancient Wisdom Matters in the Modern World*, CBC Massey Lectures (Toronto: House of Anansi Press, Inc., 2009), p. 79-115.

42. See Richard Louv's best-selling book *Last Child in the Woods* (Chapel Hill: Algonquin Books of Chapel Hill, 2005, 2008) about the importance of trees, forests and woodlands for the mental and physical health and creativity of children.

43. See <http://www.arocha.org/gh-en/9753-DSY.html> and <http://www.arocha.org/int-en/12069-DSY>

44. Luci Shaw, "Amazed by Love" in *Water Lines* (Grand Rapids: Eerdmans, 2003), p. 92.

45. Walter Brueggemann, *The Message of the Psalms* (Minneapolis: Augsburg Publishing House, 1984), p. 32.

46. "The Great Hymn to Aten" is 110 lines – too long to print here, but it can be found on the Internet. See <www.templeofaten.org/hymns-to-aten.php>.

47. See C. S. Lewis, *Reflections on the Psalms* (London: Fontana Books, 1958), p. 73-76.

48. John Barber, *Reformed Perspectives Magazine*, Volume 8, #26, June 25-July 1, 2006, p. 4. <http://thirdmill.org/newfiles/joh_barber/PT.joh_barber.Luther.Calvin.Music.Worship.pdf> accessed on September 2, 2011.

49. Pearce, 43.

50. These numbers are really hard to grasp. A couple of crazy ways to try to visualize them would be '42,000 fully loaded 747's every second' or 'the combined weight of every person in North America – every two seconds'. Not only is water heavy, there's a lot of it moving around.

51. Douglas Adams, *So Long, and Thanks for All the Fish*, Chapter 33 in *The Hitch Hiker's Guide to the Galaxy: A Trilogy in Four Parts* (London: William Heinemann Ltd. 1986), p. 569.

52. Abraham Heschel, *Man is Not alone: A Philosophy of Religion* (New York: Macmillan, 1976).

53. Andrew R. Parker, "Water Capture by a Desert Beetle" *Nature*, November 1, 2001. Reported in National Geographic News at <http://news.nationalgeographic.com/news/2001/11/1101_TVdesertbeetle.html>
For *Nature* article see < http://www.nature.com/nature/journal/v414/n6859/pdf/414033a0.pdf>.

54. See Janine M. Benyus, *Biomimicry: Innovation Inspired by Nature*, New York: HarperCollins 1998.

55. Check out Lebbrecht's snowflake slide-show in *Scientific American*. <http://www.scientificamerican.com/slideshow.cfm?id=no-two-alike-snowflake-photography>.

56. I've often wondered how this common assertion can be verified. The answer is based on a simple matter of mathematics. Because of the vast number of possible permutations in the formation of the crystalline structure, the odds of any two snowflakes forming identical patterns is about a million times the number of drops of water in the universe. It wouldn't surprise me if here and there such astonishing odds occurred, but how would we ever know?

57. Adam Gopnik, *Winter: Five Windows On the Season*, CBC Massey Lectures (Toronto: House of Anansi Press, Inc., 2011), p.50.

58. Mason, p. 15.

59. Olly McGilloway, *McGilloway's Ireland* (Belfast: The Blackstaff Press, 1994), p. 233.

60. Brueggemann, p. 142.

61. Berry, p. 13.

62. Kenneth Grahame, *The Wind in the Willows* (New York: Aladdin Paperbacks, 1999). Also available at <www.gutenberg.org/files/289/289-h/289-h.htm> Accessed December 15, 2011.

63. J Barton Payne, "rahab" in *Theological Wordbook of the Old Testament*, p. 835. Payne likens this usage to Milton's use of Greek mythological figures in *Paradise Lost*. See also William Albright, *Yahweh and the Gods of Canaan*, 183-193.

64. Derek Kidner, *Psalms 73-150* Tyndale Old Testament Commentary (Leicester: Inter-Varsity Press, 1973), p. 321.

65. G. K. Chesterton, at the end of "The Diabolist". Brennan Manning uses a similar phrase as the title of his book, *The Furious Longing of God: A Love Story for the Brokenhearted* (Colorado Springs: David C. Cook, 2009).

66. Everett Fox, *The Five Books of Moses* (Dallas: Schocken Books Inc., 1995) Translator's Preface, xix. Fox points out the verbal repetition that underscores God's measure-for-measure response. Five times the narrator uses the word *shachath* which means to ruin, corrupt or destroy.

v.11 - The earth was '*shachath*' – corrupt
v.12 – God saw how '*shachath*' – corrupted – the earth had become
v.12 – The people had '*shachath*' - corrupted their ways
v.13 – God said 'I will '*shachath*' - detroy both them and the earth
v.17 – I will bring a flood to '*shachath*' – destroy – all life.

The earth as God had designed it had been *corrupted* by the ruinous conduct of the people. The same word is used to tell how God also will *destroy* the ruined earth. God will give us what we seek and will bring down upon the heads of the perpetrators the natural outcome of their destructive actions.

67. Tremper Longman III, *How to Read Genesis* (Downers Grove: InterVarsity Press, 2005), p. 87.

68. Frederick Buechner, 'A Sprig of Hope' in *Secrets in the Dark: A Life in Sermons* (New York: HarperSanFrancisco, 2006), p. 46.

69. Walter Brueggemann, *Genesis* (Atlanta: John Knox Press, 1982), p. 79.

70. Y. B. Yeats, "The Second Coming" in *A Little Treasury of Modern Poetry*, p. 72.

71. Buechner, p. 47.

72. Brueggemann, *Genesis*, p. 81.

73. Emily Dickinson, "Hope is the Thing with Feathers" in *The Complete Poems of Emily Dickenson.*

74. Lesslie Newbigin, *The Open Secret* (Grand Rapids: Eerdmans, 1982), p. 31.

75. Charles Shultz, *Peanuts* Syndicated Cartoon, 1950's.

76. Sally Lloyd-Jones, *The Jesus Storybook Bible* (Grand Rapids: Zondervan, 2007), p. 47.

77. Abraham Kuyper, "Sphere Sovreignty" in James D Bratt, *Abraham Kuyper, A Centennial Reader* (Grand Rapids: Eerdmans, 1998), p.488. See <http://en.wikipedia.org/wiki/Abraham_Kuyper>. Accessed November 4, 2011.

78. Thomas Cahill, *The Gifts of the Jews* (New York: Doubleday, 1998). p.59.

79. Brueggemann, *Genesis*, p. 132.

80. Madeline L'Engle, *And It Was Good* (Wheaton: Harold Shaw Publishers, 1983), p. 187-197.

81. The Hebrew word for personal space, *rachab*, occurs over 50 more times in the Old Testament. It is God's gift of breathing room. A few of my favorites include: Exodus 3:8, 1 Chronicles 4:40, Job 36:16, Psalm 18:19 and Psalm 31:8. Space connotes not just legroom, but freedom from the encroaching demands and offenses of others.

82. Caedmon's Call, "Share the Well" 2004, Essential Records.

83. Nader El-Khateeb, "The Condition of Streams and Prospects for Restoration in Palestine" in Alon Tal and Alfred Abed Rabbo, (eds) *Water Wisdom* (New Brunswick, NJ.: Rutgers University Press, 2010), p. 127-135. See also www.foeme.org/projects.php

84. Frederick Buechner, *The Son of Laughter* (New York: HarperSanFranciso, 1993), p. 103.

85. See Michael Frost and Alan Hirsch, *The Faith of Leap: Embracing a Theology of Risk, Adventure and Courage* (Grand Rapids: Baker Books, 2011), p. 19.

86. In his lectures on the Fall in Genesis 3 in the 1930's under the shadow of the growing Third Reich, Dietrich Bonhoeffer said, "Humankind conducts itself not in peace but with enmity and struggle against God. [...]To be sure, this battles leaves humankind wounded, for the serpent, though defeated, still bites it in the heel. [...] Human beings are to be ... locked in dogged battle, knowing victory again

and again but also being wounded again and again; that is how things are to be for every member of the human race." *Creation and Fall*, p. 133.

87. Brueggemann, *Genesis*, 327.

88. Walter Brueggemann, "The Power of Dreams" <www.religiononline.org/showarticle.asp?title=3218>

89. Ibid.

90. See <http://eoimages.gsfc.nasa.gov/ve/6566/Egypt.A2004201.0830.1km.jpg>

91. See <www.nilebasin.org>

92. For fascinating accounts of such reconciliation, google "Reconcilation Village Rwanda". Reconciliation Village was started by Prison Fellowship International.

93. N. T. Wright, *Simply Christian (New York, HarperSan Francisco, 2006), p.* 212.

94. Lawrence Hill, *The Book of Negroes* (Toronto: HarperCollins, 2007). This book is published in the USA, Australia and New Zealand under the title *Someone Knows My Name*.

95. See, for example "Did anthrax Plague the Egyptians?" at <http://www.biblearchaeology.org/post/2007/10/17/Did-Anthrax-Plague-the-Egyptians.aspx>

96. Lynn White, Jr., "The Historical Roots of Our Ecologic Crisis" *Science*, March 10, 1967: Vol. 155 no. 3767 pp. 1203-1207. <http://www.sciencemag.org/content/155/3767/1203.citation>.

97. Godfrey Ashby, *Go Out and Meet God – A Commentary on the Book of Exodus* [International Theological Commentary] (Grand Rapids, Eerdmans Publishing, 1998), p. 64.

98. Ibid.

99. Some Biblical scholars such as Ellen Frankel, *The Five Books of Miriam: A Woman's Commentary on the Torah*. (New York: HarperSanFrancisco, 1996) propose that Miriam was much more

important in Israel's emergence as a nation than our Bible suggests, but that her story was largely expunged from the sacred text by patriarchal bias. Rabbi Bradley Shavit Artson agrees, noting that Miriam's prophecy was one of deed. Miriam focused on teaching her people how to sing in moments of joy. See <http://judaism.ajula.edu/Content/ContentUnit.asp?CID=935&u=2336&t=0>.

It is becoming more common today for progressive Jews to include a "Miriam's cup" of water in the Passover Seder alongside Elijah's cup, to make the celebration more inclusive and to remind the faithful of Miriam's role in watching over Moses and generally to highlight Miriam's importance and the importance of other righteous women who are often overlooked in telling Israel's story.

100. C. S. Lewis, *The Lion, the Witch and the Wardrobe* (London: Geoffrey Bles, 1950).

101. See <http://www.imjl.com/cwib/countries/haiti/images/zg-1074.jpg>

102. Greg Mortenson, *Three Cups of Tea* (New York: Penguin Books, 2006), p. 214-224.

103. Wendell Berry "The Real Work" in *Collected Poems* (Berkely: North Point Press, 1987).

104. John and Janet Wallach, *Still Small Voices* (San Diego, Harcourt Brace Jovanovich, Publishers, 1989), p. 208. For more information on the work of Rabbi Riskin, see <http://cjcuc.com/site/join-us-in-making-history/>

105. Ibid.

106. See Psalm 81:7, 95:8 and 106:32.

107. The *'Targum of Onkelos'* and in the Mishna tractate, *Tosefta Sukka iii, 11,12*. Quoted from James Moffat's *The First Epistle of Paul to the Corinthians* (London, Hodder and Stoughton, 1938), p. 130.

108. Rashi on Numbers 20:2; b. Ta'anit 9a; Song of Song Rabba 4:14, 27.

109. See Deuteronomy 32:4, 15, 18, 32; 1 Samuel 2:2, 22:47, 23:3; Psalm 18:31, 46, 28:1, 42:9, 78:35, 89:26, 92:15, 95:1, etc.

110. Raymond Brown, *Commentary on John* [1966, 1970] Vol 1, 322, quoted in Gary Burge, *The NIV Application Commentary: John,* (Grand Rapids: Zondervan, 2000), p. 228. For further commentary on this and other Early Christian catacomb art see <www.oneonta.edu/faculty/farberas/arth/smarthistory/early_christianity_smarthistory.html>

111. Brueggemann, *Psalms,* p. 142.

112. T. S. Eliot, "East Coker" *Four Quartets* (London: Faber, 1954), p. 32.

113. Elizabeth Barrett Browning, *Aurora Leigh, (London: J. Miller, 1864). Also available at* <http://digital.library.upenn.edu/women/barrett/aurora/aurora.html>

114. Gordon MacDonald, *Facing Turbulent Times* (Wheaton: Tyndale House Publishers, Inc. 1981).

115. Fred Pearce, *When The Rivers Run Dry* (Toronto: Key Porter Books, 2006), p. 48.

116. Recommended reading on this subject is a 2010 book, *Water Wisdom* (New Brunswick, NJ: Rutgers University Press, 2010), a fascinating collection of essays by thirty leading Israeli and Palestinian water scientists. They agree that Israel's past and present water policies have left Palestinians with inadequate water resources. Per capita water consumption in the Palestinian West Bank is only one third of the World Health Organization minimum value, and in Gaza it is less than one tenth of this standard. As the Palestinian peace process bogs down perennially, water remains a critical political, environmental and human rights issue. This book is a balanced and hopeful analysis of many aspects of water management in Israel and Palestine.

117. Dr. Tom Baskett, "Lifta, a poem" See <www.zochrot.org/en/content/lifta-poem> used by author's permission.

118. I am indebted John Hamlin, *Inheriting the Land,* (Grand Rapids: Eerdmans, 1983), p. 124 for this perspective.

119. Lucy Shaw, *Water My Soul* (Vancouver: Regent College Publishing, 1998), p. 90.

120. Hermann J Austel, "shaphak" in *Theological Wordbook of the Old Testament*, 950.

121. Joyce Baldwin, *1 & 2 Samuel* (Leicester: Inter-Varsity Press, 1988), p. 203.

122. Ibid.

123. Mark Buchanan, in an address at the "Thinking Shrewdly" conference in 2008 sponsored by Vision Ministries Canada.

124. I am indebted to Martin Ellgar and his blog <www.entergrace.org> for some of these thoughts.

125. John Bunyan, *The Pilgrim's Progress* in L. Edward Hazelbaker's *The Pilgrim's Progress in Modern English* (Gainesville, FL: Bridge-Logos, 1998), p. 206.

126. Bonhoeffer, *Creation and Fall*, 143.

127. The title of Psalm 72 calls it 'a Psalm of Solomon'. Whether he wrote it or we don't know, but the spirit of the psalm does correspond to his prayer in 1 Kings 3:9.

128. The 1955 variation by "The Travellers" on Woody Guthrie's, "This Land is Your Land" 1940.

129. Old Testament scholar John Bright writes, 'one gains the impression that the national structure was poisoned through and through' *A History of Israel*, Third Edition, (Philadelphia: Westminster Press, 1981), p. 245-6.

130. Harry Fernhout, *Of Kings and Prophets.* (Toronto: The Joy in Learning and Curriculum Development and Training Centre, 1979) p. 121.

131. David Ruis, "Mercy is Falling", Mercy Vineyard Publishing, 1994.

132. Iain Poivan, V. Philips Long, Tremper Longman III, *A Biblical History of Israel* (Louisville: Westminster John Knox Press, 2003), p. 267.

133. Peterson, *The Message Remix* (Colorado Springs, CO: NavPress Publishing Group, 2003), p. 1330.

134. J. Alec Motyer, *The Prophecy of Isaiah* (Downers Grove: Inter Varsity Press, 1993), p. 91.

135. For more detail see <www.jewishvirtuallibrary.org/jsource/Archaeology/jerwater.html> and <www.adsabs.harvard.edu/abs/2010HydJ...18.1465A>

136. For supplementary reading on this subject consult The Olive Branch Forum in the Wall Street Journal at <http://theolivebranch.myfastforum.org/archive/wall-st-journal-jerusalem-underground-secrets-of-an-ancient__o_t__t_1037.html>

137. See Dallas Willard, *The Spirit of the Disciplines* (New York: HarperCollins, 1988), p. 158-191.

138. See <www.bloodwatermission.com/> and <www.bloodwatermission.com/blog/2009/02/a-challenge-40-days-of-water.php>

139. See Herman Melville's *Moby Dick,* Chapter 9 for a vivid sermon based on the Jonah story.

140. The poem "Reluctant Prophet" is used by permission of the author, from the book *Polishing the Petoskey Stone,* (Copyright Luci Shaw, Regent College Publishing, 2003), p. 108.

141. Eugene Peterson, *The Jesus Way* (Grand Rapids: Eerdmans, 2007), p. 90-91.

142. Nicholas Wolterstorff, *Lament for a Son* (Grand Rapids, Eerdmans, 1987), p. 81.

143. Walter Brueggemann points out that Nebuchadnezzar's dream echoes the dream of Pharaoh centuries earlier at the front end of Israel's story. Both kings live "a settled life of exploitative power that expects not to be disrupted. Dreams are dangerous for such a ruler, coming when they least expect them, and coming as God's warning to act with justice. "The Power of Dreams" <http://www.religion-online.org/showarticle.asp?title=3218>

144. John Calvin, "Lecture 22" in *Daniel I.* [D. F. Wright (ed.) Calvin's Old Testament Commentaries, Vol 20], (Grand Rapids: Eerdmans, 1993), p. 199.

145. Visit the web-site of the European Community's Friends of the Earth (Middle East) <http://www.foeme.org/projects.php?ind=123> where they describe their vision for the Jordan River Peace Park – a contemporary parallel to Ezekiel's prophecy of a transformed future.

146. "Filled with Your Glory" on "Starfield" CD, Sparrow Records, 2004.

147. *The Book of Alternate Services of the Anglican Church of Canada,* (Toronto: Anglican Book Centre, 1985), p. 146.

148. C. S. Lewis, *The Voyage of the Dawn Treader,* (New York: Penguin Books, 1952), p. 81. Subsequent quotes come from page 94-96 of this edition.

149. See John Bowen's *The Spirituality of Narnia* (Vancouver: Regent College Publishing, 2007) for further insights into the deeper magic of C.S. Lewis.

150. Anne Lamott, *Traveling Mercies: Some Thoughts on Faith* (New York: Random House, 1999), p. 231-2.

151. Thanks to my brother-in-law Dr. Timothy Ralston for some of the insights into this story.

152. See <www.darwinawards.com>.

153. Josephus, *Antiquities of the Jews,* VIII, iv, 1.

154. Rob Bell and Don Golden, *Jesus Wants to Save Christians: A Manifesto for the Church in Exile* (Grand Rapids, Zondervan, 2008). I have also seen these words attributed to Anne Lamott, but I haven't been able to confirm the source.

155. Isak Dinesen, *Babette's Feast and Other Anecdotes of Destiny* (New York: Random House, 1988).

156. John Ortberg, *If You Want to Walk on Water, You Have to Get Out of the Boat* (Grand Rapids: Zondervan, 2001), p. 17.

157. See <http://www.italian-renaissance-art.com/Charge-to-Peter.html>

158. F. F. Bruce, *The Book of Acts* [The New International Commentary on the New Testament], (Grand Rapids: Eerdmans, 1979), p. 519.

159. This story of shipwreck and survival is the climax of the journey theme that Luke traces in parallel ways in his Gospel and the Book of Acts. Luke 9-24 relates the journey of Jesus from Galilee to Jerusalem where his death and resurrection occur and where Jesus tells his disciples to take the story on from there to the ends of the earth. The Book of Acts tells how the disciples undertook that mission, especially through the labors of Peter and Paul. Luke parallels both Peter and Paul's mission careers on that of Jesus. The first recorded miracle of each is the raising of a lame man (Acts 3:1-10 and 14:8), both raise someone from death (Acts 9:36-42 and 20:7-12) and both take the message of Jesus to the Gentiles (Acts 10 and 13). Both endure prison and trial for their witness and both face almost certain death – but miraculously escape (Acts 12:5-17 and 27:20-44) – a kind of symbolic resurrection. Luke shows how both Peter and Paul are extending the work and mission of Jesus. The shipwreck story brings this motif to its conclusion by bringing Paul eventually to Rome.

160. Leonard Cohen, "Hallelujah" See "http://www.leonardcohenfiles.com/halldraft.html". Cohen's song with its beautiful haunting melody is an ironic hallelujah, disillusioned and melancholic; it is stoical, but a "cold and broken hallelujah". Christian praise is grounded in the victory of Jesus, even when it is sung in the midst of suffering.

161. William Hendrickson, *More Than Conquerors* (Grand Rapids: Baker Book House, 1940), p.142.

162. Gerhard Krodel, *Revelation* (Augsburg Commentary on the New Testament; Minneapolis, Minn.: Fortress Press), p. 245, quoted in Darrell Johnson, *Discipleship on the Edge*, (Vancouver: Regent College Publishing, 2004), p. 226.

163. Wallace Stegner, "Wilderness Letter" in *The Sound of Mountain Water* (New York: Penguin Books, 1946), p. 153.

164. Brian McLaren, *Naked Spirituality: A Life with God in 12 Simple Words* (New York: Harper-One, 2011), p. 240.

165. Carl Shultz, "eden" in *Theological Wordbook of the Old Testament,* p. 646.

166. Ibid.

167. David Toshio Tsumura, *The Earth and the Waters in Genesis 1 and 2.,* 137, quoted in John H. Walton, *The NIV Application Commentary: Genesis* (Grand Rapids: Zondervan, 2001), p. 167.

168. Vishal Mangalwadi, *Truth and Transformation – A Manifesto for Ailing Nations* (Seattle: YWAM Publishing, 2009).

169. The quote is ubiquitous on the Internet and always attributed to Wendell Berry, but I have been unable to locate the source.

170. See Sandra Postel and Brian Richter, *Rivers for Life, Managing Water for People and Nature* (Washington, D.C.: Island Press, 2003), about which Harvard professor Robert France says, "a wisdom runs through it".

171. Quoted in Betsy Shirley, "Sister Act", *Sojourners,* April 2011. <http://www.sojo.net/index.cfm?action=magazine.article&issue=soj1104&article=sister-act>

172. See <http://benedictinewomen.org/care-for-the-earth/natural-environment/>

173. Genesis has two complementary creation stories. In the first story, Genesis 1, which we explored in the opening chapters of this book, vegetation emerges three days before human beings are created; in the second story, Genesis 2, people come first. Two stories with two very different themes - the first is a panoramic prologue that sets the stage for the human drama that unfolds in the second. The first culminates in the creation of humanity; the second focuses on the priority of human beings as custodians and stewards of creation.

174. See John Oswalt, "*kabash*" in *Theological Wordbook of the Old Testament*, p. 430.

175. Loren Wilkinson, *Earthkeeping in the '90s: Stewardship of Creation* (Grand Rapids: Eerdmans, 1980), p. 286.

176. Dawn, p. 46.

177. C. S. Lewis, *The Abolition of Man* (1944) (New York: HarperCollins, 2001), Chapter 3.

178. Walton, *Genesis*, p. 172.

179. Ibid., p. 172-5.

180. Gene E. Veith, *God at Work: Your Christian Vocation in All of Life* (Crossway Books, 2002), p. 17.

181. See http://seattletimes.nwsource.com/special/mlk/king/words/blueprint.html.

182. Tony Campolo, *How to Rescue the Earth Without Worshiping Nature* (Nashville: Thomas Nelson Publishers, 1992), p. 127.

183. Arthur F. Glasser, *Announcing the Kingdom* (Grand Rapids, Baker Academic, 2003), p. 38.

184. Ibid.

185. Sandra Postel, *Last Oasis: Facing Water Scarcity* (New York: W.W. Norton & Company, 1992), p.185.

186. Ibid., p. 184.

187. Ibid., p. 191.

188. Hubbard, p. 477.

189. Eugene Peterson, *The Message Remix* (Colorado Springs, CO: NavPress Publishing Group, 2003), p. 1356.

190. Tim Keller, *Kings Cross* (New York: Dutton, 2011), p. 148.

191. Ibid., p. 149.

192. Gleason Archer Jr., 'Micah' in *The New Bible Commentary Revised* (London: Inter-Varsity Press, 1970), p. 758.

193. See Isaiah 44:28 – 45:5.

194. See Psalm 1:3, Proverbs 5:6 and Isaiah 30:25 for other uses of this phrase.

195. See John McPhee's insightful essay on "The Control of Nature: Atchafalaya in February 23, 1987 issue of *The New Yorker* <http://www.newyorker.com/archive/1987/02/23/1987_02_23_039_TNY_CARDS_000347146>

196. Martin Luther King Jr., "I Have a Dream". See <www.usconstitution.net/dream.html>.

197. Ibid.

198. Augustine, *Saint Augustine's Confessions.* [translated by Henry Chadwick] (Oxford: Oxford University Press, 1991), p. 3.

199. Stegner, "Wilderness Letter".

200. Hubbard, p. 88.

201. Ibid., p. 276.

202. *Ibid.*

203. John Milton, *Paradise Regained,* Book IV, 240.

204. See <www.uoguelph.ca/news/2009/06/ddddd/html>.

205. I have resisted the temptation at this point to comment beyond my expertise about the controversial practice of hydraulic fracturing, commonly called fracking – a technique for more economically extracting natural gas from deep lying shale formations by creating thousands of conductive fractures in the shale. One of the effects of this process is that the residual chemicals used to shatter the shale, remain behind, potentially compromising deep groundwater.

206. See http://www.mrbauld.com/keatsva.html.

207. Kidner, *Psalms 73-150,* p. 305.

208. "Protecting Groundwater: The Invisible but Vital Resource" February, 2011. The C.D.Howe Institute, at http://www.cdhowe.org/pdf/Backgrounder_136.pdf Accessed Sept 5, 2011.

209. See Thomas H Green's *When the Well Runs Dry* (Notre Dame: Ave Maria Press, 1979), p. 38-59, for a helpful commentary on Theresa's metaphor. Fr. Green is a seasoned spiritual director, and this book, as the title suggests, is full of wise counsel on how to pray when the inner life feels barren and dry.

210. This interpretation is elaborated in S. Craig Glickman *A Song for Lovers*, (Downers Grove: IVPress, 1977), p. 22-24.

211. Before Shania Twain recorded her 1993 song "Dance With the One That Brought You", the phrase was attributed to University of Texas football coach Darrell Royal. It was also the title of a popular song in the 1920's.

212. Sara Teasdale, "The Kiss" in *Rivers to the Sea*, 1915.

213. Hubbard, p. 214.

214. Parker Palmer, "The Politics of the Brokenhearted: On Holding the Tensions of Democracy." Fetzer Institute, 2005. Palmer says, "the holiest thing we have to offer the world is a broken-open heart, emptied of fear and vengeance, filled with forgiveness and a willingness to take the risks of love. And we can offer our hearts only by becoming disciples of the heart's own imperatives."

215. See McGrath, p. 147-149, and Denton, p. 31.

216. Iain Poivan, *1 and 2 Kings* (Peabody, MA: Hendickson Publishers, 1995), p. 72.

217. These words are the third verse of the hymn "The Love of God" by Frederick M Lehman in 1917. Lehman tells us that this third verse comes from a Jewish poem *Haddamut* written in 1050, by a Jewish cantor in Worms, Germany, Meir Ben Isaac Nehorai.

218. Rob Moll, "A Culture of Resurrection – How the Church Can Help its People Die Well" in *Christianity Today*, July 6, 2010, http://www.christianitytoday.com/ct/2010/june/5.35.html?start=3 Accessed Sept 2, 2011.

219. Excerpted from the *Book of Alternative Services*. Copyright 1985 by the General Synod of the Anglican Church of Canada. Published by ABC Publishing (Anglican Book Centre). Used with permission.

220. Martin Nystrom, "As the Deer", Maranatha Singers, 1984.

221. See <www.gfwa.org/memorial/site.html>.

222. Luci Shaw, "Puzzle: Tuolumne River" in *Water Lines*, p. 63.

223. E. J. Pratt, "Erosion" 1932 in Carl Klinck and Reginald Watters (eds) *Canadian Anthology* (Toronto: W.J. Gage, 1966), p.228.

224. "God is Our Refuge" in *Hymns II* (Downers Grove: InterVarsity Press, 1976), #201. See Internet article on the Chefoo School at <http://www.suite101.com/content/chefoo-school-the-world-war-ii-years-in-weihsien-internment-camp-a337593>. Last accessed on Sept 5, 2011.

225. Motyer, p. 331.

226. Nelson Mandela, *Long Walk to Freedom*, (Boston: Little, Brown and Company, 1994), p. 414.

227. Paul Simon, "The Sound of Silence", in *Sounds of Silence*, Columbia Records, 1966.

228. T. S. Eliot, "Gerontion" in *Poems* (New York: Knopf, 1920).

229. N.T. Wright, *Simply Christian* (New York: HarperSanFrancisco, 2006), p. 18-27.

230. James Houston, "The Bible in its Environment" in *The Lion Handbook to the Bible* (Berkhamsted, Herts: Lion Publishing, 1973), p. 14-15.

231. Bob Goudzwaard, *Idols of Our Time* (Sioux Center, Iowa: Dordt College Press, 1989), p. 11.

232. Ed Firmage Jr, "Will we be ready when drought comes to stay?" *Salt Lake Tribune*, April 23, 2010.

233. Banyan, <http://www.economist.com/blogs/banyan/2010/05/aral_sea_ecological_disaster>

234. Professor Michal Marek, head of CzechGlobe, a climate change research project, quoted in IPS reported in *WaterWired*, a blog devoted to all things water-related, on Jan 23 2011.

235. Glandion Carney and Wm R Long, *The Renovaré Spiritual Formation Bible* (New York: HarperSanFrancisco, 2005).

236. Wendell Berry, "Water" in *Farming: A Handbook* (Berkeley: Counterpoint, 1971), p. 35.

237. Including RSV, NASB, NIVUK, and NIV 1984.

238. Pete Kipley and Bart Millard, "Word of God Speak" Integrity Media, 2002.

239. Eugene Peterson, *A Long Obedience in the Same Direction* (Downers Grove: IVPress, 1980) p. 96.

240. Scott Sabin, *Tending to Eden* (Valley Forge PA: Judson Press, 2010), p. 71-72.

241. C. S. Lewis, *The Silver Chair*, (New York: Penguin Books, 1953), p. 201-203.

242. Robert Frost, "Fire and Ice" (1920) in *A Little of Modern Poetry*, p. 174.

243. The word '*stoikeion*' is used only five other times in the New Testament – *Galatians* 4:3 and 4:9, *Colossians* 2:8 and 2:20 and *Hebrews* 5:12. In each of these, the word 'elements' refers to 'things that are elementary', the ABC's of Christian faith or the ceremonial and purity laws of Israel. If Peter is using the word in this sense, he means that everything primitive that is not required in the new creation will melt away, not that the universe is going to disintegrate.

244. G. B. Caird, *The Revelation of St John the Divine*, Second Edition. (London: A & C Black, 1984), p. 64.

245. Darrell Johnson, *Discipleship on the Edge*, p. 137.

246. Craig Koester, *Revelation and the End of All Things* (Grand Rapids: Eerdmans, 2001), p. 192.

247. See Revelation 1:20, 7:2, 9:11, 14:18, and 16:5. See also Daniel 10:13, 20.

248. Koester, p. 102.

249. Caird, p. 129.

250. The *Qur'an* uses a similar metaphor to speak of resurrection: Surah 41:39 – "And among his signs is this: thou seest the earth barren and desolate; but when We send down rain to it, it is stirred to life and yields increase. Truly, He Who gives life to the (dead) earth can surely give life to (men) who are dead. For He has power over all things." 'Abdullah Yusef 'Ali, *The Meaning of the Holy Qur'an*, (Brentwood, MD: Amana Corporation, 1991).

251. Peterson, *Reversed Thunder* (San Francisco: Harper & Row Publishers, 1988), p. 169.

252. Johnson, p. 362.

253. *Ibid.*

254. A number of these concepts of God's urban vision come from Dr. Glenn Smith and his colleagues at Christian Direction, an urban ministry in Montreal whose vision is "to see God transform urban communities by the concerted actions of committed Christians". For more information on this ministry see <www.direction.ca>

255. The subtitle of Richard Louv's *Last Child in the Woods* is 'saving our children from 'Nature-deficit Disorder'!

256. Caird, p. 267.

257. C. S. Lewis, *The Silver Chair*, p. 26-27.

258. C. S. Lewis, *The Voyage of the Dawn Treader* (New York: Penguin Books, 1952), p. 193-198.

259. From "The Sands of Time are Sinking" by Anne Ross Cousin, 1857, Public domain.

260. See footnote 5 and <www.un.org/milleniumgoals/> - especially Goal 7 - Environmental Sustainability.

261. Carl Safina, *Song for the Blue Ocean* (New York: Henry Holt & Company, 1997). See especially the Epilogue, p. 435-440.

262. Kidner, *Psalms 73-150*, p. 353.

CPSIA information can be obtained at www.ICGtesting.com
Printed in the USA
LVOW052006080612

285147LV00002BB/7/P

9 781449 745653